FTCE Elementary Education K-6

Teacher Certification Exam

Property of
Lake City
Community College

By: Sharon Wynne, M.S.
Southern Connecticut State University

"And, while there's no reason yet to panic, I think it's only prudent that we make preparations to panic."

XAMonline, Inc.

Boston

D1621619

Copyright © 2007 XAMonline, Inc.

All rights reserved. No part of the material protected by this copyright notice may be reproduced or utilized in any form or by any means, electronic or mechanical, including photocopying, recording or by any information storage and retrievable system, without written permission from the copyright holder.

To obtain permission(s) to use the material from this work for any purpose including workshops or seminars, please submit a written request to:

XAMonline, Inc.
21 Orient Ave.
Melrose, MA 02176
Toll Free 1-800-509-4128
Email: info@xamonline.com
Web www.xamonline.com
Fax: 1-781-662-9268

Library of Congress Cataloging-in-Publication Data

Wynne, Sharon A.
  Elementary Education K-6: Teacher Certification / Sharon A. Wynne. -2nd ed.
  ISBN 978-1-58197-907-7
  1. Elementary Education K-6.   2. Study Guides.   3. FTCE
  4. Teachers' Certification & Licensure.   5. Careers

Disclaimer:

The opinions expressed in this publication are the sole works of XAMonline and were created independently from the National Education Association, Educational Testing Service, or any State Department of Education, National Evaluation Systems or other testing affiliates.

Between the time of publication and printing, state specific standards as well as testing formats and website information may change that is not included in part or in whole within this product. Sample test questions are developed by XAMonline and reflect similar content as on real tests; however, they are not former tests. XAMonline assembles content that aligns with state standards but makes no claims nor guarantees teacher candidates a passing score. Numerical scores are determined by testing companies such as NES or ETS and then are compared with individual state standards. A passing score varies from state to state.

Printed in the United States of America   œ - 1

FTCE: Elementary Education K-6
ISBN: 978-1-58197-907-7

Table of Contents

DOMAIN II.   **MATHEMATICS**

DOMAIN III.   **SOCIAL SCIENCE**

COMPETENCY 12.0   KNOWLEDGE OF TIME, CONTINUITY, AND CHANGE

COMPETENCY 13.0   KNOWLEDGE OF PEOPLE, PLACES, AND ENVIRONMENT

DOMAIN IV.   SCIENCE AND TECHNOLOGY

DOMAIN V.   MUSIC, VISUAL ARTS, PHYSICAL EDUCATION, AND HEALTH

Great Study and Testing Tips!

What to study in order to prepare for the subject assessments is the focus of this study guide but equally important is *how* you study.

You can increase your chances of truly mastering the information by taking some simple, but effective, steps.

Study Tips:

1. Some foods aid the learning process. Foods such as milk, nuts, seeds, rice, and oats help your study efforts by releasing natural memory enhancers called CCKs (*cholecystokinin*) composed of *tryptophan*, *choline*, and *phenylalanine*. All of these chemicals enhance the neurotransmitters associated with memory. Before studying, try a light, protein-rich meal of eggs, turkey, and fish. All of these foods release the memory-enhancing chemicals. The better the connections, the more you comprehend.

Likewise, before you take a test, stick to a light snack of energy boosting and relaxing foods. A glass of milk, a piece of fruit, or some peanuts all release various memory-boosting chemicals and help you to relax and focus on the subject at hand.

2. Learn to take great notes. A by-product of our modern culture is that we have grown accustomed to getting our information in short doses (i.e. TV news sound bites or *USA Today*-style newspaper articles.)

Consequently, we've subconsciously trained ourselves to assimilate information better in neat little packages. If your notes are scrawled all over the paper, it fragments the flow of the information. Strive for clarity. Newspapers use a standard format to achieve clarity. Your notes can be much clearer through use of proper formatting. A very effective format is called the *"Cornell Method."*

Take a sheet of loose-leaf lined notebook paper and draw a line all the way down the paper about 1-2" from the left-hand edge.

Draw another line across the width of the paper about 1-2" up from the bottom. Repeat this process on the reverse side of the page.

Look at the highly effective result. You have ample room for notes, a left-hand margin for special emphasis items or inserting supplementary data from the textbook, a large area at the bottom for a brief summary, and a little rectangular space for just about anything you want.

3. <u>Get the concept then the details</u>. Too often we focus on the details and don't gather an understanding of the concept. However, if you simply memorize only dates, places, or names, you may well miss the whole point of the subject.

A key way to understand things is to put them in your own words. If you are working from a textbook, automatically summarize each paragraph in your mind. If you are outlining text, don't simply copy the author's words.

Rephrase them in your own words. You remember your own thoughts and words much better than someone else's, and subconsciously tend to associate the important details to the core concepts.

4. <u>Ask Why?</u> Pull apart written material paragraph by paragraph and don't forget the captions under the illustrations.

Example: If the heading is "Stream Erosion," flip it around to read, "Why do streams erode?" Then answer the questions.

If you train your mind to think in a series of questions and answers, not only will you learn more, but it also helps to lessen the test anxiety because you are used to answering questions.

5. <u>Read for reinforcement and future needs</u>. Even if you only have ten minutes, put your notes or a book in your hand. Your mind is similar to a computer; you have to input data in order to have it processed. *By reading, you are creating the neural connections for future retrieval.* The more times you read something, the more you reinforce the learning of ideas.

Even if you don't fully understand something on the first pass, *your mind stores much of the material for later recall.*

6. <u>Relax to learn so go into exile</u>. Our bodies respond to an inner clock called biorhythms. Burning the midnight oil works well for some people, but not everyone.

If possible, set aside a particular place to study that is free of distractions. Shut off the television, cell phone, and pager and exile your friends and family during your study period.

If you really are bothered by silence, try background music. Light classical music at a low volume has been shown to aid in concentration over other types. Music that evokes pleasant emotions without lyrics is highly suggested. Try just about anything by Mozart. It relaxes you.

7. <u>**Use arrows not highlighters**</u>. At best, it's difficult to read a page full of yellow, pink, blue, and green streaks. Try staring at a neon sign for a while and you'll soon see that the horde of colors obscure the message.

A quick note, a brief dash of color, an underline, and an arrow pointing to a particular passage is much clearer than a horde of highlighted words.

8. <u>**Budget your study time**</u>. Although you shouldn't ignore any of the material, *allocate your available study time in the same ratio that topics may appear on the test.*

Testing Tips:

1. <u>Get smart, play dumb</u>. Don't read anything into the question. Don't make an assumption that the test writer is looking for something else than what is asked. Stick to the question as written and don't read extra things into it.

2. <u>Read the question and all the choices *twice* before answering the question</u>. You may miss something by not carefully reading, and then re-reading, both the question and the answers.

If you really don't have a clue as to the right answer, leave it blank on the first time through. Go on to the other questions, as they may provide a clue as to how to answer the skipped questions.

If later on, you still can't answer the skipped ones . . . ***Guess.*** The only penalty for guessing is that you *might* get it wrong. Only one thing is certain; if you don't put anything down, you will get it wrong!

3. <u>Turn the question into a statement</u>. Look at the way the questions are worded. The syntax of the question usually provides a clue. Does it seem more familiar as a statement rather than as a question? Does it sound strange?

By turning a question into a statement, you may be able to spot if an answer sounds right, and it may also trigger memories of material you have read.

4. <u>Look for hidden clues</u>. It's actually very difficult to compose multiple-foil (choice) questions without giving away part of the answer in the options presented.

In most multiple-choice questions you can often readily eliminate one or two of the potential answers. This leaves you with only two real possibilities, and automatically your odds go to fifty-fifty for very little work.

5. <u>Trust your instincts</u>. For every fact that you have read, you subconsciously retain something of that knowledge. On questions that you aren't really certain about, go with your basic instincts. **Your first impression on how to answer a question is usually correct.**

6. <u>Mark your answers directly on the test booklet</u>. Don't bother trying to fill in the optical scan sheet on the first pass through the test.

Just be very careful not to miss-mark your answers when you eventually transcribe them to the scan sheet.

7. <u>Watch the clock</u>! You have a set amount of time to answer the questions. Don't get bogged down trying to answer a single question at the expense of 10 questions you can more readily answer.

THIS PAGE BLANK

DOMAIN I.   **LANGUAGE ARTS AND READING**

COMPETENCY 1.0   **KNOWLEDGE OF EMERGENT LITERACY**

Skill 1.1   **Identify the content of emergent literacy (e.g., oral language development, phonological awareness, alphabet knowledge, decoding, concepts of print, motivation, text structures, written language development).**

In 2000, the National Reading Panel released its now well-known report on teaching children to read. In a way, this report slightly put to rest the debate between phonics and whole language. It argued, essentially, that word-letter recognition was important, as was understanding what the text means. The report's "big 5" critical areas of reading instruction are as follows:

- **Phonemic Awareness:** The acknowledgement of sounds and words. For example, a child's realization that some words rhyme. Onset and rhyme, for example, are skills that might help students learn that the sound of the first letter "b" in the word "bad" can be changed with the sound "d" to make it "dad." The key in phonemic awareness is that when you teach it to children, it can be taught with the students' eyes closed. In other words, it's all about sounds, not about ascribing written letters to sounds.

- **Phonics:** As opposed to phonemic awareness, the study of phonics must be done with the eyes open. It's the connection between the sounds and letters on a page. In other words, students learning phonics might see the word "bad" and sound each letter out slowly until they recognize that they just said the word.

- **Comprehension:** Comprehension simply means that the reader can ascribe meaning to text. Even though students may be good with phonics and even know what many words on a page mean, some of them are not good with comprehension because they do not know the strategies that would help them to comprehend. For example, students should know that stories often have structures (beginning, middle, and end). They should also know that when they are reading something and it does not make sense, they will need to employ "fix-up" strategies where they go back into the text they just read and look for clues. Teachers can use many strategies to teach comprehension, including questioning, asking students to paraphrase or summarize, utilizing graphic organizers, and focusing on mental images.

Understanding that print carries meaning

This understanding is demonstrated every day in the elementary classroom as the teacher holds up a selected book to read it aloud to the class. The teachers explicitly and deliberately think aloud about how to hold the book, how to focus the class on looking at its cover, where to start reading, and in what direction to begin.

Even in writing the morning message on the board, the teacher targets the children on the placement of the message and its proper place at the top of the board to be followed by additional activities and a schedule for the rest of the day.

When the teacher challenges children to make letter posters of a single letter and to identify the items in the classroom, their home, or their knowledge base which start with that letter, the children are making concrete the understanding that print carries meaning.

Strategies for Promoting Awareness of the Relationship between Spoken and Written Language

- Write down what the children are saying on a chart.
- Highlight and celebrate the meanings, uses, and print products found in the classroom. These products include: posters, labels, yellow sticky pad notes, labels on shelves and lockers, calendars, rule signs, and directions.
- Intentionally read big-print and oversized books to teach print conventions such as directionality.
- Use practice exercises in reading to others (for K-1/2), where young children practice how to handle a book, how to turn pages, how to find tops and bottoms of pages, and how to tell the difference between the front and back covers of a book.
- Create search and discuss adventures in word awareness and close observation where children are challenged to identify and talk about the length, appearance, and boundaries of specific words and the letters which comprise them.
- Have children match oral words to printed words by forming an echo chorus. As the teacher reads the story aloud, they echo the reading. Often this works best with poetry or rhymes.
- Have the children combine, manipulate, switch, and move letters to change words and spelling patterns.
- Work with letter cards to create messages and respond to the messages that the children create.

Methods used to teach these skills are often featured in a "balanced literacy" curriculum that focuses on the use of skills in various instructional contexts. For example, with independent reading, students independently choose books that are at their reading levels; with guided reading, teachers work with small groups of students to help them with their particular reading problems; with whole group reading, the entire class will read the same text, and the teacher will incorporate activities to help students learn phonics, comprehension, fluency, and vocabulary. In addition to these components of balanced literacy, teachers incorporate writing so that students can learn the structures of communicating through text.

Skill 1.2 Identify instructional methods for developing emergent literacy.

The typical variation in literacy backgrounds that children bring to reading can make teaching more difficult. Often a teacher has to choose between focusing on the learning needs of a few students at the expense of the group or focusing on the group at the risk of leaving some students behind academically. This situation is particularly critical for children with gaps in their literacy knowledge who may be at risk in subsequent grades for becoming "diverse learners."

Areas of Emerging Evidence

1. **Experiences with print (through reading and writing) help preschool children develop an understanding of the conventions, purpose, and functions of print.** Children learn about print from a variety of sources and in the process come to realize that print carries the story. They also learn how text is structured visually (i.e., text begins at the top of the page, moves from left to right, and carries over to the next page when it is turned). While knowledge about the conventions of print enables children to understand the physical structure of language, the conceptual knowledge that printed words convey a message also helps children bridge the gap between oral and written language.

2. **Phonological awareness and letter recognition** contribute to initial reading acquisition by helping children develop efficient word recognition strategies (e.g., detecting pronunciations and storing associations in memory). Phonological awareness and knowledge of print-speech relations play an important role in facilitating reading acquisition. Therefore, phonological awareness instruction should be an integral component of early reading programs. Within the emergent literacy research, viewpoints diverge on whether acquisition of phonological awareness and letter recognition are preconditions of literacy acquisition or whether they develop interdependently with literacy activities such as story reading and writing.

3. **Storybook reading affects children's knowledge about, strategies for, and attitudes towards reading.** Of all the strategies intended to promote growth in literacy acquisition, none is as commonly practiced, nor as strongly supported across the emergent literacy literature as storybook reading. Children in different social and cultural groups have differing degrees of access to storybook reading. For example, it is not unusual for a teacher to have students who have experienced thousands of hours of story reading time, along with other students who have had little or no such exposure.

Design Principles in Emergent Literacy

Conspicuous Strategies

As an instructional priority, conspicuous strategies are a sequence of teaching events and teacher actions used to help students learn new literacy information and relate it to their existing knowledge. Conspicuous strategies can be incorporated in beginning reading instruction to ensure that all learners have basic literacy concepts. For example, during storybook reading, teachers can show students how to recognize the fronts and backs of books, locate titles, or look at pictures and predict the story, rather than assume children will learn this through incidental exposure. Similarly, teachers can teach students a strategy for holding a pencil appropriately or checking the form of their letters against an alphabet sheet on their desks or the classroom wall.

Mediated Scaffolding

Mediated scaffolding can be accomplished in a number of ways to meet the needs of students with diverse literacy experiences. To link oral and written language, for example, teachers may use texts that simulate speech by incorporating oral language patterns or children's writing. Or teachers can use daily storybook reading to discuss book-handling skills and directionality, concepts that are particularly important for children who are unfamiliar with printed texts. Teachers can also use repeated readings to give students multiple exposures to unfamiliar words or extended opportunities to look at books with predictable patterns, as well as provide support by modeling the behaviors associated with reading. Teachers can act as *scaffolds* during these storybook reading activities by adjusting their demands (e.g., asking increasingly complex questions or encouraging children to take on portions of the reading) or by reading more complex text as students gain knowledge of beginning literacy components.

Strategic Integration

Many children with diverse literacy experiences have difficulty making connections between old and new information. Strategic integration can be applied to help link old and new learning. For example, in the classroom, strategic integration can be accomplished by providing access to literacy materials in classroom writing centers and libraries. Students should also have opportunities to integrate and extend their literacy knowledge by reading aloud, listening to other students read aloud, and listening to tape recordings and videotapes in reading corners.

Primed Background Knowledge

All children bring some level of background knowledge (e.g., how to hold a book, awareness of directionality of print) to beginning reading. Teachers can utilize children's background knowledge to help children link their personal literacy experiences to beginning reading instruction, while also closing the gap between students with rich and students with impoverished literacy experiences. Activities that draw upon background knowledge include incorporating oral language activities (which discriminate between printed letters and words) into daily read-alouds, as well as frequent opportunities to retell stories, look at books with predictable patterns, write messages with invented spellings, and respond to literature through drawing.

Emergent Literacy

Emergent literacy research examines early literacy knowledge and the contexts and conditions that foster that knowledge. Despite differing viewpoints on the relation between emerging literacy skills and reading acquisition, strong support was found in the literature for the important contribution that early childhood exposure to oral and written language makes to the facility with which children learn to read.

Reading for comprehension of factual material - content area textbooks, reference books, and newspapers - is closely related to study strategies in the middle/junior high. Organized study models, such as the SQ3R method, a technique that makes it possible and feasible to learn the content of even large amounts of text (Survey, Question, Read, Recite, and Review Studying), teach students to locate main ideas and supporting details, to recognize sequential order, to distinguish fact from opinion, and to determine cause/ effect relationships.

Instructional Strategies

1. Teacher-guided activities that require students to organize and to summarize information based on the author's explicit intent are pertinent strategies in middle grades. Evaluation techniques include oral and written responses to standardized or teacher-made worksheets.

2. Reading of fiction introduces and reinforces skills in inferring meaning from narration and description. Teaching-guided activities in the process of reading for meaning should be followed by cooperative planning of the skills to be studied and of the selection of reading resources. Many printed reading-for-comprehension instruments as well as individualized computer software programs exist to monitor the progress of acquiring comprehension skills.

3. Older middle school students should be given opportunities for more student-centered activities, individual and collaborative selection of reading choices based on student interest, small group discussions of selected works, and greater written expression. Evaluation techniques include teacher monitoring and observation of discussions and written work samples.

4. Certain students may begin some fundamental critical interpretation: recognizing fallacious reasoning in news media, examining the accuracy of news reports and advertising, and explaining their reasons for preferring one author's writing to another's. Development of these skills may require a more learning-centered approach in which the teacher identifies a number of objectives and suggested resources from which the student may choose his course of study. Self-evaluation through a reading diary should be stressed. Teacher and peer evaluation of creative projects resulting from such study is encouraged.

5. Reading aloud before the entire class as a formal means of teacher evaluation should be phased out in favor of one-to-one tutoring or peer-assisted reading. Occasional sharing of favored selections by both teacher and willing students is a good oral interpretation basic.

Skill 1.3   Identify common difficulties in emergent literacy development.

Emergent Literacy is the concept that young children are emerging into reading and writing with no real ending or beginning point. This stage of reading is when the reader understands that print contains a consistent message. The approach for many emergent readers focuses on the idea that children develop their ability to construct meaning by sharing books they care about with responsive peers and adults. Some characteristics of emerging readers include 1) the emergent reader can attend to left-to-right directionality and features of print, 2) an emergent reader can identify some initial sounds and ending sounds in words, 3) the reader can recognize some high-frequency words, names, and simple words in context, and 4) pictures can be used to predict meaning.

As young students enter and work through this stage of literacy, some common difficulties may be noticed by the teacher. Some of these common problems include:

- Difficulty maintaining concentration
- Finding the appropriate text level
- Frustration with not being able to understand the text
- Limited vocabulary hindering comprehension

Skill 1.4   Identify methods for prevention of and intervention for common emergent literacy difficulties.

For students experiencing problems with concentration, make sure their desks are away from distractions and that their overall learning environment is comfortable and well-lit. Try to encourage the student to work for set amounts of time, and then as the student's concentration improves, increase the amounts of time.

To help students to select appropriate   reading material, it is often helpful to organize your classroom library by level. For example, simpler texts may be labeled with a yellow dot, grade-level texts may be labeled with a red dot, and challenging texts may be labeled with a green dot. This helps students see which books may best suit their comfortable reading needs.

Books can be considered one of three levels for each student: Easy, Just Right, or Challenging. Students should be encouraged to read mostly books that are a "just right" fit for them. Matching young children with "just right" books fosters their reading independently, no matter how young they are. The teacher needs to have an extensive classroom library of books. Books that emergent readers and early readers can be matched with should have fairly large print, appropriate spacing (so that the reader can easily see where word begins and ends), and few words on each page so that the young reader can focus on all-important concerns of top-to-bottom, left-to-right, directionality, and the one-to-one match of oral to print.

Students should be permitted to read easy books once in a while, as well as aided in reading challenging books from time to time. In a reading log or journal, have students record titles of books they've read and the level. This way, teachers can monitor that a student is meeting their individual reading needs.

When students become frustrated and feel they are not understanding the text, encourage students to break down the text into chunks. Then, after each chunk, encourage students to ask themselves questions about what they have read to improve understanding.

Limited vocabulary can often get in the way of a student's comprehension of a text. Have the students focus on the structure of words to help decode unfamiliar words. A helpful tip is for students to record new words in a notebook to create a personal glossary for each student. This way, students can refer to a dictionary with their list of words when necessary to help build their vocabulary.

Additional Strategies

Reading aloud to children helps them acquire information and skills such as the meaning of words, how a book works, a variety of writing styles, information about their world, differences between conversations and written language, and the knowledge of printed letters and words along with the relationship between sound and print. Using different types of books assures that each child will find at least a few books that meet his or her interests and preferences.

Children's storybooks are traditional favorites for many young students. Some children may prefer to see books that have informational text, such as those about animals, nature, transportation, careers, or travel. Alphabet books, picture dictionaries, and books with diagrams and overlays (such as those about the human body) catch the interest of children as well. Some children particularly enjoy books containing poetry, children's songs and verses, or folktales. Offering different types of books also gives flexibility in choosing one or two languages in which to read a story.

Illustrations for young children should support the meaning of the text and language patterns, and predictable text structures should make these texts appealing to young readers. Illustrations can be key supports for emergent and early readers. Teachers should not only use wordless stories (books which tell their narratives through pictures alone), but can also make targeted use of Big Books for read-alouds, so that young children become habituated in the use of illustrations as an important component for constructing meaning. The teacher should model for the child how to reference an illustration for help in identifying a word in the text the child does not recognize.

The content of the story should relate to the children's interests and experiences as the teacher knows them. The story should include lots of monosyllabic words and lots of rhyming ones. Finally, children, particularly the emergent and beginning early readers, benefit from reading books with partners. The partners sit side by side and each one takes turns reading the entire text. Only after all these considerations have been addressed, can the teacher select "just right" books from an already leveled bin or list.

Children with Special Needs

Introducing language and literacy experiences through concrete, multisensory approaches will provide many children with disabilities with the supports they need to build the foundation for decoding words and understanding meaning. Having access to early literacy activities as part of the curriculum is key to the educational success of all children, including children with mild to severe disabilities. Each child's unique learning needs should be considered in a comprehensive approach to early literacy.

COMPETENCY 2.0   KNOWLEDGE OF READING

Skill 2.1   Identify the processes, skills, and phases of word recognition that lead to effective decoding (e.g., pre-alphabetic, partial alphabetic, full alphabetic, graphophonemic, morphemic, syntactic, semantic).

Word analysis (a.k.a. phonics or decoding) is the process readers use to figure out unfamiliar words based on written patterns. Word recognition is the process of automatically determining the pronunciation and some degree of the meaning of an unknown word. In other words, fluent readers recognize most written words easily and correctly, without consciously decoding or breaking them down. These elements of literacy below are skills readers need for word recognition.

Phonological Awareness
Phonological awareness means the ability of the reader to recognize the sound of spoken language. This recognition includes how these sounds can be blended together, segmented (divided up), and manipulated (switched around). This awareness then leads to phonics, a method for teaching children to read. It helps them "sound out words."

Development of phonological skills may begin during pre-K years. Indeed by the age of five, a child who has been exposed to rhyme can recognize a rhyme. Such a child can demonstrate phonological awareness by filling in the missing rhyming word in a familiar rhyme or rhymed picture book. I surprised my mother by filling in missing rhymes in a familiar nursery rhyme book at the age of four. She was trying to rush ahead to complete the book, but I wouldn't be cheated of even one rhyme!! Little did I know that I was phonologically aware at four!!
.
You teach children phonological awareness when you teach them the sounds made by the letters, the sounds made by various combinations of letters, and to recognize individual sounds in words.

Phonological Awareness Skills include:

1. Rhyming and syllabification
2. Blending sounds into words—such as pic-tur-bo-k
3. Identifying the beginning or starting sounds of words and the ending or closing sounds of words
4. Breaking words down into sounds--also called "segmenting" words
5. Recognizing other smaller words in the big word, by removing starting sounds, such as "hear" to ear

Phonemic Awareness

Phonemic awareness is the idea that words are comprised of sounds. To be phonemically aware, means that the reader and listener can recognize and manipulate specific sounds in spoken words. Phonemic awareness deals with sounds in words that are spoken. The majority of phonemic awareness tasks, activities, and exercises are ORAL.

Theorist Marilyn Jager Adams, who researches early reading, has outlined five basic types of phonemic awareness tasks.

Task 1- Ability to hear rhymes and alliteration.
For example, the children would listen to a poem, rhyming picture book, or song and identify the rhyming words heard which the teacher might then record or list on an experiential chart.

Task 2- Ability to do oddity tasks (recognize the member of a set that is different {odd} among the group).
For example, the children would look at the pictures of a blade of grass, a garden, and a rose—which starts with a different sound?

Task 3– The ability to orally blend words and split syllables.
For example, the children can say the first sound of a word and then the rest of the word and put it together as a single word.

Task 4– The ability to orally segment words.
For example, the ability to count sounds. The children would be asked as a group to count the sounds in "hamburger."

Task 5- The ability to do phonics manipulation tasks.
For example, replace the "r" sound in rose with a "p" sound.

Since the ability to distinguish between individual sounds, or phonemes, within words is a prerequisite to association of sounds with letters and manipulating sounds to blend words—a fancy way of saying "reading"--the teaching of phonemic awareness is crucial to emergent literacy (early childhood K-2 reading instruction). Children need a strong background in phonemic awareness in order for phonics instruction (sound–spelling relationship-printed materials) to be effective.

Instructional methods that may be effective for teaching phonemic awareness can include:

- Clapping syllables in words
- Distinguishing between a word and a sound
- Using visual cues and movements to help children understand when the speaker goes from one sound to another
- Incorporating oral segmentation activities which focus on easily distinguished syllables rather than sounds
- Singing familiar songs (e.g., Happy Birthday, Knick Knack Paddy Wack) and replacing key words in it with words with a different ending or middle sound (oral segmentation)
- Dealing children a deck of picture cards and having them sound out the words for the pictures on their cards or calling for a picture by asking for its first and second sound.

Alphabet Principle

The Alphabetic Principle is sometimes called Graphophonemic Awareness. This multisyllabic technical reading foundation term details the understanding that written words are composed of patterns of letters which represent the sounds of spoken words.

Morphology, Syntax, and Semantics

Morphology is the study of word structure. When readers develop morphemic skills, they are developing an understanding of patterns they see in words. For example, English speakers realize that cat, cats, and caterpillar share some similarities in structure. This understanding helps readers to recognize words at a faster and easier rate, since each word doesn't need individual decoding.

Syntax refers to the rules or patterned relationships that correctly create phrases and sentences from words. When readers develop an understanding of syntax, they begin to understand the structure of how sentences are built, and eventually the beginning of grammar.

Example: "I am going to the movies"
This statement is syntactically and grammatically correct

Example: "They am going to the movies"
This statement is syntactically correct since all the words are in their correct place, but it is grammatically incorrect with the use of the word "They" rather than "I."

Semantics refers to the meaning expressed when words are arranged in a specific way. This is where connotation and denotation of words eventually will have a role with readers.

All of these skill sets are important to eventually developing effective word recognition skills, which help emerging readers develop fluency.

Skill 2.2   Identify instructional methods for promoting the development of decoding and encoding skills.

In the late 1960's and the 1970's, many reading specialists, most prominently Fries (1962), believed that successful decoding resulted in reading comprehension. This meant that if children could sound out the words, they would then automatically be able to comprehend the words. Many teachers of reading and many reading texts still subscribe to this theory after over thirty years.

To decode means to change communication signals into messages. Reading comprehension requires that the reader learn the code within which a message is written and be able to decode it to get the message.

Encoding involves changing a message into symbols. For example to encode oral language into writing (spelling) or to encode an idea into words or to encode a mathematical or physical idea into appropriate mathematical symbols.

Although effective reading comprehension requires identifying words automatically (Adams, 1990; Perfetti, 1985), children do not have to be able to identify every single word or know the exact meaning of every word in a text to understand it. Indeed, Nagy (1988) says that children can read a work with a high level of comprehension even if they do not fully know as many as 15 percent of the words within a given text.

Children develop the ability to decode and recognize words automatically. They then can extend their ability to decode to multisyllabic words.

Use this procedure for letter-sound investigations that support beginning decoding.

First, focus on a particular letter/s which you want the child to investigate. It is good to choose one from a shared text which the children are familiar with. Make certain that the teachers' directions to the children are clear and either focus them on looking for a specific letter or focus them on listening for sounds.

Next, begin a list of words that meet the task given to the children. Use chart paper to list the words that the children identify. This list can be continued into the next week as long as the children's focus is maintained on the list. This can be easily done by challenging the children with identifying a specific number of letters or sounds and "daring" them as a class team to go beyond those words or sounds.

Third, continue to add to the list. Focus the children at the beginning of the day on the goal of their individually adding to the list. Give them an adhesive note (sticky pad sheet) on which they can individually write down the words they find. Then they can attach their newly found words with their names on them to the chart. This provides the children with a sense of ownership and pride in their letter-sounding abilities. During shared reading, discuss the children's proposed additions and have the group decide if these meet the directed category. If all the children agree that they do meet the category, include the words on the chart.

Fourth, do a word sort from all the words generated and have the children put the words into categories that demonstrate similarities and differences. They can be prompted to see if the letter appeared at the beginning of the word, or in the middle of the word. They might also be prompted to see that one sound could have two different letter representations. The children can then "box" the word differences and similarities by drawing colors established in a chart key.

Finally, before the children go off to read, ask them to look for new words in the texts which they can now recognize because of the letter-sound relationships on their chart. During shared reading, make certain that they have time to share these words they were able to decode because of their explorations.

Strategies for helping students decode single syllable words that follow common patterns and multisyllable words (This activity is presented in detail so it can actually be implemented with children in a classroom and also to provide detail for a potential constructed response question on a certification examination.)

Skill 2.3   **Identify the components of reading fluency (e.g., accuracy, automaticity, rate, prosody).**

When students practice fluency, they practice reading connected pieces of text. In other words, instead of looking at a word as just a word, they might read a sentence straight through. The point of this is that in order for the student to comprehend what she is reading, she would need to be able to "fluently" piece words in a sentence together quickly. If a student is NOT fluent in reading, he or she would sound each letter or word out slowly and pay more attention to the phonics of each word. A fluent reader, on the other hand, might read a sentence out loud using appropriate intonations. The best way to test for fluency, in fact, is to have a student read something out loud, preferably a few sentences in a row— or more. Sure, most students just learning to read will probably not be very fluent right away, but with practice, they will increase their fluency. Even though fluency is not the same as comprehension, it is said that fluency is a good predictor of comprehension. Think about it: if you're focusing too much on sounding out each word, you're not going to be paying attention to the meaning.

Accuracy

One way to evaluate reading fluency is to look at student accuracy, and one way to do this is to record running records of students during oral reading. Calculating the reading level lets you know if the book is at the level from which the child can read it independently or comfortably with guidance or if the book is at a level where reading it frustrates the child.

As part of the informal assessment of primary grade reading, it is important to record the child's word insertions, omissions, requests for help, and attempts to get the word. In informal assessment the rate of accuracy can be estimated from the ratio of errors to total words read.

Results of running record informal assessment can be used for teaching based on Text Accuracy. If a child reads from 95-100percent correct, the child is ready for independent reading. If the child reads from 92-97percent right, the child is ready for guided reading. Below 92 percent the child needs a read-aloud or shared reading activity.

Automacity

Fluency in reading is dependent on automatic word identification, which assists the student in achieving comprehension of the material. Even slight difficulties in word identification can significantly increase the time it takes a student to read material, may require rereading parts or passages of the material, and reduces the level of comprehension expected. If the student experiences reading as a constant struggle or an arduous chore, then he or she will avoid reading whenever possible and consider it a negative experience when necessary. Obviously, the ability to read for comprehension, and learning in general, will suffer if all aspects of reading fluency are not presented to the student as acquirable skills which will be readily accomplished with the appropriate effort.

Automatic reading involves the development of strong orthographic representations, which allows fast and accurate identification of whole words made up of specific letter patterns. Most young students move easily from the use of alphabetic strategies to the use of orthographic representations, which can be accessed automatically. Initially word identification is based on the application of phonic word-accessibility strategies (letter-sound associations). These strategies are in turn based on the development of phonemic awareness, which is necessary to learn how to relate speech to print.

One of the most useful devices for developing automaticity in young students is through the visual pattern provided in the six syllable types.

EXAMPLES OF THE SIX SYLLABLE TYPES

1. **NOT** (CLOSED)
   <u>Closed</u> in by a consonant—vowel makes its **short** sound
2. **NO** (OPEN)
   <u>Ends</u> in a vowel—vowel makes its **long** sound
3. **NOTE** (SILENT "E")
   <u>Ends</u> in vowel consonant "e" —vowel makes its **long** sound
4. **NAIL** (VOWEL COMBINATION)
   <u>Two vowels together</u> make the sound
5. **BIRD** ("R" CONTROLLED)
   <u>Contains</u> a vowel plus R—vowel sound is changed
6. **TABLE** (CONSONANT "L"-"E")
   <u>Applied</u> at the end of a word

These orthographic (letter) patterns signal vowel pronunciation to the reader. Students must become able to apply their knowledge of these patterns to recognize the syllable types, to see these patterns automatically,. and ultimately, to read words as wholes. The move from decoding letter symbols to identify recognizable terms, to automatic word recognition is a substantial move toward fluency. A significant aid for helping students move through this phase was developed by Anna Gillingham when she incorporated the Phonetic Word Cards activity into the Orton-Gillingham lesson plan (Gillingham and Stillman, 1997). This activity involves having the students practice reading words (and some nonwords) on cards as wholes, beginning with simple syllables and moving systematically through the syllable types to complex syllables and two-syllable words. The words are divided into groups that correspond to the specific sequence of skills being taught.

The student's development of the elements necessary to automaticity continually moves through stages. Another important stage involves the automatic recognition of single graphemes as a critical first step to the development of the letter patterns that make up words or word parts. English orthography is made up of four basic word types:

1. Regular, for reading and spelling (e.g., <u>cat, print</u>)
2. Regular, for reading but not for spelling (e.g., <u>float, brain</u> - could be spelled "flote" or "brane," respectively)
3. Rule based (e.g., <u>canning</u> - doubling rule, <u>faking</u> - drop e rule)
4. Irregular (e.g., <u>beauty</u>).

Students must be taught to recognize all four types of words automatically in order to be effective readers. Repeated practice in pattern recognition is often necessary. Practice techniques for student development can include speed drills in which they read lists of isolated words with contrasting vowel sounds that are signaled by the syllable type. For example, several closed syllable and vowel-consonant "e" words containing the vowel *a* are arranged randomly on pages containing about twelve lines and read for one minute. Individual goals are established and charts are kept of the number of words read correctly in successive sessions. The same word lists are repeated in sessions until the goal has been achieved for several succeeding sessions. When selecting words for these lists, the use of high-frequency words within a syllable category increases the likelihood of generalization to text reading.

True automaticity should be linked with prosody and anticipation to acquire full fluency. Such things as which syllable is accented and how word structure can be predictive are necessary to true automaticity and essential to complete fluency.

A student whose reading rate is slow, or halting and inconsistent, is exhibiting a lack of reading fluency. According to an article by Mastropieri, Leinart, & Scruggs (1999), some students have developed accurate word pronunciation skills but read at a slow rate. They have not moved to the phase where decoding is automatic, and their limited fluency may affect performance in the following ways:

1. They read less text than peers and have less time to remember, review, or comprehend the text
2. They expend more cognitive energy than peers trying to identify individual words
3. They may be less able to retain text in their memories and less likely to integrate those segments with other parts of the text

The simplest means of determining a student's reading rate is to have the student read aloud from a prescribed passage which is at the appropriate reading level for age and grade and contains a specified number of words. The passage should not be too familiar for the student (some will try to memorize or "work out" difficult bits ahead of time), and should not contain more words than can be read comfortably and accurately by a normal reader in one or two minutes. Count only the words <u>correctly</u> pronounced on first reading, and divide this word count into elapsed time to determine the student's reading rate. To determine the student's standing and progress, compare this rate with the norm for the class and the average for all students who read fluently at that specific age/grade level.

The following general guidelines can be applied for reading lists of words with a speed drill and a one-minute timing: 30 correct wpm for first- and second-grade children; 40 correct wpm for third-grade children; 60 correct wpm for mid-third-grade; and 80 wpm for students in fourth grade and higher.

Various techniques are useful with students who have acquired some proficiency in decoding skill but whose levels of skill are lower than their oral language abilities. Such techniques have certain, common features:

1. Students listen to text as they follow along with the book
2. Students follow the print using their fingers as guides
3. Reading materials are used that students would be unable to read independently

Experts recommend that a beginning reading program should incorporate partner reading, practice reading difficult words prior to reading the text, timings for accuracy and rate, opportunities to hear books read, and opportunities to read to others.

Prosody concerns versification of text and involves such matters as which syllable of a word is accented. As regards fluency, it is that aspect which translates reading into the same experience as listening, within the reader's mind. It involves intonation and rhythm through such devices as syllable accent and punctuation.

In their article for *Perspectives* (Winter, 2002), Pamela Hook and Sandra Jones proposed that teachers can begin to develop awareness of the prosodic features of language by introducing a short three-word sentence with each of the three different words underlined for stress (e.g., *He is sick. He is sick. He is sick.*) The teacher can then model the three sentences while discussing the possible meaning for each variation. The students can practice reading them with different stress until they are fluent. These simple three-word sentences can be modified and expanded to include various verbs, pronouns, and tenses. (e.g., *You are sick. I am sick. They are sick.*) This strategy can also be used while increasing the length of phrases and emphasizing the different meanings (e.g., *Get out of bed. Get out of bed. Get out of bed now.*) Teachers can also practice fluency with common phrases that frequently occur in text. Prepositional phrases are good syntactic structures for this type of work (e.g., *on the _____, in the _____, over the _____ etc.*). Teachers can pair these printed phrases to oral intonation patterns that include variations of rate, intensity, and pitch. Students can infer the intended meaning as the teacher presents different prosodic variations of a sentence. For example, when speakers want to stress a concept, they often slow their rate of speech and may speak in a louder voice (e.g., *Joshua, get-out-of-bed-NOW!*). Often, the only text marker for this sentence will be the exclamation point (!), but the speaker's intent will affect the manner in which it is delivered.

Practicing oral variations and then mapping the prosodic features onto the text will assist students in making the connection when reading. This strategy can also be used to alert students to the prosodic features present in punctuation marks. In the early stages, using the alphabet helps to focus a student on the punctuation marks without having to deal with meaning. The teacher models for the students and then has them practice the combinations using the correct intonation patterns to fit the punctuation mark (e.g., ABC. DE? FGH! IJKL? or ABCD! EFGHI? KL.) Teachers can then move to simple two-word or three-word sentences. The sentences are punctuated with a period, question mark, and exclamation point, and the differences in meaning that occur with each different punctuation mark (e.g., *Chris hops. Chris hops? Chris hops!*) are discussed. It may help students to point out that the printed words convey the fact that someone named Chris is engaged in the physical activity of hopping, but the intonation patterns get their cue from the punctuation mark. The meaning extracted from an encounter with a punctuation mark is dependent upon a reader's prior experiences or background knowledge in order to project an appropriate intonation pattern onto the printed text. Keeping the text static while changing the punctuation marks helps students to attend to prosodic patterns.

Students who read word-for-word may benefit initially from practicing phrasing with the alphabet rather than words, since letters do not tax the meaning system. The letters are grouped, an arc is drawn underneath, and students recite the alphabet in chunks (e.g., ABC DE FGH IJK LM NOP QRS TU VW XYZ). Once students understand the concept of phrasing, it is recommended that teachers help students chunk text into syntactic (noun phrases, verb phrases, prepositional phrases) or meaning units until they are proficient themselves. There are no hard-and-fast rules for chunking, but syntactic units are most commonly used.

For better readers, teachers can mark the phrasal boundaries with slashes for short passages. Eventually, the slashes are used only at the beginning of long passages, and then students are asked to continue "phrase reading" even after the marks end. Marking phrases can be done together with students, or those on an independent level may divide passages into phrases themselves. Comparisons can be made to clarify reasons for differences in phrasing. Another way to encourage students to focus on phrase meaning and prosody in addition to word identification is to provide tasks that require them to identify or supply a paraphrase of an original statement.

Rate

A word count was obtained for each episode, then mean speed of words per second were computed within each episode and entire text. Participant miscue and accuracy rates were examined.

- **See** also Skill 1.2

Skill 2.4   Identify instructional methods (e.g., practice with high-frequency words, timed readings) for developing reading fluency.

At some point it is crucial that, just as the nervous, novice bike rider finally relaxes and speeds happily off; so too must the early reader integrate graphophonic cues with semantic and structural ones and move toward fluency. Before this is done, the oral quality of early readers has a stilted beat to it, which of course, does not promote reading engagement and enjoyment.

The teacher needs to be at his/her most theatrical to model for children the beauties of voice and nuance that are contained in the texts whose print they are tracking so anxiously. Children love nothing more than to mimic their teacher and can do so legitimately and without hesitation if the teacher takes time each day to theatrically recite a poem with them. The poem might be posted on chart paper and be up on the board for a week.

First the teacher can model the fluent and expressive reading of this poem. Then with a pointer, the class can recite it with the teacher. As the week progresses, the class can recite it on their own.

Awareness of the challenges and supports in a text
Illustrations can be key supports for emergent and early readers. Teachers should not only use wordless stories (books which tell their narratives through pictures alone), but can also make targeted use of Big Books for read-alouds, so that young children become habituated in the use of illustrations as an important component for constructing meaning. The teacher should model for the child how to reference an illustration for help in identifying a word in the text the child does not recognize.

Of course, children can also go on a picture walk with the teacher as part of a mini-lesson or guided reading and anticipate the story (narrative) using the pictures alone to construct meaning.

Decodability
Use literature that contains examples of letter-sound correspondences you wish to teach. First, read the literature with the children or read it aloud to them. Then take a specific example from the text and have the children reread it as you point out the letter-sound correspondence to the children. Then ask the children to go through the now familiar literature to find other letter-sound correspondences.

Once the children have correctly made the text-sound correspondence, have them share other similar correspondences they find in other works of literature. The opportunity may also be used for repeated readings of various literature works which will enhance the children's ownership of their letter-sound correspondence ability and their pleasure in oral reading.

Cooper (2004) suggests that children can be told to become word detectives so that they can independently and fluently decode on their own. The child should learn the following word detective routines so that he or she can function as an independent fluent reader who can decode words on his/her own. First the child should read on to the end of the sentence. Then the child should search for word parts that he knows and also try to decode the word from the letter sounds. As a last resort, the child should ask someone for help or go to look up the word in the dictionary.

Techniques for determining students' independent, instructional, and frustration reading levels

Instructional Reading is generally judged to be at the 95 percent accuracy level, although Taberski places it at between 92 and 97 percent. Taberski tries to enhance the independent reading levels by making sure that readers on the instructional reading levels read a variety of genres and have a range of available and interesting books with a particular genre to read.

Taberski's availability for reading conferences helps her to both assess first hand her children's frustration levels and to model ongoing teacher/reader book conversations by scheduling child-initiated reading conferences where she personally replenishes their book bags.

In order to allay children's frustration levels in their reading and to foster their independent reading, it is important to some children that the teacher personally take time out to hear them read aloud and to check for fluency and expression. Children's frustration level can be immeasurably lessened if they are explicitly told by the teacher after they have read aloud that they need to read without pointing and that they should try chunking words into phrases that mimic their natural speech.

Assessment of the reading development of individual students

For young readers who are from ELL backgrounds, even if they have been born in the United States, the use of pictures validates their story authoring and story telling skills and provides them with access and equity to the literary discussion and book talk of their native English-speaking peers. These children can also demonstrate their storytelling abilities by drawing sequels or prequels to the story detailed in the illustrations alone. They might even be given the opportunity to share the story aloud in their native language or to comment on the illustrations in their native language.

Since many stories today are recorded in two or even three languages at once, discussing story events or analyzing pictures in a different native language is a beneficial practice.

Use of pictures and illustrations can also help the K-3 educator assess the capabilities of children who are struggling readers because they are children whose learning strength is spatial. Through targeted questions about how the pictures would change if different plot twists occurred or how the child might transform the story through changing the illustrations, the teacher can begin to assess struggling-reader deficits and strengths.

Children from ELL backgrounds can benefit from listening to a recorded tape version of a particular story with which they can read along. This gives them another opportunity to "hear" the story correctly pronounced and presented and to begin to internalize its language structures. In the absence of taped versions of some key stories or texts, the teacher may want to make sound recordings.

Highly proficient readers can also be involved in creating these literature recordings for use with ELL peers or younger peers. This, of course, develops oral language proficiency, but also introduces these skilled readers into the intricacies of supporting ELL English language reading instruction. When they actually see their tapes being used by children, they will be tremendously gratified.

Skill 2.5   Identify instructional methods and strategies to increase vocabulary acquisition (e.g., word analysis, choice of words, context clues, multiple exposures) across the content areas.

Students will be better at comprehension if they have a stronger working vocabulary. Research has shown that students learn more vocabulary when it is presented in context, rather than in vocabulary lists, for example. Furthermore, the more that students get to use particular words in context, the more they will (a) remember each word, and (b) utilize it in the comprehension of sentences that contain the words.

Phonological Awareness
Phonological awareness means the ability of the reader to recognize the sound of spoken language. This recognition includes how these sounds can be blended together, segmented (divided up), and manipulated (switched around). This awareness then leads to phonics, a method for teaching students to read. It helps them "sound out words."

Instructional methods to teach phonological awareness may include any or all of the following: Auditory games and drills, during which students recognize and manipulate the sounds of words, separate or segment the sounds of words, take out sounds, blend sounds, add in new sounds, or take apart sound to recombine them in new formations..

Identification of common morphemes, prefixes, and suffixes
This aspect of vocabulary development is to help students look for structural elements within words which they can use independently to help them determine meaning.

The terms listed below are generally recognized as the key structural analysis components.

Root words: A root word is a word from which another word is developed. The second word can be said to have its "root" in the first. This structural component nicely lends itself to a tree-with-roots illustration which can concretize the meaning for students. Students may also want to literally construct root words using cardboard trees and/or actual roots from plants to create word family models. This is a lovely way to help students own their root words.

Base words: A base word is a stand-alone linguistic unit which cannot be deconstructed or broken down into smaller words. For example, in the word "re-tell," the base word is "tell."

Contractions: These are shortened forms of two words in which a letter or letters have been deleted. These deleted letters have been replaced by an apostrophe.

Prefixes: These are beginning units of meaning which can be added (the vocabulary word for this type of structural adding is "affixed") to a base word or root word. They cannot stand alone. They are also sometimes known as "bound morphemes," meaning that they cannot stand alone as a base word.

Suffixes: These are ending units of meaning which can be "affixed" or added on to the ends of root or base words. Suffixes transform the original meanings of base and root words. Like prefixes, they are also known as "bound morphemes," because they cannot stand alone as words.

Compound words: Occur when two or more base words are connected to form a new word. The meaning of the new word is in some way connected with that of the base word.

Inflectional endings: Are types of suffixes that impart a new meaning to the base or root word. These endings in particular change the gender, number, tense, or form of the base or root words. Just like other suffixes, these are also termed "bound morphemes."

The National Reading Panel (2000) has put forth the following conclusions about vocabulary instruction.

1. There is a need for direct instruction of vocabulary items required for a specific text.
2. Repetition and multiple exposure to vocabulary items are important. Students should be given items that will be likely to appear in many contexts.
3. Learning in rich contexts is valuable for vocabulary learning. Vocabulary words should be those that the learner will find useful in many contexts. When vocabulary items are derived from content learning materials, the learner will be better equipped to deal with specific reading matter in content areas.
4. Vocabulary tasks should be restructured as necessary. It is important to be certain that students fully understand what is asked of them in the context of reading rather than focusing only on the words to be learned.
5. Vocabulary learning is effective when it entails active engagement in learning tasks.
6. Computer technology can be used effectively to help teach vocabulary.
7. Vocabulary can be acquired through incidental learning. Much of a student's vocabulary will have to be learned in the course of doing things other than explicit vocabulary learning. Repetition, richness of context, and motivation may also add to the efficacy of incidental learning of vocabulary.
8. Dependence on a single vocabulary instruction method will not result in optimal learning. A variety of methods can be used effectively with emphasis on multimedia aspects of learning, richness of context in which words are to be learned, and the number of exposures to words that learners receive.

The Panel found that a critical feature of effective classrooms is the instruction of specific words that includes lessons and activities where students apply their vocabulary knowledge and strategies to reading and writing. Included in the activities were discussions where teachers and students talked about words, their features, and strategies for understanding unfamiliar words.

There are many methods for directly and explicitly teaching words. In fact, the Panel found twenty-one methods that have been found effective in research projects. Many emphasize the underlying concept of a word and its connections to other words, such as semantic mapping and diagrams that use graphics. The keyword method uses words and illustrations that highlight salient features of meaning. Visualizing or drawing a picture either by the student or by the teacher was found to be effective. Many words cannot be learned in this way, of course, so it should be used as only one method among others. Effective classrooms provide multiple ways for students to learn and interact with words. The Panel also found that computer-assisted activities can have a very positive role in the development of vocabulary.

Skill 2.6 **Identify instructional methods (e.g., summarizing, monitoring, comprehension, question answering, question generating, use of graphic and semantic organizers, recognizing story structure, use of multiple-strategy instruction) to facilitate students' reading comprehension.**

The point of comprehension instruction is not necessarily to focus just on the text(s) students are using at the very moment of instruction, but rather to help them learn the strategies that they can use independently with any other text.

Some of the most common methods of teaching instruction are as follows:

- Summarization: This is where, either in writing or verbally, students go over the main point of the text, along with strategically-chosen details that highlight the main point. This is not the same as paraphrasing, which is saying the same thing in different words. Teaching students how to summarize is very important, as it will help them look for the most critical areas in a text, in nonfiction. For example, it will help them distinguish between main arguments and examples. In fiction, it helps students to learn how to focus on the main characters and events and distinguish those from the lesser characters and events.
- Question answering: While this tends to be overused in many classrooms, it is still a valid method of teaching students to comprehend. As the name implies, students answer questions regarding a text, either out loud, in small groups, or individually on paper. The best questions are those that cause students to have to think about the text (rather than just find an answer within the text).
- Question generating: This is the opposite of question answering, although students can then be asked to answer their own questions or the questions of peer students. In general, we want students to constantly question texts as they read. This is important because it causes students to become more critical readers. To teach students to generate questions helps them to learn the types of questions they can ask, and it gets them thinking about how best to be critical of texts.

- Graphic organizers: Graphic organizers are graphical representations of content within a text. For example, Venn Diagrams can be used to highlight the difference between two characters in a novel or two similar political concepts in a social studies textbook. Or, a teacher can use flowcharts with students to talk about the steps in a process (for example, the steps of setting up a science experiment or the chronological events of a story). Semantic organizers are similar in that they graphically display information. The difference, usually, is that semantic organizers focus on words or concepts. For example, a word web can help students make sense of a word by mapping from the central word all the similar and related concepts to that word.

- Text structure: Often in nonfiction, particularly in textbooks, and sometimes in fiction, text structures will give important clues to readers about what to look for. Often, students do not know how to make sense of all the types of headings in a textbook and do not realize that, for example, the sidebar story about a character in history is not the main text on a particular page in the history textbook. Teaching students how to interpret text structures gives them tools in which to tackle other similar texts.

- Monitoring comprehension: Students need to be aware of their comprehension, or lack of it, in particular texts. So, it is important to teach students what to do when suddenly text stops making sense. For example, students can go back and re-read the description of a character. Or, they can go back to the table of contents or the first paragraph of a chapter to see where they are headed.

- Textual marking: This is where students interact with the text as they read. For example, armed with Post-it notes, students can insert questions or comments regarding specific sentences or paragraphs within the text. This helps students focus on the importance of the small things, particularly when they are reading larger works (such as novels in high school). It also gives students a reference point on which to go back into the text when they need to review something.

- Discussion: Small-group or whole-class discussion stimulates thoughts about texts and gives students a larger picture of the impact of those texts. For example, teachers can strategically encourage students to discuss concepts related to the text. This helps students learn to consider texts within larger societal and social concepts, or teachers can encourage students to provide personal opinions in discussion. By listening to various students' opinions, this will help all students in a class to see the wide range of possible interpretations and thoughts regarding one text.

Many people mistakenly believe that the terms "research-based" or "research-validated" or "evidence-based" relate mainly to specific programs, such as early reading textbook programs. While research does validate that some of these programs are effective, much research has been conducted regarding the effectiveness of particular instructional strategies. In reading, many of these strategies have been documented in the report from the National Reading Panel. However, just because a strategy has not been validated as effective by research does not necessarily mean that it is not effective with certain students in certain situations. The number of strategies out there far outweighs researchers' ability to test their effectiveness. Some of the strategies listed above have been validated by rigorous research, while others have been shown consistently to help improve students' reading abilities in localized situations. There simply is not enough space to list all the strategies out there that have been proven effective; just know that the above strategies are very commonly cited ones that work in a variety of situations.

Skill 2.7 **Identify essential comprehension skills (e.g., main idea, supporting details and facts, author's purpose, fact and opinion, point of view, inference, conclusion).**

Main Idea
A **topic** of a paragraph or story is what the paragraph or story is about.

The **main idea** of a paragraph or story states the important idea(s) that the author wants the reader to know about a topic.

The topic and main idea of a paragraph or story are sometimes directly stated.

There are times; however, that the topic and main idea are not directly stated, but simply implied.

Look at this paragraph.

> Henry Ford was an inventor who developed the first affordable automobile. The cars that were being built before Mr. Ford created his Model T were very expensive. Only rich people could afford to have cars.

The topic of this paragraph is Henry Ford. The main idea is that Henry Ford built the first affordable automobile.

The **topic sentence** indicates what the passage is about. It is the subject of that portion of the narrative. The ability to identify the topic sentence in a passage will enable the student to focus on the concept being discussed and better comprehend the information provided.

You can find the main ideas by looking at the way in which paragraphs are written. A paragraph is a group of sentences about one main idea. Paragraphs usually have two types of sentences: a topic sentence, which contains the main idea, and two or more detail sentences which support, prove, provide more information, explain, or give examples.

You can only tell if you have a detail or topic sentence by comparing the sentences with each other.

Look at this sample paragraph:
Fall is the best of the four seasons. The leaves change colors to create a beautiful display of golds, reds, and oranges. The air turns crisp and windy. The scent of pumpkin muffins and apple pies fill the air. Finally, Halloween marks the start of the holiday season. Fall is my favorite time of year!

Breakdown of sentences:
Fall is the best of the four seasons. (TOPIC SENTENCE)
The leaves change colors to create a beautiful display of golds, reds, and oranges. (DETAIL)
The air turns crisp and windy. (DETAIL)
The scent of pumpkin muffins and apple pies fill the air. (DETAIL)
Finally, Halloween marks the start of the holiday season. (DETAIL)
Fall is my favorite time of year! (CLOSING SENTENCE – Often a restatement of the topic sentence)

The first sentence introduces the main idea and the other sentences support and give the many uses for the product.

Tips for Finding the Topic Sentence

1. The topic sentence is usually first, but could be in any position in the paragraph.

2. A topic is usually more "general" than the other sentences, that is, it talks about many things and looks at the big picture. Sometimes it refers to more than one thing. Plurals and the words "many," "numerous," or "several" often signal a topic sentence.

3. Detail sentences are usually more "specific" than the topic, that is, they usually talk about one single or small part or side of an idea. Also, the words "for example," "i.e.," "that is," "first," "second," "third," etc., and "finally" often signal a detail.

4. Most of the detail sentences support, give examples, prove, talk about, or point toward the topic in some way.

How can you be sure that you have a topic sentence? Try this trick: switch the sentence you think is the topic sentence into a question. If the other sentences seem to "answer" the question, then you've got it.

For example:
Reword the topic sentence "Fall is the best of the four seasons" in one of the following ways:

"Why is fall the best of the four seasons?"
"Which season is the best season?"
"Is fall the best season of the year?"

Then, as you read the remaining sentences (the ones you didn't pick), you will find that they answer (support) your question.

If you attempt this with a sentence other than the topic sentence, it won't work

For example:
Suppose you select "Halloween marks the start of the holiday season," and you reword it in the following way:

"Which holiday is the start of the holiday season?"

You will find that the other sentences fail to help you answer (support) your question.

Summary Statements
The introductory statement should be at the beginning of the passage. An introductory statement will provide a bridge between any previous, relevant text and the content to follow. It will provide information about, and set the tone and parameters for, the text to follow. The old axiom regarding presenting a body of information suggested that you should always "tell them what you are going to tell them; tell it to them; tell them what you just told them." The introductory statement is where the writer will tell the readers what he or she is going to tell them.

The summary statement should be at or near the end of the passage, and is a concise presentation of the essential data from that passage. In terms of the old axiom, the content portion (the main body of the narrative) is where the writer will "tell it to them." The summary statement is where the writer will tell the readers what he or she has just told them.

Restating the Main Idea

An accurate restatement of the main idea from a passage will usually summarize the concept in a concise manner, and it will often present the same idea from a different perspective. A restatement should always demonstrate complete comprehension of the main idea.

To select an accurate restatement, identifying the main idea of the passage is essential (see Skill 2.2). Once you comprehend the main idea of a passage, evaluate your choices to see which statement restates the main idea while eliminating statements which restate a supporting detail. Walk through the steps below the sample paragraph from Skill 2.2 to see how to select the accurate restatement.

Sample Paragraph:

Fall is the best of the four seasons. The leaves change colors to create a beautiful display of golds, reds, and oranges. The air turns crisp and windy. The scent of pumpkin muffins and apple pies fill the air. Finally, Halloween marks the start of the holiday season. Fall is my favorite time of year!

Steps:
1. Identify the main idea. (Answer: "Fall is the best of the four seasons.")
2. Decide which statement below restates the topic sentence:
   A. The changing leaves turn gold, red, and orange.
   B. The holidays start with Halloween.
   C. Of the four seasons, fall is the greatest of them all.
   D. Crisp wind is a fun aspect of fall.

The answer is (C) because it rewords the main idea of the first sentence, the topic sentence.

Supporting Details

The **supporting details** are sentences that give more information about the topic and the main idea.

The supporting details in the aforementioned paragraph about Henry Ford would be that he was an inventor and that before he created his Model T, only rich people could afford cars because they were too expensive.

Fact and Opinion

A **fact** is something that is true and can be proved.
An **opinion** is something that a person believes, thinks, or feels.

Examine the following examples:

Joe DiMaggio, a Yankees center fielder, was replaced by Mickey Mantle in 1952.

This is a fact. If necessary, evidence can be produced to support this.

First-year players are more ambitious than seasoned players.

This is an opinion. There is no proof to support that everyone feels this way.

Author's Purpose

An author may have more than one purpose in writing. An **author's purpose** may be to entertain, to persuade, to inform, to describe, or to narrate.

There are no tricks or rules to follow in attempting to determine an author's purpose. It is up to the reader to use his or her judgment.

Read the following paragraph.

Charles Lindbergh had no intention of becoming a pilot. He was enrolled in the University of Wisconsin until a flying lesson changed the entire course of his life. He began his career as a pilot by performing daredevil stunts at fairs.

    The author wrote this paragraph primarily to:

    (A) Describe
    (B) Inform
    (C) Entertain
    (D) Narrate

    Since the author is simply telling us or informing us about the life of Charles Lindbergh, the correct answer here is (B).

Author's Tone and Point of View

The **author's tone** is his or her attitude as reflected in the statement or passage. His or her choice of words will help the reader determine the overall tone of a statement or passage.

Read the following paragraph.

I was shocked by your article, which said that sitting down to breakfast was a thing of the past. Many families consider breakfast time, family time. Children need to realize the importance of having a good breakfast. It is imperative that they be taught this at a young age. I cannot believe that a writer with your reputation has difficulty comprehending this.

The author's tone in this passage is one of

(A) concern
(B) anger
(C) excitement
(D) disbelief

Since the author directly states that he "cannot believe" that the writer feels this way, the answer is (D) disbelief.

Inferences and Conclusions
In order to draw **inferences** and make **conclusions**, a reader must use prior knowledge and apply it to the current situation. A conclusion or inference is never stated. You must rely on your common sense.

Read the following passage.

The Smith family waited patiently around carousel number seven for their luggage to arrive. They were exhausted after their five-hour trip and were anxious to get to their hotel. After about an hour, they realized that they no longer recognized any of the other passengers' faces. Mrs. Smith asked the person who appeared to be in charge if they were at the right carousel. The man replied, "Yes, this is it, but we finished unloading that baggage almost half an hour ago."

From the man's response we can infer that:
(A) The Smiths were ready to go to their hotel.
(B) The Smith's luggage was lost.
(C) The man had their luggage.
(D) They were at the wrong carousel.

Since the Smiths were still waiting for their luggage, we know that they were not yet ready to go to their hotel. From the man's response, we know that they were not at the wrong carousel and that he did not have their luggage. Therefore, though not directly stated, it appears that their luggage was lost. Choice (B) is the correct answer.

Skill 2.8   **Identify appropriate classroom organizational formats (e.g., literature circles, small groups, individuals, workshops, reading centers, multiage groups) for specific instructional objectives.**

It used to be that when teachers would think of varying instruction, they would be referring mainly to content. Methods of instruction were fairly constant: in older grade levels, lecture—and possibly some discussion—was the primary method of instructional delivery. In younger grades, independent work, as well as some group work, was standard fare for most instructional topics.

Today, however, teachers know that for the enormous varieties of content to be taught, there are enormous varieties of instructional methods that can be used. A good way to think about the variety of instructional methods is by classifying them into organizational formats. While there are literally hundreds of instructional ideas for just about any K-12 curricular topic, we can make the job easier by thinking of how organizational formats essentially organize our instructional ideas.

As the standard states, some widely used organizational formats include literature circles, small groups, individual work, workshops, reading centers, and multiage groups. Each of these will be explained; however, it is important to remember that additional ideas are possible. A quick example of an additional idea is whole-class drama, where after reading a book or story, the entire class acts out various portions of the text.

Literature circles are group activities where each individual in the group is given a particular "job." Jobs may include discussion leader, artist (for representing the discussion through art, perhaps), word leader (someone who looks up and informs the group of specific vocabulary words), and many others. The point of these jobs is to help keep a student-centered conversation of literature alive. These jobs assist the group in maintaining a conversation without teacher assistance.

Small group activities allow students to work together on any number of activities. While teachers circulate the room and assist where necessary, small group activities give students a chance to help each other and work together on a common problem. Often, small groups are beneficial in that groups can be pre-arranged by the teacher to serve various purposes. Sometimes, teachers want to have homogenous groups (groups of the same ability); other times, it is preferable to mix groups up so that highly skilled students can assist less skilled students.

Individual work should certainly not be ruled out, even though there is indeed a wider movement to get away from that. Individual work is very beneficial when we want to ensure that all students get the practice they need to become proficient on their own in a certain area.

Workshops are structures that allow students to work on different products simultaneously. For example, we commonly think of writing workshops. While there may be times when, for example, teachers want all students to work on the same writing assignment at the same time (which would be considered individual work), other times, teachers want students to have choices in what they write. In workshops, one student might be writing a short story, while another student might be writing an essay. Students can get feedback from one another in a workshop, and they can also get assistance from the teacher.

Reading centers are structured places in the room where, while the teacher is working with an individual or a small group, students can complete certain reading activities without teacher assistance. Usually, with reading centers, students spend a bit of time at each center and then rotate to the next center. Common centers include computer terminals (so that students can use reading instruction software), student desks (so that students can read silently), and reading activity tables (where students, in groups, can do a reading activity together).

Multiage groups consist of coordination among teachers. Sometimes it is preferable to have homogonous groups on certain topics. Therefore, a third grade teacher might have some of his or her students go to the fourth grade class if they read at a fourth grade level. And the fourth grade teacher would send his or her third grade readers to the third grade room. This allows teachers to work with students on their specific reading difficulties.

In summary, when classroom organizational concepts are considered, teachers are then free to expand their repertoire of classroom activities for the variety of content they teach.

Skill 2.9 Identify appropriate uses of multiple representations of information (e.g., charts, tables, graphs, pictures, print and nonprint media) for a variety of purposes.

While the teaching of writing undoubtedly involves an enormous of work on the composition of text, it also involves the general idea of ideas conveyed in the best possible manner. In other words, I could explain the results of a survey in words, but it might be easier to understand in a graph or chart. If that is the case, why would we want to present it in words? The important point is for the information to be conveyed.

So, as students write reports and respond to ideas in writing, they can learn how to incorporate multiple representations of information, including various graphic representations, into written text. While this is seemingly fairly easy to do considering the word processing technology we have available to us, students struggle with knowing how to appropriately and successfully do this. They can learn to do this in three primary ways: explanation, observation/modeling, and practice.

First, students need to have clear explanations from teachers on appropriate forms of graphical representations in text, as well as the methods in which to include those representations. They need to see plenty of examples of how it is done.

Second, they need to be able to see teacher-modeled examples where text has been replaced or enhanced by graphical representations. The more they see of examples, the clearer the concepts will be to them.

Finally, students need to get a chance to practice incorporating graphical representations in their writing. This, of course, will require technology and plenty of feedback.

Students will most likely appreciate the ability to utilize graphical representations in place of text, but they will soon realize that deciding which type of representation to use and how to actually use it will be very challenging. Generally, graphical representations should be used only if they can convey information better than written text can. This is an important principal that students will need to learn through constant practice.

Skill 2.10 Identify strategies for developing critical thinking skills (e.g., analysis, synthesis, evaluation).

Teachers should have a toolkit of instructional strategies, materials, and technologies to encourage and teach students how to problem solve and think critically about subject content. With each curriculum chosen by a district for school implementation, comes an expectation that students must master benchmarks and standards of learning skills. There is an established level of academic performance and proficiency in public schools that students are required to master in today's classrooms. Research of national and state standards indicate that there are additional benchmarks and learning objectives in the subject areas of science, foreign language, English language arts, history, art, health, civics, economics, geography, physical education, mathematics, and social studies that students are required to master in state assessments (Marzano & Kendall, 1996).

A critical thinking skill is a skill target that teachers help students develop to sustain learning in specific subject areas that can be applied within other subject areas. For example, when learning to understand algebraic concepts in solving a math word problem on how much fencing material is needed to build a fence around a backyard that has an 8' x 12' area, a math student must understand the order of numerical expression in how to simplify algebraic expressions. Teachers can provide instructional strategies that show students how to group the fencing measurements into an algebraic word problem that with minor addition, subtraction, and multiplication can produce a simple number equal to the amount of fencing materials needed to build the fence.

Higher-Ordered Thinking Skills

Developing critical thinking skills in students is not as simple as developing other simpler skills. In fact, many teachers mistakenly believe that these skills can be taught out of context (i.e., they can be taught as skills in and of themselves). Good teachers, however, realize that critical thinking skills must be taught within the contexts of specific subject matter. For example, language arts teachers can teach critical thinking skills through novels; social studies teachers can teach critical thinking skills through primary source documents or current events; and science teachers can teach critical thinking skills by having students develop hypotheses prior to conducting experiments.

First, let's start with definitions of the various types of critical thinking skills. Analysis is the systematic exploration of a concept, event, term, piece of writing, element of media, or any other complex item. Usually, people think of analysis as the exploration of the parts that make up a whole. For example, when someone analyzes a piece of literature, that person might focus on small pieces of the literature; yet, as they focus on the small pieces, they also call attention to the big picture and show how the small pieces create significance for the whole novel.

To carry this example further, if one were to analyze a novel, that person might investigate a particular character to determine how that character adds significance to the whole novel. In something more concrete like biology, one could analyze the findings of an experiment to see if the results might indicate significance for something even larger than the experiment itself. It is very easy to analyze political events, for example. A social studies teacher could ask students to analyze the events leading up to World War II; doing so would require that students look at the small pieces (e.g., smaller world events prior to World War II) and determine how those small pieces, when added up together, caused the war.

Next, let's consider synthesis. Synthesis is usually thought of as the opposite of analysis. In analysis, we take a whole and break it up into pieces and look at the pieces. With synthesis, we take different things and make them one whole thing. For example, a language arts teacher could ask students to synthesize two works of distinct literature. Let's say that we take *The Scarlett Letter* and *The Crucible*, two works both featuring life during Puritanical America, written about one century apart. A student could synthesize the two works and come to conclusions about Puritanical life. An art teacher could ask students to synthesize two paintings from the impressionist era and come to conclusions about the features that distinguish that style of art.

Finally, evaluation involves making judgments. Whereas analysis and synthesis seek answers and hypotheses based on investigations, evaluation seeks opinions. For example, a social studies teacher could ask students to evaluate the quality of Richard Nixon's resignation speech. To do so, they would judge whether or not they felt it was good. In contrast, analysis would keep judgment out of the assignment: it would have students focus possibly on the structure of the speech (i.e., Does an argument move from emotional to logical?). When evaluating a speech, a piece of literature, a movie, or a work of art, we seek to determine whether we think it is good or not. But, keep in mind, teaching good evaluation skills requires not just that students learn how to determine whether something is good or not: it requires that they learn how to support their evaluations. So, if a student claims that Nixon's speech was effective in what the president intended the speech to do, the student would need to explain how this is so. Notice that evaluation will probably utilize the skills of analysis and/or synthesis, but that the purpose is ultimately different.

Encouraging Independent Critical Thinking
Since most teachers want their educational objectives to use higher-level thinking skills, teachers need to direct students to these higher levels on the taxonomy. Questioning is an effective tool to build students up to these higher levels.

Low-order questions are useful to begin the process. They insure the student is focused on the required information and understands what needs to be included in the thinking process. For example, if the objective is for students to be able to read and understand the story "Goldilocks and the Three Bears," the teacher may wish to start with low-order questions (i.e., "What are some things Goldilocks did while in the bears' home?" [Knowledge] or "Why didn't Goldilocks like the Papa Bear's chair?" [Analysis])

Through a series of questions, the teacher can move the students up the taxonomy. (For example, "If Goldilocks had come to your house, what are some things she may have used?" [Application], "How might the story have differed if Goldilocks had visited the three fishes?" [Synthesis], or "Do you think Goldilocks was good or bad? Why?" [Evaluation]) The teacher through questioning can control the thinking process of the class. As students become more involved in the discussion they are systematically being led to higher-level thinking.

To develop a critical-thinking approach to the world, children need to know enough about valid and invalid reasoning to ask questions. Bringing into the classroom speeches or essays that demonstrate both valid and invalid examples can be useful in helping students develop the ability to question the reasoning of others. These will be published writers or televised speakers, so the students can see that they are able to question even ideas that are accepted by some adults and talk about what is wrong in the thinking of those apparently successful communicators.

If the teacher stays right on the cutting edge of children's experience, they will become more and more curious about what is out there in the world that they don't know about. A good way to introduce the outside world could be a lesson on a particular country or even a tribe that the children may not know exists. This kind of lesson would reveal to children what life is like in other countries or tribes for children their own age. The lesson could use different kinds of media for variety and greater impact. In such a presentation, positive aspects of the lives of those "other" children should be included. Perhaps correspondence with a village could be developed. It's good for children, some of whom may not live very high on the social scale in this country, to know what the rest of the world is like, and in so doing, develop an independent curiosity to know more.

In general, critical thinking skills should be taught through assignments, activities, lessons, and discussions that cause students to think on their own. While teachers can and should provide students with the tools to think critically, they will ultimately become critical thinkers if they have to use those tools themselves. But, this one last point cannot be taken lightly: teachers must provide students the tools to evaluate, analyze, and synthesize.

Let's take political speeches as an example. Students will be better analyzers, synthesizers, and evaluators if they understand some of the basics of political speeches. Therefore, a teacher might introduce concepts such as rhetoric, style, persona, audience, diction, imagery, and tone. The best way to introduce these concepts would be to provide students with multiple, good examples of these things. Once they are familiar with these critical tools, students will be in a better place to apply them individually to political speeches—and then be able to analyze, synthesize, and evaluate political speeches on their own.

Skill 2.11   Identify instructional methods to teach a variety of informational and literary text structures.

Text structure refers to the patterns of textual organization in a piece of writing. Authors will arrange their writings into various structures in order to make their content more comprehensible. For example, when explaining an historical event, an author may arrange her text in a cause-effect structure; in other words, the text presents causes of an event, and then it provides the potential or actual effects. Or, if an author is telling a story, such as in a literary narrative, the author may decide to arrange the text in basic, chronological events. The author could also provide flashbacks or other disruptions in a sequence—and that would change the text structure.

Particularly in information texts, text structure helps readers make sense of the content. When readers identify a text structure, often, they have an easier time comprehending the text. For example, let's say we are reading an essay that contains one paragraph explaining an opinion of a political issue and nine or ten paragraphs retelling stories of people. One might believe that the essay is merely a collection of stories about people. However, it is entirely possible that the text structure works like this:

OPINION
EXAMPLE
EXAMPLE
EXAMPLE
EXAMPLE
EXAMPLE
...SO FORTH

So, how do teachers help students to understand the concept of text structure and use it in their own reading? Often, modeling (and then giving students practice) in text-structure analysis is quite effective. Graphic organizers also provide a visual tool to help students make sense of text structure. In general, giving students the chance to practice with identifying the structures in texts will help them to do it on their own with the books and shorter texts they read outside of school.

COMPETENCY 3.0   KNOWLEDGE OF LITERATURE

Skill 3.1   Identify characteristics and elements of a variety of literary genres (e.g., short stories, poetry, plays, personal narratives).

The major literary genres include allegory, ballad, drama, epic, epistle, essay, fable, novel, poem, romance, and the short story.

Allegory: A story in verse or prose with characters representing virtues and vices. There are two meanings, symbolic and literal. John Bunyan's *The Pilgrim's Progress* is the most renowned of this genre.

Ballad: An *in medias res* story told or sung, usually in verse and accompanied by music. Literary devices found in ballads include the refrain, or repeated section; and incremental repetition, or anaphora, for effect. Earliest forms were anonymous folk ballads. Later forms include Coleridge's Romantic masterpiece, "The Rime of the Ancient Mariner."

Drama: Plays – comedy, modern, or tragedy - typically in five acts. Traditionalists and neoclassicists adhere to Aristotle's unities of time, place, and action. Plot development is advanced via dialogue. Literary devices include asides, soliloquies, and the chorus representing public opinion. The greatest of all dramatists/playwrights is William Shakespeare. Other dramaturges include Ibsen, Williams, Miller, Shaw, Stoppard, Racine, Moliére, Sophocles, Aeschylus, Euripides, and Aristophanes.

Epic: Long poem usually of book length reflecting values inherent in the generative society. Epic devices include an invocation to a muse for inspiration, purpose for writing, universal setting, protagonist and antagonist who possess supernatural strength and acumen, and interventions of a God or the gods. Understandably, there are very few epics: Homer's *Iliad* and *Odyssey*, Virgil's *Aeneid*, Milton's *Paradise Lost*, Spenser's *The Fairie Queene*, Barrett Browning's *Aurora Leigh*, and Pope's mock epic, *The Rape of the Lock*.

Epistle: A letter that is not always originally intended for public distribution, but due to the fame of the sender and/or recipient, becomes public domain. Paul wrote epistles that were later placed in the *Bible*.

Essay: Typically a limited-length prose work focusing on a topic and propounding a definite point of view and authoritative tone. Great essayists include Carlyle, Lamb, DeQuincy, Emerson, and Montaigne, who is credited with defining this genre.

Fable: A terse tale offering up a moral or exemplum. Chaucer's "The Nun's Priest's Tale" is a fine example of a *bete fabliau*, or beast fable, in which animals speak and act characteristically human, illustrating human foibles.

Legend: A traditional narrative or collection of related narratives, popularly regarded as historically factual but actually a mixture of fact and fiction.

Myth: Stories that are more or less universally shared within a culture to explain its history and traditions.

Novel: The longest form of fictional prose containing a variety of characterizations, settings, local color, and regionalism. Most have complex plots, expanded description, and attention to detail. Some of the great novelists include Austin, the Brontes, Twain, Tolstoy, Hugo, Hardy, Dickens, Hawthorne, Forster, and Flaubert.

Poem: The only requirement is rhythm. Sub-genres include fixed types of literature, such as the sonnet, elegy, ode, pastoral, and villanelle. Unfixed types of literature include blank verse and dramatic monologue.

Romance: A highly imaginative tale set in a fantastical realm dealing with the conflicts between heroes, villains and/or monsters. "The Knight's Tale" from Chaucer's *Canterbury Tales*, *Sir Gawain and the Green Knight* and Keats's "The Eve of St. Agnes" are prime representatives.

Short Story: Typically a terse narrative, with less developmental background about characters. May include description, author's point of view, and tone. Poe emphasized that a successful short story should create one focused impact. Considered to be great short story writers are Hemingway, Faulkner, Twain, Joyce, Shirley Jackson, Flannery O'Connor, de Maupasssant, Saki, Edgar Allen Poe, and Pushkin.

Children's Literature is a genre of its own and emerged as a distinct and independent form in the second half of the 18th century. *The Visible World in Pictures* by John Amos Comenius, a Czech educator, was one of the first printed works and the first picture book. For the first time, educators acknowledged that children are different from adults in many respects. Modern educators acknowledge that introducing elementary students to a wide range of reading experiences plays an important role in their mental/social/psychological development. Some of the most common forms of literature specifically for children follow:

- **Traditional Literature:** Traditional literature opens up a world where right wins out over wrong, where hard work and perseverance are rewarded, and where helpless victims find vindication—all worthwhile values that children identify with even as early as kindergarten. In traditional literature, children will be introduced to fanciful beings, humans with exaggerated powers, talking animals, and heroes that will inspire them. For younger elementary children, these stories in Big Book format are ideal for providing predictable and repetitive elements that can be grasped by these children.

- **Folktales/Fairy Tales:** Some examples: *The Three Bears, Little Red Riding Hood, Snow White, Sleeping Beauty, Puss in Boots, Rapunzel* and *Rumpelstiltskin*. Adventures of animals or humans and the supernatural characterize these stories. The hero is usually on a quest and is aided by other-worldly helpers. More often than not, the story focuses on good and evil and reward and punishment.

- **Fables:** Animals that act like humans are featured in these stories and usually reveal human foibles or sometimes teach a lesson. Example: *Aesop's Fables*.

- **Myths:** These stories about events from the earliest times, such as the origin of the world, are considered true in their own societies.

- **Legends:** These are similar to myths except that they tend to deal with events that happened more recently. Example: Arthurian legends.

- **Tall tales:** Examples: Paul Bunyan, John Henry, and Pecos Bill. These are purposely exaggerated accounts of individuals with superhuman strength.

- **Modern Fantasy:** Many of the themes found in these stories are similar to those in traditional literature. The stories start out based in reality, which makes it easier for the reader to suspend disbelief and enter worlds of unreality. Little people live in the walls in *The Borrowers* and time travel is possible in *The Trolley to Yesterday*. Including some fantasy tales in the curriculum helps elementary-grade children develop their senses of imagination. These often appeal to ideals of justice and issues having to do with good and evil; and because children tend to identify with the characters, the message is more likely to be retained.

- **Science Fiction:** Robots, spacecraft, mystery, and civilizations from other ages often appear in these stories. Most presume advances in science on other planets or in a future time. Most children like these stories because of their interest in space and the "what if" aspect of the stories. Examples: *Outer Space and All That Junk* and *A Wrinkle in Time*.

- **Modern Realistic Fiction:** These stories are about real problems that real children face. By finding that their hopes and fears are shared by others, young children can find insight into their own problems. Young readers also tend to experience a broadening of interests as the result of this kind of reading. It's good for them to know that a child can be brave and intelligent and can solve difficult problems.

- **Historical Fiction:** *Rifles for Watie* is an example of this kind of story. Presented in an historically-accurate setting, it is about a young boy who serves in the Union Army. He experiences great hardship but discovers that his enemy is an admirable human being. It provides a good opportunity to introduce children you history in a beneficial way.

- **Biography:** Reading about inventors, explorers, scientists, political and religious leaders, social reformers, artists, sports figures, doctors, teachers, writers, and war heroes helps children to see that one person can make a difference. They also open new vistas for children to think about when they choose an occupation to fantasize about.

- **Informational Books:** These are ways to learn more about something you are interested in or something that you know nothing about. Encyclopedias are good resources, of course, but a book like *Polar Wildlife* by Kamini Khanduri shows pictures and facts that will capture the imaginations of young children.

Skill 3.2   Identify the terminology and appropriate use of literary devices.

Imagery can be described as a word or sequence of words that refers to any sensory experience—that is, anything that can be seen, tasted, smelled, heard, or felt on the skin or fingers. While writers of prose may also use these devices, it is most distinctive of poetry. The poet intends to make an experience available to the reader. In order to do that, he/she must appeal to one of the senses. The most-often-used one, of course, is the visual sense. The poet will deliberately paint a scene in such a way that the reader can see it. However, the purpose is not simply to stir the visceral feeling but also to stir the emotions. A good example is "The Piercing Chill" by Taniguchi Buson (1715-1783):

> *The piercing chill I feel:*
> *My dead wife's comb, in our bedroom,*
> *Under my heel . . .*

In only a few short words, the reader can feel many things: the shock that might come from touching the corpse, a literal sense of death, and the contrast between her death and the memories he has of her when she was alive. Imagery might be defined as speaking of the abstract in concrete terms, a powerful device in the hands of a skillful poet.

A **symbol** is an object or action that can be observed with the senses, in addition to its suggesting many other things. The lion is a symbol of courage; the cross a symbol of Christianity; the color green a symbol of envy. These can almost be defined as metaphors because society pretty much agrees on the one-to-one meaning of them. Symbols used in literature are usually of a different sort. They tend to be private and personal; their significance is only evident in the context of the work where they are used. A good example is the huge pair of spectacles on a sign board in Fitzgerald's *The Great Gatsby*. They are interesting as a part of the landscape, but they also symbolize divine myopia. A symbol can certainly have more than one meaning, and the meaning may be as personal as the memories and experiences of the particular reader. In analyzing a poem or a story, it's important to identify the symbols and their possible meanings.

Looking for symbols is often challenging, especially for novice poetry readers. However, these suggestions may be useful: First, pick out all the references to concrete objects, such as a newspaper, black cats, etc. Note any that the poet emphasizes by describing in detail, by repeating, or by placing at the very beginning or ending of a poem. Ask yourself, "What is the poem about? What does it add up to?" Paraphrase the poem and determine whether or not the meaning depends upon certain concrete objects. Then ponder what the concrete object symbolizes in this particular poem. Look for a character with the name of a prophet who does little but utter prophecy or a trio of women who resemble the Three Fates. A symbol may be a part of a person's body, such as the eye of the murder victim in Poe's story *The Tell-Tale Heart* or a look, a voice, or a mannerism.

The following are some things a symbol is not: an abstraction such as truth, death, and love; in narrative, a well-developed character who is not at all mysterious; and the second term in a metaphor. In Emily Dickenson's *The Lightning is a Yellow Fork*, the symbol is the lightning, not the fork.

An **allusion** is very much like a symbol, and the two sometimes tend to run together. An allusion is defined by Merriam Webster's *Encyclopedia of Literature* as "an implied reference to a person, event, thing, or a part of another text." Allusions are based on the assumption that there is a common body of knowledge shared by poet and reader and that a reference to that body of knowledge will be immediately understood. Allusions to the *Bible* and classical mythology are common in western literature on the assumption that they will be immediately understood. This is not always the case, of course. T. S. Eliot's *The Wasteland* requires research and annotation for understanding. He assumed more background on the part of the average reader than actually exists. However, when Michael Moore on his web page headlines an article on the war in Iraq: "Déjà Fallouja: Ramadi surrounded, thousands of families trapped, no electricity or water, onslaught impending," we understand immediately that he is referring first of all to a repeat of the human disaster in New Orleans, although the "onslaught" is not a storm but an invasion by American and Iraqi troops. The use of allusion is a sort of shortcut for poets. They can use an economy of words and count on meaning to come from the reader's own experience.

Figurative language is also called figures of speech. If all figures of speech that have ever been identified were listed, it would be a very long list. However, for purposes of analyzing poetry, a few are sufficient.

1. Simile: Direct comparison between two things. "My love is like a red-red rose."

2. Metaphor: Indirect comparison between two things. The use of a word or phrase denoting one kind of object or action in place of another to suggest a comparison between them. While poets use them extensively, they are also integral to everyday speech. For example, chairs are said to have "legs" and "arms," although we know that it's humans and other animals that have these appendages.

3. Parallelism: The arrangement of ideas in phrases, sentences, and paragraphs that balance one element with another of equal importance and similar wording. The following is an example from Francis Bacon's *Of Studies:* "Reading maketh a full man, conference a ready man, and writing an exact man."

4. Personification: Human characteristics are attributed to an inanimate object, an abstract quality, or animal. Examples: John Bunyan wrote characters named Death, Knowledge, Giant Despair, Sloth, and Piety in his classic tale, *Pilgrim's Progress.* The metaphor of an arm of a chair is a form of personification.

5. Euphemism: The substitution of an agreeable or inoffensive term for one that might offend or suggest something unpleasant. Many euphemisms are used to refer to death to avoid using the real word, such as "passed away," "crossed over," or nowadays "passed."

6. Hyperbole: Deliberate exaggeration for effect or comic effect. The following is an example from Shakespeare's *The Merchant of Venice*:

> Why, if two gods should play some heavenly match
> And on the wager lay two earthly women,
> And Portia one, there must be something else
> Pawned with the other, for the poor rude world
> Hath not her fellow.

7. Climax: A number of phrases or sentences are arranged in ascending order of rhetorical forcefulness. Example from Melville's *Moby Dick*:

All that most maddens and torments; all that stirs up the lees of things; all truth with malice in it; all that cracks the sinews and cakes the brain; all the subtle demonisms of life and thought; all evil, to crazy Ahab, were visibly personified and made practically assailable in Moby Dick.

8. Bathos: A ludicrous attempt to portray pathos—that is, to evoke pity, sympathy, or sorrow. It may result from inappropriately dignifying the commonplace, using elevated language to describe something trivial, or greatly exaggerating pathos.

9. Oxymoron: A contradiction in terms deliberately employed for effect. It is usually seen in a qualifying adjective whose meaning is contrary to that of the noun it modifies, such as wise folly.

10. Irony: Expressing something other than and particularly opposite the literal meaning, such as words of praise when blame is intended. In poetry, it is often used as a sophisticated or resigned awareness of contrast between what is and what ought to be and expresses a controlled pathos without sentimentality. It is a form of indirection that avoids overt praise or censure. An early example: the Greek comic character Eiron, a clever underdog who by his wit repeatedly triumphs over the boastful character Alazon.

11. Alliteration: The repetition of consonant sounds in two or more neighboring words or syllables. In its simplest form, it reinforces one or two consonant sounds. Example: Shakespeare's Sonnet #12:

When I do count the clock that tells the time.

Some poets have used more complex patterns of alliteration by creating consonants both at the beginning of words and at the beginning of stressed syllables within words. Example: Shelley's "Stanzas Written in Dejection Near Naples":

The City's voice itself is soft like Solitude's

12. Onomatopoeia: The naming of a thing or action by a vocal imitation of the sound associated with it, such as buzz or hiss, or the use of words whose sound suggests the sense. A good example: from "The Brook" by Tennyson:

I chatter over stony ways,
In little sharps and trebles,
I bubble into eddying bays,
I babble on the pebbles.

13. Malapropism: A verbal blunder in which one word is replaced by another word that is similar in sound but different in meaning. Thinking of the geography of contiguous countries, Sheridan's Mrs. Malaprop in *The Rivals* (1775)spoke of the "geometry" of "contagious countries."

Poets use figures of speech to sharpen the effect and meaning of their poems and to help readers see things in ways they have never seen them before. Marianne Moore observed that a fir tree has "an emerald turkey foot at the top." Her poem makes us aware of something we probably had never noticed before. The sudden recognition of the likeness yields pleasure in the reading. Figurative language allows for the statement of truths that more literal language cannot. Skillfully used, a figure of speech will help the reader see more clearly and focus upon particulars. Figures of speech add many dimensions of richness to our reading and understanding of a poem; they also allow many opportunities for worthwhile analysis. The approach to take in analyzing a poem on the basis of its figures of speech is to ask the questions What does it do for the poem? Does it underscore meaning? Does it intensify understanding? Does it increase the intensity of our response?

Skill 3.3   Identify and apply professional guidelines for selecting multicultural literature.

Living and working, as we do, in a multicultural society, it is important that teachers think beyond the classics of literature (or even simply the works of literature they personally enjoy and are familiar with) and consider literature that is (1) representative of the cultures in this country and their classrooms, and (2) instructive to students about how to interact with people who are not like themselves.

When selecting multicultural literature, a few things need to be considered. First, is the literature, in general, appropriate? Second, does the literature accurately portray a particular culture? Third, will students be able to utilize the literature for a greater social purpose? Each of these questions is discussed below.

When selecting any piece of literature for classroom use, we want to make sure that it is appropriate, in general. Has the board of education in the teacher's district approved the text for classroom use? If that decision is open to the teacher, does the text contain violence, vulgar language, sexual explicitness, negative values, or racism? If so, teachers should strongly consider not using the text. In addition, is the text at the appropriate reading level for the class? These considerations should be given for any text, whether representative of a multicultural selection or not.

The next issue to consider when selecting multicultural literature is the extent to which the text accurately portrays other cultures. Often, in general literature, we find gross misunderstandings of cultures. If, by chance, certain students have not had opportunities to interact with others in those misrepresented cultures, they may develop incorrect perceptions. In addition, even if there is an opportunity for students to interact with people representing those cultures, will students in those cultures feel that they were portrayed correctly? If not, it could be damaging to those students, as well as the relationships they have with other students who get that misinformation.

Finally, we want to make sure that the literature helps students learn how to live in a multicultural society. The literature students read in classrooms could be one of the few places students have to learn how to interact with people in different cultures in a variety of situations. We want to make sure that they have good role models in the literature and that the literature assists in positively developing students' habits of mind. While not all literature should serve this purpose, it is important that at various times throughout the school year, students do get some "life instruction" through their classroom reading materials.

Skill 3.4   Identify appropriate techniques for encouraging students to respond to literature in a variety of ways.

While literature is often a vehicle for teaching reading comprehension and writing, it is often overlooked that a very important reason for teaching literature is to help students understand how to appreciate written text, complex ideas, poetic language and ideas, and unique perspectives. However, just presenting good literature to students is not enough. They need active involvement with the literature. They also need to have a chance to respond to the literature in a variety of ways. Response helps students personalize the literature (in other words, it helps students to understand that the literature comes from human instincts and issues), it helps them as they make sense of meaning, and it helps them to appreciate the literature more.

Appropriate response to literature comes in many forms. There are really too many forms to mention here, but we will provide a good overview of possible responses. Many students learn quite a bit by responding with additional works of art—whether it is further literature (poetry, fiction, etc.), visual art, or music. For example, students can write a poem expressing the mood of a character. Or they can draw a picture that portrays a scene in a novel. Or they can rewrite the end of a story. Giving students the opportunity to be creative in this way helps them to "enter" into the literature more fully. It gives them a real opportunity to interact with the ideas, characters, setting, and author.

Analytic writing is also a good way to respond to literature. Of course, this may not seem as fun for students, but analytic writing allows students to see that there is not just one way to view literature. However, they learn even more when they understand that their possibly unconventional ways of understanding literature should still be defended with clear examples from the text.

Drama is a very effective tool for responding to literature. When students act out scenes from a novel, for example, they begin to understand character motives more clearly.

As you can see, the list of appropriate responses to literature could go on and on. It is important for teachers to match up appropriate responses with the literature and their students. Not every type of response will work well for all students and for all pieces of literature, so careful selection is important.

COMPETENCY 4.0   KNOWLEDGE OF WRITING

Skill 4.1   Demonstrate knowledge of the developmental stages of writing.

Writing is a recursive process. As students engage in the various stages of writing, they develop and improve not only their writing skills, but their thinking skills as well. Students must understand that writing is a process and typically involves many steps when writing quality work. No matter the level of writer, students should be experienced in the following stages of the writing process:

Prewriting
Students gather ideas before writing. Prewriting may include clustering, listing, brainstorming, mapping, free writing, and charting. Providing many ways for a student to develop ideas on a topic will increase his/her chances for success.

Remind students that as they prewrite, they need to consider their audience. Prewriting strategies assist students in a variety of ways. Listed below are the most common prewriting strategies students can use to explore, plan, and write on a topic. It is important to remember when teaching these strategies that not all prewriting must eventually produce a finished piece of writing. In fact, in the initial lesson of teaching prewriting strategies, it might be more effective to have students practice prewriting strategies without the pressure of having to write a finished product.

- Keep an idea book so that they can jot down ideas that come to mind
- Write in a daily journal
- Write down whatever comes to mind; this is called free writing. Students do not stop to make corrections, or interrupt the flow of ideas.

A variation of this technique is focused free writing - writing on a specific topic - to prepare for an essay.

- Make a list of all ideas connected with their topic (brainstorming)
- Make sure students know that this technique works best when they let their mind work freely. After completing the list, students should analyze the list to see a pattern or way to group the ideas
- Ask the questions Who? What? When? Where? When? and How? Help the writer approach a topic from several perspectives
- Create a visual map on paper to gather ideas. Cluster circles and lines to show connections between ideas. Students should try to identify the relationship that exists between their ideas. If they cannot see the relationships, have them pair up, exchange papers, and have their partners look for some related ideas
- Observe details of sight, hearing, taste and touch

- Visualize by making mental images of something and write down the details in a list

After they have practiced with each of these prewriting strategies, ask them to pick out the ones they prefer and ask them to discuss how they might use the techniques to help them with future writing assignments. It is important to remember that they can use more than one prewriting strategy at a time. Also they may find that different writing situations may suggest certain techniques.

Drafting
Students compose the first draft. Students should follow their notes/writing plan from the prewriting stage.

Revision and Editing
Revise comes from the Latin word *revidere*, meaning, "to see again." Revision is probably the most important step for the writer in the writing process. Here, students examine their work and make changes in wording, details, and ideas. So many times, students write a draft and then feel they're done. On the contrary, students must be encouraged to develop, change, and enhance their writing as they go, as well as once they've completed a draft.

Therefore, effective teachers realize that revision and editing go hand-in-hand, and that students often move back and forth between these stages during the course of one written work. Also, these stages must be practiced in small groups, pairs, and/or individually. Students must learn to analyze and improve their own work as well as the works of their peers. Some methods to use include the following

1. Students, working in pairs, analyze sentences for variety.
2. Students work in pairs or groups to ask questions about unclear areas in the writing or to help students add details, information, etc.
3. Students perform final edit.

Many teachers introduce Writer's Workshop to their students to maximize learning about the writing process. Writer's Workshops vary across classrooms, but the main idea is for students to become comfortable with the writing process and to produce written work. A basic Writer's Workshop will include a block of classroom time committed to writing various projects (i.e., narratives, memoirs, book summaries, fiction, book reports, etc.). Students use this time to write, meet with others to review/edit writing, make comments on writing, revise their own work, proofread, meet with the teacher, and publish their work.
Teachers who facilitate effective Writer's Workshops are able to meet with students one at a time and can guide them in their individual writing needs. This approach allows the teacher to differentiate instruction for each student's writing level.

Students need to be trained to become effective at proofreading, revising, and editing strategies. Begin by training them using both desk-side and scheduled conferences. Listed below are some strategies to use to guide students through the final stages of the writing process (and these can easily be incorporated into Writer's Workshop).

- Provide some guide sheets or forms for students to use during peer responses
- Allow students to work in pairs and limit the agenda
- Model the use of the guide sheet or form for the entire class
- Give students a time limit or number of written pieces to be completed in a specific amount of time
- Have the students read their partners' papers and ask at least three who, what, when, why, how questions. The students answer the questions and use them as a place to begin discussing the piece
- At this point in the writing process, a mini-lesson that focuses on some of the problems your students are having would be appropriate

To help students revise, provide students with a series of questions that will assist them in revising their writing.

1. Do the details give a clear picture? Add details that appeal to more than just the sense of sight.

2. How effectively are the details organized? Reorder the details if it is needed.

3. Are the thoughts and feelings of the writer included? Add personal thoughts and feelings about the subject.

As you discuss revision, you begin with discussing the definition of revise. Also, state that all writing must be revised to improve it. After students have revised their writing, it is time for the final editing and proofreading.

Proofreading
Students proofread the draft for punctuation and mechanical errors. There are a few key points to remember when helping students learn to edit and proofread their work.
- It is crucial that students are not taught grammar in isolation, but in the context of the writing process
- Ask students to read their writing and check for specific errors, like using a subordinate clause as a sentence
- Provide students with a proofreading checklist to guide them as they edit their work

Publishing

Students may have their work displayed on a bulletin board, read aloud in class, or printed in a literary magazine or school anthology.

It is important to realize that these steps are recursive; as a student engages in each aspect of the writing process, he or she may begin with prewriting and then write, revise, write, revise, edit, and publish. They do not engage in this process in a lockstep manner; it is more circular.

Skill 4.2   **Demonstrate knowledge of the writing process.**

○   *See Skill 4.1*

Skill 4.3   **Distinguish between revising and editing.**

In addition to the discussion of the revising and editing processes in Skill 4.1, both teachers and students should be aware of the difference between these two writing processes. Revising typically entails substantial changes to a written draft, and it is during this process that the look, idea, and feel of a draft may be altered, sometimes significantly. Like revising, editing continues to make changes to a draft; however the changes made during the editing process do more to enhance the ideas in the draft, rather than change or alter them. Finally, proofreading is the stage where grammatical and technical errors are addressed.

Skill 4.4   **Identify characteristics of the modes of writing (e.g., narrative, descriptive, expository, persuasive).**

Discourse, whether in speaking or writing, falls naturally into four different forms: narrative, descriptive, expository, and persuasive. The first question to be asked when *reading* a written piece, *listening* to a presentation, or *writing* is "What's the point?" This is usually called the thesis. If you are reading an essay, when you've finished, you want to be able to say, "The point of this piece is that the foster-care system in America is a disaster." If it's a play, you should also be able to say, "The point of that play is that good overcomes evil." The same is true of any written document or performance. If it doesn't make a point, the reader/listener/viewer is confused or feels that it's not worth the effort. Knowing this is very helpful when you are sitting down to write your own document, be it essay, poem, or speech. What point do you want to make? We make these points in the forms that have been the structure of western thinking since the Greek rhetoricians.

Persuasion is a piece of writing, a poem, a play, or a speech whose purpose is to change the minds of the audience members or to get them to do something. This is achieved in many ways: (1) The credibility of the writer/speaker might lead the listeners/readers to a change of mind or a recommended action. (2) Reasoning is important in persuasive discourse. No one wants to believe that he accepts a new viewpoint or goes out and takes action just because he likes and trusts the person who recommended it. Logic comes into play in reasoning that is persuasive. (3) The third and most powerful force that leads to acceptance or action is emotional appeal. Even if a person has been persuaded logically, reasonably, that he should believe in a different way, he is unlikely to act on it unless he is moved emotionally. A man with resources might be convinced that people suffered in New Orleans after Katrina, but he will not be likely to do anything about it until he is moved emotionally, until he can see dead bodies floating in the dirty water or elderly people stranded in houses. Sermons are good examples of persuasive discourse.

Exposition is discourse whose only purpose is to inform. *Expository writing* is not interested in changing anyone's mind or getting anyone to take a certain action. It exists to give information. Some examples are driving directions to a particular place or the directions for putting together a toy that arrives unassembled. The writer doesn't care whether you do or don't follow the directions. She only wants to be sure you have the information in case you do decide to use it.

Narration is discourse that is arranged chronologically: something happened, and then something else happened, and then something else happened. It is also called a story. News reports are often narrative in nature, as are records of trips, etc.

Description is discourse whose purpose is to make an experience available through one of the five senses: seeing, smelling, hearing, feeling (as with the fingers), and tasting. Descriptive words are used to make it possible for the reader to "see" with her own mind's eye, hear through her own mind's ear, smell through her own mind's nose, taste with her mind's tongue, and feel with her mind's fingers. This is how language moves people. Only by experiencing an event can the emotions become involved. Poets are experts in descriptive language.

Persuasive writing often uses all forms of discourse. The introduction may be a history or background of the idea being presented—*exposition*. Details supporting some of the points may be stories—*narrations*. *Descriptive writing* will be used to make sure the point is established emotionally.

Paraphrase is the rewording of a piece of writing. The result will not necessarily be shorter than the original. It will use different vocabulary and possibly different arrangement of details. *Paraphrases* are sometimes written to clarify a complex piece of writing. Sometimes, material is paraphrased because it cannot be borrowed as is for purposes of copyright restraints.

Summary is a distilling of the elements of a piece of writing or speech. It will be much shorter than the original. To write a good summary, the writer must determine what the "bones" of the original piece are. What is its structure? What is the thesis, and what are the sub-points? A summary does not make judgments about the original; it simply reports the original in condensed form.

Letters are often expository in nature—their purpose is to give information. However, letters are also often persuasive—the writer wants to persuade or get the recipient to do something. They are also sometimes descriptive or narrative—the writer will share an experience or tell about an event.

Research reports are a special kind of expository writing. A topic is researched—explored by some appropriate means such as searching literature, interviewing experts, or even conducting experiments--and the findings will be written up in such a way that a particular audience may know what was discovered. They can be very simple, such as delving into the history of an event or very complex, such as a report on a scientific phenomenon that requires complicated testing and reasoning to explain. A research report often reports possible conclusions but puts forth one as the best answer to the question that inspired the research in the first place, which will become the thesis of the report.

Skill 4.5   **Select the appropriate mode of writing for a variety of occasions, purposes, and audiences.**

   ○   *See Skill 4.4*

Skill 4.6   **Identify elements and appropriate use of rubrics to assess writing.**

Teacher Assessment
When assessing and responding to student writing, there are several guidelines to remember.

- Use a rating system. For example, a scale from 1 to 4 (where 1=unsatisfactory and 4=excellent).
- Monitor their use of source material
- Evaluate the structure and development of their writing
- Ensure that their writing style is appropriate for the task assigned
- Check for grammatical correctness
- Provide follow-up support for any weaknesses detected

Below are a few more tips for assessing students' writing:

Responding to nongraded writing (formative)
1. Avoid using a red pen. Whenever possible use a #2 pencil.
2. Explain in advance the criteria that will be used for assessment.
3. Read the writing once while asking the question, "Is the student's response appropriate for the assignment?"
4. Reread and make note at the end whether the student met the objective of the writing task.
5. Responses should be noncritical and use supportive and encouraging language.
6. Resist writing on or over the students' writing.
7. Highlight the ideas you wish to emphasize, question, or verify.
8. Encourage your students to take risks.

Responding to and evaluating graded writing (summative)
1. Ask students to submit prewriting and rough-draft materials including all revisions with their final draft.
2. For the first reading, use a holistic method, examining the work as a whole.
3. When reading the draft for the second time, assess it using the standards previously established.
4. Responses to the writing should be written in the margin and should use supportive language.
5. Make sure you address the process as well as the product. It is important that students value the learning process as well as the final product.
6. After scanning the piece a third time, write final comments at the end of the draft.

Rubrics
Subjective tests put the student in the driver's seat. These types of assessments usually consist of short answer, longer essays, or problem solving that involves critical-thinking skills requiring definitive proof from the short reading passages to support the student's answer. Sometimes teachers provide rubrics that include assessment criteria for high scoring answers and projects. Sometimes, the rubric is as simple as a checklist, and other times, a maximum point value is awarded for each item on the rubric. Either way, rubrics provide a guideline of the teacher's expectations for the specifics of the assignment. The teacher usually discusses and/or models what is expected to fulfill each guideline, as well as provides a detailed outline of these expectations for reference.

For example, students being asked to write a research paper might be provided with a rubric. An elementary teacher may assign a total of fifty points for the entire paper. The rubric may award ten points for note-taking quality, ten points for research skills, twenty points for content covered, five points for creative elements, and five points for organization and presentation. Then a certain number of points will be awarded in accordance with the students' performance. Rubrics allow students to score in multiple areas, rather than simply on a final product.

Holistic scoring involves assessing a child's ability to construct meaning through writing. It uses a scale called a RUBRIC, which ranges from 0 to 4:

0- This rubric would be for a piece which cannot be scored. It does not respond to the topic asked or is illegible.

1- Would be a writing which does respond to the topic, but does not cover it accurately.

2- Would be for a response which is on the question, but lacks sufficient details to convey the purpose and to accomplish the writing task requested.

3- Would be a paper which in general fulfills the purpose of the writing assignment and demonstrates that the reader correctly constructed meaning. The reader showed that he or she understands the writer's purpose and message.

4- This response has the most details, best organization, and presents a well-expressed reaction to the original writer's piece.

COMPETENCY 5.0   KNOWLEDGE AND USE OF READING ASSESSMENT

Skill 5.1   Identify measurement concepts, characteristics, and uses of norm-referenced, criterion-referenced, and performance-based assessments.

The process of collecting, quantifying, and qualifying student performance data using multiple assessment information on student learning is called assessment. A comprehensive assessment system must include a diversity of assessment tools, such as norm-referenced, criterion-referenced, performance-based, or any student-generated alternative assessments that can measure learning outcomes and goals for student achievement and success in school communities. There are mainly four kinds of assessment:

1. Observation: noticing someone and judging his or her action.
2. Informal continuous assessment: less structured assessment. Informal continuous assessment is informal because it is informal - not formal like a test or exam. It is continuous because it occurs periodically - on a daily or weekly basis.
3. Informal continuous assessment: more structured, and means setting up assessment situations periodically. An assessment situation is an activity you organize so that the learners can be assessed. It could be a quiz. It could also be a group activity, where the participants will be assessed.
4. Formal assessment is a structured infrequent measure of learner achievement. It involves the use of test and exam. Exams are used to measure the learner's progress.

The purpose of informal assessment is to help our learners learn better. This form of assessment helps the teacher to know how well the learners are learning and progressing. Informal assessment can be applied to homework assignments, field journals, and daily class work, which are good indicators of student progress and comprehension.

Formal assessment, on the other hand, is highly structured, keeping the learner in mind. It must be done at regular intervals, and if the progress is not satisfactory, parent involvement is absolutely essential. A test or exam is a good example of formal assessment. A science project is also a formal assessment.

Examples of Formal Assessments

Norm-referenced Assessments

Norm-referenced tests (NRT) are used to classify student learners into a ranking category for homogenous groupings based on ability levels or basic skills. In many school communities, NRTs are used to classify students into AP (Advanced Placement), honors, regular, or remedial classes that can significantly impact student future educational opportunities or success. NRTs are also used by national testing companies such as Iowa Test of Basic Skills (Riverside), Florida Achievement Test (McGraw-Hill) and other major test publishers to test a national sample of students to norm against standard test-takers. Stiggins (1994) states "Norm-referenced tests (NRT) are designed to highlight achievement differences between and among students to produce a dependable rank order of students across a continuum of achievement from high achievers to low achievers."

Educators may select NRTs to focus on student learners with lower basic skills, which could limit the development of curriculum content that needs to provide students with academic learning that accelerates student skills from basic to higher skill application in order to address the state assessments and core subject expectations. NRT ranking ranges from 1 to 99 with 25 percent of students scoring in the lower ranking of 1 to 25 and 25 percent of students scoring in the higher ranking of 76 to 99. Florida uses a variety of NRTs for student assessments that range from Iowa Basic Skills Testing to California Battery Achievement testing to measure student learning in reading and math.

Criterion-referenced Assessments

Criterion-referenced assessments look at specific student learning goals and performance compared to a norm group of student learners. According to Bond (1996), "Educators or policy makers may choose to use a Criterion-referenced test (CRT) when they wish to see how well students have learned the knowledge and skills which they are expected to have mastered." Many school districts and state legislation use CRTs to ascertain whether schools are meeting national and state learning standards. The latest national educational mandate of "No Child Left Behind" (NCLB) and Adequate Yearly Progress (AYP) use CRTs to measure student learning, school performance, and school improvement goals as structured accountability expectations in school communities. CRTs are generally used in learning environments to reflect the effectiveness of curriculum implementation and learning outcomes.

Performance-based Assessments

Performance-based assessments are currently being used in a number of state testing programs to measure the learning outcomes of individual students in subject content areas. Washington State uses performance-based assessments for the WASL (Washington Assessment of Student Learning) in reading, writing, math and science to measure student-learning performance. Attaching a graduation requirement to passing the required state assessment for the class of 2008 has created a high-stakes testing and educational accountability for both students and teachers in meeting the expected skill-based requirements for tenth grade students taking the test.

In today's classrooms, performance-based assessments in core subject areas must have established specific performance criteria that start with pre-testing in a subject area and maintain daily or weekly testing to gauge student learning goals and objectives. To understand a student's learning is to understand how a student processes information. Effective performance assessments will show the gaps or holes in student learning which allows for an intense concentration on providing fillers to bridge nonsequential learning gaps. Typical performance assessments include oral and written student work in the form of research papers, oral presentations, class projects, journals, student portfolio collections of work, and community service projects.

| Skill 5.2 | Identify oral and written methods for assessing student progress (e.g., informal reading inventories, fluency checks, think alouds, rubrics, running records, story retelling, portfolios). |

It is useful to consider the types of assessment procedures that are available to the classroom teacher. The types of assessment discussed below represent many of the more common types, but the list is not comprehensive.

Anecdotal records

These are notes recorded by the teacher concerning an area of interest or concern with a particular student. These records should focus on observable behaviors and should be descriptive in nature. They should not include assumptions or speculations regarding effective areas such as motivation or interest. These records are usually compiled over a period of several days to several weeks.

Rating scales & checklists

These assessments are generally self-appraisal instruments completed by the students or observations-based instruments completed by the teacher. The focus of these is frequently on behavior or effective areas such as interest and motivation.

Portfolio assessment

The use of student portfolios for some aspects of assessment has become quite common. The purpose, nature, and policies of portfolio assessment vary greatly from one setting to another. In general, though, a student's portfolio contains samples of work collected over an extended period of time. The nature of the subject, age of the student, and scope of the portfolio all contribute to the specific mechanics of analyzing, synthesizing, and otherwise evaluating the portfolio contents.

In most cases, the student and teacher make joint decisions as to which work samples go into the student's portfolios. A collection of work compiled over an extended time period allows teacher, student, and parents to view the student's progress from a unique perspective. Qualitative changes over time can be readily apparent from work samples. Such changes are difficult to establish with strictly quantitative records typical of the scores recorded in the teacher's grade book.

Questioning

One of the most frequently occurring forms of assessment in the classroom is oral questioning by the teacher. As the teacher questions the students, she collects a great deal of information about the degree of student learning and potential sources of confusion for the students. While questioning is often viewed as a component of instructional methodology, it is also a powerful assessment tool.

Tests

Tests and similar direct-assessment methods represent the most easily identified types of assessment. Thorndike (1997) identifies three types of assessment instruments:

1. Standardized achievement tests
2. Assessment material packaged with curricular materials
3. Teacher-made assessment instruments
   Pencil and paper tests
   Oral tests
   Product evaluations
   Performance tests
   Effective measures (p.199)

Kellough and Roberts (1991) take a slightly different perspective. They describe "three avenues for assessing student achievement:
   a) what the learner says
   b) what the learner does, and
   c) what the learner writes..." (p.343)

Types of tests

Formal tests are those tests that have been standardized on a large sample population. The process of standardization provides various comparative norms and scales for the assessment instrument. The term "informal test" includes all other tests. Most publisher-provided tests and teacher-made tests are informal tests by this definition. Note clearly that an "informal" test is not necessarily unimportant. A teacher-made final exam, for example, is informal by definition because it has not been standardized, but is a very important assessment tool.

Skill 5.3   Interpret assessment data (e.g., screening, progress monitoring, diagnostic) to guide instructional decisions.

Purposes for assessment

There are a number of different classification systems used to identify the various purposes for assessment. A compilation of several lists identifies some common purposes such as the following:

1. Diagnostic assessments are used to determine individual weakness
2. and strengths in specific areas.
3. Readiness assessments measure prerequisite knowledge and skills.
4. Interest and Attitude assessments attempt to identify topics of high
5. interest or areas in which students may need extra motivational activities.
6. Evaluation assessments are generally program or teacher focused.
7. Placement assessments are used for purposes of grouping students or determining appropriate beginning levels in leveled materials.
8. Formative assessments provide on-going feedback on student progress and the success of instructional methods and materials.
9. Summative assessments define student accomplishment with the intent to determine the degree of student mastery or learning that has taken place.

Assessment language has deep-rooted meaning in a diversity of key terms such as the following:

- Formative- sets targets for student learning and creates an avenue to provide data on whether students are meeting the targets.
- Diagnostic- testing used to determine student's skill levels and current knowledge.
- Normative- establishes rankings and comparatives of student performances against an established norm of achievement.
- Alternative- non-traditional method of helping students construct responses to problem solving.
- Authentic- real-life assessments that are relevant and meaningful in a student's life. (For example, calculating a 20 percent discount on a Texas instrument calculator, for a student learning math percentages, creates a more personalized approach to learning.)
- Performance- based-judged according to pre-established standards.
- Traditional- diversity of teacher assessments that either come with the textbooks or ones that are directly created from the textbooks.

Assessment skills should be an integral part of teacher training, where teachers are able to monitor student learning using pre and post assessments of content areas, to analyze assessment data in terms of individualized support for students and instructional practice for teachers, and to design lesson plans that have measurable outcomes and definitive learning standards. Assessment information should be used to provide performance-based criteria and academic expectations for all students in evaluating whether students have learned the expected skills and content of the subject area.

For example in an Algebra I class, teachers can use assessment to see whether students have learned the prior knowledge to engage in the subject area. If the teacher provides students with a pre-assessment on algebraic expression and ascertains whether the lesson plan should be modified to include a pre-algebraic expression lesson unit to refresh student understanding of the content area, then the teacher can create, if needed, quantifiable data to support the need of additional resources to support student learning. Once the teacher has taught the unit on algebraic expression, a post-assessment test can be used to test student learning, and a mastery exam can be used to test how well students understand and can apply the knowledge to the next unit of math content learning.

Teachers can use assessment data to inform and impact instructional practices by making inferences on teaching methods and gathering clues for student performance. By analyzing the various types of assessments, teachers can gather more definitive information on projected student academic performance. Instructional strategies for teachers would provide learning targets for student behavior, cognitive thinking skills, and processing skills that can be employed to diversify student learning opportunities.

- **See also** Skills 5.1 and 5.2

Skill 5.4   Use individual student reading data to differentiate instruction.

There are a number of reliable reading tests that can be administered to provide empirical data to let you know where your students' reading skills lie. Your school or your district can probably recommend some. Some of these can be given at the beginning of the school year and again at the end to let you know what impact your teaching is having.

Assessment and evaluation should be ongoing in the reading classroom. When a teacher asks a student to retell a story, it is a form of assessment. After the child retells the story, the teacher can judge how accurate it is and give it a grade or score and make anecdotal comments in the course of listening to the child's retelling of the story.

Informal assessment utilizes observations and other nonstandardized procedures to compile anecdotal and observation data/evidence of children's progress and may include checklists, observations, and performance assessments and tasks. Formal assessment involves standardized tests and procedures carried out under circumscribed conditions and includes state tests, standardized achievement tests, NAEP tests, etc.

Effective assessment should have the following characteristics:

1. It should be an ongoing process with the teacher making some kind of informal or formal assessment almost every time the student speaks, listens, reads, writes, or views something in the classroom. The assessment should be a natural part of the instruction and not intrusive.
2. The most effective assessment is integrated into the ongoing instruction. Throughout the teaching and learning day, the child's written, spoken, and reading contributions to the class or lack thereof need to be continually assessed.
3. Assessment should reflect the actual reading and writing experiences that classroom learning has prepared the student for.
4. Assessment needs to be a collaborative and reflective process. Teachers can learn from what the students reveal about their own individual assessments. Students should be supported by their teacher to continually and routinely ask themselves questions assessing their reading progress.
5. Quality valid assessment is multidimensional and may include samples of writing, student retellings, running records, anecdotal teacher observations, self-evaluations, etc. This not only enables the teacher to derive a consistent level of performance but also to design additional instruction that will enhance that level of performance.
6. Assessment must take into account the student's age and ethnic/cultural patterns of learning.
7. Assess to teach students from their strengths, not their weaknesses. Find out what reading behaviors students demonstrate well and then design instruction to support those behaviors.
8. Assessment should be part of children's learning process and not done on them but rather done with them.

Skill 5.5 **Interpret a student's formal and informal assessment results to inform students and parents.**

Communicating with Students

How can a teacher provide good feedback so that students will learn from their assessments? First, language should be helpful and constructive. Critical language does not necessarily help students learn. They may become defensive or hurt, and therefore, they may be more focused on the perceptions than the content. Language that is constructive and helpful will guide students to specific actions and recommendations that would help them improve in the future.

When teachers provide timely feedback, they increase the chance that students will reflect on their thought processes as they were when they originally produced the work. When feedback comes weeks after the production of an assignment, the student may not remember what it is that caused him or her to respond in a particular way.

Specific feedback is particularly important. Comments like "This should be clearer" and "Your grammar needs to be worked on" provide information that students may already know. They may already know they have a problem with clarity. What students can benefit from is commentary that provides very specific actions they could take to make something more clear or to improve his or her grammar.

When teachers provide feedback on a set of assignments, for example, they enhance their students' learning by teaching students how to use the feedback. For example, returning a set of papers can actually do more than provide feedback to students on their initial performance. Teachers can ask students to do additional things to work with their original products, or they can even ask students to take small sections and rewrite based on the feedback. While written feedback will enhance student learning, having students do something with the feedback encourages even deeper learning and reflection.

Experienced teachers may be reading this and thinking, "When will I ever get the time to provide so much feedback?" Although detailed and timely feedback is important—and necessary—teachers do not have to provide it all the time to increase student learning. They can also teach students how to use scoring guides and rubrics to evaluate their own work, particularly before they turn it in. One particularly effective way of doing this is to have students examine models and samples of proficient work. Over years, teachers should collect samples, remove names and other identifying factors, and show these to students so that they understand what is expected of them. Often, when teachers do this, they will be surprised to see how much students gain from this in terms of their ability to assess their own performance.

Finally, teachers can help students develop plans for revising and improving upon their work, even if it is not evaluated by the teacher in the preliminary stages. For example, teachers can have students keep track of words they commonly misspell, or they can have students make personal lists of areas they feel on which they need to focus.

Communicating with Parents

The major questions for parents in understanding student performance criterion-referenced data assessment are, "Are students learning?" and "How well are students learning?" Providing parents with a collection of student learning assessment data related to student achievement and performance is a quantifiable response to the questions. The National Study of School Evaluation (NSSE) 1997 research study, "School Improvement: Focusing on Student Performance," adds the following additional questions for parent focus on student learning outcomes:

- What are the types of assessments of student learning that are used in the school?
- What do the results of the data assessments indicate about the current levels of student learning performance? About future predictions? What were the learning objectives and goals?
- What are the strengths and limitations in student learning and achievement?
- How prepared are students for further education or promotion to the next level of education?
- What are the trends seen in student learning in various subject areas or overall academic learning?

Providing parents with opportunities to attend in-service workshops on data discussions with teachers and administrators creates additional opportunity for parents to ask questions and become actively involved in monitoring their student's educational progress. With state assessments, parents should look for the words "passed" or "met/exceeded standards" in interpreting the numerical data on student reports. Parents who maintain an active involvement in their student's education will attend school opportunities to promote their understanding of academic and educational achievement.

Skill 5.6   **Evaluate the appropriateness (e.g., curriculum alignment, cultural bias) of assessment instruments and practices.**

For most teachers, assessment purposes vary according to the situation. It may be helpful to consult several sources to help formulate an overall assessment plan. Kellough and Roberts (1991) identify six purposes for assessment:.

1. To evaluate and improve student learning
2. To identify student strengths and weaknesses
3. To assess the effectiveness of a particular instructional strategy
4. To evaluate and improve program effectiveness
5. To evaluate and improve teacher effectiveness
6. To communicate to parents their children's progress (p.341)

Bias

Bias exists in assessment when, after getting the results, it is obvious that demographic variables account for score variation. In other words, test bias would exist if a test question assumes that the test taker understands some of the contextual information in the question. For example, let's say a test question is trying to assess a student's understanding of a science concept that has been taught in class. However, to set up the question, the teacher uses an example that assumes all students have the same cultural background. This test question would be assumed to be biased.

There are a few ways to systematically notice potential bias. First, when test questions are developed, they should focus on assessing discrete skills or areas of knowledge that have been taught. With teacher-created test materials, teachers should not include elements on the test that might require students to access information that they may not have. While some students possibly could know that additional information, not all students will, and it will instead look like those other students did not know the material the teacher really intended for the student to know. So, test questions should be simply written, contain basic vocabulary, and not include elements that pertain to any one culture or religion.

On a wider level, teachers may notice that an entire demographic group has performed worse compared to other demographic groups on a particular question. This might be a clue to possible bias.

How can teachers eliminate bias on their own assessments that they create? They can work to ensure that everything tested has been taught. This is an important task. Teachers should carefully examine their tests for material that students would have no way of knowing. Teachers should also be very sensitive to the things that they take for granted. Something as simple as forgetting that different religions celebrate different holidays can lead to bias.

DOMAIN II.   **MATHEMATICS**

COMPETENCY 6.0   KNOWLEDGE OF NUMBER SENSE, CONCEPTS, AND OPERATIONS

Skill 6.1   Associate multiple representations of numbers using word names, standard numerals, and pictorial models for real numbers (whole numbers, decimals, fractions, and integers).

	Word Name	Standard Numeral	Pictorial Model
Decimal	Three-tenths	0.3	
Fraction	One-half	$\frac{1}{2}$	
Integer or Whole Number	Three	3	

Skill 6.2   Compare the relative size of integers, fractions, and decimals, numbers expressed as percents, numbers with exponents, and/or numbers in scientific notation

The expanded form of a number may be expressed in words or numbers. In words, the expanded form of 4, 213 would be 4 thousands and 2 hundreds and 1 ten and 3 ones. In numeric form, it would be 4 x 1000 + 2 x 100 + 1 x 10 + 3 x 1.

The following are different representations of expressions with exponents and square roots:

$$x^3 = x \cdot x \cdot x$$

$$x^{-2} = \frac{1}{x^2}$$

$$x^{\frac{1}{2}} = \sqrt{x}$$

If we compare numbers in various forms, we see the following:

The integer $400 = \dfrac{800}{2}$ (fraction) = 400.0 (decimal) = 400% (percent) = 20^2 (number with exponent) = 4×10^2 (scientific notation), and

$1 > \dfrac{7}{8} > 0.65 > 60\% > 2^{-2} > 1 \times 10^{-2}$

Skill 6.3   Apply ratios, proportions, and percents in real-world situations.

The unit rate for purchasing an item is its price divided by the number of pounds/ounces, etc. in the item. The item with the lower unit rate is the lower price.

Example: Find the item with the best unit price:

$1.79 for 10 ounces
$1.89 for 12 ounces
$5.49 for 32 ounces

$\dfrac{1.79}{10} = .179$ per ounce $\dfrac{1.89}{12} = .158$ per ounce $\dfrac{5.49}{32} = .172$ per ounce

$1.89 for 12 ounces is the best price.

A second way to find the better buy is to make a proportion with the price over the number of ounces, etc. Cross multiply the proportion, writing the products above the numerator that is used. The better price will have the smaller product.

Example: Find the better buy:

$8.19 for 40 pounds or $4.89 for 22 pounds

Find the unit price.

$\dfrac{40}{8.19} = \dfrac{1}{x}$ $\dfrac{22}{4.89} = \dfrac{1}{x}$

$40x = 8.19$ $22x = 4.89$

$x = .20475$ $x = .22\overline{227}$

Since $.20475 < .22\overline{227}$, $8.19 is less and is a better buy.

To find the amount of sales tax on an item, change the percent of sales tax into an equivalent decimal number. Then multiply the decimal number times the price of the object to find the sales tax. The total cost of an item will be the price of the item plus the sales tax.

Example: A guitar costs $120 plus 7% sales tax. How much are the sales tax and the total bill?

> 7% = .07 as a decimal
> (.07)(120) = $8.40 sales tax
> $120 + $8.40 = $128.40 ← total price

Example: A suit costs $450 plus 6½% sales tax. How much are the sales tax and the total bill?

> 6½% = .065 as a decimal
> (.065)(450) = $29.25 sales tax
> $450 + $29.25 = $479.25 ← total price

Ratios

Example: The road map Mr. Richards is reading states that 3 inches represent 125 miles. Mr. Richards estimates that the distance to his destination is approximately 5.5 inches on the map. Approximately how many miles would this be?

Solution:	Represent the map scale as a ratio:	$\dfrac{3}{125}$
	Set the problem up as a proportion:	$\dfrac{3}{125} = \dfrac{5.5}{x}$
	Cross multiply:	$3x = 687.5$
	Solve:	$x \approx 229$ miles

Skill 6.4   **Represent numbers in a variety of equivalent forms, including whole numbers, integers, fractions, decimals, percents, scientific notation, and exponents.**

The real number system includes all rational and irrational numbers.

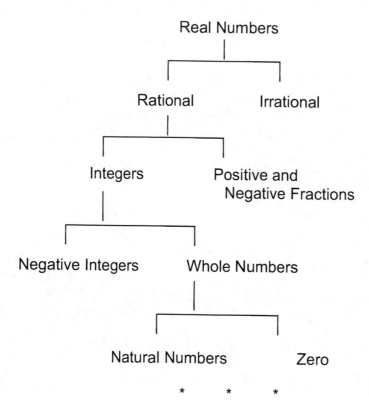

```
                        Real Numbers
                             |
           ┌─────────────────┴─────────────────┐
       Rational                            Irrational
           |
     ┌─────┴──────────┐
  Integers      Positive and
                Negative Fractions
     |
 ┌───┴────────────┐
Negative Integers   Whole Numbers
                        |
                 ┌──────┴──────┐
           Natural Numbers    Zero

              *      *      *
```

Rational numbers can be expressed as the ratio of two integers, $\frac{a}{b}$, where b 0. For example: $\frac{2}{3}$, $-\frac{4}{5}$, $\frac{5}{1}$ = 5.

The rational numbers include integers, fractions and mixed numbers, and terminating and repeating decimals. Every rational number can be expressed as a repeating or terminating decimal and can be shown on a number line.

Integers are positive and negative whole numbers and zero.
   ...-6, -5, -4, -3, -2, -1, 0, 1, 2, 3, 4, 5, 6, ...

Whole numbers are natural numbers and zero.
   0, 1, 2, 3, 4, 5 ,6 ...

Natural numbers are the counting numbers.
   1, 2, 3, 4, 5, 6, ...

Irrational numbers are real numbers that cannot be written as the ratio of two integers. These are infinite non-repeating decimals.

Examples: $\sqrt{5} = 2.2360..$,   pi $= \Pi = 3.1415927...$

Percent = per 100 (written with the symbol %). Thus $10\% = \dfrac{10}{100} = \dfrac{1}{10}$.

Decimals = deci = part of ten. To find the decimal equivalent of a fraction, use the denominator to divide the numerator as shown in the following examples.

Example: Find the decimal equivalent of $\dfrac{7}{10}$.

$$
\begin{array}{r}
.7 \\
10\overline{)7.0} \\
70 \\
\hline
00
\end{array}
$$

Since 10 cannot divide into 7 evenly, put a decimal point in the answer row on top; put a 0 behind 7 to make it 70. Continue the division   process. If a remainder occurs, put a 0 by the last digit of the remainder and continue the division.

Thus $\dfrac{7}{10} = 0.7$

It is a good idea to write a 0 before the decimal point so that the decimal point is emphasized.

Example: Find the decimal equivalent of $\dfrac{7}{125}$.

$$
\begin{array}{r}
.056 \\
125\overline{)7.000} \\
625 \\
\hline
750 \\
750 \\
\hline
0
\end{array}
$$

Example: Convert 0.056 to a fraction.

Multiplying 0.056 by $\dfrac{1000}{1000}$ to get rid of the decimal point:

$$0.056 \times \dfrac{1000}{1000} = \dfrac{56}{1000} = \dfrac{7}{125}$$

Example: Find 23% of 1000.

$$= \dfrac{23}{100} \times \dfrac{1000}{1} = 23 \times 10 = 230$$

Example: Convert 6.25% to a fraction and to a mixed number.

$$6.25\% = 0.0625 = 0.0625 \times \dfrac{10000}{10000} = \dfrac{625}{10000} = \dfrac{1}{16}$$

A **decimal** can be converted to a **percent** by multiplying by 100, or merely moving the decimal point two places to the right. A **percent** can be converted to a **decimal** by dividing by 100, or moving the decimal point two places to the left.

Examples:
$$0.375 = 37.5\%$$
$$0.7 = 70\%$$
$$0.04 = 4\%$$
$$3.15 = 315\%$$

$$84\% = 0.84$$
$$3\% = 0.03$$
$$60\% = 0.6$$
$$110\% = 1.1$$
$$\tfrac{1}{2}\% = 0.5\% = 0.005$$

A **percent** can be converted to a **fraction** by placing it over 100 and reducing to simplest terms.

Examples:
$$32\% = \tfrac{32}{100} = \tfrac{8}{25}$$
$$6\% = \tfrac{6}{100} = \tfrac{3}{50}$$
$$111\% = \tfrac{111}{100} = 1\tfrac{11}{100}$$

Common Equivalents

$$\frac{1}{2} = 0.5 = 50\%$$

$$\frac{1}{3} = 0.33\frac{1}{3} = 33\frac{1}{3}\%$$

$$\frac{1}{4} = 0.25 = 25\%$$

$$\frac{1}{5} = 0.2 = 20\%$$

$$\frac{1}{6} = 0.16\frac{2}{3} = 16\frac{2}{3}\%$$

$$\frac{1}{8} = 0.12\frac{1}{2} = 12\frac{1}{2}\%$$

$$\frac{1}{10} = 0.1 = 10\%$$

$$\frac{2}{3} = 0.66\frac{2}{3} = 66\frac{2}{3}\%$$

$$\frac{5}{6} = 0.83\frac{1}{3} = 83\frac{1}{3}\%$$

$$\frac{3}{8} = 0.37\frac{1}{2} = 37\frac{1}{2}\%$$

$$\frac{5}{8} = 0.62\frac{1}{2} = 62\frac{1}{2}\%$$

$$\frac{7}{8} = 0.87\frac{1}{2} = 87\frac{1}{2}\%$$

$$1 = 1.0 = 100\%$$

The **exponent form** is a shortcut method to write repeated multiplication. The basic form is b^n, where b is called the base and n is the exponent. The b and n are both real numbers. The symbol b^n implies that the base b is multiplied by itself n times.

Examples: $3^4 = 3 \times 3 \times 3 \times 3 = 81$

$2^3 = 2 \times 2 \times 2 = 8$

$(^-2)^4 = (^-2) \times (^-2) \times (^-2) \times (^-2) = 16$

$^-2^4 = ^-(2 \times 2 \times 2 \times 2) = ^-16$

When 10 is raised to any power, the exponent tells the numbers of zeroes in the product.

Example: $10^7 = 10,000,000$

Caution: Unless the negative sign is inside the parentheses and the exponent is outside the parentheses, the product's sign depends on whether the exponent is even or odd, whereas if the negative sign and exponenet have no parentheses, the answer will be negative regardless of the nature of the exponent.

$(^-2)^4$ implies that -2 is multiplied by itself four times.

$^-2^4$ implies that 2 is multiplied by itself four times, and then the answer is negated.

Scientific notation is a more convenient method for writing very large and very small numbers. It employs two factors. The first factor is a number between 1 and 10. The second factor is a power of 10. This notation is a "shorthand" for expressing large numbers (like the weight of 100 elephants) or small numbers (like the weight of an atom in pounds).

Recall that:

$10^n = (10)^n$ Ten multiplied by itself n times.

$10^0 = 1$ Any nonzero number raised to power of zero is 1.

$10^1 = 10$

$10^2 = 10 \times 10 = 100$

$10^3 = 10 \times 10 \times 10 = 1000$ (kilo)

$10^6 = 1,000,000$ (mega)

$10^{-1} = 1/10$ (deci)

$10^{-2} = 1/100$ (centi)

$10^{-3} = 1/1000$ (milli)

$10^{-6} = 1/1,000,000$ (micro)

Key exponent rules:

For 'a' nonzero, and 'm' and 'n' real numbers:

1) $a^m \cdot a^n = a^{(m+n)}$ Product rule

2) $\dfrac{a^m}{a^n} = a^{(m-n)}$ Quotient rule

3) $\dfrac{a^{-m}}{a^{-n}} = \dfrac{a^n}{a^m}$

Scientific notation format:

Convert a number to a form of $b \times 10^n$, where b is a number between -9.9 and 9.9 and n is an integer.

Example: 356.73 can be written in various forms.

$$356.73 = 3567.3 \times 10^{-1}$$
$$= 35673 \times 10^{-2}$$
$$= 35.673 \times 10^1$$
$$= 3.5673 \times 10^2$$
$$= 0.35673 \times 10^3 \qquad ($$

Only (4) is written in proper scientific notation format. The following examples illustrate how to write in scientific notation format:

Example: Write 46,368,000 in scientific notation.

1)   Introduce a decimal point and decimal places.
       46,368,000 = 46,368,000.0000

2)   Make a mark between the two digits that give a number between -9.9 and 9.9.
       4 ∧ 6,368,000 .0000

3)   Count the number of digit places between the decimal point and the ∧ mark. This number is the 'n'-the power of 10.

       So, $46,368,000 = 4.6368 \times 10^7$

Example: Write 0.00397 in scientific notation.

1)   Decimal place is already in place.

2)   Make a mark between 3 and 9 to get a number between -9.9 and 9.9.

3)   Move decimal place to the mark (three hops).

       0.003 ∧ 97

Motion is to the right, so the n of 10^n is negative.

Therefore, $0.00397 = 3.97 \times 10^{-3}$.

<u>Example:</u>   Evaluate $\dfrac{3.22 \times 10^{-3} \times 736}{0.00736 \times 32.2 \times 10^{-6}}$

Since we have a mixture of large and small numbers, convert each number to scientific notation:

$736 = 7.36 \times 10^2$

$0.00736 = 7.36 \times 10^{-3}$

$32.2 \times 10^{-6} = 3.22 \times 10^{-5}$ thus we have,

$$\dfrac{3.22 \times 10^{-3} \times 7.36 \times 10^2}{7.36 \times 10^{-3} \times 3.22 \times 10^{-5}}$$

$$= \dfrac{3.22 \times 7.36 \times 10^{-3} \times 10^2}{7.36 \times 3.22 \times 10^{-3} \times 10^{-5}}$$

$$= \dfrac{3.22 \times 7.36}{7.36 \times 3.22} \times \dfrac{10^{-1}}{10^{-8}}$$

$$= \dfrac{3.22 \times 7.36}{7.36 \times 3.22} \times 10^{-1} \times 10^8$$

$$= \dfrac{23.6992}{23.6992} \times 10^7$$

$$= 1 \times 10^7 = 10,000,000$$

Skill 6.5   **Recognize the effects of operations on rational numbers and the relationships among these operations (i.e., addition, subtraction, multiplication, and division).**

Mathematical operations include addition, subtraction, multiplication, and division. Addition can be indicated by the expressions: sum, greater than, and, more than, increased by, added to. Subtraction can be expressed by: difference, fewer than, minus, less than, decreased by. Multiplication is shown by: product, times, multiplied by, twice. Division is used for: quotient, divided by, ratio.

Examples:	7 added to a number	$n + 7$
	a number decreased by 8	$n - 8$
	12 times a number divided by 7	$12n \div 7$
	28 less than a number	$n - 28$
	the ratio of a number to 55	$\dfrac{n}{55}$
	4 times the sum of a number and 214	$(n + 21)$

Skill 6.6 **Select the appropriate operation(s) to solve problems involving ratios, proportions, and percents and the addition, subtraction, multiplication, and division of rational numbers.**

Ratios:

Problems involving ratios are solved using multiplication and division.

Example: The ratio of the length of a rectangle to its width is 3:2. If the length of the rectangle is 12 meters, what is the width?

Set up the ratios: $\dfrac{3}{2} = \dfrac{length}{width}$

Substitute: $\dfrac{3}{2} = \dfrac{12}{x}$

Cross multiply: $3x = 24$

Solve by dividing: $x = 8$

Proportions:

Problems involving proportions are solved in the same manner as those involving ratios, since proportions are two ratios set equal to each other.

Example: The weight of artificial sweetener in a box of 400 identical sweetener bags is 14 ounces. What is the weight, in ounces, of the sweetener in 12 bags?

Set up two ratios: $\dfrac{12}{400} = \dfrac{x}{14}$

Cross multiply: $400x = 168$

Solve by dividing: $x = 0.42$

Percents: Percents are also ratios; for example $75\% = \dfrac{75}{100}$. Therefore, problems involving percents are solved in a manner similar to ratios and proportions.

<u>Example:</u>   15 is what percent of 75?

Set up two ratios: $\dfrac{15}{75} = \dfrac{x}{100}$

Cross multiply: $75x = 1500$

Solve by dividing: $x = 0.20$ or 20%

Addition and subtraction of rational numbers:

If fractions have the same denominators, only the operations of addition and subtraction are necessary. However, if a common denominator must be determined, then multiplication is needed to convert the fractions.

Multiplication and division of rational numbers:

Multiplication of fractions is the easiest operation involving fractions. You merely multiply the numerators by each other and the denominators by each other.

Division of fractions, on the other hand, calls for multiplication. To divide two fractions, you must multiply the dividend by the reciprocal of the divisor.

<u>Example:</u>

$$\dfrac{2}{3} \div \dfrac{3}{4} =$$

$$\dfrac{2}{3} \times \dfrac{4}{3} =$$

$$\dfrac{8}{9}$$

Skill 6.7   Use estimation in problem-solving situations.

Estimation and approximation may be used to check the reasonableness of answers.

Example: Estimate the answer.

$$\frac{58 \times 810}{1989}$$

58 becomes 60, 810 becomes 800 and 1989 becomes 2000.

$$\frac{60 \times 800}{2000} = 24$$

Word problems: An estimate may sometimes be all that is needed to solve a problem.

Example: Janet goes into a store to purchase a CD on sale for $13.95. While shopping, she sees two pairs of shoes, prices $19.95 and $14.50. She only has $50.00. Can she purchase everything?

Solve by rounding:

$19.95→$20.00
$14.50→$15.00
$13.95→$14.00
$49.00   Yes, she can purchase the CD and the shoes.

Skill 6.8 **Apply number theory concepts (e.g., primes, composites, multiples, factors, number sequences, number properties, and rules of divisibility).**

Prime numbers are numbers that can only be factored into 1 and the number itself. When factoring into prime factors, all the factors must be numbers that cannot be factored again (without using 1). Initially numbers can be factored into any two factors. Check each resulting factor to see if it can be factored again. Continue factoring until all remaining factors are prime. This is the list of prime factors. Regardless of what way the original number was factored, the final list of prime factors will always be the same.

Example: Factor 30 into prime factors.

Factor 30 into any two factors.
   5 x 6   Now factor the 6.
 5 x 2 x 3   These are all prime factors.
Factor 30 into any two factors.
   3 x 10   Now factor the 10.
3 x 2 x 5   These are the same prime factors even though the
                 original factors were different.

Example: Factor 240 into prime factors.

Factor 240 into any two factors.
  24 x 10   Now factor both the 24 and the 10.
 4 x 6 x 2 x 5   Now factor both the 4 and the 6.
2 x 2 x 2 x 3 x 2 x 5 These are prime factors.

This can also be written as $2^4 \cdot 3 \times 5$.

GCF is the abbreviation for the **greatest common factor**. The GCF is the largest number that is a factor of all the numbers given in a problem. The GCF can be no larger than the smallest number given in the problem. If no other number is a common factor, then the GCF will be the number 1. To find the GCF, list all possible factors of the smallest number given (include the number itself). Starting with the largest factor (which is the number itself), determine if it is also a factor of all the other given numbers. If so, that is the GCF. If that factor doesn't work, try the same method on the next smaller factor. Continue until a common factor is found. That is the GCF. Note: There can be other common factors besides the GCF.

Example: Find the GCF of 12, 20, and 36.

The smallest number in the problem is 12. The factors of 12 are 1,2,3,4,6, and 12. The largest factor is 12, but it does not divide evenly into 20. Neither does 6, but 4 will divide into both 20 and 36 evenly.

Therefore, 4 is the GCF.

Example: Find the GCF of 14 and 15.

Factors of 14 are 1,2,7, and 14. The largest factor is 14, but it does not divide evenly into 15. Neither does 7 or 2. Therefore, the only factor common to both 14 and 15 is the number 1, the GCF.

LCM is the abbreviation for **least common multiple**. The least common multiple of a group of numbers is the smallest number that all of the given numbers will divide into. The least common multiple will always be the largest of the given numbers or a multiple of the largest number.

Example: Find the LCM of 20, 30, and 40.

The largest number given is 40, but 30 will not divide evenly into 40. The next multiple of 40 is 80 (2 x 40), but 30 will not divide evenly into 80 either. The next multiple of 40 is 120. Divisible by both 20 and 30, 120 is the LCM (least common multiple).

Example: Find the LCM of 96, 16, and 24.

The largest number is 96, which is divisible by both 16 and 24, so 96 is the LCM.

Rules of Divisibility:

a) A number is divisible by 2 if that number is an even number (which means it ends in 0,2,4,6 or 8).

1,354 ends in 4, so it is divisible by 2. The number 240,685 ends in a 5, so it is not divisible by 2.

b) A number is divisible by 3 if the sum of its digits is evenly divisible by 3.

The sum of the digits of 964 is 9 + 6 + 4 = 19. Since 19 is not divisible by 3, neither is 964. The digits of 86,514 is 8 + 6 +5+ 1 + 4 = 24. Since 24 is divisible by 3, then 86,514 is also divisible by 3.

c) A number is divisible by 4 if the number in its last two digits is evenly divisible by 4.

The number 113,336 ends with the number 36 in the last 2 columns. Since 36 is divisible by 4, then 113,336 is also divisible by 4. The number 135,627 ends with the number 27 in the last 2 columns. Since 27 is not evenly divisible by 4, then 135,627 is also not divisible by 4.

d) A number is divisible by 5 if the number ends in either a 5 or a 0.

225 ends with a 5, so it is divisible by 5. The number 470 is also divisible by 5 because its last digit is a 0. The number 2,358 is not divisible by 5 because its last digit is an 8, not a 5 or a 0.

e) A number is divisible by 6 if the number is even and the sum of its digits is evenly divisible by 3.

4,950 is an even number and its digits add up to 18 (4 + 9 + 5 + 0 = 18). Since the number is even, and the sum of its digits is 18 (which is divisible by 3), then 4950 is divisible by 6. The number 326 is even , but its digits add up to 11. Since 11 is not divisible by 3, then 326 is not divisible by 6. The number 698,135 is not an even number, so it cannot possibly be divided evenly by 6.

f) A number is divisible by 8 if the number in its last 3 digits is evenly divisible by 8.

The number 113,336 ends with the three digit number 336 in the last 3 places. Since 336 is divisible by 8, then 113,336 is also divisible by 8. The number 465,627 ends with the number 627 in the last 3 places. Since 627 is not evenly divisible by 8, then 465,627 is also not divisible by 8.

g) A number is divisible by 9 if the sum of its digits is evenly divisible by 9.

The sum of the digits of 874 is 8 + 7 + 4 = 19. Since 19 is not divisible by 9, neither is 874. The digits of 116,514 are 1 + 1 + 6 + 5 + 1 +4 = 18. Since 18 is divisible by 9, the number 116,514 is also divisible by 9.

h) A number is divisible by 10 if the number ends in the digit 0.

305 ends with a 5 so it is not divisible by 10. The number 2,030,270 is divisible by 10 because its last digit is a 0. The number 42,978 is not divisible by 10 because its last digit is an 8, not a 0.

i) Why these rules work:

All even numbers are divisible by 2 by definition. A two digit number (with T as the tens digit and U as the ones digit) has as its sum of the digits, T + U. Suppose this sum of T + U is divisible by 3. Then it equals 3 times some constant, K. So, T + U = 3K. Solving this for U, U = 3K - T. The original two digit number would be represented by 10T + U. Substituting 3K - T in place of U, this two digit number becomes 10T + U = 10T + (3K - T) = 9T + 3K. This two digit number is clearly divisible by 3, since each term is divisible by 3. Therefore, if the sum of the digits of a number is divisible by 3, then the number itself is also divisible by 3. Since 4 divides evenly into 100, 200, or 300, it will divide evenly into any amount of hundreds. The only part of a number that determines if 4 will divide into it evenly is the number in the last two places. Numbers divisible by 5 end in 5 or 0. This is clear if you look at the answers to the multiplication table for 5.

Answers to the multiplication table for 6 are all even numbers. Since 6 factors into 2 times 3, the divisibility rules for 2 and 3 must both work. Any number of thousands is divisible by 8. Only the last 3 places of the number determine whether or not it is divisible by 8. A two digit number (with T as the tens digit and U as the ones digit) has as its sum of the digits, T + U. Suppose this sum of T + U is divisible by 9. Then it equals 9 times some constant, K. So, T + U = 9K.

Solving this for U, U = 9K - T. The original two digit number would be represented by 10T + U. Substituting 9K - T in place of U, this two digit number becomes 10T + U = 10T + (9K - T) = 9T + 9K. This two digit number is clearly divisible by 9, since each term is divisible by 9. Therefore, if the sum of the digits of a number is divisible by 9, then the number itself is also divisible by 9. Numbers divisible by 10 must be multiples of 10 which all end in a zero.

Prime numbers are whole numbers greater than 1 that have only two factors, 1 and the number itself. Examples of prime numbers are 2,3,5,7,11,13,17, or 19. Note that 2 is the only even prime number.

Composite numbers are whole numbers that have more than two different factors. For example 9 is composite because besides factors of 1 and 9, 3 is also a factor. 70 is also composite because besides the factors of 1 and 70, the numbers 2,5,7,10,14, and 35 are also all factors.

Remember that the number 1 is neither prime nor composite.

Skill 6.9   Apply the order of operations.

The Order of Operations is to be followed when evaluating algebraic expressions. Follow these steps in order:

> 1. Simplify inside grouping characters such as parentheses, brackets, square root, fraction bar, etc.
>
> 2. Multiply out expressions with exponents.
>
> 3. Do multiplication or division, from left to right.
>
> 4. Do addition or subtraction, from left to right.

Samples of simplifying expressions with exponents:

<u>Example:</u> $3^3 - 5(b + 2)$

$= 3^3 - 5b - 10$

$= 27 - 5b - 10 = 17 - 5b$

<u>Example:</u> $2 - 4 \times 2^3 - 2(4 - 2 \times 3)$

$= 2 - 4 \times 2^3 - 2(4 - 6) = 2 - 4 \times 2^3 - 2(^-2)$

$= 2 - 4 \times 2^3 + 4 = 2 - 4 \times 8 + 4$

$= 2 - 32 + 4 = 6 - 32 = ^- 26$

COMPETENCY 7.0   KNOWLEDGE OF MEASUREMENT

Skill 7.1   Apply given measurement formulas for perimeter, circumference, area, volume, and surface area in problem situations.

Examining the change in area or volume of a given figure requires first to find the existing area given the original dimensions, and then finding the new area given the increased dimensions.

Sample problem:

Given the rectangle below determine the change in area if the length is increased by 5 and the width is increased by 7.

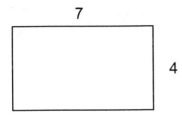

Draw and label a sketch of the new rectangle.

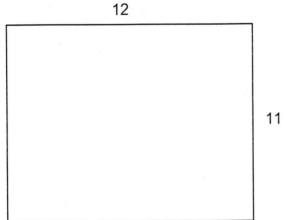

Find the areas.

Area of original = LW   Area of enlarged shape = LW
= (7)(4)   = (12)(11)
= 28 units^2 = 132 units^2

The change in area is $132 - 28 = 104$ units^2.

Skill 7.2   **Evaluates how a change in length, width, height, or radius affects perimeter, circumference, area, surface area, or volume**

The perimeter of a figure is found by adding the sides of a figure. For a rectangle, this would be

$$l + w + l + w$$

If we add 2 units to the length, we then get

$$l + 2 + w + l + 2 + w \text{ or } 2l + 2w + 4$$

The perimeter of a figure will change by the total number of units added or subtracted from each side.

The area of a polygon is a product of the length, width, and height. Therefore, a change in any of those dimensions has a multiple effect on the area.

Example: The area of a triangle is equal to

$$\frac{1}{2}bh \text{ where } b \text{ is the base and } h \text{ is the height}$$

If we double the height, the area becomes

$$\frac{1}{2}b(2h) = bh$$

Doubling the height doubles the area.

Circumference and **area** of a circle are products involving the radius. As in the case of polygons, the factor by which the radius changes will be the factor by which the circumference changes.

The formula for circumference is

$$2\pi r$$

If we multiply the radius by 3, we get

$$2\pi(3r) = 6\pi r$$

Tripling the radius triples the circumference.

The formula for area is

$$\pi r^2$$

If we multiply the radius by 3, we get

$$\pi(3r)^2 = 9r^2\pi$$

The area of a circle changes by a factor equal to the square of the number by which we multiply the radius.

Surface area is the sum of all the faces of a prism or sphere. In the case of a rectangular prism, this is

$$2lw + 2lh + 2wh$$

If we double the width, the surface area becomes

$$2l(2w) + 2lh + 2(2w)h = 4lw + 2lh + 4wh$$

Since the formula for the surface area of a rectangular prism is a combination of addition and multiplication, we cannot easily determine a factor by which the surface area changes.

However, we can determine a factor of change for the surface area of a sphere.

The surface area of a sphere is equal to

$$4\pi r^2$$

If we triple the radius, the surface area becomes

$$4\pi(3r)^2 = 4\pi(9r^2) = 36\pi r^2$$

The surface area changes by a factor equal to the square of the number by which we multiply the radius.

Volume is a three-dimensional measurement. The volume of a rectangular prism is equal to

$$lwh$$

If we double the width, we get

$$l(2w)h = 2lwh$$

The volume has doubled. The volume changes by the factor that the length, width, or height changes.

The volume of a sphere is equal to

$$\frac{4}{3}\pi r^3$$

If we double the radius, we get

$$\frac{4}{3}\pi(2r)^3 = \frac{4}{3}\pi(8r^3) = \frac{32\pi r^3}{3}$$

The volume changes by a factor equal to the cube of the number by which we multiply the radius.

Skill 7.3   **Within a given system, solve real-world problems involving measurement, with both direct and indirect measures, and make conversions to a larger or smaller unit (metric and customary).**

Example: Students are trying to determine the volume of a block.

Direct measurement:
Students pour water into a graduated cylinder and note the volume of the cylinder. They then place the block in the cylinder and note the new volume. By deducting the first reading from the second reading, they can determine the volume of the block by displacement.

Indirect measurement:
Students measure the length, height, and width of the block. They then determine the volume by multiplying the length times the width times the height.

Converting from larger units to smaller units (metric):
To convert larger units to smaller units, multiply.

Example: If a packet of sugar weighs 0.5 grams, how many milligrams does it weigh?

        1 gram = 1000 milligrams
        0.5 grams x 1000 milligrams = 500 milligrams

Converting from smaller units to larger units (customary):
To convert smaller units to larger units, divide.

Example: If an adult Kodiak bear weighs 1150 pounds, how many tons does it weigh?

        1 ton = 2000 pounds
        1150 pounds / 2000 pounds = 0.575 tons

Skill 7.4   Solve real-world problems involving estimates and exact measurements.

Example of a real-world problem where an estimate is more appropriate than an exact measurement:

Mrs. Jackson wants to make a 5' x 10' braided rug using 1"- wide braid.

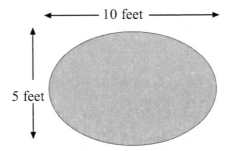

She can estimate how much braid she will need by determining the approximate area of the rug. If the rug were rectangular, the area would be 50 sq. ft., or 7200 sq. in. (50 x 144). Mrs. Jackson may use this estimate to make or purchase the amount of braid she needs for the rug.

Example of a real-world problem where an exact measurement is more appropriate than an estimate:

A carpenter is building a stairway to reach the second floor of a house. If the carpenter estimates instead of using an exact measurement and overestimates the length of the stairway, the stairway will not fit against the second floor. If he underestimates the length, the stairway will not reach to the second floor.

Skill 7.5   Select appropriate units to solve problems.

Students should be able to determine what unit of measurement is appropriate for a particular problem, as indicated by the following table:

Problem Type	Unit (Customary System)	Unit (Metric System)
Length	Inch Foot Yard	Millimeter Centimeter Meter
Distance	Mile	Kilometer
Area	Square inches Square feet Square yards Square miles	Square millimeters Square centimeters Square meters Square kilometers
Volume	Cubic inches Cubic feet Cubic yards	Cubic millimeters Cubic centimeters Cubic meters
Liquid volume	Fluid ounces Cups Pints Quarts Gallons	Milliliters Liters
Mass		Milligrams Centigrams Grams Kilograms
Weight	Ounces Pounds Tons	Milligrams Centigrams Grams Kilograms
Temperature	Degrees Fahrenheit	Degrees Celsius or Kelvin

COMPETENCY 8.0   KNOWLEDGE OF GEOMETRY AND SPATIAL SENSE

Skill 8.1   Identify angles or pairs of angles as adjacent, complementary, supplementary, vertical, corresponding, alternate interior, alternate exterior, obtuse, acute, or right

The classifying of angles refers to the angle measure. The naming of angles refers to the letters or numbers used to label the angle.

Sample Problem:

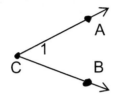

$\overrightarrow{CA}$ (read ray CA) and $\overrightarrow{CB}$ are the sides of the angle.
The angle can be called $\angle ACB$, $\angle BCA$, $\angle C$ or $\angle 1$.

Angles are classified according to their size as follows:

acute:	greater than 0 and less than 90 degrees.
right:	exactly 90 degrees.
obtuse:	greater than 90 and less than 180 degrees.
straight:	exactly 180 degrees.

Angles can be classified in a number of ways. Some of those classifications are outlined here.

Adjacent angles have a common vertex and one common side but no interior points in common.

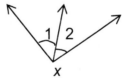

Complimentary angles add up to 90 degrees.

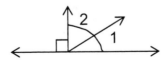

Supplementary angles add up to 180 degrees.

Vertical angles have sides that form two pairs of opposite rays.

Corresponding angles are in the same corresponding position on two parallel lines cut by a transversal.

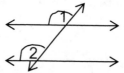

Alternate interior angles are diagonal angles on the inside of two parallel lines cut by a transversal.

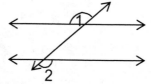

Alternate exterior angles are diagonal angles on the outside of two parallel lines cut by a transversal.

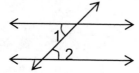

Skill 8.2   Identify lines and planes as perpendicular, intersecting, or parallel.

Parallel lines or planes do not intersect.

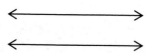

Perpendicular lines or planes form a 90 degree angle to each other.

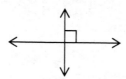

Intersecting lines share a common point, and intersecting planes share a common set of points or line.

Skew lines do not intersect and do not lie on the same plane.

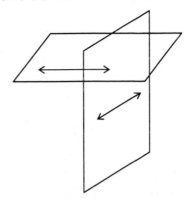

Skill 8.3 **Apply geometric properties and relationships, such as the Pythagorean Theorem, in solving problems.**

The Pythagorean Theorem states that the square of the length of the hypotenuse is equal to the sum of the squares of the lengths of the legs. Symbolically, this is stated as:

$$c^2 = a^2 + b^2$$

Given the right triangle below, find the missing side.

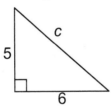

$c^2 = a^2 + b^2$	1. write formula
$c^2 = 5^2 + 6^2$	2. substitute known values
$c^2 = 61$	3. take square root
$c = \sqrt{61}$ or 7.81	4. solve

The converse of the Pythagorean Theorem states that if the square of one side of a triangle is equal to the sum of the squares of the other two sides, then the triangle is a right triangle.

Example: Given $\triangle XYZ$, with sides measuring 12, 16, and 20 cm., is this a right triangle?

$$c^2 = a^2 + b^2$$
$$20^2 \underline{\ ?\ } 12^2 + 16^2$$
$$400 \underline{\ ?\ } 144 + 256$$
$$400 = 400$$

Yes, the triangle is a right triangle.

This theorem can be expanded to determine if triangles are obtuse or acute.
If the square of the longest side of a triangle is greater than the sum of the squares of the other two sides, then the triangle is an obtuse triangle.
and
If the square of the longest side of a triangle is less than the sum of the squares of the other two sides, then the triangle is an acute triangle.

Example: Given $\triangle LMN$ with sides measuring 7, 12, and 14 inches, is the triangle right, acute, or obtuse?

$$14^2 \underline{\ ?\ } 7^2 + 12^2$$
$$196 \underline{\ ?\ } 49 + 144$$
$$196 > 193$$

Therefore, the triangle is obtuse.

<u>Real-World Example:</u> Find the area and perimeter of a rectangle if its length is 12 inches and its diagonal is 15 inches.

1. Draw and label sketch.

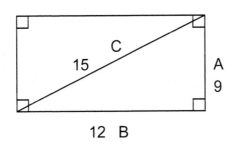

2. Since the height is still needed, use Pythagorean formula to find missing leg of the triangle.

$$A^2 + B^2 = C^2$$
$$A^2 + 12^2 = 15^2$$
$$A^2 = 15^2 - 12^2$$
$$A^2 = 81$$
$$A = 9$$

Now use this information to find the area and perimeter.

$A = LW$	$P = 2(L + W)$	1. write formula
$A = (12)(9)$	$P = 2(12 + 9)$	2. substitute
$A = 108\ \text{in}^2$	$P = 42$ inches	3. solve

<u>Real-World Example:</u> Given the figure below, find the area by dividing the polygon into smaller shapes.

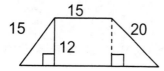

1. divide the figure into two triangles and a rectangle.

2. find the missing lengths.

3. find the area of each part.

4. find the sum of all areas.

Find the base of both right triangles using the Pythagorean Formula:

$$a^2 + b^2 = c^2$$
$$a^2 + 12^2 = 15^2$$
$$a^2 = 225 - 144$$
$$a^2 = 81$$
$$a = 9$$

$$a^2 + b^2 = c^2$$
$$a^2 + 12^2 = 20^2$$
$$a^2 = 400 - 144$$
$$a^2 = 256$$
$$a = 16$$

Area of triangle 1   Area of triangle 2   Area of rectangle

$$A = \frac{1}{2}bh$$

$$A = \frac{1}{2}(9)(12)$$

$A = 54$ sq. units

$$A = \frac{1}{2}bh$$

$$A = \frac{1}{2}(16)(12)$$

$A = 96$ sq. units

$$A = LW$$

$$A = (15)(12)$$

$A = 180$ sq. units

Find the sum of all three figures.

$$54 + 96 + 180 = 330 \text{ square units}$$

Skill 8.4 **Identify the basic characteristics of, and relationships pertaining to, regular and irregular geometric shapes in two and three dimensions.**

We can represent any two-dimensional geometric figure in the **Cartesian** or **rectangular coordinate system**. The Cartesian or rectangular coordinate system is formed by two perpendicular axes (coordinate axes): the X-axis and the Y-axis. If we know the dimensions of a two-dimensional, or planar, figure, we can use this coordinate system to visualize the shape of the figure.

Example: Represent an isosceles triangle with two sides of length 4.

Draw the two sides along the x- and y- axes and connect the points (vertices).

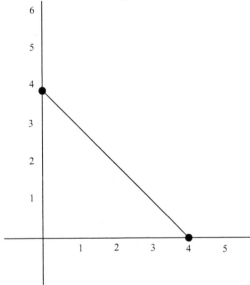

We refer to three-dimensional figures in geometry as **solids**. A solid is the union of all points on a simple closed surface and all points in its interior. A **polyhedron** is a simple closed surface formed from planar polygonal regions. Each polygonal region is called a **face** of the polyhedron. The vertices and edges of the polygonal regions are called the **vertices** and **edges** of the polyhedron.

We may form a cube from three congruent squares. However, if we tried to put four squares about a single vertex, their interior angle measures would add up to 360°; i.e., four edge-to-edge squares with a common vertex lie in a common plane and therefore cannot form a corner figure of a regular polyhedron.

There are five ways to form corner figures with congruent regular polygons:

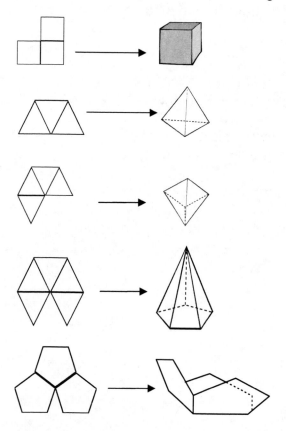

When creating a three-dimensional figure, if we know any two values of the vertices, faces, and edges, we can find the remaining value by using **Euler's Formula**: $V + F = E + 2$.

Example:

We want to create a pentagonal pyramid, and we know it has six vertices and six faces. Using Euler's Formula, we compute:

$$V + F = E + 2$$
$$6 + 6 = E + 2$$
$$12 = E + 2$$
$$10 = E$$

Thus, we know that our figure should have 10 edges.

Skill 8.5   Apply the geometric concepts of symmetry, congruency, similarity, tessellations, transformations, and scaling.

A **Tessellation** is an arrangement of closed shapes that completely covers the plane without overlapping or leaving gaps. Unlike **tilings**, tessellations do not require the use of regular polygons. In art the term is used to refer to pictures or tiles mostly in the form of animals and other life forms, which cover the surface of a plane in a symmetrical way without overlapping or leaving gaps. M. C. Escher is known as the "father" of modern tessellations. Tessellations are used for tiling, mosaics, quilts, and art.

If you look at a completed tessellation, you will see the original motif repeats in a pattern. There are 17 possible ways that a pattern can be used to tile a flat surface, or "wallpaper."

There are four basic transformational symmetries that can be used in tessellations: **translation, rotation, reflection,** and **glide reflection**. The transformation of an object is called its image. If the original object was labeled with letters, such as $ABCD$, the image may be labeled with the same letters followed by a prime symbol, $A'B'C'D'$.

The tessellation below is a combination of the four types of transformational symmetry we have discussed:

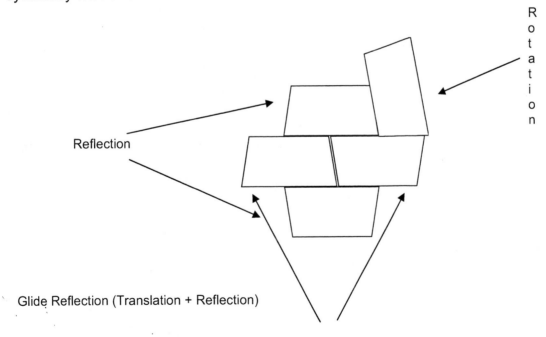

Reflection

Rotation

Glide Reflection (Translation + Reflection)

A **transformation** is a change in the position, shape, or size of a geometric figure. **Transformational geometry** is the study of manipulating objects by flipping, twisting, turning, and scaling. **Symmetry** is exact similarity between two parts or halves, as if one were a mirror image of the other.

A **translation** is a transformation that "slides" an object a fixed distance in a given direction. The original object and its translation have the same shape and size, and they face in the same direction.

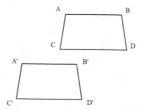

An example of a translation in architecture would be stadium seating. The seats are the same size and the same shape and face in the same direction.

A **rotation** is a transformation that turns a figure about a fixed point called the center of rotation. An object and its rotation are the same shape and size, but the figures may be turned in different directions. Rotations can occur in either a clockwise or a counterclockwise direction.

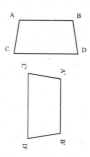

Rotations can be seen in wallpaper and art, and a Ferris wheel is an example of rotation.

An object and its **reflection** have the same shape and size, but the figures face in opposite directions.

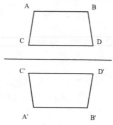

The line (where a mirror may be placed) is called the **line of reflection**. The distance from a point to the line of reflection is the same as the distance from the point's image to the line of reflection.

A **glide reflection** is a combination of a reflection and a translation.

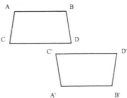

Another type of transformation is **dilation**. Dilation is a transformation that "shrinks" or "makes it bigger."

<u>Example:</u> Using dilation to transform a diagram.

Starting with a triangle whose center of dilation is point P,

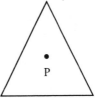

we dilate the lengths of the sides by the same factor to create a new

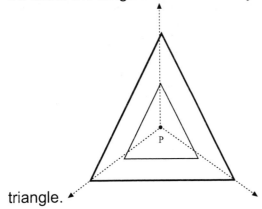

triangle.

Skill 8.6   **Determine and locate ordered pairs in all four quadrants of a rectangular coordinate system.**

Example:

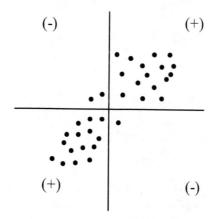

Horizontal and vertical lines are drawn through the point of averages, which is the point on the averages of the x and y values. This divides the scatter plot into four quadrants. If a point is in the lower left quadrant, the product of two negatives is positive; in the upper right, the product of two positives is positive. The positive quadrants are depicted with the positive sign (+). In the two remaining quadrants (upper left and lower right), the product of a negative and a positive is negative. The negative quadrants are depicted with the negative sign (-). If r is positive, then there are more points in the positive quadrants, and if r is negative, then there are more points in the two negative quadrants.

An **ordered pair** is made up of an x-coordinate and a y-coordinate (x, y). The x-coordinate is plotted along the x-axis, and the y-coordinate is plotted along the y-axis.

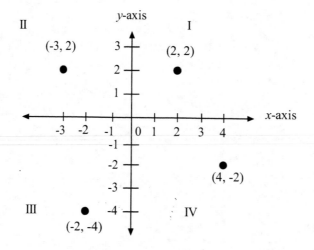

With (0, 0) as the intersection of the two axes, the right side on the *x*-axis is positive, and the left side is negative. The top part of the *y*-axis is positive, and the bottom part is negative. Accordingly, any ordered pair in Quadrant I is made up of a positive *x*-coordinate and a positive *y*-coordinate; any ordered pair in Quadrant II is made up of a negative *x*-coordinate and a positive *y*-coordinate; any ordered pair in Quadrant III is made up of a negative *x*-coordinate and a negative *y*-coordinate; and any ordered pair in Quadrant IV is made up of a positive *x*-coordinate and a negative *y*-coordinate.

Example: To locate the point (4, -2), from the origin, (0, 0), you would move to the right 4 units and move down 2 units.

COMPETENCY 9.0   KNOWLEDGE OF ALGEBRAIC THINKING

Skill 9.1   Extend and generalize patterns or functional relationships.

Example: Conjecture about pattern presented in tabular form.

Kepler discovered a relationship between the average distance of a planet from the sun and the time it takes the planet to orbit the sun.

The following table shows the data for the six planets closest to the sun:

	Mercury	Venus	Earth	Mars	Jupiter	Saturn
Average distance, x	0.387	0.723	1	1.523	5.203	9.541
x^3	0.058	.378	1	3.533	140.852	868.524
Time, y	0.241	0.615	1	1.881	11.861	29.457
y^2	0.058	0.378	1	3.538	140.683	867.715

Looking at the data in the table, we see that $x^3 = y^2$. We can conjecture the following function for Kepler's relationship: $y = \sqrt{x^3}$.

-Representation of patterns using symbolic notation:

Example: Find the recursive formula for the sequence 1, 3, 9, 27, 81...

We see that any term other than the first term is obtained by multiplying the preceding term by 3. Then, we may express the formula in symbolic notation as

$$a_n = 3a_{n-1}, \; a_1 = 1$$

where a represents a term, the subscript n denotes the place of the term in the sequence, and the subscript $n-1$ represents the preceding term.

-Identification of patterns of change created by functions (e.g., linear, quadratic, exponential):

A **linear function** is a function defined by the equation $f(x) = mx + b$.

Example: A model for the distance traveled by a migrating monarch butterfly looks like $f(t) = 80t$, where t represents time in days. We interpret this to mean that the average speed of the butterfly is 80 miles per day, and distance traveled may be computed by substituting the number of days traveled for t . In a linear function, there is a **constant** rate of change.

The standard form of a **quadratic function** is $f(x) = ax^2 + bx + c$.

Example: What patterns appear in a table for $y = x^2 - 5x + 6$?

x	y
0	6
1	2
2	0
3	0
4	2
5	6

We see that the values for y are **symmetrically** arranged.

An **exponential function** is a function defined by the equation $y = ab^x$, where a is the starting value, b is the growth factor, and x tells how many times to multiply by the growth factor.

Example: $y = 100(1.5)^x$

x	y
0	100
1	150
2	225
3	337.5
4	506.25

This is an **exponential** or multiplicative pattern of growth.

-Iterative and recursive functional relationships (e.g., Fibonacci numbers):

The **iterative process** involves repeated use of the same steps. A **recursive function** is an example of the iterative process. A recursive function is a function that requires the computation of all previous terms in order to find a subsequent term. Perhaps the most famous recursive function is the **Fibonacci sequence**. This is the sequence of numbers 1,1,2,3,5,8,13,21,34 … for which the next term is found by adding the previous two terms.

Skill 9.2   Interpret tables, graphs, equations, and verbal descriptions to explain real-world situations involving functional relationships.

A relationship between two quantities can be shown using a table, graph, or rule. In this example, the rule y = 9x describes the relationship between the total amount earned, y, and the total amount of $9.00 sunglasses sold, x.

A table using this data would appear as:

number of sunglasses sold	1	5	10	15
total dollars earned	9	45	90	135

Each *(x,y)* relationship between a pair of values is called the coordinate pair and can be plotted on a graph. The coordinate pairs *(1,9)*, *(5,45)*, *(10,90)*, and *(15,135)* are plotted on the graph below.

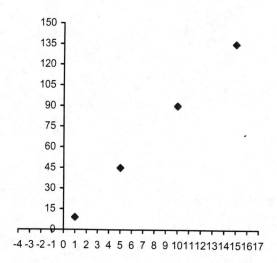

The graph above shows a linear relationship. A linear relationship is one in which two quantities are proportional to each other. Doubling *x* also doubles *y*. On a graph, a straight line depicts a linear relationship.

Another type of relationship is a nonlinear relationship. This is one in which change in one quantity does not affect the other quantity to the same extent. Nonlinear graphs have a curved line, such as the graph below.

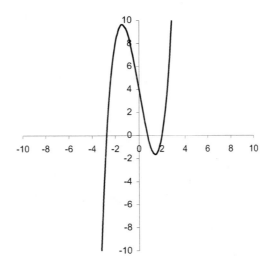

Skill 9.3   Select a representation of an algebraic expression, equation, or inequality that applies to a real-world situation.

Many algebraic procedures are similar to and rely upon number operations and algorithms. Two examples of this similarity are the adding of rational expressions and division of polynomials.

Addition of rational expressions is similar to fraction addition. The basic algorithm of addition for both fractions and rational expressions is the common denominator method. Consider an example of the addition of numerical fractions.

$$\frac{3}{5}+\frac{2}{3}=\frac{3(3)}{3(5)}+\frac{5(2)}{5(3)}=\frac{9}{15}+\frac{10}{15}=\frac{19}{15}$$

To complete the sum, we first find the least common denominator.

Now, consider an example of rational expression addition.

$$\frac{(x+5)}{(x+1)}+\frac{2x}{(x+3)}=\frac{(x+3)(x+5)}{(x+3)(x+1)}+\frac{(x+1)2x}{(x+1)(x+3)}$$

$$=\frac{x^2+8x+15}{(x+3)(x+1)}+\frac{2x^2+2x}{(x+3)(x+1)}=\frac{3x^2+10x+15}{(x+3)(x+1)}$$

Note the similarity to fractional addition. The basic algorithm, finding a common denominator and adding numerators, is the same.

Division of polynomials follows the same algorithm as numerical long division. Consider an example of numerical long division.

$$
\begin{array}{r}
720 \\
6\overline{)4321} \\
\underline{42} \\
12 \\
\underline{12} \\
01
\end{array}
$$

⟶ 720 1/6 = final quotient

Compare the process of numerical long division to polynomial division.

$$
\begin{array}{r}
x-9 \\
x+1\overline{)x^2-8x-9} \\
\underline{-x^2-x} \\
-9x-9 \\
\underline{+9x+9} \\
0+0
\end{array}
$$

⟶ x – 9 = final quotient

Note that the step-by-step process is identical in both cases.

Concrete and visual representations can help demonstrate the logic behind operational algorithms. Blocks or other objects modeled on the base ten system are useful concrete tools. Base ten blocks represent ones, tens, and hundreds. For example, modeling the partial sums algorithm with base ten blocks helps clarify the thought process. Consider the sum of 242 and 193. We represent 242 with two one-hundred blocks, four ten blocks and two one blocks. We represent 193 with one one-hundred block, nine ten blocks and three one blocks. In the partial sums algorithm, we manipulate each place value separately and total the results. Thus, we group the hundred blocks, ten blocks and one blocks and derive a total for each place value. We combine the place values to complete the sum.

An example of a visual representation of an operational algorithm is the modeling of a two-term multiplication as the area of a rectangle. For example, consider the product of 24 and 39. We can represent the product in geometric form. Note that the four sections of the rectangle equate to the four products of the partial products method.

	30	9
20	A = 600	A = 180
4	A = 120	A = 36

Thus, the final product is the sum of the areas, or 600 + 180 + 120 + 36 = 936.

COMPETENCY 10.0   KNOWLEDGE OF DATA ANALYSIS AND PROBABILITY

Skill 10.1   Apply the concepts of range and central tendency (mean, median, and mode).

Mean, median, and mode are three measures of central tendency. The **mean** is the average of the data items. The **median** is found by putting the data items in order from smallest to largest and selecting the item in the middle (or the average of the two items in the middle). The **mode** is the most frequently occurring item.

Range is a measure of variability. It is found by subtracting the smallest value from the largest value.

Sample problem:

Find the mean, median, mode, and range of the test scores listed below:

85	77	65
92	90	54
88	85	70
75	80	69
85	88	60
72	74	95

Mean (X) = sum of all scores ÷ number of scores = 78

Median = put numbers in order from smallest to largest. Pick middle number.
54, 60, 65, 69, 70, 72, 74, 75, 77, 80, 85, 85, 85, 88, 88, 90, 92, 95
                                         -- --
                                    both in middle
Therefore, median is average of two numbers in the middle, or 78.5.

Mode = most frequent number
     = 85

Range = largest number minus smallest number
       = 95 − 54
       = 41

Skill 10.2   Determine probabilities of dependent or independent events.

Dependent events occur when the probability of the second event depends on the outcome of the first event. For example, consider the following two events: (A) it is sunny on Saturday, and (B) you go to the beach. If you intend to go to the beach on Saturday, rain or shine, then A and B may be independent. If, however, you plan to go to the beach only if it is sunny, then A and B may be dependent. In this situation, the probability of event B will change depending on the outcome of event A.

Suppose you have a pair of dice, one red and one green. If you roll a three on the red die and then roll a four on the green die, we can see that these events do not depend on each other. The total probability of the two independent events can be found by multiplying the separate probabilities.

$$P(A \text{ and } B) = P(A) \times P(B)$$
$$= 1/6 \times 1/6$$
$$= 1/36$$

Many times, however, events are not independent. Suppose a jar contains 12 red marbles and 8 blue marbles. If you randomly pick a red marble, replace it, and then randomly pick again, the probability of picking a red marble the second time remains the same. However, if you pick a red marble and then pick again without replacing the first red marble, the second pick becomes dependent upon the first pick.

P(Red and Red) with replacement = P(Red) × P(Red)
$$= 12/20 \times 12/20$$
$$= 9/25$$

P(Red and Red) without replacement = P(Red) × P(Red)
$$= 12/20 \times 11/19$$
$$= 33/95$$

Skill 10.3   Determines odds for and odds against a given situation

Odds are defined as the ratio of the number of favorable outcomes to the number of unfavorable outcomes. The sum of the favorable outcomes and the unfavorable outcomes should always equal the total possible outcomes.

For example, given a bag of 12 red and 7 green marbles compute the odds of randomly selecting a red marble.

$$\text{Odds of red} = \frac{12}{19} : \frac{7}{19} \text{ or } 12:7.$$

$$\text{Odds of not getting red} = \frac{7}{19} : \frac{12}{19} \text{ or } 7:12.$$

In the case of flipping a coin, it is equally likely that a head or a tail will be tossed. The odds of tossing a head are 1:1. This is called even odds.

Skill 10.4   Applies fundamental counting principles such as combinations to solve probability problems

In probability, the **sample space** is a list of all possible outcomes of an experiment. For example, the sample space of tossing two coins is the set {HH, HT, TT, TH}, the sample space of rolling a six-sided die is the set {1, 2, 3, 4, 5, 6}, and the sample space of measuring the height of students in a class is the set of all real numbers {R}.

When conducting experiments with a large number of possible outcomes it is important to determine the size of the sample space. The size of the sample space can be determined by using the fundamental counting principle and the rules of combinations and permutations.

The **fundamental counting principle** states that if there are m possible outcomes for one task and n possible outcomes of another, there are (m x n) possible outcomes of the two tasks together.

A **permutation** is the number of possible arrangements of items, without repetition, where order of selection is important.

A **combination** is the number of possible arrangements, without repetition, where order of selection is not important.

Permutations and combinations are covered in detail in Skill 9.4.

Examples:

1. Find the size of the sample space of rolling two six-sided die and flipping two coins.

Solution:
List the possible outcomes of each event:

each dice: {1, 2, 3, 4, 5, 6}
each coin: {Heads, Tails}

Apply the fundamental counting principle:
size of sample space = 6 x 6 x 2 x 2 = 144

Skill 10.5   Interprets information fom tables, charts, line graphs, bar graphs, circle graphs, box and whisker graphs, and stem and leaf plots.

To read a bar graph or a pictograph, read the explanation of the scale that was used in the legend. Compare the length of each bar with the dimensions on the axes and calculate the value each bar represents. On a pictograph count the number of pictures used in the chart and calculate the value of all the pictures.

To read a circle graph, find the total of the amounts represented on the entire circle graph. To determine the actual amount that each sector of the graph represents, multiply the percent in a sector times the total amount number.

To read a chart read the row and column headings on the table. Use this information to evaluate the given information in the chart.

Histograms are used to summarize information from large sets of data that can be naturally grouped into intervals. The vertical axis indicates **frequency** (the number of times any particular data value occurs), and the horizontal axis indicates data values or ranges of data values. The number of data values in any interval is the **frequency of the interval**.

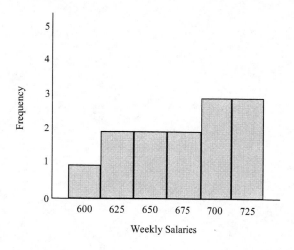

Skill 10.6   Makes accurate predictions and draw conclusions from data

The absolute probability of some events cannot be determined. For instance, one cannot assume the probability of winning a tennis match is ½ because, in general, winning and losing are not equally likely. In such cases, past results of similar events can be used to help predict future outcomes. The **relative frequency** of an event is the number of times an event has occurred divided by the number of attempts.

Relative frequency =   number of successful trials
                                    total number of trials

For example, if a weighted coin flipped 50 times lands on heads 40 times and tails 10 times, the relative frequency of heads is 40/50 = 4/5. Thus, one can predict that if the coin is flipped 100 times, it will land on heads 80 times.

Example:

Two tennis players, John and David, have played each other 20 times.
John has won 15 of the previous matches and David has won 5.
        (a) Estimate the probability that David will win the next match.
        (b) Estimate the probability that John will win the next 3 matches.

Solution:

   (a) David has won 5 out of 20 matches. Thus, the relative frequency of David winning is 5/20 or ¼. We can estimate that the probability of David winning the next match is ¼.

   (b) John has won 15 out of 20 matches. The relative frequency of John winning is 15/20 or ¾. We can estimate that the probability of John winning a future match is ¾. Thus, the probability that John will win the next three matches is ¾ x ¾ x ¾ = 27/64.

COMPETENCY 11.0   KNOWLEDGE OF INSTRUCTION AND ASSESSMENT

Skill 11.1   Identifies alternative instructional strategies.

It is important to realize that not all students learn the same way and, therefore, alternative instructional strategies may be appropriate. These strategies should provide alternatives to conventional basic skills instruction by emphasizing meaning and understanding, teaching discrete skills in context, and making real-world connections. Alternative methodologies include the use of:

- simulations
- group, cooperative, collaborative learning
- strategy and role-playing games
- peer tutoring
- toolkits
- learning by design
- multimedia
- storytelling structures
- coaching and scaffolding
- case studies

In addition, the following may be incorporated into instruction:

- use open-ended questions
- have students record, represent, or analyze data
- have students explain their reasoning when giving an answer
- have students work on longer mathematics investigations (a week or more in duration)
- encourage mathematical communication
- have students engage in hands-on mathematics activities
- encourage students to explore alternative methods for solutions
- have students share ideas or solve problems in small groups
- help students see connections between mathematics and other disciplines.

Skill 11.2   Selects manipulatives, mathematical and physical models, and other classroom teaching tools

The use of supplementary materials in the classroom can greatly enhance the learning experience by stimulating student interest and satisfying different learning styles. Manipulatives, models, and technology are examples of tools available to teachers.

Manipulatives are materials that students can physically handle and move. Manipulatives allow students to understand mathematic concepts by allowing them to see concrete examples of abstract processes. Manipulatives are attractive to students because they appeal to the students' visual and tactile senses. Available for all levels of math, manipulatives are useful tools for reinforcing operations and concepts. They are not, however, a substitute for the development of sound computational skills.

Models are another means of representing mathematical concepts by relating the concepts to real-world situations. Teachers must choose wisely when devising and selecting models because, to be effective, models must be applied properly. For example, a building with floors above and below ground is a good model for introducing the concept of negative numbers. It would be difficult, however, to use the building model in teaching subtraction of negative numbers.

Finally, there are many forms of **technology** available to math teachers. For example, students can test their understanding of math concepts by working on skill specific computer programs and websites. Graphing calculators can help students visualize the graphs of functions. Teachers can also enhance their lectures and classroom presentations by creating multimedia presentations.

MANIPULATIVES

<u>Example</u>:
Using tiles to demonstrate both geometric ideas and number theory.

Give each group of students 12 tiles and instruct them to build rectangles.
Students draw their rectangles on paper.

12 × 1

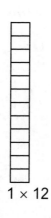

1 × 12

3 × 4

4 × 3

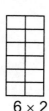

6 × 2

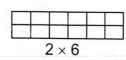

2 × 6

Encourage students to describe their reactions. Extend to 16 tiles. Ask students
to form additional problems.

Skill 11.3   Identifies ways that calculators, computers, and other technology can be used in instruction.

Calculators are an important tool. They should be encouraged in the classroom and at home. They do not replace basic knowledge but they can relieve the tedium of mathematical computations, allowing students to explore more challenging mathematical directions. Students will be able to use calculators more intelligently if they are taught how. Students need to always check their work by estimating. The goal of mathematics is to prepare the child to survive in the real world. Technology is a reality in today's society

Skill 11.4   Identifies a variety of methods of assessing mathematical knowledge, including analyzing student thinking processes to determine strengths and weaknesses.

Teachers of mathematics should be aware of alternative positive assessment techniques that are performance-based and focus on conceptual understanding. These techniques include:

1) open-ended questions – allow students to express answers in their own words along with diagrams and/or pictures and express how they can apply their knowledge
2) mathematical investigations and projects – provide evidence of communication in mathematics
3) writing activities in mathematics – logbooks, journals, expository writing, creative writing to demonstrate writing ability and communication in mathematics

4) observations and interviews – checklists used over time to measure a student's attitude and aptitude
5) enhanced multiple-choice questions – require not only knowledge of basic facts, but also the ability to apply higher-order thinking skills to make sense of those facts
6) portfolio assessments – collections of students' work, showing progress over time, allowing students to demonstrate their ability to do major pieces of work as opposed to short exercises

DOMAIN III.   SOCIAL SCIENCE

COMPETENCY 12.0   KNOWLEDGE OF TIME, CONTINUITY, AND CHANGE

Skill 12.1   Identify major historical events that are related by cause and effect

Historic causation is the concept that events in history are linked to one another by an endless chain of cause and effect. The root causes of major historical events cannot always be seen immediately, and are only apparent when looking back from many years later.

When Columbus landed in the New World in 1492, the full effect of his discovery could not have been measured at that time. By opening the Western Hemisphere to economic and political development by Europeans, Columbus changed the face of the world. The native populations that had existed before Columbus arrived were quickly decimated by disease and warfare. Over the following century, the Spanish conquered most of South and Central America, and English and French settlers arrived in North America, eventually displacing the native people. This gradual displacement took place over many years and could not have been foreseen by those early explorers. Looking back it can be said that Columbus caused a series of events that greatly impacted world history.

In some cases, individual events can have an immediate, clear effect. In 1941, Europe was embroiled in war. On the Pacific Rim, Japan was engaged in military occupation of Korea and other Asian countries. The United States took a position of isolation, choosing not to become directly involved with the conflicts. This position changed rapidly, however, on the morning of December 7, 1941, when Japanese forces launched a surprise attack on the US naval base at Pearl Harbor in Hawaii. The United States immediately declared war on Japan and became involved in Europe shortly afterwards. The entry of the United States into the Second World War undoubtedly contributed to the eventual victory of the Allied forces in Europe, and the defeat of Japan after two atomic bombs were dropped there by the US. The surprise attack on Pearl Harbor affected the outcome of the war and the shape of the modern world.

Interaction between cultures, either by exploration and migration or war, often contribute directly to major historical events, but other forces can influence the course of history, as well. Religious movements such as the rise of Catholicism in the Middle Ages created social changes throughout Europe and culminated in the Crusades and the expulsion of Muslims from Spain. Technological developments can lead to major historical events, as in the case of the Industrial Revolution which was driven by the replacement of water power with steam power. Social movements can also cause major historical shifts. Between the Civil War and the early 1960s in the United States, racial segregation was practiced legally in many parts of the country through "Jim Crow" laws.

Demonstrations and activism opposing segregation began to escalate during the late 1950s and early 1960s, eventually leading to the passage in the Congress of the Civil Rights Act of 1964, which ended legal segregation in the United States.

Skill 12.2 Evaluate examples of primary source documents for historical perspective

The resources used in the study of history can be divided into two major groups: primary sources and secondary sources.

Primary sources are works, records, etc. that were created during the period being studied or immediately after it. Secondary sources are works written significantly after the period being studied and based upon primary sources. "Primary sources are the basic materials that provide the raw data and information for the historian. Secondary sources are the works that contain the explications of, and judgments on, this primary material." [Source: Norman F Cantor & Richard I. Schneider. HOW TO STUDY HISTORY, Harlan Davidson, Inc., 1967, pp. 23-24.]

Primary sources include the following kinds of materials:
- Documents that reflect the immediate, everyday concerns of people: memoranda, bills, deeds, charters, newspaper reports, pamphlets, graffiti, popular writings, journals or diaries, records of decision-making bodies, letters, receipts, snapshots, etc.
- Theoretical writings which reflect care and consideration in composition and an attempt to convince or persuade. The topic will generally be deeper and more pervasive values than is the case with "immediate" documents. These may include newspaper or magazine editorials, sermons, political speeches, philosophical writings, etc.
- Narrative accounts of events, ideas, trends, etc. written with intentionality by someone contemporary with the events described.
- Statistical data, although statistics may be misleading.
- Literature and nonverbal materials, novels, stories, poetry and essays from the period, as well as coins, archaeological artifacts, and art produced during the period.

Guidelines for the use of primary resources:
1. Be certain that you understand how language was used at the time of writing and that you understand the context in which it was produced.
2. Do not read history blindly; but be certain that you understand both explicit and implicit referenced in the material.
3. Read the entire text you are reviewing; do not simply extract a few sentences to read.
4. Although anthologies of materials may help you identify primary source materials, the full original text should be consulted.

Secondary sources include the following kinds of materials:
- Books written on the basis of primary materials about the period of time.
- Books written on the basis of primary materials about persons who played a major role in the events under consideration.
- Books and articles written on the basis of primary materials about the culture, the social norms, the language, and the values of the period.
- Quotations from primary sources.
- Statistical data on the period.
- The conclusions and inferences of other historians.
- Multiple interpretations of the ethos of the time.

Guidelines for the use of secondary sources:
1. Do not rely upon only a single secondary source.
2. Check facts and interpretations against primary sources whenever possible.
3. Do not accept the conclusions of other historians uncritically.
4. Place greatest reliance on secondary sources created by the best and most respected scholars.
5. Do not use the inferences of other scholars as if they were facts.
6. Ensure that you recognize any bias the writer brings to his/her interpretation of history.
7. Understand the primary point of the book as a basis for evaluating the value of the material presented in it to your questions.

Skill 12.3 Identify cultural contributions and technological developments of Africa, the Americas, Asia, including the Middle East and Europe

African civilizations during these centuries were few and far between. Most of northern coastal Africa had been conquered by Moslem armies. The preponderance of deserts and other inhospitable lands restricted African settlements to a few select areas. The city of Zimbabwe became a trading center in south-central Africa in the fifth century but didn't last long. More successful was **Ghana**, a Muslim-influenced kingdom that arose in the ninth century and lasted for nearly 300 years. Ghanaians had large farming areas and also raised cattle and elephants. They traded with people from Europe and the Middle East. Eventually overrunning Ghana was Mali, whose trade center Timbuktu survived its own empire's demise and blossomed into one of the world's caravan destinations. Iron, tin, and leather came out of **Mali** with a vengeance. The succeeding civilization of the **Songhai** had relative success in maintaining the success of their predecessors. Religion in all of these places was definitely Muslim; and even after extended contact with other cultures, technological advancements were few and far between.

The civilizations of the Sumerians, Amorites, Hittites, Assyrians, Chaldeans, and Persians controlled various areas of the land we call Mesopotamia. With few exceptions, tyrants and military leaders controlled the vast majority of aspects of society, including trade, religions, and the laws. Each Sumerian city-state (and there were a few) had its own god, with the city-state's leader doubling as the high priest of worship of that local god. Subsequent cultures had a handful of gods as well, although they had more of a national worship structure, with high priests centered in the capital city as advisers to the tyrant.

Trade was vastly important to these civilizations, since they had access to some but not all of the things that they needed to survive. Some trading agreements led to occupation, as was the case with the Sumerians, who didn't bother to build walls to protect their wealth of knowledge. Egypt and the Phoenician cities were powerful and regular trading partners of the various Mesopotamian cultures.

Legacies handed down to us from these people include:

- The first use of writing, the wheel, and banking (Sumeria);
- The first written set of laws (Code of Hammurabi);
- The first epic story (*Gilgamesh*);
- The first library dedicated to preserving knowledge (instituted by the Assyrian leader Ashurbanipal);
- The Hanging Gardens of Babylon (built by the Chaldean Nebuchadnezzar)

The ancient civilization of the **Sumerians** invented the wheel; developed irrigation through use of canals, dikes, and devices for raising water; devised the system of cuneiform writing; learned to divide time; and built large boats for trade. The Babylonians devised the famous Code of Hammurabi, a code of laws

Egypt made numerous significant contributions including construction of the great pyramids; development of hieroglyphic writing; preservation of bodies after death; making paper from papyrus; contributing to developments in arithmetic and geometry; the invention of the method of counting in groups of 1-10 (the decimal system); completion of a solar calendar; and laying the foundation for science and astronomy.

The earliest historical record of **Kush** is in Egyptian sources. They describe a region upstream from the first cataract of the Nile as "wretched." This civilization was characterized by a settled way of life in fortified mud-brick villages. They subsisted on hunting and fishing, herding cattle, and gathering grain. Skeletal remains suggest that the people were a blend of Negroid and Mediterranean peoples. This civilization appears to be the second-oldest in Africa (after Egypt).

The Kushite religion was polytheistic, including all of the primary Egyptian gods. There were, however, regional gods which were the principal gods in their regions. Derived from other African cultures, there was also a lion warrior god.

The ancient **Assyrians** were warlike and aggressive due to a highly organized military and used horse drawn chariots.

The **Hebrews**, also known as the ancient Israelites instituted monotheism, which is the worship of one God, Yahweh, and combined the 66 books of the Hebrew and Christian Greek scriptures into the Bible we have today.

The **Minoans** had a system of writing using symbols to represent syllables in words. They built palaces with multiple levels containing many rooms, water and sewage systems with flush toilets, bathtubs, hot and cold running water, and bright paintings on the walls.

The **Mycenaeans** changed the Minoan writing system to aid their own language and used symbols to represent syllables.

The **Phoenicians** were sea traders well known for their manufacturing skills in glass and metals and the development of their famous purple dye. They became so very proficient in the skill of navigation that they were able to sail by the stars at night. Further, they devised an alphabet using symbols to represent single sounds, which was an improved extension of the Egyptian principle and writing system.

In **India**, the caste system was developed, the principle of zero in mathematics was discovered, and the major religion of Hinduism was begun. In India, Hinduism was a continuing influence along with the rise of Buddhism. Industry and commerce developed along with extensive trading with the Near East. Outstanding advances in the fields of science and medicine were made along with being one of the first to be active in navigation and maritime enterprises during this time.

China is considered by some historians to be the oldest, uninterrupted civilization in the world and was in existence around the same time as the ancient civilizations founded in Egypt, Mesopotamia, and the Indus Valley. The Chinese studied nature and weather; stressed the importance of education, family, and a strong central government; followed the religions of Buddhism, Confucianism, and Taoism; and invented such things as gunpowder, paper, printing, and the magnetic compass. China began building the Great Wall; practiced crop rotation and terrace farming; increased the importance of the silk industry, and developed caravan routes across Central Asia for extensive trade. Also, they increased proficiency in rice cultivation and developed a written language based on drawings or pictographs (no alphabet symbolizing sounds as each word or character had a form different from all others).

The ancient **Persians** developed an alphabet; contributed the religions/philosophies of Zoroastrianism, Mithraism, and Gnosticism; and allowed conquered peoples to retain their own customs, laws, and religions.

The classical civilization of **Greece** reached the highest levels in man's achievements based on the foundations already laid by such ancient groups as the Egyptians, Phoenicians, Minoans, and Mycenaeans. Among the more important contributions of Greece were the Greek alphabet derived from the Phoenician letters which formed the basis for the Roman alphabet and our present-day alphabet. Extensive trading and colonization resulted in the spread of the Greek civilization. The love of sports, with emphasis on a sound body, led to the tradition of the Olympic Games. Greece was responsible for the rise of independent, strong city-states. Note the complete contrast between independent, freedom-loving Athens with its practice of pure democracy i.e. direct, personal, active participation in government by qualified citizens and the rigid, totalitarian, militaristic Sparta.

Other important areas that the Greeks are credited with influencing include drama, epic and lyric poetry, fables, myths centered on the many gods and goddesses, science, astronomy, medicine, mathematics, philosophy, art, architecture, and recording historical events. The conquests of Alexander the Great spread Greek ideas to the areas he conquered and brought to the Greek world many ideas from Asia Above all, the value of ideas, wisdom, curiosity, and the desire to learn as much about the world as possible.

The ancient civilization of **Rome** lasted approximately 1,000 years including the periods of republic and empire, although its lasting influence on Europe and its history was for a much longer period. There was a very sharp contrast between the curious, imaginative, inquisitive Greeks and the practical, simple, down-to-earth, no-nonsense Romans, who spread and preserved the ideas of ancient Greece and other culture groups. The contributions and accomplishments of the Romans are numerous but their greatest included language, engineering, building, law, government, roads, trade, and the "Pax Romana". Pax Romana was the long period of peace which enabled free travel and trade and spread people, cultures, goods, and ideas over a vast area of the known world.

The civilization in **Japan** appeared during this time having borrowed much of their culture from China. It was the last of these classical civilizations to develop. Although they used, accepted, and copied Chinese art, law, architecture, dress, and writing, the Japanese refined these into their own unique way of life, including incorporating the religion of Buddhism into their culture. Early Japanese society focused on the emperor and the farm, in that order. The Sea of Japan protected Japan from more than Chinese invasion, including the famous Mongol one that was blown back by the "divine wind." The power of the emperor declined as it was usurped by the era of the Daimyo and his loyal soldiers, the Samurai. Japan flourished economically and culturally during many of these years, although the policy of isolation the country developed kept the rest of the world from knowing such things. Buddhism and local religions were joined by Christianity in the sixteenth century, but it wasn't until the mid-nineteenth century that Japan rejoined the world community.

The civilizations in **Africa** south of the Sahara were developing the refining and use of iron, especially for farm implements and later for weapons. Trading was overland using camels and at important seaports. The Arab influence was extremely important, as was their later contact with Indians, Christian Nubians, and Persians. In fact, their trading activities were probably the most important factor in the spread of and assimilation of different ideas and stimulation of cultural growth.

The people who lived in the Americas before Columbus arrived had a thriving, connected society. The civilizations in North America tended to spread out more and were in occasional conflict but maintained their sovereignty, for the most part. The South American civilizations, however, tended to migrate into empires, with the strongest city or tribe assuming control of the lives and resources of the rest of the nearby peoples. One of the best known of the North American tribes was the **Pueblo**, who lived in what is now the American Southwest. They are perhaps best known for the challenging vista-based villages that they constructed from the sheer faces of cliffs and rocks and for their *adobes*, mud-brick buildings that housed their living and meeting quarters. The Pueblos chose their own chiefs. This was perhaps one of the oldest representative governments in the world.

Known also for their organized government were the **Iroquois**, who lived in the American Northeast. The famous Five Nations of the Iroquois made treaties among themselves and shared leadership of their peoples.

We know the most about the empires of South America, the Aztec, Inca, and Maya. People lived in South America before the advent of these empires, of course. One of the earliest people of record were the Olmecs, who left behind little to prove their existence except a series of huge carved figures.

The **Aztecs** dominated Mexico and Central America. They weren't the only people living in these areas, just the most powerful ones. The Aztecs had many enemies, some of whom were only too happy to help Hernan Cortes precipitate the downfall of the Aztec society. The Aztecs had access to large numbers of metals and jewels, and they used these metals to make weapons and these jewels to trade for items they didn't already possess. Actually, the Aztecs didn't do a whole lot of trading; rather, they conquered neighboring tribes and demanded tribute from them; this is the source of so much of the Aztec riches. They also believed in a handful of gods and believed that these gods demanded human sacrifice in order to continue to smile on the Aztecs. The center of Aztec society was the great city of Tenochtitlan, which was built on an island so as to be easier to defend and boasted a population of 300,000 at the time of the arrival of the conquistadors. Tenochtitlan was known for its canals and its pyramids, none of which survive today.

The **Inca** Empire stretched across a vast period of territory down the western coast of South America and was connected by a series of roads. A series of messengers ran along these roads, carrying news and instructions from the capital, Cusco, another large city along the lines of but not as spectacular as Tenochtitlan. The Incas are known for inventing the *quipu*, a string-based device that provided them with a method of keeping records. The Inca Empire, like the Aztec Empire, was very much a centralized state, with all income going to the state coffers and all trade going through the emperor as well. The Incas worshiped the dead, their ancestors, and nature and often took part in what we could consider strange rituals.

The most advanced Native American civilization was the **Maya**, who lived primarily in Central America. They were the only Native American civilization to develop writing, which consisted of a series of symbols that has still not been deciphered. The Mayas also built huge pyramids and other stone figures and sculptures, mostly of the gods they worshiped. The Mayas are most famous, however, for their calendars and for their mathematics. The Mayan calendars were the most accurate on the planet until the 16th Century. The Mayas also invented the idea of zero, which might sound like a small thing except that no other culture had thought of such a thing. Maya worship resembled the practices of the Aztec and Inca, although human sacrifices were rare. The Mayas also traded heavily with their neighbors.

Skill 12.4   Relate physical and human geographic factors to major historical events and movements

○ *Please refer to the section on Geography and also Skill 14.11 for physical geographic factors.*

The **Agricultural Revolution**, initiated by the invention of the plow, led to a thoroughgoing transformation of human society by making large-scale agricultural production possible and facilitating the development of agrarian societies. During the period during which the plow was invented, the wheel, numbers, and writing were also invented. Coinciding with the shift from hunting wild game to the domestication of animals, this period was one of dramatic social and economic change.

Numerous changes in lifestyle and thinking accompanied the development of stable agricultural communities. Rather than gathering a wide variety of plants as hunter-gatherers, agricultural communities become dependent on a limited number of plants or crops that are harvested. Subsistence becomes vulnerable to the weather and dependent upon planting and harvesting times. Agriculture also required a great deal of physical labor and the development of a sense of discipline. Agricultural communities become sedentary or stable in terms of location. This makes the construction of dwellings appropriate. These tend to be built relatively close together, creating villages or towns. Stable communities also freed people from the need to carry everything with them and the move from hunting ground to hunting ground. This facilitates the invention of larger, more complex tools. As new tools are envisioned and developed it begins to make sense to have some specialization within the society. Skills begin to have greater value, and people begin to do work on behalf of the community that utilizes their particular skills and abilities. Settled community life also gives rise to the notion of wealth. It is now possible to keep possessions.

In the beginning of the transition to agriculture, the tools that were used for hunting and gathering were adequate to the tasks of agriculture. The initial challenge was in adapting to a new way of life. Once that challenge was met, attention turned to the development of more advanced tools and sources of energy. Six thousand years ago the first plow was invented in Mesopotamia. This plow was pulled by animals. Agriculture was now possible on a much larger scale. Soon tools were developed that make such basic tasks as gathering seeds, planting, and cutting grain faster and easier. It also becomes necessary to maintain social and political stability to ensure that planting and harvesting times are not interrupted by internal discord or a war with a neighboring community. It also becomes necessary to develop ways to store the crop and prevent its destruction by the elements and animals. And then it must be protected from thieves.

Settled communities that produce the necessities of life are self-supporting. Advances in agricultural technology and the ability to produce a surplus of produce create two opportunities: first, the opportunity to trade the surplus goods for other desired goods, and second, the vulnerability to others who steal to take those goods. Protecting domesticated livestock and surplus, as well as stored, crops become an issue for the community. This, in turn, leads to the construction of walls and other fortifications around the community. The ability to produce surplus crops creates the opportunity to trade or barter with other communities in exchange for desired goods. Traders and trade routes begin to develop between villages and cities. The domestication of animals expands the range of trade and facilitates an exchange of ideas and knowledge.

The **Scientific Revolution** and the Enlightenment were two of the most important movements in the history of civilization, resulting in a new sense of self-examination and a wider view of the world than ever before. The Scientific Revolution was, above all, a shift in focus from belief to evidence. Scientists and philosophers wanted to see the proof, not just believe what other people told them. It was an exciting time, if you were a forward-looking thinker.

The **Industrial Revolution** of the eighteenth and nineteenth centuries resulted in even greater changes in human civilization and even greater opportunities for trade, increased production, and the exchange of ideas and knowledge. The first phase of the Industrial Revolution (1750-1830) saw the mechanization of the textile industry, vast improvements in mining, with the invention of the steam engine, and numerous improvements in transportation, with the development and improvement of turnpikes, canals, and the invention of the railroad.
The second phase (1830-1910) resulted in vast improvements in a number of industries that had already been mechanized through such inventions as the Bessemer steel process and the invention of steam ships. New industries arose as a result of the new technological advances, such as photography, electricity, and chemical processes. New sources of power were harnessed and applied, including petroleum and hydroelectric power. Precision instruments were developed and engineering was launched. It was during this second phase that the Industrial Revolution spread to other European countries, Japan, and the US.

The direct results of the industrial revolution, particularly as they affected industry, commerce, and agriculture, included:
- Enormous increases in productivity
- Huge increases in world trade
- Specialization and division of labor
- Standardization of parts and mass production
- Growth of giant business conglomerates and monopolies
- A new revolution in agriculture facilitated by the steam engine, machinery, chemical fertilizers, processing, canning, and refrigeration

The political results included:

- Growth of complex government by technical experts
- Centralization of government, including regulatory administrative agencies
- Advantages to democratic development, including extension of franchise to the middle class, and later to all elements of the population, mass education to meet the needs of an industrial society, the development of media of public communication, including radio, television, and cheap newspapers
- Dangers to democracy included the risk of manipulation of the media of mass communication, facilitation of dictatorial centralization and totalitarian control, subordination of the legislative function to administrative directives, efforts to achieve uniformity and conformity, and social impersonalization.

The economic results were numerous:

- The conflict between free trade and low tariffs and protectionism
- The issue of free enterprise against government regulation
- Struggles between labor and capital, including the trade-union movement
- The rise of socialism
- The rise of the utopian socialists
- The rise of Marxian or scientific socialism

The social results of the Industrial Revolution include:

- Increase of population, especially in industrial centers
- Advances in science applied to agriculture, sanitation and medicine
- Growth of great cities
- Disappearance of the difference between city dwellers and farmers
- Faster tempo of life and increased stress from the monotony of the work routine
- The emancipation of women
- The decline of religion
- Rise of scientific materialism
- Darwin's theory of evolution

Skill 12.5   Identify significant historical leaders and events that have influenced Eastern and Western civilizations

India began this period recovering from the invasion of **Alexander the Great**. One strong man who met the great Alexander was Chandragupta Maurya, who began one of his country's most successful dynasties. Chandragupta conquered most of what we now call India. His grandson, Asoka, was more of a peaceful ruler but powerful nonetheless. He was also a great believer in the practices and power of Buddhism, sending missionaries throughout Asia to preach the ways of the Buddha. Succeeding the Mauryas were the Guptas, who ruled India for a longer period of time and brought prosperity and international recognition to their people.

The **Guptas** were great believers in science and mathematics, especially their uses in production of goods. They invented the decimal system and had a concept of zero, two things that put them ahead of the rest of the world on the mathematics timeline. They were the first to make cotton and calico, and their medical practices were much more advanced than those in Europe and elsewhere in Asia at the time. These inventions and innovations made Indian goods in high demand throughout Asia and Europe.

The idea of a united India continued after the Gupta Dynasty ended. It was especially favorable to the invading Muslims, who took over in the eleventh century, ruling the country for hundreds of years through a series of **sultanates.** The most famous Muslim leader of India was **Tamerlane**, who founded the Mogul Dynasty and began a series of conquests that expanded the borders of India. Tamerlane's grandson **Akbar** is considered the greatest Mogul. He believed in freedom of religion and is perhaps most well-known for the series of buildings that he had built, including mosques, palaces, forts and tombs, some of which are still standing today. During the years that Muslims ruled India, Hinduism continued to be respected, although it was a minority religion; Buddhism, however, died out almost entirely from the country that begot its founder. The imposing mountains to the north of India served as a deterrent to Chinese expansion. India was more vulnerable to invaders who came from the west or by sea from the south. The Indian people were also vulnerable to the powerful monsoons, which came driving up from the south a few times every year, bringing howling winds and devastation in their wake.

The story of China during this time is one of dynasties controlling various parts of what is now China and Tibet. The Tang Dynasty was one of the most long-lasting and the most proficient, inventing the idea of civil service and the practice of block printing. Next up was the Sung Dynasty, which produced some of the world's greatest paintings and porcelain pottery but failed to unify China in a meaningful way. This would prove instrumental in the takeover of China by the Mongols, led by Genghis Khan and his most famous grandson, Kublai.

Genghis Khan was known as a conqueror and Kublai was known as a uniter. They both extended the borders of their empire, however; and at its height, the Mongol Empire was the largest the world has ever seen, encompassing all of China, Russia, Persia, and central Asia. Following the Mongols were the Ming and Manchu Dynasties, both of which focused on isolation. As a result, China at the end of the eighteenth century knew very little of the outside world, and vice versa. Ming artists created beautiful porcelain pottery, but not much of it saw its way into the outside world until much later. The **Manchus** were known for their focus on farming and road-building, two practices that were instituted in greater numbers in order to try to keep up with expanding population. Confucianism, Taoism, and ancestor worship—the staples of Chinese society for hundreds of years—continued to flourish during all this time.

A Polish astronomer, **Nicolaus Copernicus**, began the Scientific Revolution. He crystallized a lifetime of observations into a book that was published about the time of his death; in this book, Copernicus argued that the Sun, not the Earth, was the center of a solar system and that other planets revolved around the Sun, not the Earth. This flew in the face of established (read: Church-mandated) doctrine. The Church still wielded tremendous power at this time, including the power to banish people or sentence them to prison or even death.

The Danish astronomer **Tycho Brahe** was the first to catalog his observations of the night sky, of which he made thousands. Building on Brahe's data, German scientist Johannes Kepler instituted his theory of planetary movement, embodied in his famous Laws of Planetary Movement. Using Brahe's data, Kepler also confirmed Copernicus's observations and argument that the Earth revolved around the Sun.

The most famous defender of this idea was **Galileo Galilei**, an Italian scientist who conducted many famous experiments in the pursuit of science. He is most well-known, however, for his defense of the heliocentric (sun-centered) idea. He wrote a book comparing the two theories, but most readers could tell easily that he favored the new one. He was convinced of this mainly because of what he had seen with his own eyes. He had used the relatively new invention of the telescope to see four moons of Jupiter. They certainly did not revolve around the Earth, so why should everything else? His ideas were not at all favored with the Church, which continued to assert its authority in this and many other matters. The Church was still powerful enough at this time, especially in Italy, to order Galileo to be placed under house arrest.

Galileo died under house arrest, but his ideas didn't die with him. Picking up the baton was an English scientist named **Isaac Newton**, who became perhaps the most famous scientist of all. He is known as the discoverer of gravity and a pioneering voice in the study of optics (light), calculus, and physics. More than any other scientist, Newton argued for (and proved) the idea of a mechanistic view of the world: You can see how the world works and prove how the world works through observation; if you can see these things with your own eyes, they must be so. Up to this time, people believed what other people told them; this is how the Church was able to keep control of people's lives for so long. Newton, following in the footsteps of Copernicus and Galileo, changed all that.

This naturally led to the **Enlightenment**, a period of intense self-study that focused on ethics and logic. More so than at any time before, scientists and philosophers questioned cherished truths, widely held beliefs, and their own sanity in an attempt to discover why the world worked—from within. "I think, therefore I am" was one of the famous sayings of that or any day. It was uttered by Rene Descartes, a French scientist-philosopher whose dedication to logic and the rigid rules of observation were a blueprint for the thinkers who came after him.

One of the giants of the era was England's **David Hume**, a pioneer of the doctrine of empiricism (believing things only when you've seen the proof for yourself). The Enlightenment thinker who might be the most famous is Immanuel Kant of Germany. He was both a philosopher and a scientist, and he took a definite scientific view of the world. He wrote the movement's most famous essay, "Answering the Question: What Is Enlightenment?" and he answered his famous question with the motto "Dare to Know." For Kant, the human being was a rational being capable of hugely creative thought and intense self-evaluation. He encouraged all to examine themselves and the world around them. He believed that the source of morality lay not in nature of in the grace of God but in the human soul itself. He believed that man believed in God for practical, not religious or mystical, reasons.

Also prevalent during the Enlightenment was the idea of the "social contract," the belief that government existed because people wanted it to, that the people had an agreement with the government that they would submit to it as long as it protected them and didn't encroach on their basic human rights. This idea was first made famous by the Frenchman Jean-Jacques Rousseau but was also adopted by England's **John Locke** and America's Thomas Jefferson. John Locke was one of the most influential political writers of the seventeenth century who put great emphasis on human rights and put forth the belief that when governments violate those rights people should rebel. He wrote the book "Two Treatises of Government" in 1690, which had tremendous influence on political thought in the American colonies and helped to shape the U.S. Constitution and Declaration of Independence

Louis XIV acceded to the throne shortly before his fifth birthday. His mother and the First Minister, Mazarin, controlled the government until Mazarin's death in 1661, at which time Louis XIV declared that he would rule the country. He has been referred to alternately as Louis the Great, the Great Monarch and as The Sun King. During his reign, France attained cultural dominance, as well as military and political superiority. Louis XIV created a centralized government that he ruled with absolute power. He is often considered "the archetype of an absolute monarch." He is quoted as claiming "I am the State." However, many scholars believe this statement was falsely attributed to him by political opponents. It did, however, summarize the absolute power he held.

Louis XIV reigned as an absolute monarch. To be sure, he and his advisors moved France to economic strength and political power and influence in Europe. But the claim of absolute power by divine right combined with his distrust of others led to unique actions to maintain power and to control any who might instigate rebellion against him. One of his tactics to control the nobility was to require them to remain at the Palace of Versailles, where he could watch them and prevent them from plotting unrest in their communities. He spent lavishly on parties and distractions to keep the nobility occupied and to strengthen his control over them. He was determined to undercut the power and influence of the nobility. He tried to fill high offices with commoners or members of the new aristocracy because he believed that if commoners got out of hand, they could be dismissed. He knew he could not mitigate the influence of great nobles. By forcing the powerful nobles to remain at court he effectively reduced their power and influence. By appointing commoners and new aristocracy to government functions, he increased his control over both the functions and those who held them. He controlled the nobles to such an extent that he was able to ensure that there would never be another Fronde.

Louis also tried to control the Church. He called an assembly of the clergy in 1681. By the time the assembly ended, he had won acceptance of the "Declaration of the Clergy of France," by which the power of the Pope was greatly reduced and his power was greatly enhanced. This Declaration was never accepted by the Pope.

Perhaps the great mistake of Louis' reign was his attitude toward Protestantism and his handling of the Huguenots. In 1685 he revoked the Edict of Nantes. This resulted in the departure from the country of these French Protestants, who were among the wealthiest and most industrious people in the nation. He also alienated the Protestant countries of Europe, particularly England.

Catherine the Great (Catherine II) has often been called the "enlightened despot." She came to power through a coup that removed her husband (Peter III) from the throne, had herself proclaimed Empress with the help of the military and other politically powerful persons with whom Catherine had cultivated relationships. Shortly after the coup, Peter was murdered.

Catherine revised Russian law in an effort to make it more logical and more humane. She built many hospitals and orphanages, encouraged the people to be inoculated against smallpox, and wanted to establish schools throughout the nation to teach the people the responsibilities of citizenship. Despite her sympathy for the peasants, she did nothing to free them from serfdom. In fact, to maintain control of the nobility, she made large land grants, which increased serfdom. She divided Russia into 50 provinces. She claimed to want each district to control its own local affairs. Yet she empowered the governors she appointed. The end result was broader despotism rather than enlightenment.

Because Catherine's power relied upon the loyalty of the nobles, they must be pleased with land grants. She did not enforce her more humanitarian ideas when her subordinates did not enforce them. Although she was "enlightened," she never forgot that she ruled an empire of "barbarous peoples." She corresponded with leading thinkers of the day throughout Europe and read widely. This resulted in some influence of European culture and technology, philosophy and social theory. But the influence of these ideas was limited to a very small number of professional and intellectual circles.

Tokugawa *Ieyasu* came to power in Japan in 1600 by defeating a coalition that sought political power in Japan. His rise to power marks the beginning of the Tokugawa shogunate, which held power as military rulers in Japan until 1868. In the 16th century, Japan had absorbed a great deal of European influence. The Portuguese had arrived in 1543 and Francis Xavier, a Jesuit priest, brought a mission to Japan in 1549. By 1600 there were about 300,000 Christians, including a number of the military aristocracy. Hideyoshi began to suppress Christianity as a foreign threat in 1587, and banished the Portuguese missionaries. The Tokugawa shoguns persecuted Christianity more extensively by executing thousands of Christians and driving the Church underground. An uprising in 1637-38 culminated in a massive slaughter. After this event, foreigners were banned from the country, except for a small number of Dutch merchant traders who were strictly confined to an island.

Skill 12.6 Identify the causes and consequences of exploration, settlement, and growth

Columbus' first trans-Atlantic voyage was to try to prove his theory or idea that Asia could be reached by sailing west. And to a certain extent, his idea was true. It could be done but only after figuring how to go around or across or through the landmass in between. Long after Spain dispatched explorers and her famed conquistadors to gather the wealth for the Spanish monarchs and their coffers, the British were searching valiantly for the "Northwest Passage," a land-sea route across North America and the eventual open sea to the wealth of Asia. It wasn't until after the Lewis and Clark Expedition when Captains Meriwether Lewis and William Clark proved conclusively that there simply was no Northwest Passage. It did not exist.

However, this did not deter exploration and settlement. Spain, France, and England along with some participation by the Dutch led the way with expanding Western European civilization in the New World. These three nations had strong monarchial governments and were struggling for dominance and power in Europe. With the defeat of Spain's mighty Armada in 1588, England became undisputed mistress of the seas. Spain lost its power and influence in Europe and it was left to France and England to carry on the rivalry, leading to eventual British control in Asia as well.

Spain's influence in the New World was in Florida, the Gulf Coast, from Texas to California, south to the tip of South America, and included some of the islands of the West Indies. French control centered from New Orleans north to what is now northern Canada and included the entire Mississippi Valley, St. Lawrence Valley, Great Lakes and land that was part of the Louisiana Territory. A few West Indies islands were also part of France's empire. England settled the eastern seaboard of North America, including parts of Canada and from Maine to Georgia. Some of the West Indies islands came under British control. The Dutch had New Amsterdam for a period, but later ceded it to British hands. One interesting aspect of this was that in each of these three nations, especially England, land claims extended partly or all the way across the continent, regardless of the fact that others had claimed the same land. The wars for dominance and control of power and influence in Europe undoubtedly would eventually extend to the Americas, especially North America.

Spanish settlement had its beginnings in the Caribbean, with the establishment of colonies on Hispaniola (at Santo Domingo, which became the capital of the West Indies), Puerto Rico and Cuba. There were a number of reasons for Spanish involvement in the Americas, to name just a few: the spirit of adventure; the desire for land; expansion of Spanish power, influence and empire; the desire for great wealth; the expansion of Roman Catholic influence; and conversion of native peoples.

The first permanent settlement in what is now the United States was in 1565 at St. Augustine, Florida. A later permanent settlement, in the southwestern United States, was in 1609 in Santa Fe, New Mexico. At the peak of Spanish power, the area in the United States claimed, settled and controlled by Spain included Florida, and all land west of the Mississippi River; quite a piece of choice real estate. Of course, France and England also laid claim to the same areas. Nonetheless, ranches and missions were built. The Indians who came in contact with the Spaniards were introduced to animals, plants and seeds from the Old World that they had never seen before. Animals brought to the United States included: horses, cattle, donkeys, pigs, sheep, goats and poultry.

Spain's control over New World colonies lasted more than 300 years, longer than England or France. To this day, Spanish influence in names of places, art, architecture, music, literature, law and cuisine remains. The Spanish settlements in North America were not commercial enterprises, but were for protection and defense of the trading and wealth from their colonies in Mexico and South America. Russians hunting seals came down the Pacific coast, English moved into Florida and west into and beyond the Appalachians, and French traders and trappers made their way from Louisiana and other parts of New France into the Spanish territory. The Spanish never realized or understood that self-sustaining economic development and colonial trade was so important. Consequently, the Spanish settlements in the U.S. never really prospered.

The Dutch West India Company founded a colony in what is now New York, establishing it as New Holland. It was eventually captured by English settlers and renamed New York, but many of the Dutch families that had been granted large segments of land by the Dutch government were allowed to keep their estates. As hostility built between England and the colonies over the taxation of tea, colonists turned to the Dutch to supply them with this important import.

The part of North America claimed by France was called New France and consisted of the land west of the Appalachian Mountains. This area of claims and settlement included the St. Lawrence Valley, the Great Lakes, the Mississippi Valley and the entire region of land westward to the Rocky Mountains. They established the permanent settlements of Montreal and New Orleans, thus giving them control over these two major gateways into the heart of North America, the vast rich interior. The St. Lawrence River, the Great Lakes and the Mississippi River along with its tributaries made it possible for the French explorers and traders to roam at will, virtually unhindered in exploring, trapping and trading to further the interests of France.

The English colonies, with only a few exceptions, were considered commercial ventures to make a profit for the crown or the company or whoever financed their beginnings. One was strictly a philanthropic enterprise, three others were primarily for religious reasons, but the other nine were started for economic reasons. Settlers in these unique colonies came for different reasons:

    a) religious freedom
    b) political freedom
    c) economic prosperity
    d) land ownership

Colonists from England, France, Holland, Sweden and Spain all settled in North America on lands once frequented by Native Americans. Spanish colonies were mainly in the south, French colonies were mainly in the extreme north and in the middle of the continent, and the rest of the European colonies were in the northeast and along the Atlantic coast. These colonists got along with their new neighbors with varying degrees of success.

The colonies were divided generally into the three regions of New England, Middle Atlantic and Southern. The culture of each was distinct and affected attitudes, ideas towards politics, religion and economic activities. The geography of each region also contributed to its unique characteristics. The **New England colonies** consisted of Massachusetts, Rhode Island, Connecticut and New Hampshire. Life in these colonies was centered on the towns. What farming was done was completed by each family on their own plot of land, but a short summer growing season and a limited amount of good soil gave rise to other economic activities such as manufacturing, fishing, shipbuilding and trade.

The vast majority of the settlers shared similar origins, coming from England and Scotland. Towns were carefully planned and laid out the same way. The form of government was the town meeting, where all adult males met to make the laws. The legislative body and the General Court consisted of an Upper and Lower House.

The **Middle or Middle Atlantic colonies** included New York, New Jersey, Pennsylvania, Delaware and Maryland. New York and New Jersey were at one time the Dutch colony of New Netherlands and Delaware at one time was New Sweden. These five colonies from their beginnings were considered "melting pots" with settlers from many different nations and backgrounds. The main economic activity was farming, with the settlers scattered over the countryside cultivating rather large farms. The Indians were not as much of a threat as they were in New England so the colonists did not have to settle in small farming villages. The soil was very fertile, the land was gently rolling, and a milder climate provided a longer growing season. These farms produced a large surplus of food, not only for the colonists themselves, but also for sale. This colonial region became known as the "breadbasket" of the New World. The New York and Philadelphia seaports were constantly filled with ships being loaded with meat, flour and other foodstuffs for the West Indies and England.

There were other economic activities such as shipbuilding, iron mines and factories producing paper, glass and textiles. The legislative body in Pennsylvania was unicameral or consisted of one house. In the other four colonies, the legislative body had two houses. Also, units of local government were in counties and towns.

The **Southern colonies** were Virginia, North and South Carolina and Georgia. Virginia was the first permanent successful English colony and Georgia was the last. The year 1619 was a very important year in the history of Virginia and the United States, featuring three very significant events. First, sixty women were sent to Virginia to marry and establish families. Second, twenty Africans, the first of thousands, arrived. Third, and most importantly, the Virginia colonists were granted the right to self-govern and began electing their own representatives to the House of Burgesses, which was their own legislative body.

By the 1750s in Europe, Spain was "out of the picture," no longer the most powerful nation and not a contender. The remaining rivalry was between Britain and France. For nearly 25 years, between 1689 and 1748, a series of "armed conflicts" involving these two powers had been taking place. These conflicts had spilled over into North America. The War of the League of Augsburg in Europe, 1689 to 1697, had been King William's War. The War of the Spanish Succession, 1702 to 1713, had been Queen Anne's War. The War of the Austrian Succession, 1740 to 1748, was called King George's War in the colonies. The two nations fought for possession of colonies, especially in Asia and North America and for control of the seas, but none of these conflicts was decisive.

The final conflict, which decided once and for all who was the most powerful, began in North America in 1754 in the Ohio River Valley. It was known in America as the French and Indian War. In Europe it was known as the **Seven Years' War** since it began there in 1756. In America, both sides had advantages and disadvantages. The British colonies were well established and consolidated in a smaller area. British colonists outnumbered French colonists 23 to 1. Except for a small area in Canada, French settlements were scattered over a much larger area (roughly half of the continent) and were smaller; however, the French settlements were united under one government and were quick to act and cooperate when necessary. Additionally, the French had many more Indian allies than the British. The British colonies had separate individual governments and very seldom cooperated, even when needed. In Europe, at that time, France was the more powerful of the two nations.

In Paris in 1763, Spain, France and Britain met to draw up the **Treaty of Paris**. Great Britain got most of India and all of North America east of the Mississippi River, except for New Orleans. Britain received control of Florida from Spain and returned Cuba and the islands of the Philippines, taken during the war to Spain. France lost nearly all of its possessions in America. India was allowed to keep four islands: Guadeloupe, Martinique, Haiti on Hispaniola and Miquelon on St. Pierre. France gave New Orleans and the vast territory of Louisiana, west of the Mississippi River to Spain. Britain was now the most powerful nation, period.

Where did all of this leave the British colonies? Their colonial militias had fought with the British and they too benefited. The militias and their officers gained much experience in fighting, which was very valuable later. The thirteen colonies began to realize that cooperating with each other was the only way to defend their selves. They didn't really understand that until the war for independence and setting up a national government, but a start had been made. At the start of the war in 1754, Benjamin Franklin proposed to the thirteen colonies that they unite permanently to be able to defend themselves. This was after the French and their Indian allies had defeated Major George Washington and his militia at Fort Necessity. This left the entire northern frontier of the British colonies vulnerable and open to attack.

Delegates from seven of the thirteen colonies met at Albany, New York, along with the representatives from the Iroquois Confederation and British officials. Franklin's proposal, known as the **Albany Plan of Union**, was totally rejected by the colonists, along with a similar proposal from the British. They simply did not want each of the colonies to lose the right to act independently; however, the seed was planted.

The war for independence occurred due to a number of changes, the two most important ones being economic and political. By the end of the French and Indian War in 1763, Britain's American colonies were thirteen out of a total of thirty-three scattered around the earth. Like all other countries, Britain strove for having a strong economy and a favorable balance of trade. To have that delicate balance a nation needs wealth, self-sufficiency, and a powerful army and navy. This is why the overseas colonies developed. The colonies would provide raw materials for the industries in the Mother Country, be a market for finished products by buying them, and assist the Mother Country in becoming powerful and strong. In the case of Great Britain, a strong merchant fleet would be a school for training providing bases of operation for the Royal Navy.

The foregoing explained the major reason for British encouragement and support of colonization, especially in North America. So between 1607 and 1763, at various times for various reasons, the British Parliament enacted different laws to assist the government in getting and keeping this trade balance.

The **Navigation Acts** of 1651 put restrictions on shipping and trade within the British Empire by requiring that it was allowed only on British ships. This increased the strength of the British merchant fleet and greatly benefited the American colonists. Since they were British citizens, they could have their own vessels, building and operating them as well. By the end of the war in 1763, the shipyards in the colonies were building one third of the merchant ships under the British flag. There were quite a number of wealthy American colonial merchants.

The Navigation Act of 1660 restricted the shipment and sale of colonial products to England only. In 1663, another Navigation Act stipulated that the colonies had to buy manufactured products only from England and that any European goods going to the colonies had to go to England first. These acts were a protection from enemy ships and pirates and from competition from European rivals.

The New England and Middle Atlantic colonies at first felt threatened by these laws. They had started producing many of the products already being produced in Britain, but they soon found new markets for their goods and began what was known as **triangular trade**. Colonial vessels started the first part of the triangle by sailing for Africa loaded with kegs of rum from colonial distilleries. On Africa's West Coast, the rum was traded for either gold or slaves. The second part of the triangle was from Africa to the West Indies where slaves were traded for molasses, sugar or money. The third part of the triangle was home, bringing sugar or molasses (to make more rum), gold and silver.

The British had been extremely lax and totally inconsistent in enforcement of the mercantile or trade laws passed in the years before 1754. The government itself was not particularly stable so actions against the colonies occurred in anger and their attitude was one of a moral superiority that they knew how to manage America better than the Americans did themselves. This of course pointed to a lack of sufficient knowledge of conditions and opinions in America. The colonists had been left on their own for nearly 150 years and by the time the Revolutionary War began, they were quite adept at self-government and adequately handling the affairs of their daily lives. The Americans equated ownership of land or property with the right to vote. Property was considered the foundation of life and liberty; in the colonial mind and tradition these went together.

These colonists also had their own tradition of publishing the views and sentiments of individuals regarding issues of parochial interest and matters of concern that crossed colonial boundaries. In print—via newspapers and pamphlets—dialogue and debate over matters quite trivial or quite significant became common public practice in the American colonies. As strains with the Mother Country began to develop and increase—especially after the French and Indian War—the resulting issues became increasingly focused in print throughout the colonies. No doubt the discussions and debates published carried their sentiments over to the homes, taverns and other places where the people met to discuss events of the day. An important result of this was a growing "Americanism" in the sentiments of those writers published, and a sense of connection among American people that transcended colonial boundaries.

From the initial Stamp Act in 1765, through the "Boston Massacre" in 1770, to the time of the Tea Act in 1773 (which resulted in the "Boston Tea Party") and beyond, colonial presses were rife with discussion and debate about what they considered to be an unacceptable situation. Parliament intended to assert its right to tax and legislatively control the colonies of Great Britain in whatever manner it saw as prudent and appropriate. Most American colonists, believing their selves to be full British subjects, would deny Parliaments assertions so long as they were not provided with full and equal representation within Parliament.

One of the most notable spokesmen for the American cause was, in fact, an Englishman. **Thomas Paine** (1737-1809) was born in England and came to America in November 1774. He was immediately taken up by the social issues and politics in the American colonies and insinuated himself into the dialogue of current issues, which was ongoing in the colonies and conducted via newspapers and pamphlets. Within months of his arrival, he published his first article in America. Interestingly, his first address to the American public would presage the elaborate exposition of tyranny versus the natural rights of humans to be and act free, which would color and popularize his writings during the war years. But his topic at the time—his bold statement and unusual public stand—was about African slavery.

He is best remembered for "**Common Sense**." In a series of publications, spanning the war years (from 1776 through 1783), Thomas Paine wrote of a series of addresses, inspiring the American people and reprimanding British authorities. One of his most famous publications, produced at a time of ill fortune for the American cause, and disenchantment for many members of the fledgling American Army, began, "THESE are the times that try men's souls. The summer soldier and the sunshine patriot will, in this crisis, shrink from the service of their country; but he that stands it now, deserves the love and thanks of man and woman. Tyranny, like hell, is not easily conquered; yet we have this consolation with us, that the harder the conflict, the more glorious the triumph."

Therefore, when an indirect tax on tea was made, the British felt that since it wasn't a direct tax, there should be no objection to it. The colonists viewed any tax, direct or indirect, as an attack on their property. They felt that as a representative body, the British Parliament should protect British citizens, including the colonists, from arbitrary taxation. Since they felt they were not represented, Parliament, in their eyes, gave them no protection. So, war began. August 23, 1775, George III declared that the colonies were in rebellion and warned them to stop or else.

By 1776, the colonists and their representatives in the Second Continental Congress realized that things were past the point of no return. The **Declaration of Independence** was drafted and declared July 4, 1776. George Washington labored against tremendous odds to wage a victorious war. The turning point in the Americans' favor occurred in 1777 with the American victory at **Saratoga**. This victory decided for the French to align themselves with the Americans against the British. With the aid of **Admiral de Grasse** and French warships blocking the entrance to Chesapeake Bay, British General Cornwallis trapped at Yorktown, Virginia, surrendered in 1781 and the war was over. The **Treaty of Paris** officially ending the war was signed in 1783.

Civil War

In 1833, Congress lowered tariffs, this time at a level acceptable to South Carolina. Although President Jackson believed in states' rights, he also firmly believed in and determined to keep the preservation of the Union. A constitutional crisis had been averted, but sectional divisions were getting deeper and more pronounced. The abolition movement was growing rapidly, becoming an important issue in the North. The slavery issue was at the root of every problem, crisis, event, decision and struggle from then on. The next crisis involved the issue concerning Texas. By 1836, Texas was an independent republic with its own constitution. During its fight for independence, Americans were sympathetic to and supportive of the Texans and some recruited volunteers who crossed into Texas to help the struggle. Problems arose when the state petitioned Congress for statehood. Texas wanted to allow slavery, but Northerners in Congress opposed admission to the Union because it would disrupt the balance between free and slave states and give Southerners in Congress increased influence.

A few years later, Congress took up consideration of new territories between Missouri and present-day Idaho. Again, heated debate over permitting slavery in these areas flared up. Those opposed to slavery used the **Missouri Compromise** to prove their point showing that the land being considered for territories was part of the area the Compromise had been designated as banned to slavery. On May 25, 1854, Congress passed the infamous **Kansas-Nebraska Act,** which nullified the provision creating the territories of Kansas and Nebraska. This provided for the people of these two territories to decide for themselves whether or not to permit slavery to exist there. Feelings were so deep and divided that any further attempts to compromise would meet with little, if any, success. Political and social turmoil swirled everywhere. Kansas was called "Bleeding Kansas" because of the extreme violence and bloodshed throughout the territory. Two governments existed there, one pro-slavery, and the other anti-slavery.

The Supreme Court in 1857 handed down a decision guaranteed to cause explosions throughout the country. Dred Scott was a slave whose owner had taken him from slave state Missouri to free state Illinois into the Minnesota Territory, which was free under the provisions of the Missouri Compromise; then he returned back to the slave state Missouri. Abolitionists pursued the dilemma by presenting a court case stating that since Scott had lived in a free state and free territory he was actuality a free man. Two lower courts had ruled before the Supreme Court became involved, one ruling was in favor and one was against. The Supreme Court decided that residing in a free state and free territory did not make Scott a free man because Scott (and all other slaves) was neither a U.S. citizen nor a state citizen of Missouri. Therefore, he did not have the right to sue in state or federal courts. The Court went a step further and ruled that the old Missouri Compromise was now unconstitutional because Congress did not have the power to prohibit slavery in the Territories.

In 1858, Abraham Lincoln and Stephen A. Douglas were running for the office of U.S. Senator from Illinois and participated in a series of debates, which directly affected the outcome of the 1860 Presidential election. Douglas, a Democrat, was up for re-election and knew that if he won this race, he had a good chance of becoming President in 1860. Lincoln, a Republican, was not an abolitionist, but he believed that slavery was morally wrong and firmly believed in and supported the Republican Party principle that slavery must not be allowed to extend any further.

The final straw came with the election of Lincoln to the Presidency the next year. Due to a split in the Democratic Party, there were four candidates from four political parties. With Lincoln receiving a minority of the popular vote and a majority of electoral votes, the Southern states, one by one, voted to secede from the Union, as they had promised they would do if Lincoln and the Republicans were victorious. The die was cast.

It is ironic that South Carolina was the first state to **secede** from the Union and the first shots of the war were fired on Fort Sumter in Charleston Harbor. Both sides quickly prepared for war. The North had more in its favor a larger population; superiority in finances and transportation facilities; and manufacturing, agricultural and natural resources. The North possessed most of the nation's gold, had about 92% of all industries, and almost all known supplies of copper, coal, iron and various other minerals. Most of the nation's railroads were in the North and Mid-West. Men and supplies could be moved wherever needed, food could be transported from the farms of the Mid-West to workers in the East, and to soldiers on the battlefields. Trade with nations overseas could go on as usual due to control of the navy and the merchant fleet.

The Northern states numbered 24 and included western (California and Oregon) and border (Maryland, Delaware, Kentucky, Missouri and West Virginia) states. The Southern states numbered 11 and included South Carolina, Georgia, Florida, Alabama, Mississippi, Louisiana, Texas, Virginia, North Carolina, Tennessee and Arkansas, making up the Confederacy.

Although outnumbered in population, the South was completely confident of victory. They knew that all they had to do was fight a defensive war and protect their own territory. The North had to invade and defeat an area almost the size of Western Europe. Another advantage of the South was that a number of its best officers had graduated from the U.S. Military Academy at West Point and had had long years of army experience. Many had exercised varying degrees of command in the Indian Wars and the war with Mexico. Men from the South were conditioned to living outdoors and were more familiar with horses and firearms than men from northeastern cities. Since cotton was such an important crop, Southerners felt that British and French textile mills were so dependent on raw cotton that they would be forced to help the Confederacy in the war.

The South won decisively until the Battle of Gettysburg, July 1 - 3, 1863. Until Gettysburg, Lincoln's commanders, McDowell and McClellan, were less than desirable, Burnside and Hooker, not what was needed. Lee, on the other hand, had many able officers, Jackson and Stuart depended on heavily by him. Jackson died at Chancellorsville and was replaced by Longstreet. Lee decided to invade the North and depended on J.E.B. Stuart and his cavalry to keep him informed of the location of Union troops and their strengths.

The day after Gettysburg, on July 4, Vicksburg, Mississippi surrendered to Union General Ulysses Grant, thus severing the western Confederacy from the eastern part. In September 1863, the Confederacy won its last important victory at Chickamauga. In November, the Union victory at Chattanooga made it possible for Union troops to go into Alabama and Georgia, splitting the eastern Confederacy in two. Lincoln gave Grant command of all Northern armies in March of 1864. Grant led his armies into battles in Virginia while Phil Sheridan and his cavalry did as much damage as possible. In a skirmish at a place called

Yellow Tavern, Virginia, Sheridan's and Stuart's forces met, with Stuart being fatally wounded.

The Civil War took more American lives than any other war in history, the South losing one-third of its soldiers in battle compared to about one-sixth for the North. More than half of the total deaths were caused by disease and the horrendous conditions of field hospitals. Destruction was pervasive with towns, farms, trade, industry, lives and homes of men, women, children all destroyed and an entire Southern way of life was lost. The South had no voice in the political, social, and cultural affairs of the nation, lessening to a great degree the influence of the more traditional Southern ideals. The Northern Yankee Protestant ideals of hard work, education and economic freedom became the standard of the United States and helped influence the development of the nation into a modern, industrial power.

The effects of the Civil War were tremendous. It changed the methods of waging war and has been called the first modern war. It introduced weapons and tactics that, when improved later, were used extensively in wars of the late 1800s and 1900s. Civil War soldiers were the first to fight in trenches, first to fight under a unified command, first to wage a defense called "major cordon defense," a strategy of advance on all fronts. They were also the first to use repeating and breech loading weapons. Observation balloons were first used during the war along with submarines, ironclad ships and mines. Telegraphy and railroads were put to use first in the Civil War.

By executive proclamation and constitutional amendment, slavery was officially ended, although there remained deep prejudice and racism, still raising its ugly head today. Also, the Union was preserved and the states were finally truly united. Sectionalism, especially in the area of politics, remained strong for another 100 years, but not to the degree and with the violence as existed before 1861. It has been noted that the Civil War may have been American democracy's greatest failure for from 1861 to 1865, calm reason basic to democracy, fell to human passion. Yet, democracy did survive. The victory of the North established that no state has the right to end or leave the Union. Because of unity, the U.S. became a major global power. Lincoln never proposed to punish the South. He was most concerned with restoring the South to the Union in a program that was flexible and practical rather than rigid and unbending. In fact, he never really felt that the states had succeeded in leaving the Union but that they had left the "family circle" for a short time.

The nineteenth century was the age of **Manifest Destiny** – the belief in the divinely given right of the nation to expand westward and incorporate more of the continent into the nation. This belief had been expressed, at the end of the Revolutionary War, in the demand that Britain cede all lands east of the Mississippi River to America. The goal of expanding westward was further confirmed with the Northwest Ordinance (1787) and the Louisiana Purchase (1803).

The Red River Basin was the next acquisition of land and came about as part of a treaty with Great Britain in 1818. It included parts of North and South Dakota and Minnesota. In 1819, Florida, both east and West, was ceded to the U.S. by Spain along with parts of Alabama, Mississippi and Louisiana. Texas was annexed in 1845 and after the war with Mexico in 1848. The government paid $15 million for what would become the states of California, Utah, Nevada and parts of four other states. In 1846, the Oregon Country was ceded to the U.S., which extended the western border to the Pacific Ocean. The northern U.S. boundary was established at the 49th parallel. The states of Idaho, Oregon and Washington were formed from this territory. In 1853, the **Gadsden Purchase** rounded out the present boundary of the 48 conterminous states with payment to Mexico of $10 million for land that makes up the present states of New Mexico and Arizona.

World War I - 1914 to 1918

The origins of World War I are complex and drawn mainly along the lines of various alliances and treaties that existed between the world powers. Imperialism, nationalism and economic conditions of the time led to a series of sometimes shaky alliances among the powerful nations, each wishing to protect its holdings and provide mutual defense from smaller powers.

On June 28, 1914, Serbian Gavrilo Princip assassinated Archduke Ferdinand of Austria-Hungary, while on a visit to Sarajevo, Serbia. Serbian nationalism had led the country to seek dominance on the Balkan Peninsula, a movement that had been opposed by Austria-Hungary. Seeing an opportunity to move on Serbia, Austria-Hungary issued an ultimatum after the assassination, demanding that they be allowed to perform a complete investigation. Serbia refused, and in July, Austria-Hungary, with the backing of its ally Germany, declared war on Serbia. Serbia called on its ally Russia to come to its defense and Russia began to move troops into the area.

Germany, allied with Austria-Hungary, viewed the Russian mobilization as an act of war, and declared war on Russia. A few days afterwards, Germany declared war of France, which was allied with Russia by treaty. Germany invaded Belgium, a neutral country, so as to be closer to Paris. Britain, bound by treaty to defend both Belgium and France, subsequently declared war on Germany.

The United States, under President Woodrow Wilson, declared neutrality in the affair, and did not enter the war immediately. Not until Germany threatened commercial shipping with submarine warfare did the US join the fray, in 1917. Fighting continued until November 1918, when Germany petitioned for armistice. Peace negotiations began in early 1919, and the Treaty of Versailles was signed in June of that year. Also, growing out of the peace negotiations was the **League of Nations**, a group of countries agreeing to avoid armed conflict through disarmament and diplomacy.

World War II - 1939 to 1945

The Treaty of Versailles that ended the First World War was in part the cause of the second. Severely limited by the treaty, Germany grew to resent its terms, which required reparations and limited the size of its army, and worked constantly to revise them. This was done through diplomacy and negotiation through the 1920's. In 1933, Adolf Hitler became Chancellor of Germany, and shortly thereafter was granted dictatorial powers. Hitler was determined to remove all restrictions imposed by the treaty and to unify the German speaking people of the surrounding countries into a single country. Toward this end, Hitler marched into Austria in 1938, and was welcomed. He later made claims on the Sudetenland, a German-speaking area of Czechoslovakia, a claim that was supported internationally; however, Hitler continued to march into the whole of Czechoslovakia, to which he had no claim.

France and Britain, who had followed a policy of appeasing Hitler in the hopes that he would be content with Austria, were now concerned as Germany looked next to Poland. They pledged to fight Germany if Hitler invaded Poland, which he did in September 1939, after signing a pact with the Soviet Union. Days later, France and Britain declared war on Germany, and the fighting began. Again, the United States stayed out of the fighting at first. Only when Japan, an ally of Germany, attacked a US naval base in Pearl Harbor, Hawaii, did the US enter the war.

The European Theater of WWII ended in 1945, when Allied troops invaded Germany and Hitler committed suicide. In the Pacific, the US dropped two atomic bombs on Japan in August of that year, forcing the Japanese to surrender.

WWII left the British and European economies in ruins, and established the United States and the Soviet Union as the two major powers of the world, laying the foundation for the Cold War. Dismayed at the failure of the League of Nations ability to prevent war, a stronger organization was created. The United Nations was provided with the ability to raise peacekeeping forces. Under the Marshall plan, the United States helped rebuild Europe into an industrial, reliable economy again.

Korean War - 1950 to 1953

With the surrender of Japan at the end of WWII, its 35-year occupation of Korea came to an end. The Soviet Union and the United States assumed trusteeship of the country, with the Soviets occupying the northern half and the US controlling the south. Elections were ordered by the United Nations to elect a unified government, but with each occupying country backing different candidates, the result was the formation of two separate states divided along the 38th parallel of latitude. Each claimed sovereignty over the whole country. These conflicting claims to sovereignty led to occasional military skirmishes along the common border throughout 1949, with each side aiming to unify the country under its own government. In June 1950, North Korea mounted a major attack across the 38th parallel, marking what is considered the beginning of the war.

The North Korean faction received military aid and backing from the Soviet Union, which aroused the United States' fear that communism and Soviet influence might spread. In August 1950, American troops arrived in South Korea to join the fight, along with British, Australian, and UN forces.

Control of the peninsula see-sawed over the next year and North Korea captured the South Korean capital of Seoul. The North Koreans were pushed to the north, with southern forces eventually capturing the North Korean capital Pyongyang. They were driven as far as the border of China. China had already announced its intention to get involved should forces enter North Korea and the Chinese army mounted a push that reclaimed the North.

In 1953, peace negotiations resulted in a cease-fire and created a buffer zone between the two countries along the 38th parallel. This cease-fire has been in effect for over fifty years. The war has never officially ended; since the cease-fire, North Korea has become an increasingly isolated communist dictatorship, while South Korea has grown into a major world economy.

The Vietnam War - U.S. Involvement - 1957 to 1973

Like Korea, Vietnam became a divided country after WWII, with a Soviet and Chinese-backed communist government in the north led by Ho Chi Minh and a western-backed government in the south. As the communist backed north drove out the occupying French and maintained more and more insurgency in the south, the larger powers became increasingly involved, with the United States sending advisors and small numbers of troops between 1955 and 1964.

In 1964, following an attack on US ships by North Vietnamese forces in the Gulf of the United States escalated its military involvement, sending more and more troops over the next four years. As fighting continued, with no decisive progress, opposition to the war began to grow among the American public. President Richard Nixon began to make reductions in troops while trying to assist the South Vietnamese Army in building enough strength to fight on its own. In January 1973, the Paris Peace Accords were signed, ending offensive action by the US in Vietnam. Nixon promised defensive assistance, but in 1974 Congress cut off all funding to the South Vietnamese government after Nixon had resigned the presidency following the Watergate scandal.

The withdrawal of the United States left South Vietnam without economic or military support, and the North Vietnamese army was able to overrun and control the entire country. North Vietnamese forces took Saigon, the southern capital, in April 1975. North and South were unified under one socialist government.

The social impact of the Vietnam War was considerable in the United States. Opposition to the draft and to US involvement led to large protests, particularly among young people, and returning veterans found they were not treated as heroes, as other vets had been.

Skill 12.7 Identify individuals and events that have influenced economic, social, and political institutions in the United States

George Washington (1789-1797) faced a number of challenges during his two terms as President. There were boundary disputes with Spain over the Southeast and wars with the Indians on the western frontier.

The French Revolution and the ensuing war between France and England created great turmoil within the new nation. Thomas Jefferson, Secretary of State, was pro-French and believed the U.S. should enter the fray. Alexander Hamilton, Secretary of the Treasury, was pro-British and wanted to support England. Washington took a neutral course, believing the U.S. was not strong enough to be engaged in a war. Washington did not interfere with the powers of the Congress in establishing foreign policy. Two political parties were beginning to form by the end of his first term. In his farewell address he encouraged Americans to put an end to regional differences and exuberant party spirit. He also warned the nation against long-term alliances with foreign nations.

John Adams, of the Federalist Party, was elected President in 1796. When he assumed office, the war between England and France was in full swing. The British were seizing American ships that were engaging in trade with France; however, France was refusing to receive the American envoy and had suspended economic relationships. The people were divided in their loyalties to either France or England. Adams focused on France and the diplomatic crisis known as the XYZ Affair. During his administration, Congress appropriated money to build three new frigates and additional ships, authorized the creation of a provisional army, and passed the Alien and Sedition Acts, which were intended to drive foreign agents from the country and to maintain dominance over the Republican Party. When the war ended, Adams sent a peace mission to France. This angered the Republicans. The Election of 1800 pitted a unified and effective Republican Party against a divided and ineffective Federalist Party.

Thomas Jefferson won the election of 1800. Jefferson opposed a strong centralized government as a champion of States' Rights. He supported a strict interpretation of the Constitution. He reduced military expenditures, made budget cuts, and eliminated a tax on whiskey. At the same time, he reduced the national debt by one third. The Louisiana Purchase doubled the size of the nation. During his second term, the administration focused on keeping the U.S. out of the Napoleonic Wars. Both the French and the British were seizing American ships and trying to deny the other access to trade. The U.S. Jefferson's solution was to impose an embargo on all foreign commerce. The cost to the northeast was great and the embargo was both ineffective and unpopular.

James Madison won the election of 1808 and inherited the foreign policy issues with England. During the first year of his administration, trade was prohibited with both Britain and France. In 1810, Congress authorized trade with both England and France. They directed the President that, if either nation would accept America's view of neutrality, he was to forbid trade with the other nation. Napoleon pretended to comply. Madison thus banned trade with Great Britain. The British continued to harass American ships and captured sailors and forced them to become members of the British Navy (impressment). In June of 1812, Madison asked Congress to declare war on Great Britain. The nation was really not prepared to fight a war, especially with the strong British army.

The **American Revolution** resulted in the successful efforts of the English colonists in America to win their freedom from Great Britain. After more than one hundred years of mostly self-government, the colonists resented the increased British meddling and control, they declared their freedom, won the Revolutionary War with aid from France, and formed a new independent nation.

The **French Revolution** was the revolt of the middle and lower classes against the gross political and economic excesses of the rulers and the supporting nobility. It ended with the establishment of the First in a series of French Republics. Conditions leading to revolt included extreme taxation, inflation, lack of food, and the total disregard for the impossible, degrading, and unacceptable condition of the people on the part of the rulers, nobility and the Church.

The **Judiciary Act** set up the U.S. Supreme Court by providing for a Chief Justice and five associate justices. It also established federal district and circuit courts. One of the most important acts of Congress was the first 10 amendments to the Constitution called the Bill of Rights which emphasized and gave attention to the rights of individuals.

Supreme Court Chief Justice John Marshall made extremely significant contributions to the American judiciary. He set or established three basic principles of law, which became the foundation of the judicial system and the federal government. He started the power of judicial review; the right of the Supreme Court to determine the constitutionality of laws passed by Congress. He stated that only the Supreme Court had the power to set aside laws passed by state legislatures when they contradicted the U.S. Constitution. He established the right of the Supreme Court to reverse decisions of state courts.

After the U.S. purchased the Louisiana Territory, Jefferson appointed Captains Meriwether Lewis and William Clark to explore it, to find out exactly what had been bought. The Corps of Discovery expedition went all the way to the Pacific Ocean, returning two years later with maps, journals and artifacts. This led the way for future explorers to make available more knowledge about the territory and resulted in the Westward Movement and the later belief in the doctrine of Manifest Destiny.

The **Industrial Revolution** had spread from Great Britain to the United States. Before 1800, most manufacturing activities were done in small shops or in homes; however, starting in the early 1800s, factories with modern machines were built making it easier to produce goods faster. The eastern part of the country became a major industrial area, although some developed in the West. At about the same time, improvements began to be made in building roads, railroads, canals, and steamboats. The increased ease of travel facilitated the westward movement and boosted the economy with faster and cheaper shipment of goods and products, covering larger areas. Some of the innovations include the Erie Canal, which connects the interior and Great Lakes with the Hudson River and coastal port of New York.

Westward expansion occurred for a number of reasons, most important being economic. Cotton had become most important to many of the people who lived in the southern states. The effects of the Industrial Revolution, which began in England, were now being felt in the United States. With the invention of power-driven machines, the demand for cotton fiber greatly increased for the yarn needed in spinning and weaving. Eli Whitney's cotton gin made the separation of the seeds from the cotton much more efficient and faster. This, in turn, increased the demand and more and more farmers became involved in the raising and selling of cotton.

The innovations and developments of better methods of long-distance transportation moved the cotton in greater quantities to textile mills in England as well as the areas of New England and Middle Atlantic States in the U.S. As prices increased along with increased demand, southern farmers began expanding by clearing increasingly more land to grow more cotton. Movement, settlement, and farming headed west to utilize the fertile soils. This, in turn, demanded increased need for a large supply of cheap labor. The system of slavery expanded, both in numbers and in the movement to lands "west" of the South.

Following is just a partial list of well-known Americans who contributed their leadership and talents in various fields and reforms:

- Lucretia Mott and Elizabeth Cady Stanton for **women's rights**
- Emma Hart Willard, Catharine Esther Beecher and Mary Lyon for **education for women**
- Dr. Elizabeth Blackwell, the **first woman doctor**
- Antoinette Louisa Blackwell, the **first female minister**
- Dorothea Lynde Dix for **reforms in prisons and insane asylums**
- Elihu Burritt and William Ladd for **peace movements**
- Robert Owen for a **Utopian society**
- Horace Mann, Henry Barmard, Calvin E. Stowe, Caleb Mills and John Swett for **public education**
- Benjamin Lundy, David Walker, William Lloyd Garrison, Isaac Hooper, Arthur and Lewis Tappan, Theodore Weld, Frederick Douglass, Harriet Tubman, James G. Birney, Henry Highland Garnet, James Forten, Robert Purvis, Harriet Beecher Stowe, Wendell Phillips and John Brown for **abolition of slavery and the Underground Railroad**
- Louisa Mae Alcott, James Fenimore Cooper, Washington Irving, Walt Whitman, Henry David Thoreau, Ralph Waldo Emerson, Herman Melville, Richard Henry Dana, Nathaniel Hawthorne, Henry Wadsworth Longfellow, John Greenleaf Whittier, Edgar Allan Poe and Oliver Wendell Holmes, **famous writers**
- John C. Fremont, Zebulon Pike, Kit Carson, **explorers**

- Henry Clay, Daniel Webster, Stephen Douglas, John C. Calhoun, American **statesmen**
- Robert Fulton, Cyrus McCormick, Eli Whitney, **inventors**
- Noah Webster, American **dictionary and spellers**
- The list could go on and on, but the contributions of these and many, many others greatly enhanced the unique American culture.

Skill 12.8   Identify immigration and settlement patterns that have shaped the history of the United States

Between 1870 and 1916, more than 25 million immigrants came into the United States adding to the phenomenal population growth taking place. This tremendous growth aided business and industry in two ways: 1) the number of consumers increased creating a greater demand for products thus enlarging the markets for the products, and 2) with increased production and expanding business, more workers were available for newly created jobs. The completion of the nation's transcontinental railroad in 1869 contributed greatly to the nation's economic and industrial growth. Some examples of the benefits of using the railroads include raw materials that were shipped quickly by the mining companies and finished products that were sent to all parts of the country. Many wealthy industrialists and railroad owners saw tremendous profits steadily increasing due to this improved method of transportation. Another impact of interstate railroad expansion was the standardization of time zones, in order to maintain the reliability and accuracy of train schedules across vast east-west routes.

Innovations in new industrial processes and technology. grew at a pace unmatched at any other time in American history. Thomas Edison was the most prolific inventor of that time, using a systematic and efficient method to invent and improve on current technology in a profitable manner. The abundance of resources, together with growth of industry and the pace of capital investments led to the growth of cities. Populations were shifting from rural agricultural areas to urban industrial areas and by the early 1900's, a third of the nation's population lived in cities. Industry needed workers in its factories, mills and plants and rural workers were being displaced by advances in farm machinery and their increasing use and other forms of automation.

The dramatic growth of population in cities was fueled by growing industries, more efficient transportation of goods and resources, and the people who migrated to those new industrial jobs, that were from rural areas of the United States or immigrants from foreign lands. Increased urban populations, often packed into dense tenements, often without adequate sanitation or clean water, led to public health challenges that required cities to establish sanitation, water and public health departments in order to cope with and prevent epidemics. Political organizations also saw advantages through mobilizing the new industrial working class and creating vast patronage programs. These programs sometimes became notorious for corruption in big-city machine politics like Tammany Hall in New York.

The Dutch settlers of the early colonial period introduced many goods to North America that profoundly affected the nature of the development of both the state and the nation. The trade of the Dutch West India Company provided the foundation for an economy based on trade and commerce.

As one of the first colonized areas in the nation, New York was a major point of entry for immigrants. The melding of the Dutch, French and British settlers into a unified colony was the first-step along the way to becoming the melting pot that New York has been to this day. With the large harbor and reputation of the state for business, industry and commerce made New York a place of special opportunity for immigrants who were seeking freedom and opportunity.

The development of **Ellis Island** as an immigrant processing center made it the point of entry for millions who came to America in search of political or religious freedom, safe haven from political oppression, and the quest for the American dream. The gift of the Statue of Liberty and its placement in New York harbor made New York the symbol of American opportunity and freedom. Throughout the history of America, the nation has welcomed a population that has been repeatedly enriched by the cultural mix.

As African Americans left the rural South and migrated to the North in search of opportunity, many settled in Harlem in New York City. By the 1920s Harlem had become a center of life and activity for persons of color. The music, art and literature of this community gave birth to a cultural movement known as the Harlem Renaissance. The artistic expressions that emerged from this community in the 1920s and 1930s celebrated the black experience, black traditions and the voices of black America. Major writers and works of this movement include:

- Claude McKay
- Countee Cullen
- Jean Toomer
- Langston Hughes – *The Weary Blues*
- Nella Larsen – *Passing*
- Zora Neale Hurston – *Their Eyes Were Watching God*

The Irish Famine of 1845-1849 is alternately referred to as the Irish Potato Famine, The Great Famine or the Great Hunger. The immediate cause of the famine was the appearance of "the blight." This was the destruction of the potato crops due to a fungus. The potato was the primary food source for much of the population of Ireland at the time. Deaths were not officially recorded, but are believed to be in the range of 500,000 to one million during the five years from 1846 to 1851. Although estimates vary, the number of people who emigrated from Ireland is in the neighborhood of two million.

The Irish who emigrated to the U.S. for the most part became residents of cities. With no money, they were forced to remain in the port cities where they arrived. By 1850, the Irish accounted for one quarter of the population of Boston, New York City, Philadelphia and Baltimore.

On the West Coast, there was a steady increase in the number of **Japanese immigrants** in the early part of the twentieth century. As the number of Japanese in California grew, anti-Japanese sentiment also grew. A series of actions were taken against the Japanese immigrants:

- Labor leaders in San Francisco formed an "Asiatic Exclusion League" in 1905 and demanded public policies against the Japanese. They pressured the city into requiring that Japanese children attend only segregated schools with other Asian children. Protests from Japan led to intervention by President Theodore Roosevelt. The city agreed to suspend the segregation act in exchange for a law that would limit Japanese immigration. Japan agreed in 1907 to prohibit its workers from coming to the U.S.

- The Japanese immigrants were capable farmers. White farmers tried to eliminate the competition. In 1913 the state legislature passed a law prohibiting anyone who was not eligible for citizenship from owning land in the state. Asians were ineligible for naturalization (under federal law).

- In 1924, U.S. Congress passed the "National Origins Quota Act." This law prohibited all further immigration from Japan.

This period of rapid economic growth and industrial expansion in California came to an abrupt end with the **Stock Market crash of 1929**. The worst depression in the history of the country and of California ensued. With 20-25% of the population unemployed and losing everything, nativism and a fear of foreigners rose quickly. The first to be subjected to the hostility of the natives were the **Filipinos**. White workers complained that the recent immigrants posed an economic threat to native-born workers. Numerous riots broke out. Congress passed the "Filipino Repatriation Act" in 1935. The government offered to pay transportation expenses for any Filipinos who wished to return home.

Then **Mexican** immigrants became the targets. The federal government created a program of repatriation. Some left voluntarily, others were forced to leave. Up to 100,000 deportees left California and returned to Mexico.

But another occurrence in the 1930s created yet another, less desirable influx of people to California. **Dust Bowl refugees** came by the hundreds of thousands in search of a better life in California. The situation in California was not what they expected, and they were unwelcome to many Californians. But these refugees held on to the culture of the Southwest and created their own subculture in California. They were called "Okies" because many came from Oklahoma, although they came from several states.

Although **Puerto Rico** became a territory of the U.S. at the end of the Spanish American War, there was little immigration during the first half of the century. The transition from Spanish colony to U.S. possession was not easy for the people of Puerto Rico. Residents have been U.S. citizens since 1917, but they have no representation in the Congress. Technically, moving from the island to the U.S. mainland is considered internal migration rather than immigration. This does not, however, recognize that leaving an island with a distinct culture and identity involves the same cultural conflicts and intellectual, language and other adjustments as those faced by most immigrants. A severe economic depression created widespread poverty in the early part of the twentieth century. Few Puerto Ricans were able to afford the fare to travel by boat to the mainland. In 1910, there were only about 2,000 Puerto Ricans living on the mainland; most created small enclaves in New York City. By 1945, there were 13,000 Puerto Ricans in New York City, but by 1946, there were more than 50,000. And, for each of the next ten years, over 25,000 more would immigrate each year. By the mid-1960s, there were more than a million Puerto Ricans on the mainland.

Many of the immigrant Puerto Ricans established communities in major east coast cities and mid-Atlantic farming regions, and also in the mill towns of New England. A very large number of these immigrants settled in the northeastern part of Manhattan that came to be known as Spanish Harlem. They quickly became an important factor in the city's political and cultural life. Although the first generation of migrants faced prejudice, unemployment, discrimination and poverty, most remained and learned to thrive.

Today, Puerto Rican immigrants and their descendants have developed several means of preserving and teaching their heritage. Their communities are strong and integrated into the mainstream of the society. They have contributed to the growth of the nation and the inclusion within every area of American life from politics to education to sports and the arts.

Skill 12.9   Identify how various cultures contributed to the unique social, cultural, economic, and political features of Florida

Florida's first human inhabitants were Indians, as shown by the burial mounds found in varying locations around the state. When Europeans eventually arrived, there were about 10,000 Indians (Native Americans) belonging to as many as five major tribes. In the south, were the Calusa and the Tequesta. The Ais were found on the Atlantic coast in the central part of the peninsula. The Timucans were in the central and northeast area of the state. And, in the northwest part of Florida dwelled the Apalachee.

Written records about life in Florida began with the arrival in 1513 of the first European, Spanish explorer and adventurer Juan Ponce de León who was searching for the fabled fountain of youth. Sometime between April 2 and April 8, Ponce de León waded ashore on the northeast coast of Florida, possibly near present-day St. Augustine. He called the area la Florida, in honor of Pascua Florida ("feast of the flowers"), Spain's Easter time celebration. Other Europeans may have reached Florida earlier, but no firm evidence of such achievement has been found.

The Spanish flag flew over Florida for the next 250 years. Other Spanish explorers who spent time in Florida included Panfilo de Narvaez, Hernando de Soto (who became the first European to reach the Mississippi River), and Pedro Menendez de Aviles (who put an end to French attempts to settle in eastern Florida and founded the first permanent European settlement in the present-day United States, St. Augustine).

On another voyage in 1521, Ponce de León landed on the southwestern coast of the peninsula, accompanied by two-hundred people, fifty horses and numerous beasts of burden. His colonization attempt quickly failed because of attacks by native people; however, Ponce de León's activities served to identify Florida as a desirable place for explorers, missionaries and treasure seekers.

In 1539, Hernando de Soto began another expedition in search of gold and silver, which took him on a long trek through Florida and what is now the southeastern United States. For four years, de Soto's expedition wandered in hopes of finding the fabled wealth of the Indian people. De Soto and his soldiers camped for five months in the area now known as Tallahassee. De Soto died near the Mississippi River in 1542. Survivors of his expedition eventually reached Mexico.

No great treasure troves awaited the Spanish conquistadores who explored Florida; however, their stories helped inform Europeans about Florida and its relationship to Cuba, Mexico and Central and South America, from which Spain regularly shipped gold, silver and other products. Groups of heavily-laden Spanish vessels, called plate fleets, usually sailed up the Gulf Stream through the straits that parallel Florida's Keys.

Aware of this route, pirates preyed on the fleets. Hurricanes created additional hazards, sometimes wrecking the ships on the reefs and shoals along Florida's eastern coast.

In 1559, Tristán de Luna y Arellano led another attempt by Europeans to colonize Florida. He established a settlement at Pensacola Bay, but a series of misfortunes caused his efforts to be abandoned after two years.

Spain was not the only European nation that found Florida attractive. In 1562, the French Protestant Jean Ribault explored the area. Two years later, fellow Frenchman René Goulaine de Laudonnière established Fort Caroline at the mouth of the St. Johns River, near present-day Jacksonville.

These French adventurers prompted Spain to accelerate her plans for colonization. Pedro Menéndez de Avilés hastened across the Atlantic, his sights set on removing the French and creating a Spanish settlement. Menéndez arrived in 1565 at a place he called San Augustín (St. Augustine) and established the first permanent European settlement in what is now the United States. He accomplished his goal of expelling the French, attacking and killing all settlers except for non-combatants and Frenchmen who professed belief in the Roman Catholic faith. Menéndez captured Fort Caroline and renamed it San Mateo.

French response came two years later, when Dominique de Gourgues recaptured San Mateo and made the Spanish soldiers stationed there pay with their lives. This incident did not halt the Spanish advance. Their pattern of constructing forts and Roman Catholic missions continued. Spanish missions established among native people soon extended across north Florida and north along the Atlantic coast to what we now call South Carolina.

The English, also eager to exploit the wealth of the Americas, increasingly came into conflict with Spain's expanding empire. In 1586 the English captain Sir Francis Drake looted and burned the tiny village of St. Augustine; however, Spanish control of Florida was not diminished.

In fact, as late as 1600, Spain's power over what is now the southeastern United States was unquestioned. When English settlers came to America, they established their first colonies well to the North—at Jamestown (in the present state of Virginia) in 1607 and Plymouth (in the present state of Massachusetts) in 1620. English colonists wanted to take advantage of the continent's natural resources and gradually pushed the borders of Spanish power southward into present-day southern Georgia. At the same time, French explorers were moving down the Mississippi River valley and eastward along the Gulf Coast.

The English colonists in the Carolina colonies were particularly hostile toward Spain. Led by Colonel James Moore, the Carolinians and their Creek Indian allies attacked Spanish Florida in 1702. They destroyed the town of St. Augustine, but could not capture the fort, named Castillo de San Marcos. Two years later, they destroyed the Spanish missions between Tallahassee and St. Augustine, killing many native people and enslaving many others. The French continued to harass Spanish Florida's western border and captured Pensacola in 1719, twenty-one years after the town had been established.

Spain's adversaries moved even closer when England founded Georgia in 1733, its southernmost continental colony. Georgians attacked Florida in 1740, assaulting the Castillo de San Marcos at St. Augustine for almost a month. While the attack was not successful, it did point out the growing weakness of Spanish Florida.

Britain gained control of Florida in 1763 in exchange for Havana, Cuba, which the British had captured from Spain during the Seven Years' War (1756–63). Spain evacuated Florida after the exchange, leaving the province virtually empty. At that time, St. Augustine was still a garrison community with fewer than five hundred houses, and Pensacola also was a small military town.

The British had ambitious plans for Florida. First, it was split into two parts: East Florida, with its capital at St. Augustine; and West Florida, with its seat at Pensacola. British surveyors mapped much of the landscape and coastline and tried to develop relations with a group of Indian people who were moving into the area from the North. The British called these people of Creek Indian descent Seminolies or Seminoles. Britain attempted to attract white settlers by offering land to settle on and to help those who produced products for export. Given enough time, this plan might have converted Florida into a flourishing colony, but British rule lasted only twenty years.

The two Floridas remained loyal to Great Britain throughout the War for American Independence (1776–83); however, Spain—participating indirectly in the war as an ally of France—captured Pensacola from the British in 1781. In 1784, it regained control of the rest of Florida as part of the peace treaty that ended the American Revolution. The second period of Spanish control lasted until 1821.

On one of those military operations, in 1818, General Andrew Jackson made a foray into Florida. Jackson's battles with Florida's Indian people later would be called the First Seminole War. When the British evacuated Florida, Spanish colonists as well as settlers from the newly formed United States came pouring in. Many of the new residents were lured by favorable Spanish terms for acquiring property, called land grants. Others who came were escaped slaves, trying to reach a place where their U.S. masters had no authority and effectively could not reach them. Instead of becoming more Spanish, the two Floridas increasingly became more "American." Finally, after several official and unofficial U.S. military expeditions into the territory, Spain formally ceded Florida to the United States in 1821, according to terms of the Adams-Onís Treaty.

Andrew Jackson returned to Florida in 1821 to establish a new territorial government on behalf of the United States. What the U.S. inherited was a wilderness sparsely dotted with settlements of native Indian people, African Americans and Spaniards.

As a territory of the United States, Florida was particularly attractive to people from the older Southern plantation areas of Virginia, the Carolinas and Georgia who arrived in considerable numbers. After territorial status was granted, the two Floridas were merged into one entity with a new capital city in Tallahassee. Established in 1824, Tallahassee was chosen because it was halfway between the existing governmental centers of St. Augustine and Pensacola.

As Florida's population increased through immigration, so did pressure on the federal government to remove the Indian people from their lands. The Indian population was made up of several groups—primarily, the Creek and the Miccosukee people; and many African American refugees who lived with the Indians. Indian removal was popular with white settlers because the native people occupied lands that white people wanted and because their communities often provided a sanctuary for runaway slaves from northern states.

Among Florida's native population, the name of Osceola has remained familiar after more than a century and a half. Osceola was a Seminole war leader who refused to leave his homeland in Florida. Seminoles, already noted for their fighting abilities, won the respect of U.S. soldiers for their bravery, fortitude and ability to adapt to changing circumstances during the Second Seminole War (1835–42). This war, the most significant of the three conflicts between Indian people and U.S. troops in Florida, began over the question of whether Seminoles should be moved westward across the Mississippi River into what is now Oklahoma.

Under President Andrew Jackson, the U.S. government spent $20 million and the lives of many U.S. soldiers, Indian people and U.S. citizens to force the removal of the Seminoles. In the end, the outcome was not as the federal government had planned. Some Indians migrated "voluntarily." Some were captured and sent west under military guard; and others escaped into the Everglades, where they made a life for themselves away from contact with whites. Today, reservations occupied by Florida's Indian people exist at Immokalee, Hollywood, Brighton (near the city of Okeechobee), and along the Big Cypress Swamp. In addition to the Seminole people, Florida also has a separate Miccosukee tribe.

By 1840 white Floridians were concentrating on developing the territory and gaining statehood. The population had reached 54,477 people, with African American slaves making up almost one-half of the population. Steamboat navigation was well established on the Apalachicola and St. Johns Rivers, and railroads were planned.

Florida now was divided informally into three areas: East Florida, from the Atlantic Ocean to the Suwannee River; Middle Florida, between the Suwannee and the Apalachicola Rivers; and West Florida, from the Apalachicola to the Perdido River. The southern area of the territory (south of present-day Gainesville) was sparsely settled by whites. The territory's economy was based on agriculture. Plantations were concentrated in Middle Florida and their owners established the political tone for all of Florida until after the Civil War. Florida became the twenty-seventh state in the United States on March 3, 1845. William D. Moseley was elected the new state's first governor, and David Levy Yulee, one of Florida's leading proponents for statehood, became a U.S. Senator. By 1850, the population had grown to 87,445, which included about 39,000 African American slaves and 1,000 free blacks.

The slavery issue began to dominate the affairs of the new state. Most Florida voters—who were white males, ages twenty-one years or older—did not oppose slavery; however, they were concerned about the growing feeling against it in the North and during the 1850s they viewed the new anti-slavery Republican Party with suspicion. In the 1860 presidential election, no Floridians voted for Abraham Lincoln, although this Illinois Republican won at the national level. Shortly after his election, a special convention drew up an ordinance that allowed Florida to secede from the Union on January 10, 1861. Within several weeks, Florida joined other southern states to form the Confederate States of America.

During the Civil War, Florida was not ravaged as several other southern states were. Indeed, no decisive battles were fought on Florida soil. While Union forces occupied many coastal towns and forts, the interior of the state remained in Confederate hands.

Florida provided an estimated 15,000 troops and significant amounts of supplies— including salt, beef, pork and cotton—to the Confederacy, but more than 2,000 Floridians, both African American and white, joined the Union army. Confederate and foreign merchant ships slipped through the Union navy blockade along the coast, bringing in needed supplies from overseas ports. Tallahassee was the only southern capital east of the Mississippi River to avoid capture during the war, spared by southern victories at Olustee (1864) and Natural Bridge (1865). Ultimately, the South was defeated, and federal troops occupied Tallahassee on May 10, 1865.

Before the Civil War, Florida had been well on its way to becoming another of the southern cotton states. Afterward, the lives of many residents changed. The ports of Jacksonville and Pensacola again flourished due to the demand for lumber and forest products to rebuild the nation's cities. Those who had been slaves were declared free. Plantation owners tried to regain prewar levels of production by hiring former slaves to raise and pick cotton; however, such programs did not work well and much of the land came under cultivation by tenant farmers and sharecroppers, both African American and white.

Beginning in 1868, the federal government instituted a congressional program of "reconstruction" in Florida and the other southern states. During this period, Republican officeholders tried to enact sweeping changes, many were aimed at improving conditions for African Americans.

At the time of the 1876 presidential election, federal troops still occupied Florida. The state's Republican government and recently enfranchised African American voters helped to put Rutherford B. Hayes in the White House. Democrats gained control of enough state offices to end the years of Republican rule and prompt the removal of federal troops the following year. A series of political battles in the state left African Americans with little voice in their government. During the final quarter of the nineteenth century, large-scale commercial agriculture in Florida, especially cattle-raising, grew in importance. Industries such as cigar manufacturing took root in the immigrant communities of the state. Large phosphate deposits were discovered, citrus groves were planted and cultivated, swamplands were drained, and Henry Plant and Henry Flagler built railroad lines opening the state for further growth and development.

Potential investors became interested in enterprises that extracted resources from the water and land. These extractive operations were as widely diverse as sponge harvesting in Tarpon Springs and phosphate mining in the southwestern part of the state. The Florida citrus industry grew rapidly, despite occasional freezes and economic setbacks. The development of industries throughout the state prompted the construction of roads and railroads on a large scale. Jobs created by the state helped develop the natural resources. Private industries' construction of paper mills resulted in conservation programs for the state's forests and to help preserve perishable fruits and vegetables, cooling plants were built. To aid farmers, cooperative markets and cooperative farm groups were established.

The growth of Florida's transportation industry had its origins in 1855, when the state legislature passed the Internal Improvement Act. Like legislation passed by several other states and the federal government, Florida's act offered cheap or free public land to investors, particularly those interested in transportation. The act, and other legislation like it, had its greatest effect in the years between the end of the Civil War and the beginning of World War I. During this period, many railroads were constructed throughout the state by companies owned by Henry Flagler and Henry B. Plant, who also built lavish hotels near their railroad lines. The Internal Improvement Act stimulated the initial efforts to drain the southern portion of the state in order to convert it to farmland.

These development projects had far-reaching effects on the agricultural, manufacturing, and extractive industries of late-nineteenth-century Florida. The citrus industry especially benefited, since it was now possible to pick oranges in south Florida; put them on a train heading north; and eat them in Baltimore, Philadelphia or New York in less than a week.

In 1898, national attention focused on Florida, as the Spanish-American War began. The port city of Tampa served as the primary staging area for U.S. troops bound for the war in Cuba. Many Floridians supported the Cuban peoples' desire to be free of Spanish colonial rule.

By the turn of the century, Florida's population and per capita wealth were increasing rapidly; the potential of the "Sunshine State" appeared endless. By the end of World War I, land developers had descended on this virtual gold mine. With more Americans owning automobiles, it became commonplace to vacation in Florida. Many visitors stayed on; exotic projects sprang up in southern Florida. Some people moved onto land made from drained swamps. Others bought canal-crossed tracts through what had been dry land. The real estate developments quickly attracted buyers and land in Florida was sold and resold. Profits and prices for many developers reached inflated levels. The early 1900s saw the settlement and economic development of south Florida, especially along the East Coast. A severe depression in 1926, 1926, and 1928 hurricanes and the Great Depression of the 1930s burst the economic bubble.

During World War II, many military bases were constructed as part of the vital defense interests of the state and nation. After the War, prosperity and population grew resulting in tourism becoming the most important industry. It remains so today. Continued agricultural development and industrial expansion also played an important role in the state's economy. Such industries as paper and paper products, chemicals, electronics and ocean and space exploration gave a tremendous boost to the labor force. From the 1950s to the present day, The Kennedy Space Center at Cape Canaveral has been a space and rocket center with the launching of orbiting satellites, manned space flights and today's space shuttles.

There are serious problems to be faced, many immigrants from places like Cuba and Haiti entered the state by the thousands since the early 1960s, both legally and illegally. Increasing population growth puts a strain on public and social services. Pollution and overbuilding has threatens the environment in Florida. Tremendous growth occurred during the 1970s with the opening of Walt Disney World. With other tourist attractions and the resulting need for hotels, restaurants and a larger airport—Orlando leads Tampa, Miami, Jacksonville, Fort Lauderdale and West Palm Beach as the fastest growing region of the state. Although the state's economy continues to rely mainly on tourism and the citrus industry, stable growth remains consistent due to the expanding trade, financial and service industries.

COMPETENCY 13.0 KNOWLEDGE OF PEOPLE, PLACES AND ENVIRONMENT

Skill 13.1 Identify the five themes of geography, including the specific terms for each theme

The five themes of geography are:

1) **Location** - including relative and absolute location. A relative location refers to the surrounding geography, (e.g., "on the banks of the Mississippi River"). Absolute location refers to a specific point, such as 41 degrees North latitude, 90 degrees West longitude or 123 Main Street.

2) **Place** - A place has both human and physical characteristics. Physical characteristics include features such as mountains, rivers, deserts and etc. Human characteristics are the features created by human interaction with their environment such as canals and roads.

3) **Human-Environmental Interaction** - The theme of human-environmental interaction has three main concepts: humans adapt to the environment (wearing warm clothing in a cold climate, for instance,) humans modify the environment (planting trees to block a prevailing wind, for example,) and humans depend on the environment (for food, water and raw materials.)

4) **Movement** - The theme of movement covers how humans interact with one another through trade, communications, emigration and other forms of interaction.

5) **Regions** - A region is an area that has some kind of unifying characteristic, such as a common language, a common government or other. There are three main types of regions: 1) formal regions are areas defined by actual political boundaries, such as a city, county, or state, 2) functional regions are defined by a common function, such as the area covered by a telephone service, and 3) vernacular regions are less formally defined areas that are formed by people's perception, (e.g., "the Middle East" and "the South").

Geography - involves studying location and how living things and the earth's features are distributed throughout the earth. It includes where animals, people and plants live and the effects of their relationship with earth's physical features. Geographers explore the locations of earth's features, how they developed, and why they are important.

Skill 13.2   Interpret maps and other graphic representations and identify tools and technologies to acquire, process, and report information from a spatial perspective

We use **illustrations** of various sorts because it is often easier to demonstrate a given idea visually instead of orally. Sometimes, it is even easier to do so with an illustration than a description; this is especially true in the areas of education and research because humans are visually stimulated. It is a fact that any idea presented visually in some manner is always easier to understand and to comprehend than simply getting an idea across verbally, by hearing it or reading it. Illustrations in this section have been presented to explain an idea in a more precise way. Sometimes these demonstrate the types of illustrations available for use in the arena of political science. Among the more common illustrations used in political science are various types of **maps, graphs and charts**. Photographs and globes are useful, but are limited in what kind of information that they can show so they are rarely used. Unless, as in the case of a photograph, it is of a particular political figure or a time that one wishes to visualize.

Although maps have advantages over globes and photographs, they do have a major disadvantage. This problem must be considered as well. The major problem of all maps comes about because most maps are flat and the Earth is a sphere. It is impossible to reproduce exactly on a flat surface an object shaped like a sphere. In order to put the earth's features onto a map they must be stretched in some way. This stretching is called **distortion.** Distortion does not mean that maps are wrong; it simply means that they are not perfect representations of the Earth or its parts. **Cartographers** or mapmakers, understand the problems of distortion. They try to design them so that there is as little distortion as possible in the maps.

The process of putting the features of the Earth onto a flat surface is called **projection**. All maps are really map projections. There are many different types. Each one deals in a different way with the problem of distortion. Map projections are made in a number of ways. However, the basic ideas behind map projections can be understood by looking at the three most common types:

1) <u>**Cylindrical Projections**</u> - These are created by taking a cylinder of paper and wrapping it around a globe. A light is used to project the globe's features onto the paper. Distortion is least where the paper touches the globe. For example, suppose that the paper was wrapped so that it touched the globe at the equator, the map from this projection would have just a little distortion near the equator; however, in moving north or south of the equator, the distortion would increase as you moved further away from the equator. The best known and most widely used cylindrical projection is the **Mercator Projection**. It was first developed in 1569 by Gerardus Mercator, a Flemish mapmaker

2) **Conical Projections** - The name for these maps comes from the fact that the projection is made onto a cone of paper. The cone is made so that it touches a globe at the base of the cone only. It can also be made so that it cuts through part of the globe in two different places. Again, the least distortion is where the paper touches the globe. If the cone touches at two different points, there is some distortion at both points. Conical projections are most often used to map areas in the **middle latitudes**. Maps of the United States are most often conical projections. This is because most of the country lies within these latitudes.

3) **Flat-Plane Projections** - These are made with a flat piece of paper. It touches the globe at one point only. Areas near this point show little distortion. Flat-plane projections are often used to show the areas of the north and south poles. One such flat projection is called a **Gnomonic Projection**. On this kind of map all meridians appear as straight lines, Gnomonic projections are useful because any straight line drawn between points on it forms a **Great-Circle Route**.

Great-Circle Routes can best be described by thinking of a globe and when using the globe the shortest route between two points on it can be found by simply stretching a string from one point to the other. If the string were to be extended in reality so that it took into effect the globe's curvature, it would then make a great-circle. A great-circle is any circle that cuts a sphere, such as the globe, into two equal parts. Because of distortion, most maps do not show great-circle routes as straight lines. Gnomonic Projections, however, do show the shortest distance between the two places as a straight line, because of this they are valuable for navigation. They are called Great-Circle Sailing Maps.

Maps
The Title - All maps should have a title, just like all books should. The title tells you what information is to be found on the map.

The Legend - Most maps have a legend. A legend tells the reader about the various symbols that are used on that particular map and what the symbols represent (also called a *map key*).

The Grid - A grid is a series of lines that are used to find exact places and locations on the map. There are several different kinds of grid systems in use; however, most maps do use the longitude and latitude system, known as the **Geographic Grid System**.

Directions - Most maps have some directional system to show the way the map is being presented. Often on a map, a small compass will be present with arrows showing the four basic directions: north, south, east and west.

The Scale - This is used to show the relationship between a unit of measurement on the map versus real world measurement on the Earth. Maps are drawn to many different scales. Some maps show a lot of detail for a small area. Others show a greater span of distance, whichever is being used, one should always be aware of what scale is being used. For instance, the scale might be something like 1 inch = 10 miles for a small area or for a map showing the whole world it might have a scale in which 1 inch = 1,000 miles. The point is that one must look at the map key in order to see what units of measurements the map is using.

Equal areas - One property maps can have is that of equal areas. In an equal area map, the meridians and parallels are drawn so that the areas shown have the same proportions as they do on the Earth. For example, Greenland is about 118th the size of South America, thus it will be show as 118th the size on an equal area map. The **Mercator Projection** is an example of a map that does not have equal areas. In it, Greenland appears to be about the same size of South America. This is because the distortion is very bad at the poles and Greenland lies near the North Pole.

Conformal Maps - A second map property is conformal or correct shapes. There are no maps that show very large areas of the earth in their exact shapes. Only globes can really do that; however, Conformal Maps are as close as possible to true shapes. The United States is often shown by a Lambert Conformal Conic Projection Map.

Consistent Scales - Many maps attempt to use the same scale on all parts of the map. Generally, this is easier when maps show a relatively small part of the earth's surface. For example, a map of Florida might be a Consistent Scale Map. Generally maps showing large areas are not consistent-scale maps. This is because of distortion. Often such maps will have two scales noted in the key. One scale, for example, might be accurate to measure distances between points along the Equator. Another might be used to measure distances between the North Pole and the South Pole.

Relief Maps - Show the shape of the land surface, flat, rugged or steep. Relief maps usually give more detail than simply showing the overall elevation of the land's surface. Relief is also sometimes shown with colors, but another way to show relief is by using **contour lines**. These lines connect all points of a land surface which are the same height surrounding the particular area of land.

Thematic Maps - These are used to show more specific information, often on a single **theme** or topic. Thematic maps show the distribution or amount of something over a certain given area, such as population density, climate, economic information, cultural, political information, or other criteria.

Political science would be almost impossible without maps. Information can be gained looking at a map that might take hundreds of words to explain otherwise. Maps reflect the great variety of knowledge covered by political science. To show such a variety of information maps are made in many different ways. Because of this variety, maps must be understood in order to make the best sense of them. Once they are understood, maps provide a solid foundation for political science studies.

To apply information obtained from **graphs** one must understand the two major reasons why graphs are used:

1. To present a model or theory visually in order to show how two or more variables interrelate.
2. To present real world data visually in order to show how two or more variables interrelate.

Most often used are those known as **bar graphs** and **line graphs** (charts are often used for similar reasons and are explained in the next section). Graphs themselves are most useful when one wishes to demonstrate the sequential increase or decrease of a variable or to show specific correlations between two or more variables in a given circumstance.

Most common is the **bar graph** because it has an easy to see and understand way of visually showing the difference in a given set of variables; however, it is limited in that it can not really show the actual proportional increase or decrease of each given variable to each other (in order to show a decrease, a bar graph must show the "bar" under the starting line, thus removing the ability to really show how the various different variables would relate to each other).

Thus in order to accomplish this one must use a **line graph**. Line graphs can be of two types a **linear** or **non-linear** graph. A linear line graph uses a series of straight lines and a non-linear line graph uses a curved line. Though the lines can be either straight or curved, all of the lines are called **curves**.

A line graph uses a number line or **axis**. The numbers are generally placed in order, equal distances from one another, the number line is used to represent a number, degree or some such other variable at an appropriate point on the line. Two lines are used, intersecting at a specific point. They are referred to as the X-axis and the Y-axis. The Y-axis is a vertical line the X-axis is a horizontal line. Together they form a **coordinate system**. The difference between a point on the line of the X-axis and the Y-axis is called the **slope** of the line or the change in the value on the vertical axis divided by the change in the value on the horizontal axis. The Y-axis number is called the **rise** and the X-axis number is called the **run**.

To use **charts** correctly, one should remember the reasons one uses graphs. The general ideas are similar. It is usually a question as to which, a graph or chart, is more capable of adequately portraying the information one-wants to illustrate. One can see the difference between them and realize that in many ways graphs and charts are interrelated. One of the most common types, because it is easiest to read and understand, even for the lay person, is the **pie-chart**. You can see pie-charts used often, especially when one is trying to illustrate the differences in percentages among various items or when one is demonstrating the divisions of a whole.

As stated before, in political science and related fields, all type of illustrations, maps, graphs and charts are useful tools for both education and research. As such, they quite often are used to better demonstrate an idea than simply stating it since there are some problems and situations that are easier to understand visually than verbally. They are also better in trying to show relationships between any given set of variables or circumstances; however, one must always remember that though a picture may "be worth a thousand words," it still can't say everything and one should always be aware of the limits of any diagrammatic model. In other words, *"seeing is not always, necessarily, believing."*

Spatial organization is a description of how things are grouped in a given space. In geographical terms, this can describe people, places and environments anywhere and everywhere on Earth.

The most basic form of spatial organization for people is where they live. The vast majority of people live near other people, in villages, towns, cities and settlements. These people live near others in order to take advantage of the goods and services that naturally arise from cooperation. These villages, towns, cities and settlements are, to varying degrees, near bodies of water. Water is a staple of survival for every person on the planet and is also a good source of energy for factories and other industries, as well as a form of transportation for people and goods.

Skill 13.3   Identify the factors that influence the selection of a location for a specific activity

One way to describe where people live is by the **geography** and **topography** around them. The vast majority of people on the planet live in areas that are very hospitable. Yes, people live in the Himalayas and in the Sahara, but the populations in those areas are small indeed when compared to the plains of China, India, Europe and the United States. People naturally want to live where they won't have to work really hard just to survive and world population patterns reflect this.

Geography can lend itself to many other disciplines. One of the foremost examples is the application of geography to economics. People looking to locate manufacturing plants will naturally consider **geographic factors** when making their final decision. We can examine the spatial organization of the places where people live. For example, in a city: where are the factories and heavy industry buildings? Are they near airports or train stations? Are they on the edge of town, near major roads? What about housing developments? Are they near industries or are they far away? Where are the other industry buildings? Where are the schools, hospitals and parks? What about the police and fire stations? How close are homes to each of these? Towns, and especially cities, are routinely organized into neighborhoods so that each house or home is near to most things that residents might need on a regular basis. This means that large cities have multiple schools, hospitals, grocery stores, fire stations and other resources.

Related to this is the distance between cities, towns, villages or settlements. In certain parts of the United States, and definitely in many countries in Europe, the population settlement patterns achieve megalopolis standards with no clear boundaries from one town to the next. Other, more sparsely populated areas have towns that are few and far between and have relatively few people in them. Some exceptions to this exist, of course, like oases in the deserts; for the most part population centers tend to be relatively near one another or at least near smaller towns.

Simpler decisions take place when a group of people seek to open a new business or shopping mall. Practical considerations such as the locations of nearby homes and possible competitors factor into the decision of where to locate that new business or shopping mall. Is the city an urban hub, with shoppers already coming from nearby towns? If the answer is yes, the new business can count on more than just the local population for business. If the business is a grocery store, can the owners count on a steady supply of varied foods and liquids to keep customers keeping back? If the business is a niche market, then is the local population large enough to sustain such a niche?

Most places in the world are in some manner close to agricultural land as well. Food makes the world go round and some cities are more agriculturally inclined than others. Rare is the city that grows absolutely no crops. The kind of food grown is almost entirely dependent on the kind of land available and the climate surrounding that land. Rice doesn't grow well in the desert for instance, nor do bananas grow well in snowy lands. Certain crops are easier to transport than others and the ones that aren't are usually grown near ports or other areas of export.

Skill 13.4   Identify the relationship between natural physical processes and the environment

When human, other population and migration changes; climate changes; or natural disasters disrupt the delicate balance of a habitat or an ecosystem, species either adapt or become extinct.

Natural changes can occur that alter habitats (floods, volcanoes, storms and earthquakes). These changes can affect the species that exist within the habitat, either by causing extinction or by changing the environment in a way that will no longer support the life systems. Climate changes can have similar effects. Inhabiting species can also alter habitats, particularly through migration.

Plate tectonics is a geological theory that explains **continental drift**, which are the large movements of the solid portions of the Earth's crust floating on the molten mantle. There are ten major tectonic plates, with several smaller plates. The surface of the earth can be drastically affected at the boundaries of these plates. There are three types of plate boundaries (convergent, divergent and transform). Convergent boundaries are where plates are moving toward one another. When this happens, the two plates collide and fold up against one another, called **continental collision** or one plate slides under the other, called **subduction**. Continental collision can create high mountain ranges, such as the Andes and Himalayas. Subduction often results in volcanic activity along the boundary, as in the "Ring of Fire" along the northern coasts of the Pacific Ocean.

Divergent boundaries occur where plates are moving away from one another, creating **rifts** in the surface. The Mid-Atlantic Ridge on the floor of the Atlantic Ocean, and the Great Rift Valley in east Africa, are examples of rifts at divergent plate boundaries. Transform boundaries are where plates are moving in opposite directions along their boundary, grinding against one another. The tremendous pressures that build along these types of boundaries often lead to earthquake activity when this pressure is released. The San Andreas Fault along the West Coast of North America is an example of a transform boundary.

Erosion is the displacement of solid earth surfaces such as rock and soil. Erosion is often a result of wind, water or ice acting on surfaces with loose particles (sand, loose soils or decomposing rock). Gravity can cause erosion on loose surfaces. Factors such as slope, soil and rock composition, plant cover, and human activity all affect erosion.

Weathering is the natural decomposition of the Earth's surface from contact with the atmosphere. It is not the same as erosion, but can be a factor in erosion. Heat, water, ice and pressure are all factors that can lead to weathering. Chemicals in the atmosphere can also contribute to weathering.

Transportation is the movement of eroded material from one place to another by wind, water or ice. Examples of transportation include pebbles rolling down a streambed and boulders being carried by moving glaciers.

Deposition is the result of transportation and occurs when the material being carried settles on the surface and is deposited. Sand dunes and moraines are formed by transportation and deposition of glacial material.

Skill 13.5 Interpret statistics that show how places differ in their human and physical characteristics

Demography is the branch of science of statistics most concerned with the social well being of people. **Demographic tables** may include:

1. Analysis of the population on the basis of age, parentage, physical condition, race, occupation and civil position, giving the actual size and the density of each separate area.
2. Changes in the population as a result of birth, marriage and death.
3. Statistics on population movements and their effects and their relations to given economic, social, and political conditions.
4. Statistics of crime, illegitimacy and suicide.
5. Levels of education, economic, and social statistics.

Such information is similar to that area of science known as **vital statistics** and is indispensable in studying social trends and making important legislative, economic, and social decisions. Such demographic information is gathered from census, registrar reports and by state laws. Such information, especially the vital kind, is kept by physicians, attorneys, funeral directors, members of the clergy, and similar professional people. In the United States such demographic information is compiled, kept and published by the Public Health Service of the United States Department of Health, Education and Welfare.

The most important element of this information is the so-called **rate**, which customarily represents the average of births and deaths for a unit of 1000 population over a given calendar year. These general rates are called **crude rates**, which are then sub-divided into *sex, color, age, occupation, locality and other criteria*. They are then known as **refined rates**.

In examining **statistics** and sources of statistical data one must be aware of the methods of statistical information gathering. For instance, there are many good sources of raw statistical data. Books such as *The Statistical Abstract of the United States,* published by the United States Chamber of Commerce, *The World Fact Book,* published by the Central Intelligence Agency or *The Monthly Labor Review* published by the United States Department of Labor are excellent examples, which contain much raw data. Many such yearbooks on various topics are readily available from any library or from the government itself; however, knowing how that data and information was gathered is at least as equally as important as the figures themselves. Because only by having knowledge of statistical language and methodology, can one really be able to gauge the usefulness of any given piece of data presented. Thus we must first understand just what statistics are, and what they can or cannot, tell us.

In collecting any such statistical information and data, care and adequate precautions must always be taken in order to assure that the knowledge obtained is complete and accurate. It is important to be aware of how much data is necessary to collect in order to establish the idea that being formulated. One important idea to understand is that statistics usually deal with a specific **model**, **hypothesis** or **theory** that is being attempted to be proven. Though one should be aware that a theory could never actually be proved correct, it can only really be corroborated (**corroboration** means that the data presented is more consistent with this theory than with any other theory, so it makes sense to use this theory.) One should be aware of what is known as **correlation** (the joint movement of various data points) does not infer **causation** (the change in one of those data points caused the other data points to change). It is important that one take these aspects into account so that one can be in a better position to appreciate what the collected data is really saying.

Once collected, data must then be arranged, tabulated, and presented to permit ready and meaningful analysis and interpretation. Often tables, charts or graphs will be used to present the information in a concise easy to see manner, with the information sometimes presented in raw numerical order as well. **Tests of reliability** are used, bearing in mind the manner in which the data has been collected and the inherent biases of any artificially created model to be used to explain real world events.

Skill 13.6   Identify how conditions of the past, such as wealth and poverty, land tenure, exploitation, colonialism and independence, affect present human characteristics of places

Human characteristics of a place include: architecture, roads, patterns of settlement, and land use. These characteristics can be shaped by conditions of the past that affect how humans interact with the geography of their home. The relative wealth and poverty of a person or a community can determine the type of architecture encountered, for example. A formerly poor area that finds prosperity may demolish older, less desirable buildings, and replace them with newer ones. Likewise, a formerly prosperous area that falls on hard times may still be living among older buildings, lacking resources to replace them.

Land use in the past can affect settlement patterns. Small villages often arose among open agricultural areas. As agriculture gave way to industry, these villages emerged into towns and cities, even though their original reason for existing had passed. The narrow, wandering streets of Greenwich Village in Manhattan, for instance, are remnants of the country lanes that existed before New York City expanded into the area, replacing the lanes with paved streets.

Language and religion are human characteristics that define a place. These social aspects of a place are greatly affected by traditions of the region, but can be influenced by other regions through colonial settlement or conquest. For example, present day Central and South America are largely Spanish-speaking and Roman Catholic, a result of the region having been conquered and colonized by Spain in the sixteenth century.

Cultural identity is the identification of individuals or groups as they are influenced by their belonging to a particular group or culture. This refers to the sense of who one is, what values are important, and what racial or ethnic characteristics are important in one's self-understanding and manner of interacting with the world and with others. In a nation with a well-deserved reputation as a "melting pot" the attachment to cultural identities can become a divisive factor in communities and societies. Cosmopolitanism, its alternative, tends to blur those cultural differences in the creation of a shared new culture.

Throughout the history of the nation, groups have defined themselves and/or assimilated into the larger population to varying degrees. In order for a society to function as a cohesive and unifying force, there must be some degree of enculturation of all groups. The alternative is a competing, and often conflicting, collection of sub-groups that are not able to cohere into a society. This failure to assimilate will often result in culture wars as values and lifestyles come into conflict.

Cross-cultural exchanges can enrich every involved group of persons with the discovery of shared values and needs, as well as an appreciation for unique cultural characteristics of each. For the most part, the history of the nation has been the story of successful enculturation and cultural enrichment. The notable failures, often resulting from one sort of prejudice and intolerance or another, are well known. For example, cultural biases have led to the oppression of the Irish or the Chinese immigrants in various parts of the country. Racial biases have led to various kinds of disenfranchisement and oppression of other groups of immigrants. Perhaps most notably, the bias of the European settlers against the civilization and culture of the Native peoples of North America has caused mass extermination, relocation, and isolation.

Skill 13.7   Identify ways in which people adapt to an environment through the production and use of clothing, food and shelter

Human communities subsisted initially as gatherers – gathering berries, leaves and etc. With the invention of tools it became possible to dig for roots, hunt small animals, and catch fish from rivers and oceans. Humans observed their environments and soon learned to plant seeds and **harvest crops**. As people migrated to areas where game and fertile soil were abundant, communities began to develop. When people had the knowledge to grow crops and skills to hunt game, they began to understand the division of labor. Some of the people in the community tended to agricultural needs while others hunted game.

As habitats attracted larger numbers of people, environments became crowded, and there was competition. The concept of division of labor and sharing of **food** soon came, in more heavily populated areas, to be managed. Groups of people focused on growing crops while others concentrated on hunting. Experience led to the development of skills and of knowledge that make work easier. Farmers began to develop new plant species and hunters began to protect animal species from other predators for their own use. This ability to manage the environment led people to settle down, guard their resources, and manage them.

Camps soon became villages. **Villages** became year-round settlements. Animals were domesticated and gathered into herds that met the needs of the village. With the settled life it was no longer necessary to "travel light." Pottery was developed for storing and cooking food. As farming and animal husbandry skills increased, the dependence upon wild game and food gathering declined. With this change came the realization that a larger number of people could be supported on the produce of farming and animal husbandry.

By 8000 BCE culture was beginning to evolve in these villages. Agriculture was developed for the production of grain crops, which led to a decreased reliance on wild plants. Domesticating animals for various purposes decreased the need to hunt wild game. Life became more settled. It was then possible to turn attention to such matters as managing water supplies, producing tools, **making cloth**, and other.

There was both social interaction and opportunity to reflect upon existence. Mythologies arose and various kinds of belief systems. Rituals arose that re-enacted the mythologies that gave meaning to life.

Two things seem to have come together to produce cultures and civilizations (a society and culture based on agriculture and the development of centers of the community with literate social and religious structures). The members of these hierarchies then managed **water supply** and irrigation, ritual and religious life, and exerted their own right to use a portion of the goods produced by the community for their own subsistence in return for their management. Sharpened skills, development of more sophisticated tools, commerce with other communities, and increasing knowledge of their environment, the resources available to them, and responses to the needs to share good, order community life, and protect their possessions from outsiders led to further division of labor and community development.

As trade routes developed and travel between cities became easier, trade led to specialization. Trade enables a people to obtain goods they desire in exchange for the goods they are able to produce. This, leads to increased attention to refinements of technique and sharing of ideas. The knowledge of a new discovery or invention provides knowledge and technology that increases the ability to produce goods for trade.

Skill 13.8   Identify how tools and technology affect the environment

Human civilization, population growth, and efforts to control the environment can have many negative effects on various habitats. Humans change their environments to suit their particular needs and interests. This can result in changes that result in the extinction of species or changes to the habitat itself. For example, **deforestation** damages the stability of mountain surfaces. One particularly devastating example is in the removal of the grasses of the Great Plains for agriculture. Tilling the ground and planting crops left the soil unprotected. Sustained drought dried out the soil into dust. When windstorms occurred, the topsoil was stripped away and blown all the way to the Atlantic Ocean. In extreme cases, erosion can leave a plot of agricultural land unsuitable for use. Technological advances have led to a modern method of farming that relies less on plowing the soil before planting, but more on chemical fertilizers, pesticides and herbicides. These **chemicals** can find their way into groundwater, affecting the environment.

Cities are large examples of how technological change has allowed humans to modify their environment to suit their needs. At the end of the eighteenth century, advances made in England in the **construction of canals** were brought to New York, and an ambitious project to connect Lake Erie with the Hudson River by canal was planned. The Erie Canal was built through miles of virgin wilderness, opening natural areas to settlement, and commerce. Towns along the canal grew and thrived, including Buffalo, Rochester, and Albany. The canal opened westward expansion beyond the borders of New York by opening a route between the Midwest and the East Coast.

Further advances **in transportation and building** methods allow for larger and denser communities, which in many ways impact the environment. Concentrated consumption of fuels by automobiles and home heating systems affect the quality of the air in and around cities. The lack of exposed ground means that rainwater runs off of roads and rooftops into sewer systems instead of seeping into the ground and often makes its way into nearby streams or rivers, carrying urban debris with it. New York City, the nation's largest city, has had considerable impact on its island environment and is making extensive use of new technology to reduce its energy use. New York City has the world's largest mass transit system, including hybrid buses that reduce emissions. New "clean" methods of energy production are being explored, such as underwater turbines that are run by tidal forces, and wind power. Cities like New York impact the surrounding areas that supply resources such as water. A large portion of the Catskill Mountains in New York is restricted from development because the watershed supplies water to New York City.

Skill 13.9   Identify physical, cultural, economic, and political reasons for the movement of people in the world, nation or state

Social scientists use the term **culture** to describe the way of life of a group of people. This would include not only art, music and literature, but also beliefs, customs, languages, traditions, inventions; in short, any way of life, whether complex or simple. The term **geography** is defined as the study of earth's features and living things as to their location, relationship with each other, how they came to be there, and why it is so important.

Physical geography is concerned with the locations of such earth features as climate, water and land; how these relate to and affect each other and human activities; and what forces shaped and changed them. All three of these earth features affect the lives of all humans and have a direct influence on what is made and produced, where it occurs, how it occurs, and what makes it possible. The combination of the different climate conditions and types of landforms as well as other surface features work together all around the earth to give the many varied cultures unique characteristics and distinctions.

Cultural geography studies the location, characteristics, and influence of the physical environment on different cultures around the earth. Also included in these studies are comparisons and influences of the many varied cultures. Ease of travel and up-to-the-minute, state-of-the-art communication techniques, ease the difficulties of understanding cultural differences making it easier to come in contact with them.

A **population** is a group of people living within a certain geographic area. Populations are usually measured on a regular basis by census, which also measures age, economic, ethnic, and other data. Populations change over time due to many factors and these changes can have significant impact on cultures.

When a population grows in size, it becomes necessary for it to either expand its geographic boundaries to make room for new people or to increase its density. Population density is simply the number of people in a population divided by the geographic area in which they live. Cultures with a high population density are likely to have different ways of interacting with one another than those with low density, as people live in closer to proximity to one another.

As a population grows, its economic needs change. More basic needs are required and more workers are needed to produce them. If a population's production or purchasing power does not keep pace with its growth, its economy can be adversely affected. The age distribution of a population can impact the economy as well, if the number of young and old people who are not working is disproportionate to those who are.

Growth in some areas may spur **migration** to other parts of a population's geographic region that are less densely populated. This redistribution of population also places demands on the economy, as infrastructure is needed to connect these new areas to older population centers, and land is put to new use.

Populations can grow naturally, when the rate of birth is higher than the rate of death or by adding new people from other populations through **immigration**. Immigration is often a source of societal change as people from other cultures bring their institutions and language to a new area. Immigration impacts a population's educational and economic institutions as immigrants enter the workforce and place their children in schools.

Populations can decline in number, when the death rate exceeds the birth rate, or when people migrate to another area. War, famine, disease and natural disasters can dramatically reduce a population. The economic problems from population decline can be similar to those from over population because economic demands may be higher than can be met. In extreme cases, a population may decline to the point where it can no longer perpetuate itself and its members and their culture either disappear or are absorbed into another population. When human and other population and migration changes, climate changes or natural disasters disrupt the delicate balance of a habitat or an ecosystem, species either adapt or become extinct.

Skill 13.10   Identify how transportation and communication networks contribute to the level of economic development in different regions

The global economy had its origins in the early twentieth century, with the advent of the airplane, which made travel and trade easier and less time-consuming than ever. With the recent advent of the Internet, the world might be better termed a global neighborhood. Airplanes travel the fastest of any mode of transportation on the planet. Flight has made possible global commerce and goods exchange on a level never before seen. Foods from all around the world can be flown literally around the world and with the aid of refrigeration techniques are kept fresh enough to sell in markets nearly everywhere. The same is true of medicine and unfortunately, weapons. Being able to ship goods quickly and efficiently means that businesses can conduct business overseas more efficiently than they ever could. Trucks, trains and ships carry cargo all over the world. Trains travel faster than ever, as do ships. Roads are more prevalent and usually in better repair than they have ever been, making truck and even car travel not the dead-end option that it once was.

With all of this capability has come increasing demand. People traditionally had gotten their goods using their own means or from traders who lived nearby. As technology improved, trade routes got longer and demand for things from overseas grew. This demand feeds the economic imperative of creating more supply and vice versa. As more people discovered goods from overseas, the demand for those foreign goods increased.

An incredible increase in demand for something is not always a good thing, however, especially if what is being demanded is in limited supply. A good example is wood, paper and other goods that are made from trees. The demand for paper especially these days is staggering. In order to fulfill that demand, companies are cutting down more and more trees. An example of nonrenewable resources like coal and oil are in worldwide demand these days and the supplies won't last forever. Making it easier to ship goods all over the world has made demand grow at an unbelievable rate, raising concerns about supply. Because resources have a limited supply, they are in danger of becoming extinct without being replaced.

Globalization has brought about welcome and unwelcome developments in the field of epidemiology. Vaccines and other cures for diseases can be shipped relatively quickly all around the world. For example, this has made it possible for HIV vaccines to reach the remotest areas of the world. Unfortunately, the preponderance of global travel has also meant that the threat of spreading a disease to the world by an infected person traveling on an international flight is quite real.

The most recent example of technology contributing to globalization is the development of the **Internet**. Instant communication between people millions of miles apart is possible just by plugging in a computer and connecting to the Net. The Internet is an extension of the telephone and cell phone revolutions; all three are developments that have brought faraway places closer together. All three allow people to communicate no matter the distance. This communication can facilitate friendly chatter and, of course, trade. A huge number of businesses use cell phones and the Internet to do business these days, also using computers to track goods and receipts quickly and efficiently.

Globalization has brought financial and cultural exchange on a worldwide scale. A large number of businesses have investments in countries around the world. Financial transactions are conducted using a variety of currencies. The cultures of the countries of the world are increasingly viewed by people elsewhere in the world through the wonders of television and the Internet. Not only goods, but also belief systems, customs and practices are being exchanged.

With this exchange of money, goods and culture has come an increase in immigration. Many people who live in less-developed nations see what is available in other places and want to move there, in order to fully take advantage of all that those more-developed nations have to offer. This can conceivably create an increase in immigration. Depending on the numbers of people who want to immigrate and the resources available, this could become a problem. The technological advances in transportation and communications have made such immigration easier than ever.

Economic mobility refers to the ability of factors, particularly labor to move around the country in response to employment opportunities. The U.S. economy is so big that there can be unemployment in one part of the country, while there are labor shortages in other parts of the country. In many cases there are institutional rigidities, like lack of information that prevents workers from migrating in response to employment opportunities. State job services exist to provide information about available job opportunities, even though many workers are reluctant to migrate due to family situations.

Tremendous progress in communication and transportation has drawn all parts of the earth closer. There are still vast areas of the former Soviet Union that have unproductive land, extreme poverty, food shortages, rampant diseases, violent friction between cultures, the ever-present nuclear threat, environmental pollution, rapid reduction of natural resources, urban over-crowding, acceleration in global terrorism, and violent crimes, and a diminishing middle class.

Skill 13.11   Compare and contrast major regions of the world

Mountains are landforms with rather steep slopes at least 2,000 feet or more above sea level. Mountains are found in groups called mountain chains or mountain ranges. At least one range can be found on six of the earth's seven continents. North America has the Appalachian and Rocky Mountains; South America the Andes; Asia the Himalayas; Australia the Great Dividing Range; Europe the Alps; and Africa the Atlas, Ahaggar and Drakensburg Mountains.

Hills are elevated landforms rising to an elevation of about 500 to 2000 feet. They are found everywhere including Antarctica where they are covered by ice.

Plateaus are elevated landforms usually level on top. Depending on location, they range from being an area that is very cold to one that is cool and healthful. Some plateaus are dry because mountains that keep out any moisture surround them. Some examples include the Kenya Plateau in East Africa, which is very cool. The plateau extending north from the Himalayas is extremely dry while those in Antarctica and Greenland are covered with ice and snow.

Plains are described as areas of flat or slightly rolling land, usually lower than the landforms next to them. Sometimes called lowlands they support the majority of the world's people. Some are found inland and many have been formed by large rivers. This resulted in extremely fertile soil for successful cultivation of crops and numerous large settlements of people. In North America, the vast plains areas extend from the Gulf of Mexico north to the Arctic Ocean and between the Appalachian and Rocky Mountains. In Europe, rich plains extend east from Great Britain into central Europe on into the Siberian region of Russia. Plains in river valleys are found in China (the Yangtze River valley), India (the Ganges River valley), and Southeast Asia (the Mekong River valley).

Valleys are land areas found between hills and mountains. Some have gentle slopes containing trees and plants; others have steep walls and are referred to as canyons. One example is Arizona's Grand Canyon of the Colorado River.

Deserts are large dry areas of land receiving ten inches or less of rainfall each year. Among the better known deserts are Africa's large Sahara Desert, the Arabian Desert on the Arabian Peninsula and the Outback in Australia.

Deltas are areas of lowlands formed by soil and sediment deposited at the mouths of rivers. The soil is generally very fertile and most fertile river deltas are important crop-growing areas. One well-known example is the delta of Egypt's Nile River, known for its production of cotton.

Mesas are the flat tops of hills or mountains usually with steep sides. Sometimes plateaus are also called mesas. Basins are considered to be low areas drained by rivers or low spots in mountains. Foothills are generally considered a low series of hills found between a plain and a mountain range. Marshes and swamps are wet lowlands providing growth of such plants as rushes and reeds.

Oceans are the largest bodies of water on the planet. The four oceans of the earth are the **Atlantic Ocean**, one-half the size of the Pacific and separating North and South America from Africa and Europe; the **Pacific Ocean**, covering almost one-third of the entire surface of the earth and separating North and South America from Asia and Australia; the **Indian Ocean**, touching Africa, Asia and Australia; and the ice-filled **Arctic Ocean,** extending from North America and Europe to the North Pole. The waters of the Atlantic, Pacific and Indian Oceans also touch the shores of Antarctica.

Seas are smaller than oceans and are surrounded by land. Some examples include the Mediterranean Sea found between Europe, Asia and Africa; and the Caribbean Sea, touching the West Indies, South and Central America. A lake is a body of water surrounded by land. The Great Lakes are a good example.

Rivers, considered a nation's lifeblood, usually begin as very small streams, formed by melting snow and rainfall, flowing from higher to lower land, emptying into a larger body of water, usually a sea or an ocean. Examples of important rivers for the people and countries affected by and/or dependent on them include the Nile, Niger and Zaire Rivers of Africa; the Rhine, Danube and Thames Rivers of Europe; the Yangtze, Ganges, Mekong, Hwang He and Irrawaddy Rivers of Asia; the Murray-Darling in Australia; and the Orinoco in South America. River systems are made up of large rivers and numerous smaller rivers or tributaries flowing into them. Examples include the vast Amazon Rivers system in South America and the Mississippi River system in the United States.

Canals are man-made water passages constructed to connect two larger bodies of water. Famous examples include the **Panama Canal** across Panama's isthmus connecting the Atlantic and Pacific Oceans and the **Suez Canal** in the Middle East between Africa and the Arabian Peninsula connecting the Red and Mediterranean Seas.

COMPETENCY 14.0   KNOWLEDGE OF GOVERNMENT AND THE CITIZEN

Skill 14.1   Identify the structure, functions and purposes of government

Historically the functions of government, or people's concepts of government and its purpose and function, have varied considerably. In the theory of political science, the function of government is to secure the common welfare of the members of the given society over which it exercises control. In different historical eras, governments have attempted to achieve the common welfare by various means in accordance with the traditions and ideology of the given society. Among *primitive peoples*, systems of control were rudimentary at best. They arose directly from the ideas of right and wrong that had been established in the group and was common in that particular society. Control being exercised most often by means of group pressure, most often in the forms of taboos and superstitions and in many cases by ostracism, or banishment from the group. Thus, in most cases, because of the extreme tribal nature of society in those early times, this lead to very unpleasant circumstances for the individual so treated. Without the protection of the group, a lone individual was most often in for a sad and very short, fate (no other group would accept such an individual into their midst and survival alone was extremely difficult if not impossible).

Among more *civilized peoples*, governments began to assume more institutional forms. They rested on a well-defined legal basis. They imposed penalties on violators of the social order. They used force, which was supported and sanctioned by their people. The government was charged to establish the social order and was supposed to do so in order to be able to discharge its functions.

Eventually the ideas of government, who should govern and how, came to be considered by various thinkers and philosophers. The most influential of these and those who had the most influence on our present society were the ancient Greek philosophers such as Plato and Aristotle.

Aristotle's conception of government was based on a simple idea. The function of government was to provide for the general welfare of its people. A good government, and one that should be supported, was one that did so in the best way possible, with the least pressure on the people. Bad governments were those that subordinated the general welfare to that of the individuals who ruled. At no time should any function of any government be that of personal interest of any one individual, no matter who that individual was. This does not mean that Aristotle had no sympathy for the individual or individual happiness (as at times Plato has been accused by those who read his "***Republic,***" which was the first important philosophical text to explore these issues). Rather Aristotle believed that a society is greater than the sum of its parts, or that "the good of the many outweighs the good of the few and also of the one."

Yet, a good government, and one that is carrying out its functions well, will always weigh the relative merits of what is good for a given individual in society and what is good for the society as a whole.

This basic concept has continued to our own time and has found its fullest expression in the idea of representative democracy and political and personal freedom. In addition, a government that maintains good social order, while allowing the greatest possible exercise of autonomy for individuals to achieve.

Skill 14.2   Demonstrate knowledge of the rights and responsibilities of a citizen in the world, nation, state and/or community

In the United States, the Bill of Rights guarantees every US citizen the freedoms defined following. The **Bill Of Rights** is the first ten amendments to the United States Constitution dealing with civil liberties and civil rights. They were written mostly by James Madison. They are in brief:

1. Freedom of Religion.
2. Right To Bear Arms.
3. Security from the quartering of troops in homes.
4. Right against unreasonable search and seizures.
5. Right against self-incrimination.
6. Right to trial by jury, right to legal council.
7. Right to jury trial for civil actions.
8. No cruel or unusual punishment allowed.
9. These rights shall not deny other rights the people enjoy.
10. Powers not mentioned in the Constitution shall be retained by the states or the people.

A citizen in a democratic society is expected to follow the laws of that society. Citizens have a responsibility to themselves and if government is infringing on their basic rights, they have a natural right to speak up and do something about it. Related to this is the idea that the government of a democratic society exists in part to protect the rights of its citizens. Real terms include civil and countrywide defense, and virtual terms include laws and the people who make them. Citizens of a democratic society are expected to participate in the political process, either directly or indirectly. In theory, anyone who is a citizen of a democratic society can get himself or herself elected to *something*, be it at the local, state or federal level. Other ways to participate in the political process include donating time and/or money to the political campaigns of others and speaking out on behalf of or against certain issues. The most basic level of participation in the political process is to vote.

Skill 14.3   Identify major concepts of the U.S. Constitution and other historical documents

Authors, printers and publishers, and other factions were quite active in promoting the new American attitude toward independence. Of significant note, was the **Virginia Declaration of Rights**, drafted by George Mason in May 1776 and amended by Thomas Ludwell Lee and the Virginia Convention. Thomas Jefferson was influenced by it when he drafted the Declaration of Independence only a month later. This document would also influence James Madison when drawing up the **Bill of Rights** (1789) and the Marquis de Lafayette when drafting the **French Declaration of the Rights of Man** (1789).

The Declaration's text can be divided into three main parts:

1. Statements of the general state of humanity and the natural rights inherent in all civil societies. Jefferson talks about "self-evident" truths, unalienable rights of people to "Life, Liberty and the pursuit of Happiness," which show considerable influence from primarily French thinkers of the Enlightenment during the seventeenth and eighteenth centuries. He clearly states that a government that no longer respects these inherent rights loses its legitimacy and becomes despotic. And, that the governed have the right to throw off such a government and impose a call for insurrection against the sovereign.

2. An enumeration of specific and detailed grievances, which point out why the current sovereign has lost the right to govern and that lists how the king even subverted English Common Law and legal traditions dating back to antiquity.

3. The last part of the text states that the colonists had exhausted all civil and legal means of having their grievances addressed by British government and now had the right, and duty, to break with the crown and be a free and independent nation.

The final section of the Declaration contains the signatures of the representatives of the colonies to the Continental Congress in Philadelphia. Realizing that they had committed an act of treason, punishable by death by hanging, Benjamin Franklin counseled unity, lest they all hang separately. It should be noted that at that moment, open hostilities between British and Colonists had already been underway for over a year. **George Washington** had taken command of the Continental Army, organized on June 14, 1775 at Harvard Yard, and in the same year, the Continental Navy and the Marine Corps had been organized.

During the war, and after independence was declared, the former colonies now found themselves independent states.

The Declaration of Independence was the founding document of the United States of America. The Articles of Confederation were the first attempt of the newly independent states to reach a new understanding amongst their selves. The Declaration was intended to demonstrate the reasons that the colonies were seeking separation from Great Britain. Conceived by, and written for, the most part by Thomas Jefferson, it is not only important for what it says, but also for how it says it. The Declaration is in many respects a poetic document. Instead of a simple recitation of the colonists' grievances, it set out clearly the reasons why the colonists were seeking their freedom from Great Britain. They had tried all means to resolve the dispute peacefully. It was the right of a people, when all other methods of addressing their grievances have been tried and failed, to separate themselves from that power that was keeping them from fully expressing their rights to **"life, liberty and the pursuit of happiness."**

During the war, and after independence was declared, the former colonies now found themselves independent states. The Second Continental Congress was conducting a war with representation by delegates from thirteen separate states. The Congress had no power to act for the states or to require them to accept and follow its wishes. A permanent united government was desperately needed. On November 15, 1777, the **Articles of Confederation** were adopted, creating a league of free and independent states.

The central government of the new United States of America consisted of a **Congress** of two to seven delegates from each state with each state having just one vote. The government under the Articles solved some of the postwar problems, but had serious weaknesses. Some of its powers included: borrowing and coining money, directing foreign affairs, declaring war and making peace, building and equipping a navy, regulating weights and measures, asking the states to supply men and money for an army. The delegates to Congress had no real authority as each state carefully and jealously guarded its own interests and limited powers under the Articles. Also, the delegates to Congress were paid by their states and had to vote as directed by their state legislatures. The serious weaknesses were the lack of power: to regulate finances, over interstate trade, over foreign trade, to enforce treaties, and military power. Something better and more efficient was needed.

In May of 1787, delegates from all states except Rhode Island began meeting in Philadelphia. At first, they met to revise the Articles of Confederation as instructed by Congress; but they soon realized that much more was needed. Abandoning the instructions, they set out to write a new Constitution, a new document, the foundation of all government in the United States, and a model for representative government throughout the world.

Within a few months from the adoption of the Articles of Confederation, it became apparent that there were serious defects in the system of government established for the new republic. There was a need for changes that would create a national government with adequate powers to replace the Confederation, which was actually only a League of Sovereign States. In 1786, an effort to regulate interstate commerce ended in what is known as the **Annapolis Convention**. Because only five states were represented, this Convention was not able to accomplish definitive results. The debates, however, made it clear that foreign and interstate commerce could not be regulated by a government with as little authority as the government established by the Confederation. Congress was, therefore, asked to call a convention to provide a constitution that would address the emerging needs of the new nation.

The convention met under the presidency of George Washington, with fifty-five of the sixty-five appointed members present. A constitution was written in four months. **The Constitution of the United States** is the fundamental law of the republic. It is a precise, formal, written document of the *extraordinary*, or *supreme*, type of constitution. The founders of the Union established it as the highest governmental authority. There is no national power superior to it. The foundations were so broadly laid as to provide for the expansion of national life and to make it an instrument that would last for all time. To maintain its stability, the framers created a difficult process for making any changes to it. No amendment can become valid until it is ratified by three fourths of all of the states. The British system of government was part of the basis of the final document, but significant changes were necessary to meet the needs of a partnership of states that were tied together as a single federation--yet sovereign in their own local affairs. This constitution established a system of government that was unique and advanced far beyond other systems of its day.

There were, to be sure, differences of opinion. The **compromises** that resolved these conflicts are reflected in the final document. The first point of disagreement and compromise was related to the Presidency. Some wanted a strong, centralized, individual authority. Others feared autocracy or the growth of monarchy. The compromise was to give the President broad powers, but to limit the amount of time, through term of office, that any individual could exercise that power. The power to make appointments and to conclude treaties was controlled by the requirement of the consent of the Senate.

The second conflict was between large and small states. The large states wanted power proportionate to their voting strength; the small states opposed this plan. The compromise was that all states should have equal voting power in the Senate, but to make the membership of the House of Representatives determined in proportion to population.

The third conflict was about slavery. The compromise was that a) fugitive slaves should be returned by states to which they might flee for refuge, and b) no law would be passed for 20 years prohibiting the importation of slaves.

The fourth major area of conflict was how the President would be chosen. One side of the disagreement argued for election by direct vote of the people. The other side thought the President should be chosen by Congress. One group feared the ignorance of the people; the other feared the power of a small group of people. The Compromise was the **Electoral College**.

The Constitution binds the states in a governmental unity in everything that affects the welfare of all. At the same time, it recognizes the right of the people of each state to independence of action in matters that relate only to them. Since the Federal Constitution is the law of the land, all other laws must conform to it.

The debates conducted during the Constitutional Congress represent the issues and the arguments that led to the compromises in the final document. The debates reflect the concerns of the Founding Fathers that the rights of the people be protected from abrogation by the government itself and the determination that no branch of government should have enough power to override the others. There is, therefore, a system of **checks and balances**.

The Federalist Papers were written to win popular support for the new proposed Constitution. In these publications the debates of the Congress and the concerns of the founding fathers were made available to the people of the nation. In addition to providing an explanation of the underlying philosophies and concerns of the Constitution and the compromises that were made, the Federalist Papers conducted what has frequently been called the most effective marketing and public relations campaign in human history.

The Bill of Rights consists of the first ten Amendments to the U.S. Constitution. These amendments were passed almost immediately upon ratification of the Constitution by the states. They reflect the concerns that were raised throughout the country and by the Founding Fathers during the ratification process. These Amendments reflect the fears and concerns of the people that the power and authority of the government be restricted from denying or limiting the rights of the people of the nation. The experiences of the founders of the nation as colonists formed the foundation of the concern to limit the power of government.

The Bill of Rights has been interpreted in different ways at different times by different interpreters. These, and other, Constitutional Amendments may be interpreted very strictly or very loosely. The terms of the amendments may be defined in different ways to enfranchise or to disenfranchise individuals or groups of persons.

Example: During and after Reconstruction, the interpretation of the Bill of Rights that did not include blacks in the definition of a citizen necessitated the passage of the 14th and 15th Amendments. The interpretation of these amendments was broadly interpreted by the Supreme Court in the Plessey case, resulting in the establishment of the doctrine of "separate but equal." It was not until fifty years later, in the case of Brown v. Board of Education, that a narrower interpretation of the amendment resulted in a Supreme Court decision that reversed the previous interpretation.

Skill 14.4   Identify how the Legislative, Executive and Judicial branches share powers and responsibility

In the United States, the three branches of the federal government: the **Executive**, the **Legislative** and the **Judicial** divide their powers thus:

Legislative - Article I of the Constitution established the Legislative, or law-making branch of the government called the Congress. It is made up of two houses, the House of Representatives and the Senate. Voters in all states elect the members who serve in each respective house of Congress. The Legislative branch is responsible for making laws, raising and printing money, regulating trade, establishing the postal service and federal courts, approving the President's appointments, and declaring war and supporting the armed forces. The Congress has the power to change the Constitution itself and to impeach (bring charges against) the President. Charges for impeachment are brought by the House of Representatives and are tried in the Senate.

Executive – Article II of the Constitution created the Executive branch of the government, headed by the President, who leads the country, recommends new laws, and can veto bills passed by the Legislative branch. As the Chief of State, the President is responsible for carrying out the laws of the country and the treaties and declarations of war passed by the Legislative branch. The President appoints federal judges and is Commander in Chief of the military when it is called into service. Other members of the Executive branch include the Vice-President, who is also elected. Various cabinet members as he might appoint, ambassadors, presidential advisers, members of the armed forces, and other appointed and civil servants of government agencies, departments and bureaus. Though the President appoints them, they then must be approved by the Legislative branch.

Judicial - Article III of the Constitution established the Judicial branch of government headed by the Supreme Court. The Supreme Court has the power to rule that a law passed by the Legislature, or an act of the Executive branch is illegal and unconstitutional. In an appeal capacity, citizens, businesses and government officials can also ask the Supreme Court to review a decision made in a lower court if someone believes that the ruling by a judge is unconstitutional. The Judicial branch includes lower federal courts known as federal district courts that have been established by the Congress. The courts try lawbreakers and review cases referred from other courts.

Checks and Balances - System set up by the Constitution in which each branch of the federal government has the power to check or limit the actions of other branches.

Separation of Powers - System of American government in which each branch of government has its own specifically designated powers and can not interfere with the powers of another.

Skill 14.5   Demonstrate knowledge of the U.S. electoral system and the election process

The U.S. electoral process has many and varied elements, from simple voting to complex campaigning for office. Everything in between is complex and detailed. First of all, American citizens vote. They vote for laws, statues, referenda and elected officials. They have to register in order to vote and at that time they can declare their intended membership in a political party. America has a large list of political parties, which have varying degrees of membership. The Democratic and Republican Parties are the two with the most money and power, but other political parties abound.

Candidates affiliate themselves with political parties. Candidates then go about the business of campaigning, which includes getting the word on out on their candidacy, what they believe in, and what they will do if elected. Candidates sometimes get together for debates, to showcase their views on important issues of the day and how those views differ from those of their opponents. Candidates give public speeches, attend public functions, and spout their views to reporters, for coverage in newspapers and magazines and on radio and television. On Election Day, candidates hope that what they've done is enough.

Elections take place regularly, so voters know just how long it will be before the next election. Some candidates begin planning their next campaign the day after their victory or loss. Voters technically have the option to **recall** elected candidates; such a measure, however, is drastic and requires a large pile of signatures to get the motion on the ballot and then a large number of votes to have the measure approved. As such, recalls of elected candidates are relatively rare. One widely publicized recall in recent years was that of California Governor Gray Davis, who was replaced by movie star Arnold Schwarzenegger.

Another method of removing public officials from office is **impeachment**. This is rare, but still a possibility. Both houses of the state or federal government get involved and both houses have to approve the impeachment measures by a large margin. In the case of the federal government, the House of Representatives votes to impeach a federal official and the Senate votes to convict or acquit. Conviction means that the official must leave office immediately; acquittal results in no penalties or fines.

The **College of Electors**—or the Electoral College, as it is more commonly known—has a long and distinguished history of mirroring the political will of the American voters. On some occasions, the results have not been entirely in sync with that political will.

Article II of the Constitution lists the specifics of the Electoral College. The Founding Fathers included the Electoral College as one of the famous "checks and balances" for two reasons: 1) to give states with small populations more of an equal weight in the presidential election, and 2) they didn't trust the common man (women couldn't vote then) to be able to make an informed decision on which candidate would make the best president.

First of all, the same theory that created the U.S. Senate practice of giving two Senators to each state created the Electoral College. The large-population states had their populations reflected in the House of Representatives. New York and Pennsylvania, two of the states with the largest populations, had the highest number of members of the House of Representatives. But these two states still had only two senators, the exact same number that small-population states like Rhode Island and Delaware had. This was true as well in the Electoral College. Each state had just one vote, regardless of how many members of the House represented that state. So, the one vote that the state of New York cast would be decided by an initial vote of New York's Representatives (if that initial vote was a tie, then that deadlock would have to be broken).

Technically, the electors do not have to vote for anyone. The Constitution does not require them to do so. And throughout the history of presidential elections, some have indeed voted for someone else. But tradition holds that the electors vote for the candidate chosen by their state and so the vast majority of electors do just that. The Electoral College meets a few weeks after the presidential election. Mostly, their meeting is a formality. When all the electoral votes are counted, the President with the most votes wins. In most cases, the candidate who wins the popular vote also wins in the Electoral College; however, this has not always been the case.

Most recently, in 2000 in Florida, the election was decided by the Supreme Court. The Democratic Party's nominee was Vice-President Al Gore. The Republican Party's nominee was George W. Bush, Governor of Texas and son of former President George Bush. He campaigned on a platform of a strong national defense and an end to questionable ethics in the White House. The election was hotly contested, and many states went down to the wire, being decided by only a handful of votes. The one state that seemed to be flip-flopping as Election Day turned into Election Night was Florida. In the end, Gore won the popular vote, by nearly 540,000 votes. But he didn't win the electoral vote. The vote was so close in Florida that a recount was necessary under federal law. Eventually, the Supreme Court weighed in and stopped all the recounts. The last count had Bush winning by less than a thousand votes. That gave him Florida and the White House.

Skill 14.6 Identify the structures and functions of U.S. federal, state and local governments

Powers delegated to the federal government

1. To tax.
2. To borrow and coin money.
3. To establish postal service.
4. To grant patents and copyrights.
5. To regulate interstate & foreign commerce.
6. To establish courts.
7. To declare war.
8. To raise and support the armed forces.
9. To govern territories.
10. To define and punish felonies and piracy on the high seas.
11. To fix standards of weights and measures.
12. To conduct foreign affairs.

Powers reserved to the states

1. To regulate intrastate trade.
2. To establish local governments.
3. To protect general welfare.
4. To protect life and property.
5. To ratify amendments.
6. To conduct elections.
7. To make state and local laws.

Concurrent powers of the federal government and states.

1. Both Congress and the states may tax.
2. Both may borrow money.
3. Both may charter banks and corporations.
4. Both may establish courts.
5. Both may make and enforce laws.
6. Both may take property for public purposes.
7. Both may spend money to provide for the public welfare.

Implied powers of the federal government.

1. To establish banks or other corporations implied from delegated powers to tax, borrow, and to regulate commerce.
2. To spend money for roads, schools, health, insurance and etc. implied from powers to establish post roads, to tax to provide for general welfare and defense, and to regulate commerce.
3. To create military academies, implied from powers to raise and support an armed force.
4. To locate and generate sources of power and sell surplus implied from powers, to dispose of government property, commerce and war powers.
5. To assist and regulate agriculture implied from power to tax and spend for general welfare and regulate commerce.

Skill 14.7   Identify the relationships between social, economic, and political rights and the historical documents that secure these rights

The Magna Carta - This charter has been considered the basis of English constitution liberties. It was granted to a representative group of English barons and nobles on *June 15, 1215* by the British King John, after they had forced it on him. The English barons and nobles sought to limit what they had come to perceive as the overwhelming power of the Monarchy in public affairs. The Magna Carta is considered to be the first modern document that sought to try to limit the powers of the given state authority. It guaranteed feudal rights, regulated the justice system, and abolished many abuses of the King's power to tax and regulate trade. It said that the king could not raise new taxes without first consulting a Great Council made up of nobles, barons and Church people. Significantly, the Magna Carta only dealt with the rights of the upper classes of the nobility and all of its provisions excluded the rights of the common people; however, gradually the rights won by the nobles were given to other English people.

The Great Council grew into a representative assembly called the Parliament. By the 1600s, Parliament was divided into the House of Lords, made up of nobles and the House of Commons. Members of the House of Commons were elected to office. In the beginning, only a few wealthy men could vote. Still English people firmly believed that the ruler must consult Parliament on money matters and obey the law. Thus, it did set a precedent that there was a limit to the allowed power of the state. A precedent, which would have no small effect on the history of political revolution, is notably the American Revolution.

The Petition of Right - In English history, it was the title of a petition that was addressed to the King of England **Charles I,** by the British parliament in **1628.** The Parliament demanded that the King stop proclaiming new taxes without its' consent. Parliament demanded that he cease housing soldiers and sailors in the homes of private citizens, proclaiming martial law in times of peace, and that no subject should be imprisoned without a good cause being shown. After some attempts to circumvent these demands, Charles finally agreed to them. They later had an important effect on the demands of the revolutionary colonists, as these were some of the rights that as Englishmen, they felt were being denied. The Petition of Right was also the basis of specific protections that the designers of the Constitution made a point of inserting in the document.

British Bill of Rights - Also known as the **Declaration of Rights** spelled out the rights that were considered to belong to Englishmen. It was granted by **King William III** in 1869. It had previously been passed by a convention of the Parliament. The Declaration came out of the struggle for power that took place in Great Britain and at that time was known as **The Glorious Revolution.** It was known as a revolution that was accomplished with virtually no bloodshed and led to King William III and Queen Mary II becoming joint sovereigns.

The Declaration itself was very similar in style to the later American Bill of Rights. It protected the rights of individuals and gave anyone accused of a crime the right to trial by jury. It outlawed cruel punishments; also, it stated that a ruler could not raise taxes or an army without the consent of Parliament. The colonists as Englishmen were protected by these provisions. The colonists considered abridgments of these rights that helped to contribute to the revolutionary spirit of the times.

All of these events, and the principles that arose from them, are of the utmost importance in understanding the process that eventually led to the ideals that are inherent in the Constitution of the United States. In addition, the fact is that all of these ideals are universal in nature and have become the basis for the idea of human freedoms throughout the world.

The Declaration of the Rights of Man and of the Citizen is a document created by the French National Assembly and issued in 1789. It sets forth the "natural, inalienable and sacred rights of man." It proclaims the following rights:

- Men are born and remain free and equal in rights. Social distinctions may only be founded upon the general good.

- The aim of all political association is the preservation of the natural and imprescriptible rights of man: liberty, property, security and resistance to oppression.

- All sovereignty resides essentially in the nation. No body or individual may exercise any authority which does not proceed directly from the nation.

- Liberty is the freedom to do everything which injures no one else; hence the exercise of these rights has no limits except those which assure to the other members of the society the enjoyment of the same rights. These limits can only be determined by law.

- Law can only prohibit such actions as are hurtful to society.

- Law is the expression of the general will. Every citizen has a right to participate in the formation of law. It must be the same for all. All citizens, being equal in the eyes of the law, are equally eligible to all dignities and to all public positions and occupations, according to their abilities.

- No person shall be accused, arrested or imprisoned except in the cases and according to the forms prescribed by law.

- The law shall provide for such punishments only as are strictly and obviously necessary.

- All persons are held innocent until they have been declared guilty. If it is necessary to arrest a person, all harshness not essential to the securing of the prisoner's person shall be severely repressed by law.

- No one shall be disquieted on account of his opinions, including religious views, provided their manifestation does not disturb the peace.

- The free communication of ideas and opinions is one of the most precious of the rights of man.

- The security of the rights of man and of the citizen requires public military force. These forces are, therefore, established for the good of all and not for the personal advantage of those to whom they shall be entrusted.

- A common contribution is essential for the maintenance of the public forces and for the cost of administration. This should be equitably distributed among all the citizens in proportion to their means.

- All the citizens have a right to decide, either personally or by their representatives, as to the necessity of the public contribution.

- Society has the right to require of every public agent an account of his administration.

- A society in which the observance of the law is not assured, nor the separation of powers defined, has no constitution at all.
- Since property is an inviolable and sacred right, no one shall be deprived thereof except where public necessity, legally determined, shall clearly demand it, and then only on condition that the owner shall have been previously and equitably indemnified.

The United Nations Declaration of Universal Human Rights (1948). The declaration opens with these words: "Whereas recognition of the inherent dignity and of the equal and inalienable rights of all members of the human family is the foundation of freedom, justice and peace in the world. Whereas disregard and contempt for human rights have resulted in barbarous acts which have outraged the conscience of mankind, and the advent of a world in which human beings shall enjoy freedom of speech and belief and freedom from fear and want has been proclaimed as the highest aspiration of the common people."

1. All human beings are born free and equal in dignity and rights. They are endowed with reason and conscience and should act towards one another in a spirit of brotherhood.
2. Everyone is entitled to all the rights and freedoms set forth in this Declaration, without distinction of any kind.
3. Everyone has the right to life, liberty and security of person.
4. No one shall be held in slavery or servitude.
5. No one shall be subjected to torture or to cruel, inhuman or degrading treatment or punishment.
6. Everyone has the right to recognition everywhere as a person before the law.
7. All are equal before the law and are entitled without any discrimination to equal protection of the law.
8. Everyone has the right to an effective remedy by the competent national tribunals for acts violating the fundamental rights granted him by the constitution of by law.
9. No one shall be subjected to arbitrary arrest, detention or exile.
10. Everyone is entitled in full equality to a fair and public hearing by an independent and impartial tribunal, in the determination of his rights and obligations and of any criminal charge against him.
11. Everyone charged with a penal offence has the right to be presumed innocent until proved guilty according to law in a public trial at which he has had all the guarantees necessary for his defence. No one shall be held guilty of any penal offence on account of any act or omission which did not constitute a penal offence, under national or international law, at the time when it was committed
12. No one shall be subjected to arbitrary interference with his privacy, family, home or correspondence, nor to attacks upon his honour and reputation.

13. Everyone has the right to freedom of movement and residence within the borders of each state. Everyone has the right to leave any country, including his own, and to return to his country.

14. Everyone has the right to seek and to enjoy in other countries asylum from persecution. This right may not be invoked in the case of prosecutions genuinely arising from non-political crimes or from acts contrary to the purposes and principles of the United Nations.

15. Everyone has the right to a nationality. No one shall be arbitrarily deprived of his nationality nor denied the right to change his nationality.

16. Men and women of full age have the right to marry and to found a family. They are entitled to equal rights as to marriage, during marriage and at its dissolution. Marriage shall be entered into only with the free and full consent of the intending spouses. The family is the natural and fundamental group unit of society and is entitled to protection by society and the State.

17. Everyone has the right to own property alone or in association with others. No one shall be arbitrarily deprived of his property.

18. Everyone has the right to freedom of thought, conscience and religion, including the right to change his religion or belief, and freedom to manifest his religion or belief in teaching, practice, worship and observance.

19. Everyone has the right to freedom of opinion and expression.

20. Everyone has the fight to freedom of peaceful assembly and association. No one may be compelled to belong to an association.

21. Everyone has the right to take part in the government of his country, directly or through freely chosen representatives. Everyone has the right of equal access to public service in his country. The will of the people shall be the basis of the authority of government.

22. Everyone has the right to social security and is entitled to realization of the economic, social and cultural rights indispensable for his dignity and the free development of his personality.

23. Everyone has the right to work. Everyone, without any discrimination, has the right to equal pay for equal work. Everyone who works has the right to just and favourable remuneration. Everyone has the right to form and to join trade unions for the protection of his interests.

24. Everyone has the right to rest and leisure, including reasonable limitation of working hours and periodic holidays with pay.

25. Everyone has the right to a standard of living adequate for the health and well-being of himself and his family, and the right to security in the event of unemployment, sickness, disability, widowhood, old age or other lack of livelihood in circumstances beyond his control. Motherhood and childhood are entitled to special care and assistance. All children shall enjoy the same social protection.

26. Everyone has the right to education. Education shall be directed to the full development of the human personality and to the strengthening of respect

for human rights and fundamental freedoms. Parents have a prior right to choose the kind of education that shall be given to their children.

27. Everyone has the right freely to participate in the cultural life of the community. Everyone has the right to the protection of the moral and materials interests resulting from any scientific, literary or artistic production of which he is the author.

28. Everyone is entitled to a social and international order in which the rights and freedoms set forth in this Declaration can be fully realized.

The United Nations Convention on the Rights of the Child brings together the rights of children as they are enumerated in other international documents. In this document, those rights are clearly and completely stated, along with the explanation of the guiding principals that define the way society views children. The goal of the document is to clarify the environment that is necessary to enable every human being to develop to their full potential. The Convention calls for resources and contributions to be made to ensure the full development and survival of all children. The document requires the establishment of appropriate means to protect children from neglect, exploitation and abuse. The document also recognizes that parents have the most important role in raising children.

Skill 14.8   Demonstrate knowledge of the processes of the U.S. legal system

The Federal Court System - is provided for in the Constitution of the United States on the theory that the judicial power of the federal government could not be entrusted to the individual states, many of which had opposed the idea of a strong federal government in the first place. Thus Article III, Section 1, of the Constitution says: *"the judicial power of the United States shall be vested in one Supreme Court, and in such inferior courts as the Congress may from time to time ordain and establish"*. In accordance with these provisions, Congress passed the **Judiciary Act** in 1789, organizing the Supreme Court of the United States and establishing a system of federal courts of inferior jurisdiction. The states were left to establish their own judicial systems subject to the exclusive overall jurisdiction of the federal courts and to Article VI of the Constitution declaring the judges of the state courts to be bound to the Constitution and to the laws and treaties of the United States. This created a dual system of judicial power and authority in the United States.

The jurisdiction of the federal courts is further defined in Article III, Section 2 of the Constitution as extending in law and in equity to all cases arising under the Constitution and through federal legislation to controversies in which the United States is a party, including those arising from treaties with other governments, to maritime cases on the high seas in areas under American control, to disagreements between the states, between a citizen and a state, between citizens in different states and between a citizen and a foreign nation. The federal courts were also originally empowered with jurisdiction over problems airing between citizens of one state and the government of another state. The 11th amendment to the Constitution (ratified 1795) removed from federal jurisdiction those cases in which citizens of one state were the plaintiffs and the government of another state was the defendant. The amendment did not disturb the jurisdiction of the federal courts in cases in which a state government is a plaintiff and a citizen of another state the defendant. The federal courts have exclusive jurisdiction in all patent and copyright cases. By congressional law in 1898, the federal courts were empowered with original jurisdiction in all bankruptcy cases.

The courts established under the powers granted by Article III Section 1 & 2 of the Constitution are known as Constitutional Courts. Judges of the Constitutional courts are appointed for life by the President with the approval of the Senate. These courts are the *district courts, lower courts of original jurisdiction,* the *courts of appeals* (before 1948, known as the circuit court of appeals), exercising appellate jurisdiction over the district courts, and the *Supreme Court*. A district court functions in each of the more than ninety federal judicial districts and in the District of Columbia.

A court of appeals functions in each of the ten federal judicial circuits and in the District of Columbia, (the federal district court and the circuit court of appeals of the District of Columbia performs all of the same functions discharged in the states by the state courts). All of the lower federal courts operate under the uniform rules of procedure promulgated by the Supreme Court.

The Supreme Court of the United States is the highest appellate court in the country and is a court of original jurisdiction according to the Constitution *"in all cases affecting ambassadors, other public ministers and consuls, and those in which a state shall be a party"*. By virtue of its' power to declare legislation unconstitutional, the Supreme Court is the final arbitrator of all Constitutional questions.

Other federal courts, established by Congress under powers to be implied in other articles of the Constitution, are called legislative courts. These courts are the **Court of Claims, the Court of Customs and Patent Appeals, the Customs Court,** and the territorial courts established in the federally administered territories of the United States.

The special jurisdictions of these courts are defined by the Congress of the United States. (Except in the case of the territorial courts, which are courts of general jurisdiction), the specialized functions of these courts are suggested by their titles.

The State Courts - Each State has an independent system of courts operating under the laws and constitution of that particular individual state. Broadly speaking, the state courts are based on the English judicial system as it existed in colonial times, but as modified by succeeding statues. The character and names of the various courts differ from state to state, but the state courts as a whole have general jurisdiction, except in cases in which exclusive jurisdiction has by law been vested in the federal courts. In cases involving the United States Constitution or federal laws or treaties and such, the state courts are governed by the decisions of the Supreme Court of the United States and their decisions are subject to review by it.

Cases involving the federal Constitution, federal laws or treaties and the like, may be brought to either the state courts, or the federal courts. Ordinary **civil suits** not involving any of the aforementioned elements can be brought only to the state courts, except in cases of different state citizenship between the parties, in which case the suit may be brought to a federal court. By an act of Congress suits involving different federal questions or different state citizenship may be brought to a federal court only when it is a civil suit that involves $3,000 or more. All such cases that involve a smaller amount must be brought to a state court only. In accordance with a congressional law, a suit brought before a state court may be removed to a federal court at the option of the defendant.

Bear in mind that any statements about state courts, that is trying to give a typical explanation of all of them, is subject to many exceptions. The following may be taken as a general comprehensive statement of their respective jurisdictions, functions and organization.

County courts of general original jurisdiction exercise both criminal and civil jurisdictions in most states. A few states maintain separate courts of criminal and civil law inherited from the English judicial system. Between the lower courts and the supreme appellate courts of each state in a number of states, are intermediate appellate courts. Like the federal courts of appeals, appellate courts provide faster justice for individuals by disposing of a large number of cases that would otherwise be added to the overcrowded calendars of the higher courts. Courts of last resort, the highest appellate courts for the states in criminal and civil cases are usually called *State Supreme Courts*.

The state court system includes a number of minor, local courts with limited jurisdictions; these courts dispose of minor offenses and relatively small civil actions. Included in this classification are police and municipal courts in various cities and towns, and the courts presided over by justices of the peace in rural areas.

Skill 14.9   Identify the roles of the United States in international relations

The elements of the U.S. Government that pursue and conduct foreign policy are large and varied. Some are in the Legislative Branch; others are in the Executive Branch.

The most well known foreign policy advocate is the **Secretary of State**, who resides in the Executive Branch, is appointed by the President, and is confirmed by Congress. The Secretary of State is the country's primary ambassador to other countries, having prime responsibilities in this regard for attending international meetings, brokering peace deals, and negotiating treaties. The Secretary of State often acts as the "voice of the country," speaking for the interests of the United States to the rest of the world. A political element exists in this scenario as well: since the Secretary of State is appointed by the President, he or she is expected to follow the policy directives of the President. It is usually the case that the two people are of the same political party and share political views on important issues. The result of this is that, in some cases, the views and actions of the Secretary of State are in line with a few or a great many people, but not with all U.S. citizens; such is the nature of politics.

The Executive Branch has a **National Security Council**, which advises the President on matters of foreign policy. Members of this group are not nearly as visible or well traveled as the Secretary of State, but they do provide the President and other members of the Government with valuable information on goings-on elsewhere in the world.

The most numerous of the Executive Branch members involved in foreign policy are the **ambassadors**. Most countries throughout the world have ambassadors, people who reside in other countries in order to be lobbyists for their home countries' interests. The United States has ambassadors to most countries in the world; by the same token, most countries in the world have embassies, buildings and organizations that contain offices for these ambassadors. These ambassadors attend official functions in their "adopted" countries and speak for their countries in international meetings.

The Legislative Branch plays an important role in U.S. foreign policy as well. The Senate in particular is responsible for approving treaties and ambassadorial appointments. Both houses of Congress have committees of lawmakers who specialize in foreign policy. These lawmakers make a habit of keeping abreast of happenings elsewhere in the world and advising their fellow lawmakers on foreign businesses, issues and conflicts. These foreign policy-focused lawmakers often tour other countries and attend state functions, but they don't have the voice or responsibility of ambassadors.

Increasingly, state and local governments practice foreign policy as well. Governors and lawmakers of many states have trade agreements with other countries; these agreements are not on the order of national agreements, but they do deal with foreign relations all the same, mainly with economics. Local governments, too, get involved overseas. A good example of this is the growing practice of implementing a "sister city," whereby a city in the U.S. "adopts" a city in another country and exchanges ideas, goods, services and technology and other resources with its new "companion."

The United States has influenced other nations in many ways in the more than 200 years of its existence. That influence has gone the other way as well. The areas of this influence include political, economic, and cultural elements.

The democratic government familiar to most Americans is not an American invention, but is certainly an American export. American envoys have trumpeted the virtues of representative government throughout the world. This has encouraged many countries to embrace the ideals of democracy and has also inspired distrust and even hatred in other countries that have authoritarian governments.

The market economy of the United States has been a model of efficiency and openness for other countries as well. The spirit of free enterprise that drives the American economy has been a major export to burgeoning democracies as well as a source of scorn for those living in command economies.

Perhaps the most recognizable American export, though, is American culture. Some of the more visible elements of American culture seen nearly everywhere in the world are Coca-Cola and McDonald's. Other popular products are everywhere as well, including other fast-food chains, soft drinks and the eponymous iPod. American music and films are popular in other countries as well, as are the people who make them.

Another popular element of American life that has been successfully exported, nearly from the moment of the country's inception, is "the American Dream," the idea that anyone from anywhere else can come to America and find the freedom to pursue the job and lifestyle that they want. The United States was built on the backs of immigrants and immigration continues to be popular today.

COMPETENCY 15.0   KNOWLEDGE OF PRODUCTION, DISTRIBUTION, AND CONSUMPTION

Skill 15.1   Identify ways that limited resources affects the choices made by governments and individuals

Economics is the study of how a society allocates its scarce resources to satisfy what are basically unlimited and competing wants. Economics can also be defined as a study of the production, consumption and distribution of goods and services. Both of these definitions are the same. A fundamental fact of economics is that resources are scarce and that wants are infinite. The fact that scarce resources have to satisfy unlimited wants means that choices have to be made. If society uses their resources to produce good A, then it doesn't have those resources to produce good B. This trade-off is referred to as the opportunity cost, or the value of the sacrificed alternative.

On the consumption side of the market, consumers buy the goods and services that give them satisfaction, or utility. They want to obtain the most utility they can for their dollar. The quantity of goods and services that consumers are willing and able to purchase at different prices during a given period of time is referred to as demand. Since consumers buy the goods and services that give them satisfaction, this means that, for the most part, they don't buy the goods and services that they don't want that don't give them satisfaction. Consumers are, in effect, voting for the goods and services that they want with dollars or what is called dollar voting. Consumers are basically signaling firms as to how they want society's scarce resources used with their dollar votes. A good that society wants acquires enough dollar votes for the producer to experience profits – a situation where the firm's revenues exceed the firm's costs. The existence of profits indicate to the firm that it is producing the goods and services that consumers want and that society's scarce resources are being used in accordance with consumer preferences.

This process where consumers vote with their dollars is called consumer sovereignty. Consumers are basically directing the allocation of scarce resources in the economy with their dollar spending. Firms, who are in business to earn profit, hire resources or inputs, in accordance with consumer preferences. This is the way in which resources are allocated in a market economy.

Price plays an important role in a market economy. Demand was defined above. Supply is based on production costs. The supply of a good or service is defined as the quantities of a good or service that a producer is willing and able to sell at different prices during a given period of time. Market equilibrium occurs where the buying decisions of buyers are equal to the selling decisions of sellers, or where the demand and supply curves intersect. At this point, the quantity that sellers want to sell at a price is equal to the quantity the buyers want to buy at that same price. This is the market equilibrium price.

Skill 15.2   Compare and contrast the characteristics of different economic institutions (e.g., banks, credit unions, stock markets and the Federal Reserve)

Households, businesses and government are related through the circular flow diagram. They are all integral parts of the macro economy. There are two markets. The input market is where factor owners sell their factors and employers hire their inputs. The output market is where firms sell the output they produce with their inputs. It's where factors owners spend their incomes on goods and services.

There are two sectors, households and businesses. Households sell their factors in the input market and use their income to purchase goods and services in the output market. So wages, interest, rent and profit flow from the business sector to the household sector. Households that earn their factor incomes in the factor market spend their incomes on goods and services produced by businesses and sold in the output market. Receipts for goods and services flow from households to businesses. Government receives tax payments from households and businesses and provides services to businesses and households. Each of the three is a component of the aggregate sectors of the economy and as such makes a contribution to the GDP.

Adding financial institutions to the picture shows how monetary policy is implemented by the Fed. There are three components of monetary policy: the reserve ratio, the discount rate, and open market operations. Changes in any of these three components affect the amount of money in the banking system and thus, the level of spending in the economy.

The reserve ratio refers to the portion of deposits that banks are required to hold as vault cash or on deposit with the Fed. The purpose of this reserve ratio is to give the Fed a way to control the money supply. These funds can't be used for any other purpose. When the Fed changes the reserve ratio, it changes the money creation and lending ability of the banking system. When the Fed wants to expand the money supply it lowers the reserve ratio, leaving banks with more money to loan. This is one aspect of expansionary monetary policy. When the reserve ratio is increased, this results in banks having less money to make loans with, which is a form of contractionary monetary policy, which leads to a lower level of spending in the economy.

Another way in which monetary policy is implemented is by changing the discount rate. When banks have temporary cash shortages, they can borrow from the Fed. The interest rate on the funds they borrow is called the discount rate. Raising and lowering the discount rate is a way of controlling the money supply. Lowering the discount rate encourages banks to borrow from the Fed, instead of restricting their lending to deal with the temporary cash shortage. By encouraging banks to borrow, their lending ability is increased and this results in a higher level of spending in the economy. Lowering the discount rate is a form of expansionary monetary policy. Discouraging bank lending by raising the discount rate, then is a form of contractionary monetary policy.

The final tool of monetary policy is called open market operations. This consists of the Fed buying or selling government securities with the public or with the banking system. When the Fed sells bonds, it is taking money out of the banking system. The public and the banks pay for the bonds, thus resulting in fewer dollars in the economy and a lower level of spending. The Fed selling bonds is a form of contractionary monetary policy that leads to a lower level of spending in the economy. The Fed is expanding the money supply when it buys bonds from the public or the banking system because it is paying for those bonds with dollars that enter the income-expenditures stream. The result of the Fed buying bonds is to increase the level of spending in the economy.

Skill 15.3   Identify the role of markets from production, through distribution, to consumption

Free enterprise, individual entrepreneurship, competitive markets, and consumer sovereignty are all parts of a market economy. Individuals have the right to make their own decisions as to what they want to do as a career. The financial incentives are there for individuals who are willing to take the risk. A successful venture earns profit. It is these financial incentives that serve to motivate inventors and small businesses. The same is true for businesses. They are free to determine what production technique they want to use and what output they want to produce within the confines of the legal system. They can make investments based on their own decisions. Nobody is telling them what to do.

Competitive markets, relatively free from government interference are also a manifestation of the freedom that the U.S. economic system is based on. These markets function on the basis of supply and demand to determine output mix and resource allocation. There is no commissar dictating what is produced and how. Consumers buy the goods and services that give them satisfaction. They do not buy goods and services that they do not want that do not give them satisfaction. Consumers vote for goods and services that they want with dollars or what is called dollar voting. Consumers are basically signaling firms as to how they want society's scarce resources used with their dollar votes. A good that society wants, acquires enough dollar votes for the producer to experience profits – a situation where the firm's revenues exceed the firm's costs. The existence of profits indicate to the firm that it is producing the goods and services that consumers want and that society's scarce resources are being used in accordance with consumer preferences. When a firm does not have a profitable product, it is because that product is not tabulating enough dollar votes of consumers. Consumers don't want the good or service and they don't want society's scarce resources being used in its production.

This process where consumers vote with their dollars is called consumer sovereignty. Consumers are basically directing the allocation of scarce resources in the economy with the dollar spending. Firms, who are in business to earn profit, then hire resources, or inputs, in accordance with consumer preferences. This is the way in which resources are allocated in a market economy. This is the manner in which society achieves the output mix that it desires.

Skill 15.4 Identify factors to consider when making consumer decisions

Consumers do not have enough time and money to do everything that they want and to buy everything that they want. Time and money are scarce resources. If a consumer spends his time doing one activity, he is sacrificing another activity. For example, if the consumer spends the afternoon playing golf, he is sacrificing doing the garden work. If the consumer decides to enroll in evening classes, he has less time to spend with family and friends. Devoting time to one activity means that there is another activity that has to be sacrificed. There are only twenty-four hours in the day and people can only be in one place at a time.

Scarcity is evident in personal financial management. Scarcity here refers to dollars and paying bills. There are only so many dollars available. This is why responsible people don't go on wild spending sprees. Their paycheck has to cover the bills or they find themselves in the position of paying one bill and not another bill. There aren't enough dollars to buy both a diamond ring and a new car, so which one does the consumer want? Just as consumers have to choose how to spend their time, they also have to choose how to spend their dollars.

Scarcity means that consumers can't have all of the goods that they want and do all of the activities that they want to do. This is true on both a micro and a macro level. Choices have to be made and all of these choices involve opportunity costs.

Skill 15.5 Identify the economic interdependence among nations (e.g., trade, finance and movement of labor)

The theory of comparative advantage says that trade should be based on the comparative opportunity costs between two nations. The nation that can produce a good more cheaply should specialize in the production of that good and trade for the good in which it has the comparative disadvantage. In this way, both nations will experience gains from trade. A basis for trade exists if there are differing comparative costs in each country. Suppose country A can produce 10 units of good X, or ten units of good Y, with its resources. Country B can produce 30 units of X, or 10 units of Y, with its resources. What are the relative costs in each country? In country A, one X costs one unit of Y, and in country B, one X costs three units of Y. Good Y is cheaper in country B than it is in country A, $1/3X = 1 Y$ in country B versus $1Y = 1X$ in country A. Country B has the comparative advantage in the production of Y and country A has the comparative advantage in the production of good X. According to trade theory, each country should specialize in the production of the good in which it has the comparative advantage. Country B will devote all of its resources to the production of good Y and country A will devote of its resources to the production of good X. Each country will trade for the good in which it has the comparative disadvantage.

To determine the gains from trade, we must first consider the pre-trade production and consumption positions of both countries. In A, the pre-trade position was where they could have either 10 units of X or 10 units of Y or any combination in between. Let's assume country A chose a combination of 7Y and 3X. In country B their resources allowed either 30 units of Y or 10 units of X or any combination in between. Let's assume country B chose the combination of 18Y and 4 X. Now let's consider the production and consumption situation before and after trade. Before trade, the total production of good Y was 18 from country B and 7 from country A for a total of 25Y. After trade, total world production is 30Y, with country B specializing in the production of Y. For good X, the pre-trade situation was 3 units of X from country A and 4 units of X from country B, for a total of 7 units of X. After trade, with country A specializing in the production of X, total world production of X is 10 units. Specialization and trade according to comparative advantage results in the world having 30Y rather than 25Y and 10X instead of 7X. This increase is referred to as the gains from trade. Both countries have higher consumption levels of both goods due to specialization. This example refers to free unrestricted trade. Trade barriers introduce distortions.

In today's world, markets are international. Nations are all part of a global economy. No nation exists in isolationism or is totally independent of other nations. Isolationism is referred to as autarky or a closed economy. Membership is a global economy means that what one nation does affects other nations because economies are linked through international trade, commerce and finance. They all have open economies. International transactions affect the levels of income, employment, and prices in each of the trading economies.

The relative importance of trade is based on what percentage of Gross Domestic Product (GDP) trade constitutes. In a country like the United States, trade represents only a few percent of GDP. In other nations, trade may represent over fifty percent of GDP. For those countries, changes in international transactions can cause many economic fluctuations and problems.

Trade barriers are a way in which economic problems are caused in other countries. Suppose the domestic government is confronted with rising unemployment in the domestic industry due to cheaper foreign imports. Consumers are buying the cheaper foreign import instead of the higher priced domestic good. In order to protect domestic labor, government imposes a tariff, thus raising the price of the more efficiently produced foreign good. The result of the tariff is that consumers buy more of the domestic good and less of the foreign good. The problem is that the foreign good is the product of the foreign nation's labor. A decrease in the demand for the foreign good means foreign producers don't need as much labor, so they lay-off workers in the foreign country.

The result of the trade barrier is that unemployment has been exported from the domestic country to the foreign country. Treaties like NAFTA are a way of lowering or eliminating trade barriers on a regional basis. As trade barriers are lowered or eliminated, this causes changes in labor and output markets. Some grow; some shrink. These adjustments are taking place now for Canada, the United States and Mexico. Membership in a global economy adds another dimension to economics, in terms of aiding developing countries and in terms of national policies that are implemented.

Skill 15.6   Identify human, natural and capital resources and how these resources are used in the production of goods and services

A resource is an input into the production process. Resources are limited in supply; they are scarce. There are not enough of them to produce all of the goods and services that society wants. Resources are called "factors of production" and there are four factors of production: labor, capital, land and entrepreneurship. Labor refers to all kinds of labor used in the production process. It doesn't matter if the labor is skilled or unskilled, part-time or full-time. All laborers are selling their ability to produce goods and services. Capital refers to anything that is made or manufactured to be used in the production process. Included in this definition are plant, equipment, machines, tools and etc. Included are land and all natural resources – anything that is naturally occurring, like lumber, minerals, oil and etc. The entrepreneur is the individual that has the ability to combine the land, labor and capital to produce a good or service. The entrepreneur is the one who bears the risks of failure and loss and he is the one who will gain from the profits if the product is successful. Each of these four resources is combined in the production of every good and service. Every good and service that is produced uses some combination of each of the four inputs. The combination used is called the production process. The production process refers to the way the four factors are combined to produce the output. If the production technique uses a lot of machinery with very few laborers, then the production process is called capital-intensive. If the production process requires many workers with very little machinery, then it is said to be a labor-intensive production process. Whatever the production technique is, there are not enough resources to produce all of the goods and services that a society wants.

The scarcity of resources functions as a constraint on the amounts and kinds of goods and services that the economy can produce and consume. The scarcity of resources then affects the production, distribution and consumption decisions of the society. Production is determined by the available resource supply, both quantity and quality. For example, if there are not enough workers for a particular productive technique, then the smart owner will find machinery that requires fewer workers if he is going to stay in business in that area. Consumers can't consume goods and services that can't be produced or distributed. Since the scarcity of resources determines what can be produced, distributed and consumed, then defining economics as a study of how a society allocates its scarce resources to satisfy unlimited and competing desires is saying the same thing. Unlimited wants exist by consumers, businesses and government. Consumers want more consumer goods, businesses want more investments, and government wants more public goods. More capital goods mean fewer consumer goods because there are enough resources to produce more of both.

COMPETENCY 16.0   KNOWLEDGE OF INSTRUCTION AND ASSESSMENT OF THE SOCIAL SCIENCES

Skill 16.1   Identify appropriate resources for teaching social science concepts

There are many resources available for the teaching of social science concepts. The resources used should be appropriate to the learning objectives specified. The teacher wants to use different kinds of resources in order to make the subject matter more interesting to the student and to appeal to different learning styles. First of all a good textbook is required. This gives the student something that they can refer to and something to study from. Students generally like to have a text to refer to. The use of audio-video aides is also beneficial in the classroom environment. Most people are visual learners and will retain information better when it is in visual form. Audio-visual presentations, like movies, give students concepts in pictures that they will easily retain.

Library projects are good for students also. The library has an abundance of resources that students should become familiar with at an early age, so they learn to use the library. There are books and magazines that they can look through and read to expand their knowledge beyond the textbooks. Younger children, particularly, like to look at pictures. The computer also offers abundant opportunities as a teaching tool and resource. The internet provides a wealth of information on all topics and something can be found that is suitable for any age group. Children like to play games, so presenting the material in a game-like format is also a good teaching tool. Making little puzzles for vocabulary or letting them present the information in the form of a story or even a play helps them learn and retain various concepts. Field trips, if possible, are also a good way to expose children to various aspects of social science. Trips to museums, stock markets, the Federal Reserve and etc. are things children enjoy and remember. Today's world of technology makes a myriad of resources available to the teacher. The teacher should make use of as many of them as possible to keep the material more interesting for the student and to aide in their retention of the material.

Assessment methods are always important in teaching. Assessment methods are ways to determine if the student has sufficiently learned the required material. There are different ways of accomplishing this. Assessment methods basically mean asking a question in some way and receiving a response in some way from the student, whether it is written or verbal. The test is the usual method where the student answers questions on the material he has studied. Tests, of course, can be written or verbal. Tests for younger children can be game-like.

Students can be asked to draw lines connecting various associated symbols or to pick a picture representing something like landmarks in various countries. Other methods involve writing essays on various tropics. They don't have to be long, but just long enough for the student to demonstrate that he has adequate knowledge of a subject. Verbal reports can accomplish the same goal.

Younger children studying culture or geography, or even history, can role-play or act out various parts. They can even put on a little play about certain events or aspects of culture. They can even dress in ethnic costumes. This, along with facts about the culture of a country represents a more tangible experience to the student and will help them to remember the material better. The experiences will be associated with the facts and they will be better able to answer questions. They can be assessed based on their participation and knowledge of the subject.

Assigning projects for students to do is another good way of reinforcing learning. They are required to obtain information about a subject and organize that information into some sort of report, whether it is written or verbal. Children can use their imaginations in putting together the information and can be assessed on the quality and depth of the information included in the report.

Skill 16.2   Assessment methods in teaching social science concepts

Teaching strategies useful for studying social structures in various industries and sectors is to present an overview of the industry, what that industry is about, and what are its different components. Examine the different groups that are involved in the industry or sector and how those groups interact. For example, examine the labor movement as it occurred in these industries and look at the conflicts between labor and management. Explore the reasons why these conflicts occurred and why the union organization was required to solve the problems. Explain how these groups interact differently in the presence of a union and why?

Examine the effect these industries and sectors have had on the population. Communications enhanced commerce, just as transportation did. Markets were able to expand beyond their local areas. Industrialization not only led to more jobs for people but also to increased products available for consumption. The income from the jobs created by industrialization generated the money required to buy those products. Technology results in greater output at lower costs and also creates different occupations. Witness the growth of internet providers and website developers and other internet related companies. People can now work out of their home offices instead of traveling to an office.

The social structures in economics would be the different groups that form the economy. There is government, which consists of all three levels: federal, state and local and sometimes tribal. The business sector consists of private businesses, both large and small. And then there are consumers that buy the products of businesses with the incomes they receive from working for businesses. All three sectors interact with each other, as well as with the international sectors. All of their productive activities are included in the nations Gross Domestic Product figure.

DOMAIN IV.   **SCIENCE AND TECHNOLOGY**

COMPETENCY 17.0   KNOWLEDGE OF THE NATURE OF MATTER

Skill 17.1   **Identify the physical and chemical properties of matter (e.g., mass, volume, density and chemical change)**

Everything in our world is made up of **matter**, whether it is a rock, a building, an animal, or a person. Matter is defined by its characteristics: it takes up space and it has mass.

Mass is a measure of the amount of matter in an object. Two objects of equal mass will balance each other on a simple balance scale no matter where the scale is located. For instance, two rocks with the same amount of mass that are in balance on earth will also be in balance on the moon. They will feel heavier on earth than on the moon because of the gravitational pull of the earth. So, although the two rocks have the same mass, they will have different **weight.**

Weight is the measure of the earth's pull of gravity on an object. It can also be defined as the pull of gravity between other bodies. The units of weight measurement commonly used are the pound (English measure) and the kilogram (metric measure).

In addition to mass, matter also has the property of volume. **Volume** is the amount of cubic space that an object occupies. Volume and mass together give a more exact description of the object. Two objects may have the same volume, but different mass, or the same mass but different volumes and etc. For instance, consider two cubes that are each one cubic centimeter, one made from plastic, one from lead. They have the same volume, but the lead cube has more mass. The measure that we use to describe the cubes takes into consideration both the mass and the volume. **Density** is the mass of a substance contained per unit of volume. If the density of an object is less than the density of a liquid, the object will float in the liquid. If the object is denser than the liquid, then the object will sink.

Density is stated in grams per cubic centimeter (g/cm^3) where the gram is the standard unit of mass. To find an object's density, you must measure its mass and its volume. Then divide the mass by the volume ($D = m/V$).

To discover an object's density, first use a balance to find its mass. Then calculate its volume. If the object is a regular shape, you can find the volume by multiplying the length, width and height together; however, if it is an irregular shape, you can find the volume by seeing how much water it displaces. Measure the water in the container before and after the object is submerged. The difference will be the volume of the object.

Specific gravity is the ratio of the density of a substance to the density of water. For instance, the specific density of one liter of turpentine is calculated by comparing its mass (0.81 kg) to the mass of one liter of water (1 kg):

$$\frac{\text{mass of 1 L alcohol}}{\text{mass of 1 L water}} \quad = \quad \frac{0.81 \text{ kg}}{1.00 \text{ kg}} \quad = \quad 0.81$$

Physical properties and chemical properties of matter describe the appearance or behavior of a substance. A **physical property** can be observed without changing the identity of a substance. For instance, you can describe the color, mass, shape and volume of a book. **Chemical properties** describe the ability of a substance to be changed into new substances. Baking powder goes through a chemical change as it changes into carbon dioxide gas during the baking process.

Matter constantly changes. A **physical change** is a change that does not produce a new substance. The freezing and melting of water is an example of physical change. A **chemical change** (or chemical reaction) is any change of a substance into one or more other substances. Burning materials turn into smoke; a seltzer tablet fizzes into gas bubbles.

Skill 17.2   Identify the characteristics of elements, compounds and mixtures and distinguish among the states of matter (solids, liquids and gases)

An **element** is a substance that can not be broken down into other substances. To date, scientists have identified 109 elements: 89 are found in nature and 20 are synthetic.

An **atom** is the smallest particle of the element that retains the properties of that element. All of the atoms of a particular element are the same. The atoms of each element are different from the atoms of other elements.

Elements are assigned an identifying symbol of one or two letters. The symbol for oxygen is O and stands for one atom of oxygen; however, because oxygen atoms in nature are joined together is pairs, the symbol O_2 represents oxygen. This pair of oxygen atoms is a molecule. A **molecule** is the smallest particle of substance that can exist independently and has all of the properties of that substance. A molecule of most elements is made up of one atom; however, oxygen, hydrogen, nitrogen and chlorine molecules are made of two atoms each.

A **compound** is made of two or more elements that have been chemically combined. Atoms join together when elements are chemically combined. The result is that the elements lose their individual identities when they are joined. The compound that they become has different properties.

We use a formula to show the elements of a chemical compound. A **chemical formula** is a shorthand way of showing what is in a compound by using symbols and subscripts. The letter symbols let us know what elements are involved and the number subscript tells how many atoms of each element are involved. No subscript is used if there is only one atom involved. For example, carbon dioxide is made up of one atom of carbon (C) and two atoms of oxygen (O_2), so the formula would be represented as CO_2.

Substances can combine without a chemical change. A **mixture** is any combination of two or more substances in which the substances keep their own properties. A fruit salad is a mixture. So is an ice cream sundae, although you might not recognize each part if it is stirred together. Colognes and perfumes are the other examples. You may not readily recognize the individual elements; however, they can be separated.

Compounds and **mixtures** are similar in that they are made up of two or more substances; however, they have the following opposite characteristics:

Compounds:
1. Made up of one kind of particle
2. Formed during a chemical change
3. Broken down only by chemical changes
4. Properties are different from its parts
5. Has a specific amount of each ingredient.

Mixtures:
1. Made up of two or more particles
2. Not formed by a chemical change
3. Can be separated by physical changes
4. Properties are the same as its parts.
5. Does not have a definite amount of each ingredient.

Common compounds are **acids, bases, salts** and **oxides** and are classified according to their characteristics.

An **acid** contains one element of hydrogen (H); although it is never wise to taste a substance to identify it, acids have a sour taste. Vinegar and lemon juice are both acids and acids occur in many foods in a weak state. Strong acids can burn skin and destroy materials. Common acids and their uses include:

Sulfuric acid (H_2SO_4)	Used in medicines, alcohol, dyes and car batteries.
Nitric acid (HNO_3)	Used in fertilizers, explosives, cleaning materials
Carbonic Acid (H_2CO_3)	Used in soft drinks.
Acetic acid ($HC_2H_3O_2$)	Used in making plastics, rubber, photographic film and as a solvent

Bases have a bitter taste and the stronger ones feel slippery. Like acids, strong bases can be dangerous and should be handled carefully. All bases contain the elements oxygen and hydrogen (OH). Many household cleaning products contain bases. Common bases and their uses include:

Sodium hydroxide (NaOH)	Used in making soap, paper, vegetable oils and refining petroleum
Ammonium hydroxide (NH$_4$OH)	Making deodorants, bleaching and cleaning compounds
Potassium hydroxide (KOH)	Making soaps, drugs, dyes, alkaline batteries and purifying industrial gases
Calcium hydroxide (Ca(OH)$_2$)	Making cement and plaster

An **indicator** is a substance that changes color when it comes in contact with an acid or a base. Litmus paper is an indicator. Blue litmus paper turns red in an acid. Red litmus paper turns blue in a base.

A substance that is neither acid nor base is **neutral**. Neutral substances do not change the color of litmus paper.

Salt is formed when an acid and a base combine chemically. Water is also formed. The process is called **neutralization**. Table salt (NaCl) is an example of this process. Salts are also used in toothpaste, epsom salts and cream of tartar. Calcium chloride (CaCl$_2$) is used on frozen streets and walkways to melt the ice.

Oxides are compounds that are formed when oxygen combines with another element. Rust is an oxide formed when oxygen combines with iron.

The **phase of matter** (solid, liquid or gas) is identified by its shape and volume. A **solid** has a definite shape and volume. A **liquid** has a definite volume, but no shape. A **gas** has no shape or volume because it will spread out to occupy the entire space of whatever container it is in.

While plasma is really a type of gas, its properties are so unique that it is considered a unique phase of matter. **Plasma is a gas that has been ionized**, meaning that at least on electron has been removed from some of its atoms.

Plasma shares some characteristics with gas, specifically, the **high kinetic energy** of its molecules. Thus, plasma exists as a diffuse "cloud," though it sometimes includes tiny grains (this is termed dusty plasma). What most distinguishes plasma from gas is that it is **electrically conductive** and exhibits a strong response to electromagnetic fields. This property is a consequence of the **charged particles that result from the removal of electrons** from the molecules in the plasma.

Energy is the ability to cause change in matter. Applying heat to a frozen liquid changes it from solid back to liquid. Continue heating it and it will boil and give off steam, a gas.

Evaporation is the change in phase from liquid to gas. **Condensation** is the change in phase from gas to liquid.

Skill 17.3   Identify the basic components of the atom (i.e.: electrons, neutrons, protons)

An **atom** is a nucleus surrounded by a cloud with moving electrons.

The **nucleus** is the center of the atom. The positive particles inside the nucleus are called **protons**. The mass of a proton is about 2,000 times that of the mass of an electron. The number of protons in the nucleus of an atom is called the **atomic number**. All atoms of the same element have the same atomic number.

Neutrons are another type of particle in the nucleus. Neutrons and protons have about the same mass, but neutrons have no charge. Neutrons were discovered because scientists observed that not all atoms in neon gas have the same mass. They had identified isotopes. **Isotopes** of an element have the same number of protons in the nucleus, but have different masses. Neutrons explain the difference in mass. They have mass but no charge.

The mass of matter is measured against a standard mass such as the gram. Scientists measure the mass of an atom by comparing it to that of a standard atom. The result is relative mass. The **relative mass** of an atom is its mass expressed in terms of the mass of the standard atom. The isotope of the element carbon is the standard atom. It has six (6) neutrons and is called carbon-12. It is assigned a mass of 12 **atomic mass units (amu)**. Therefore, the **amu** is the standard unit for measuring the mass of an atom. It is equal to the mass of a carbon atom.

The **mass number** of an atom is the sum of its protons and neutrons. In any element, there is a mixture of isotopes, some having slightly more or slightly fewer protons and neutrons. The **atomic mass** of an element is an average of the mass numbers of its atoms.

The following table summarizes the terms used to describe atomic nuclei:

Term	Example	Meaning	Characteristic
Atomic Number	# protons (p)	same for all atoms of a given element	Carbon (C) atomic number = 6 (6p)
Mass number	# protons + # neutrons (p + n)	changes for different isotopes of an element	C-12 (6p + 6n) C-13 (6p + 7n)
Atomic mass	average mass of the atoms of the element	usually not a whole number	atomic mass of carbon equals 12.011

Each atom has an equal number of electrons (negative) and protons (positive). Therefore, atoms are neutral. Electrons orbiting the nucleus occupy energy levels that are arranged in order and the electrons tend to occupy the lowest energy level available. A **stable electron arrangement** is an atom that has all of its electrons in the lowest possible energy levels.

Each energy level holds a maximum number of electrons; however, an atom with more than one level does not hold more than 8 electrons in its outermost shell.

Level	Name	Max. # of Electrons
First	K shell	2
Second	L shell	8
Third	M shell	18
Fourth	N shell	32

This can help explain why chemical reactions occur. Atoms react with each other when their outer levels are unfilled. When atoms either exchange or share electrons with each other, these energy levels become filled and the atom becomes more stable.

As an electron gains energy, it moves from one energy level to a higher energy level. The electron can not leave one level until it has enough energy to reach the next level. **Excited electrons** are electrons that have absorbed energy and have moved farther from the nucleus.

Electrons can also lose energy. When they do, they fall to a lower level; however, they can only fall to the lowest level that has room for them. This explains why atoms do not collapse.

COMPETENCY 18.0   KNOWLDEGE OF FORCES, MOTION AND ENERGY

Skill 18.1   Apply knowledge of temperature and heat

Heat and temperature are different physical quantities. **Heat** is a measure of energy. **Temperature** is the measure of how hot (or cold) a body is with respect to a standard object.

Two concepts are important in the discussion of temperature changes. Objects are in thermal contact if they can affect each other's temperatures. Set a hot cup of coffee on a desk top. The two objects are in thermal contact with each other and will begin affecting each other's temperatures. The coffee will become cooler and the desktop warmer. Eventually, they will have the same temperature. When this happens, they are in **thermal equilibrium**.

We can not rely on our sense of touch to determine temperature because the heat from a hand may be conducted more efficiently by certain objects, making them feel colder. **Thermometers** are used to measure temperature. A small amount of mercury in a capillary tube will expand when heated. The thermometer and the object whose temperature it is measuring are put in contact long enough for them to reach thermal equilibrium. Then the temperature can be read from the thermometer scale.

Three temperature scales are used:

- **Celsius**: The freezing point of water is set at 0 and the steam (boiling) point is 100. The interval between the two is divided into 100 equal parts called degrees Celsius.

- **Fahrenheit**: The freezing point of water is 32 degrees and the boiling point is 212. The interval between is divided into 180 equal parts called degrees Fahrenheit.

Temperature readings can be converted from one to the other as follows.

Fahrenheit to Celsius   **Celsius to Fahrenheit**
$C = 5/9 (F - 32)$ $F = (9/5) C + 32$

Kelvin Scale has degrees the same size as the Celsius scale, but the zero point is moved to the triple point of water. Water inside a closed vessel is in thermal equilibrium in all three states (ice, water and vapor) at 273.15 degrees Kelvin. This temperature is equivalent to .01 degrees Celsius. Because the degrees are the same in the two scales, temperature changes are the same in Celsius and Kelvin.

Temperature readings can be converted from Celsius to Kelvin:

Celsius to Kelvin	**Kelvin to Celsius**
K = C + 273.15	C = K - 273.15

Heat is a measure of energy. If two objects that have different temperatures come into contact with each other, heat flows from the hotter object to the cooler.

Heat Capacity of an object is the amount of heat energy that it takes to raise the temperature of the object by one degree.

Heat capacity (C) per unit mass (m) is called **specific heat** (c):

$$c = \frac{C}{m} = \frac{Q / \Delta}{m}$$

Specific heats for many materials have been calculated and can be found in tables.

There are a number of ways that heat is measured. In each case, the measurement is dependent upon raising the temperature of a specific amount of water by a specific amount. These conversions of heat energy and work are called the **mechanical equivalent of heat**.

The **calorie** is the amount of energy that it takes to raise one gram of water one degree Celsius.

The **kilocalorie** is the amount of energy that it takes to raise one kilogram of water by one degree Celsius. Food calories are kilocalories.

In the International System of Units (**SI**), the calorie is equal to 4.184 **joules**.

A **British thermal unit (BTU)** = 252 calories = 1.054 kJ

Skill 18.2   Identify the types and characteristics of contact forces (e.g., mechanical) and at-a-distance forces (e.g., magnetic, gravitational and electrostatic)

Dynamics is the study of the relationship between motion and the forces affecting motion. **Force** causes motion.

Mass and weight are not the same quantities. An object's **mass** gives it a reluctance to change its current state of motion. It is also the measure of an object's resistance to acceleration. The force that the earth's gravity exerts on an object with a specific mass is called the object's weight on earth. Weight is a force that is measured in Newtons. Weight (W) = mass times acceleration due to gravity (**W = mg**). To illustrate the difference between mass and weight, picture two rocks of equal mass on a balance scale. If the scale is balanced in one place, it will be balanced everywhere, regardless of the gravitational field; however, the weight of the stones would vary on a spring scale, depending upon the gravitational field. In other words, the stones would be balanced both on earth and on the moon; however, the weight of the stones would be greater on earth than on the moon.

Surfaces that touch each other have a certain resistance to motion. This resistance is **friction.**

1.   The materials that make up the surfaces will determine the magnitude of the frictional force.
2.   The frictional force is independent of the area of contact between the two surfaces.
3.   The direction of the frictional force is opposite to the direction of motion.
4.   The frictional force is proportional to the normal force between the two surfaces in contact.

Static friction describes the force of friction of two surfaces that are in contact, but do not have any motion relative to each other, such as a block sitting on an inclined plane. **Kinetic friction** describes the force of friction of two surfaces in contact with each other when there is relative motion between the surfaces.

When an object moves in a circular path, a force must be directed toward the center of the circle in order to keep the motion going. This constraining force is called **centripetal force**. Gravity is the centripetal force that keeps a satellite circling the earth.

Electrical force is the influential power resulting from electricity as an attractive or repulsive interaction between two charged objects. The electric force is determined using Coulomb's law. As shown below, the appropriate unit on charge is the Coulomb (C) and the appropriate unit on distance is meters (m). Use of these units will result in a force expressed in units of Newtons. The demand for these units emerges from the units on Coulomb's constant.

$$F_{elect} = k \cdot Q_1 \cdot Q_2 / d^2$$

There is something of a mystery as to how objects affect each other when they are not in mechanical contact. Newton wrestled with the concept of "action-at-a-distance" (as Electrical Force is now classified) and eventually concluded that it was necessary for there to be some form of ether or intermediate medium, which made it possible for one object to transfer force to another. We now know that no ether exists. It is possible for objects to exert forces on one another without any medium to transfer the force. From our fluid notion of electrical forces we still associate forces as being due to the exchange of something between the two objects. The electrical field force acts between two charges, in the same way that the gravitational field force acts between two masses.

Magnetic Force- Magnetized items interact with other items in very specific ways. If a magnet is brought close enough to a ferromagnetic material (that is not magnetized itself) the magnet will strongly attract the ferromagnetic material regardless of orientation. Both the north and south pole of the magnet will attract the other item with equal strength. IN opposition, diamagnetic materials weakly repel a magnetic field. This occurs regardless of the north/south orientation of the field. Paramagnetic materials are weakly attracted to a magnetic field. This occurs regardless of the north/south orientation of the field. **Calculating** the attractive or repulsive magnetic force between two magnets is, in the general case, an extremely complex operation, as it depends on the shape, magnetization, orientation and separation of the magnets.

In the **Nuclear Force** the protons in the nucleus of an atom are positively charged. If protons interact, they are usually pushed apart by the electromagnetic force; however, when two or more nuclei come VERY close together, the nuclear force comes into play. The nuclear force is a hundred times stronger than the electromagnetic force so the nuclear force may be able to "glue" the nuclei together so fusion can happen. The nuclear force is also known as the strong force. The nuclear force keeps together the most basic of elementary particles, the quarks. Quarks combine together to form the protons and neutrons in the atomic nucleus.

The **force of gravity** is the force at which the earth, moon or other massively large object attracts another object towards itself. By definition, this is the weight of the object. All objects upon earth experience a force of gravity that is directed "downward" towards the center of the earth. The force of gravity on earth is always equal to the weight of the object as found by the equation:

$$\text{Fgrav} = m * g$$

where $g = 9.8$ m/s^2 (on Earth)
and m = mass (in kg)

Skill 18.3   Apply knowledge of simple machines to solve problems involving work

Forces on objects at rest – The formula F= m/a is shorthand for force equals mass over acceleration. An object will not move unless the force is strong enough to move the mass. Also, there can be opposing forces holding the object in place. For instance, a boat may want to be forced by the currents to drift away but an equal and opposite force is a rope holding it to a dock.

Forces on a moving object - Overcoming inertia is the tendency of any object to oppose a change in motion. An object at rest tends to stay at rest. An object that is moving tends to keep moving.

Inertia and circular motion – The centripetal force is provided by the high banking of the curved road and by friction between the wheels and the road. This inward force that keeps an object moving in a circle is called centripetal force.

Work is done on an object when an applied force moves through a distance.

Power is the work done divided by the amount of time that it took to do it. (Power = Work / time)

Simple machines include the following:

1.   Inclined plane
2.   Lever
3.   Wheel and axle
4.   Pulley

Compound machines are two or more simple machines working together. A wheelbarrow is an example of a complex machine. It uses a lever, a wheel and an axle. Machines of all types ease workload by changing the size or direction of an applied force. The amount of effort saved when using simple or complex machines is called mechanical advantage or MA.

Skill 18.4   Identify the properties and characteristics of sounds as they apply to everyday situations

The **pitch** of a sound depends on the **frequency** that the ear receives. High-pitched sound waves have high frequencies. High notes are produced by an object that is vibrating at a greater number of times per second than one that produces a low note.

The **intensity** of a sound is the amount of energy that crosses a unit of area in a given unit of time. The loudness of the sound is subjective and depends upon the effect on the human ear. Two tones of the same intensity, but different pitches, may appear to have different loudness. The intensity level of sound is measured in decibels. Normal conversation is about 60 decibels. A power saw is about 110 decibels.

The **amplitude** of a sound wave determines its loudness. Loud sound waves have large amplitudes. The larger the sound wave, the more energy is needed to create the wave.

An oscilloscope is useful in studying waves because it gives a picture of the wave that shows the crest and trough of the wave. **Interference** is the interaction of two or more waves that meet. If the waves interfere constructively, the crest of each one meets the crests of the others. They combine into a crest with greater amplitude. As a result, you hear a louder sound. If the waves interfere destructively, then the crest of one meets the trough of another. They produce a wave with lower amplitude that produces a softer sound.

If you have two tuning forks that produce different pitches, then one will produce sounds of a slightly higher frequency. When you strike the two forks simultaneously, you may hear beats. **Beats** are a series of loud and soft sounds. This is because when the waves meet, the crests combine at some points and produce loud sounds. At other points, they nearly cancel each other out and produce soft sounds.

Sound waves are produced by a vibrating body. The vibrating object moves forward and compresses the air in front of it, then reverses direction so that the pressure on the air is lessened and expansion of the air molecules occurs. One compression and expansion creates one longitudinal wave. Sound can be transmitted through any gas, liquid or solid; however, it cannot be transmitted through a vacuum, because there are no particles present to vibrate and bump into their adjacent particles to transmit the wave.

The vibrating air molecules move back and forth parallel to the direction of motion of the wave as they pass the energy from adjacent air molecules (closer to the source) to air molecules farther away from the source.

Skill 18.5   Apply knowledge of light and optics to practical applications (i.e.: reflection, refraction and diffusion)

Shadows illustrate one of the basic properties of light. Light travels in a straight line. If you put your hand between a light source and a wall, you will interrupt the light and produce a shadow.

When light hits a surface, it is **reflected**. The angle of the incoming light (angle of incidence) is the same as the angle of the reflected light (angle of reflection). It is this reflected light that allows you to see objects. You see the objects when the reflected light reaches your eyes.

Different surfaces reflect light differently. Rough surfaces scatter light in many different directions. A smooth surface reflects the light in one direction. If it is smooth and shiny (like a mirror) you see your image in the surface.

When light enters a different medium, it bends. This bending, or change of speed, is called **refraction**.

Light can be **diffracted** or bent around the edges of an object. Diffraction occurs when light goes through a narrow slit. As light passes through it, the light bends slightly around the edges of the slit. You can demonstrate this by pressing your thumb and forefinger together, making a very thin slit between them. Hold them about 8 cm from your eye and look at a distant source of light. The pattern you observe is caused by the diffraction of light.

Skill 18.6   Identify the regions of the electromagnetic spectrum and the relative wavelengths and energy associated with each region

The electromagnetic spectrum is measured in frequency (f) in hertz and wavelength (λ) in meters. The frequency times the wavelength of every electromagnetic wave equals the speed of light (3.0×10^9 meters/second).

Roughly, the range of wavelengths of the electromagnetic spectrum is:

	f		$\underline{\lambda}$	
Radio waves	$10^{5} - 10^{-1}$	hertz	$10^{3} - 10^{9}$	meters
Microwaves	$10^{-1} - 10^{-3}$	hertz	$10^{9} - 10^{11}$	meters
Infrared radiation	$10^{-3} - 10^{-6}$	hertz	$10^{11.2} - 10^{14.3}$	meters
Visible light	$10^{-6.2} - 10^{-6.9}$	hertz	$10^{14.3} - 10^{15}$	meters
Ultraviolet radiation	$10^{-7} - 10^{-9}$	hertz	$10^{15} - 10^{17.2}$	meters
X-Rays	$10^{-9} - 10^{-11}$	hertz	$10^{17.2} - 10^{19}$	meters
Gamma Rays	$10^{-11} - 10^{-15}$	hertz	$10^{19} - 10^{23.25}$	meters

Skill 18.7 Identify characteristics and examples of static electricity

Electrostatics is the study of stationary electric charges. A plastic rod that is rubbed with fur or a glass rod that is rubbed with silk will become electrically charged and will attract small pieces of paper. The charge on the plastic rod rubbed with fur is negative and the charge on glass rod rubbed with silk is positive.

Electrically charged objects share these characteristics:

1. Like charges repel one another.
2. Opposite charges attract each other.
3. Charge is conserved.

A neutral object has no net change. If the plastic rod and fur are initially neutral, when the rod becomes charged by the fur a negative charge is transferred from the fur to the rod. The net negative charge on the rod is equal to the net positive charge on the fur.

Materials through which electric charges can easily flow are called **conductors**. Metals that are good conductors include silicon and boron. On the other hand, an **insulator** is a material through which electric charges do not move easily, if at all. Examples of insulators would be the nonmetal elements of the periodic table. A simple device used to indicate the existence of a positive or negative charge is called an **electroscope**. An electroscope is made up of a conducting knob and attached to it are very lightweight conducting leaves usually made of foil (gold or aluminum). When a charged object touches the knob, the leaves push away from each other because like charges repel. It is not possible to tell whether if the charge is positive or negative.

Charging by induction:

Touch the knob with a finger while a charged rod is nearby. The electrons will be repulsed and flow out of the electroscope through the hand. If the hand is removed while the charged rod remains close, the electroscope will retain the charge.

When an object is rubbed with a charged rod, the object will take on the same charge as the rod; however, charging by induction gives the object the opposite charge as that of the charged rod.

Grounding charge:

Charge can be removed from an object by connecting it to the earth through a conductor. The removal of static electricity by conduction is called **grounding**.

Skill 18.8   Apply knowledge of currents, circuits, conductors and insulators to everyday situations

Electricity can be used to change the chemical composition of a material. For instance, when electricity is passed through water, it breaks the water down into hydrogen gas and oxygen gas.

Circuit breakers in a home monitor the electric current. If there is an overload, the circuit breaker will create an open circuit, stopping the flow of electricity.

Computers can be made small enough to fit inside a plastic credit card by creating what is known as a solid state device. In this device, electrons flow through solid material such as silicon.

Resistors are used to regulate volume on a television or radio or through a dimmer switch for lights.

A bird can sit on an electrical wire without being electrocuted because the bird and the wire have about the same potential; however, if that same bird would touch two wires at the same time he would not have to worry about flying south next year.

When caught in an electrical storm, a car is a relatively safe place from lightening because of the resistance of the rubber tires. A metal building would not be safe unless there was a lightening rod that would attract the lightening and conduct it into the ground.

Skill 18.9   Identify types of magnets, their characteristics, and their applications to everyday situations

Magnets have a north pole and a south pole. Like poles repel and opposing poles attract. A **magnetic field** is the space around a magnet where its force will affect objects. The closer you are to a magnet, the stronger the force. As you move away, the force becomes weaker.

Some materials act as magnets and some do not. This is because magnetism is a result of electrons in motion. The most important motion in this case is the spinning of the individual electrons. Electrons spin in pairs in opposite directions in most atoms. Each spinning electron has the magnetic field that it creates canceled out by the electron that is spinning in the opposite direction.

In an atom of iron, there are four unpaired electrons. The magnetic fields of these are not canceled out. Their fields add up to make a tiny magnet. Their fields exert forces on each other setting up small areas in the iron called **magnetic domains** where atomic magnetic fields line up in the same direction.

You can make a magnet out of an iron nail by stroking the nail in the same direction repeatedly with a magnet. This causes poles in the atomic magnets in the nail to be attracted to the magnet. The tiny magnetic fields in the nail line up in the direction of the magnet. The magnet causes the domains pointing in its direction to grow in the nail. Eventually, one large domain results and the nail becomes a magnet.

A bar magnet has a north pole and a south pole. If you break the magnet in half, each piece will have a north and south pole.

The earth has a magnetic field. In a compass, a tiny, lightweight magnet is suspended and will line its south pole up with the North Pole magnet of the earth.

A magnet can be made out of a coil of wire by connecting the ends of the coil to a battery. When the current goes through the wire, the wire acts in the same way that a magnet does, it is called an **electromagnet**. The poles of the electromagnet will depend upon which way the electric current runs. An electromagnet can be made more powerful in three ways:

1. Make more coils.
2. Put an iron core (nail) inside the coils.
3. Use more battery power.

Telegraphs use electromagnets to work. When a telegraph key is pushed, current flows through a circuit, turning on an electromagnet which attracts an iron bar. The iron bar hits a sounding board which responds with a click. Release the key and the electromagnet turns off. Messages can be sent around the world in this way.

Scrap metal can be removed from waste materials by the use of a large electromagnet that is suspended from a crane. When the electromagnet is turned on, the metal in the pile of waste will be attracted to it. All other materials will stay on the ground.

Air conditioners, vacuum cleaners and washing machines use electric motors. An electric motor uses an electromagnet to change electric energy into mechanical energy.

Skill 18.10 Identify types of energy (e.g., chemical, electrical, nuclear, mechanical, magnetic, radiant and solar)

The law of conservation of energy states that energy is neither created nor destroyed. Thus, energy changes form when energy transactions occur in nature. The following are the major forms energy can take.

Thermal energy is the total internal energy of objects created by the vibration and movement of atoms and molecules. Heat is the transfer of thermal energy.

Acoustical energy, or sound energy, is the movement of energy through an object in waves. Energy that forces an object to vibrate creates sound.
Radiant energy is the energy of electromagnetic waves. Light, visible and otherwise, is an example of radiant energy.

Electrical energy is the movement of electrical charges in an electromagnetic field. Examples of electrical energy are electricity and lightning.

Chemical energy is the energy stored in the chemical bonds of molecules. For example, the energy derived from gasoline is chemical energy.

Mechanical energy is the potential and kinetic energy of a mechanical system. Rolling balls, car engines and body parts in motion exemplify mechanical energy.

Nuclear energy is the energy present in the nucleus of atoms. Division, combination or collision of nuclei release nuclear energy.

Because the total energy in the universe is constant, energy continually transitions between forms. For example, an engine burns gasoline converting the chemical energy of the gasoline into mechanical energy, a plant converts radiant energy of the sun into chemical energy found in glucose, or a battery converts chemical energy into electrical energy.

COMPETENCY 19.0   KNOWLEDGE OF PROCESSES THAT SHAPE THE EARTH

Skill 19.1   Identify characteristics of geologic formations, the mechanisms by which they were formed, and their relationship to the movement of tectonic plates

Orogeny is the term given to natural mountain building.

A mountain is terrain that has been raised high above the surrounding landscape by volcanic action, or some form of tectonic plate collisions. The plate collisions could be intercontinental or ocean floor collisions with a continental crust (subduction). The physical composition of mountains would include igneous, metamorphic or sedimentary rocks; some may have rock layers that are tilted or distorted by plate collision forces.

There are many different types of mountains. The physical attributes of a mountain range depends upon the angle at which plate movement thrust layers of rock to the surface. Many mountains (Adirondacks, Southern Rockies) were formed along high angle faults.

Folded mountains (Alps, Himalayas) are produced by the folding of rock layers during their formation. The Himalayas are the highest mountains in the world and contain Mount Everest which rises almost 9 km above sea level. The Himalayas were formed when India collided with Asia. The movement which created this collision is still in process at the rate of a few centimeters per year.

Fault-block mountains (Utah, Arizona and New Mexico) are created when plate movement produces tension forces instead of compression forces. The area under tension produces normal faults and rock along these faults is displaced upward.

Dome mountains are formed as magma tries to push up through the crust but fails to break the surface. Dome mountains resemble a huge blister on the earth's surface.

Upwarped mountains (Black Hills of S.D.) are created in association with a broad arching of the crust. They can also be formed by rock thrust upward along high angle faults.

Volcanism is the term given to the movement of magma through the crust and its emergence as lava onto the earth's surface. Volcanic mountains are built up by successive deposits of volcanic materials.

An active volcano is one that is presently erupting or building to an eruption. A dormant volcano is one that is between eruptions, but still shows signs of internal activity that might lead to an eruption in the future. An extinct volcano is said to be no longer capable of erupting. Most of the world's active volcanoes are found along the rim of the Pacific Ocean, which is also a major earthquake zone. This curving belt of active faults and volcanoes is often called the Ring of Fire.

The world's best known volcanic mountains include: Mount Etna in Italy and Mount Kilimanjaro in Africa. The Hawaiian Islands are actually the tops of a chain of volcanic mountains that rise from the ocean floor.

There are three types of volcanic mountains: shield volcanoes, cinder cones and composite volcanoes.

Shield Volcanoes are associated with quiet eruptions. Lava emerges from the vent or opening in the crater and flows freely out over the earth's surface until it cools and hardens into a layer of igneous rock. A repeated lava flow builds this type of volcano into the largest volcanic mountain. Mauna Loa found in Hawaii, is the largest volcano on earth.

Cinder Cone Volcanoes are associated with explosive eruptions as lava is hurled high into the air in a spray of droplets of various sizes. These droplets cool and harden into cinders and particles of ash before falling to the ground. The ash and cinder pile up around the vent to form a steep, cone-shaped hill called the cinder cone. Cinder cone volcanoes are relatively small but may form quite rapidly.

Composite Volcanoes are described as being built by both lava flows and layers of ash and cinders. Mount Fuji in Japan, Mount St. Helens in Washington, USA and Mount Vesuvius in Italy are all famous composite volcanoes.

Mechanisms of producing mountains

Mountains are produced by different types of mountain-building processes. Most major mountain ranges are formed by the processes of folding and faulting.

Folded Mountains are produced by the folding of rock layers. Crustal movements may press horizontal layers of sedimentary rock together from the sides, squeezing them into wavelike folds. Up-folded sections of rock are called anticlines; down-folded sections of rock are called synclines. The Appalachian Mountains are an example of folded mountains with long ridges and valleys in a series of anticlines and synclines formed by folded rock layers.

Faults are fractures in the earth's crust which have been created by either tension or compression forces transmitted through the crust. These forces are produced by the movement of separate blocks of crust.

Faultings are categorized on the basis of the relative movement between the blocks on both sides of the fault plane. The movement can be horizontal, vertical or oblique.

A dip-slip fault occurs when the movement of the plates is vertical and opposite. The displacement is in the direction of the inclination, or dip, of the fault. Dip-slip faults are classified as normal faults when the rock above the fault plane moves down relative to the rock below.

Reverse faults are created when the rock above the fault plane moves up relative to the rock below. Reverse faults having a very low angle to the horizontal are also referred to as thrust faults.

Faults in which the dominant displacement is horizontal movement along the trend or strike (length) of the fault are called **strike-slip faults**. When a large strike-slip fault is associated with plate boundaries it is called a **transform fault**. The San Andreas Fault in California is a well-known transform fault.

Faults that have both vertical and horizontal movement are called **oblique-slip faults**.

When lava cools, igneous rock is formed. This formation can occur either above ground or below ground.

Intrusive rock includes any igneous rock that was formed below the earth's surface. Batholiths are the largest structures of intrusive type rock and are composed of near granite materials; they are the core of the Sierra Nevada Mountains.

Extrusive rock includes any igneous rock that was formed at the earth's surface.

Dikes are old lava tubes formed when magma entered a vertical fracture and hardened. Sometimes magma squeezes between two rock layers and hardens into a thin horizontal sheet called a **sill**. A **laccolith** is formed in much the same way as a sill, but the magma that creates a laccolith is very thick and does not flow easily. It pools and forces the overlying strata creating an obvious surface dome.

A **caldera** is normally formed by the collapse of the top of a volcano. This collapse can be caused by a massive explosion that destroys the cone and empties most if not all of the magma chamber below the volcano. The cone collapses into the empty magma chamber forming a caldera.

An inactive volcano may have magma solidified in its pipe. This structure, called a volcanic neck, is resistant to erosion and today may be the only visible evidence of the past presence of an active volcano.

When lava cools, igneous rock is formed. This formation can occur either above ground or below ground.

Glaciation

A continental glacier covered a large part of North America during the most recent ice age. Evidence of this glacial coverage remains as abrasive grooves, large boulders from northern environments dropped in southerly locations, glacial troughs created by the rounding out of steep valleys by glacial scouring, and the remains of glacial sources called cirques that were created by frost wedging the rock at the bottom of the glacier. Remains of plants and animals found in warm climate have been discovered in the moraines and out wash plains help to support the theory of periods of warmth during the past ice ages.

The Ice Age began about 2 -3 million years ago. This age saw the advancement and retreat of glacial ice over millions of years. Theories relating to the origin of glacial activity include Plate Tectonics, where it can be demonstrated that some continental masses, now in temperate climates, were at one time blanketed by ice and snow. Another theory involves changes in the earth's orbit around the sun, changes in the angle of the earth's axis, and the wobbling of the earth's axis. Support for the validity of this theory has come from deep ocean research that indicates a correlation between climatic sensitive micro-organisms and the changes in the earth's orbital status.

About 12,000 years ago, a vast sheet of ice covered a large part of the northern United States. This huge, frozen mass had moved southward from the northern regions of Canada as several large bodies of slow-moving ice, or glaciers. A time period in which glaciers advance over a large portion of a continent is called an ice age. A glacier is a large mass of ice that moves or flows over the land in response to gravity. Glaciers form among high mountains and in other cold regions.

There are two main types of glaciers: valley glaciers and continental glaciers. Erosion by valley glaciers is characteristic of U-shaped erosion. They produce sharp peaked mountains such as the Matterhorn in Switzerland. Erosion by continental glaciers often rides over mountains in their paths leaving smoothed, rounded mountains and ridges.

Relationship to the movement of tectonic plates

Data obtained from many sources led scientists to develop the theory of plate tectonics. This theory is the most current model that explains not only the movement of the continents, but also the changes in the earth's crust caused by internal forces.

Plates are rigid blocks of earth's crust and upper mantle. These rigid solid blocks make up the lithosphere. The earth's lithosphere is broken into nine large sections and several small ones. These moving slabs are called plates. The major plates are named after the continents they are "transporting."

The plates float on and move with a layer of hot, plastic-like rock in the upper mantle. Geologists believe that the heat currents circulating within the mantle cause this plastic zone of rock to slowly flow, carrying along the overlying crustal plates.

Movement of these crustal plates creates areas where the plates diverge as well as areas where the plates converge. A major area of divergence is located in the Mid-Atlantic. Currents of hot mantle rock rise and separate at this point of divergence creating new oceanic crust at the rate of 2 to 10 centimeters per year. Convergence is when the oceanic crust collides with either another oceanic plate or a continental plate. The oceanic crust sinks forming an enormous trench and generating volcanic activity. Convergence also includes continent to continent plate collisions. When two plates slide past one another a transform fault is created.

These movements produce many major features of the earth's surface, such as mountain ranges, volcanoes and earthquake zones. Most of these features are located at plate boundaries, where the plates interact by spreading apart, pressing together, or sliding past each other. These movements are very slow, averaging only a few centimeters a year.

Boundaries form between spreading plates where the crust is forced apart in a process called rifting. Rifting generally occurs at mid-ocean ridges. Rifting can also take place within a continent, splitting the continent into smaller landmasses that drift away from each other, thereby forming an ocean basin between them. The Red Sea is a product of rifting. As the seafloor spreading takes place, new material is added to the inner edges of the separating plates. In this way the plates grow larger, and the ocean basin widens. This is the process that broke up the super continent Pangaea and created the Atlantic Ocean.

Boundaries between plates that are colliding are zones of intense crustal activity. When a plate of ocean crust collides with a plate of continental crust the more dense oceanic plate slides under the lighter continental plate and plunges into the mantle. This process is called **subduction** and the site where it takes place is called a subduction zone. A subduction zone is usually seen on the sea-floor as a deep depression called a trench.

The crustal movement which is identified by plates sliding sideways past each other produces a plate boundary characterized by major faults that are capable of unleashing powerful earth-quakes. The San Andreas Fault forms such a boundary between the Pacific Plate and the North American Plate.

Skill 19.2   Identify how fossils are formed and how fossils are used in interpreting the past and extrapolating to the future

A fossil is the remains or trace of an ancient organism that has been preserved naturally in the Earth's crust. Sedimentary rocks usually are rich sources of fossil remains. Those fossils found in layers of sediment were embedded in the slowly forming sedimentary rock strata. The oldest fossils known are the traces of 3.5 billion year old bacteria found in sedimentary rocks. Few fossils are found in metamorphic rock and virtually none found in igneous rocks. The magma is so hot that any organism trapped in the magma is destroyed.

The fossil remains of a woolly mammoth embedded in ice were found by a group of Russian explorers; however, the best-preserved animal remains have been discovered in natural tar pits. When an animal accidentally fell into the tar, it became trapped sinking to the bottom. Preserved bones of the saber-toothed cat have been found in tar pits.

Prehistoric insects have been found trapped in ancient amber or fossil resin that was excreted by some extinct species of pine trees. Fossil molds are the hollow spaces in a rock previously occupied by bones or shells. A fossil cast is a fossil mold that fills with sediments or minerals that later hardens forming a cast.

Fossil tracks are the imprints in hardened mud left behind by birds or animals.

Skill 19.3   Interpret geologic maps, including topographic and weather maps that contain symbols, scales, legends, directions, latitudes and longitudes

Decode map symbols

A system of imaginary lines has been developed that helps people describe exact locations on Earth. Looking at a globe of Earth, you will see lines drawn on it. The equator is drawn around Earth halfway between the North and South Poles. Latitude is a term used to describe distance in degrees north or south of the equator. Lines of latitude are drawn east and west parallel to the equator. Degrees of latitude range from 0 at the equator to 90 at either the North Pole or South Pole. Lines of latitude are also called parallels.

Lines drawn north and south at right angles to the equator and from pole to pole are called meridians. Longitude is a term used to describe distances in degrees east or west of a 0° meridian. The prime meridian is the 0° meridian and it passes through Greenwich, England.

Time zones are determined by longitudinal lines. Each time zone represents one hour. Since there are 24 hours in one complete rotation of the Earth, there are 24 international time zones. Each time zone is roughly 15° wide. While time zones are based on meridians, they do not strictly follow lines of longitude. Time zone boundaries are subject to political decisions and have been moved around cities and other areas at the whim of the electorate.

The International Date Line is the 180° meridian and it is on the opposite side of the world from the prime meridian. The International Date Line is one-half of one day or 12 time zones from the prime meridian. If you were traveling west across the International Date Line, you would lose one day. If you were traveling east across the International Date Line, you would gain one day.

Principles of contouring

A contour line is a line on a map representing an imaginary line on the ground that has the same elevation above sea level along its entire length. Contour intervals usually are given in even numbers or as a multiple of five. In mapping mountains, a large contour interval is used. Small contour intervals may be used where there are small differences in elevation.

Relief describes how much variation in elevation an area has. Rugged or high relief, describes an area of many hills and valleys. Gentle or low relief describes a plain area or a coastal region. Five general rules should be remembered in studying contour lines on a map.

1. Contour lines close around hills and basins or depressions. Hachure lines are used to show depressions. Hachures are short lines placed at right angles to the contour line and they always point toward the lower elevation. A contour line that has hachures is called a depression contour.
2. Contours lines never cross. Contour lines are sometimes very close together. Each contour line represents a certain height above sea level.
3. Contour lines appear on both sides of an area where the slope reverses direction. Contour lines show where an imaginary horizontal plane would slice through a hillside or cut both sides of a valley.
4. Contours lines form V's that point upstream when they cross streams. Streams cut beneath the general elevation of the land surface, and contour lines follow a valley.
5. All contours lines either close (connect) or extend to the edge of the map. No map is large enough to have all its contour lines close.

Interpret maps and imagery

Like photographs, maps readily display information that would be impractical to express in words. Maps that show the shape of the land are called topographic maps. Topographic maps, which are also referred to as quadrangles, are generally classified according to publication scale. Relief refers to the difference in elevation between any two points. Maximum relief refers to the difference in elevation between the high and low points in the area being considered. Relief determines the contour interval, which is the difference in elevation between succeeding contour lines that are used on topographic maps.

Map scales express the relationship between distance or area on the map to the true distance or area on the earth's surface. It is expressed as so many feet (miles, meters, km or degrees) per inch (cm) of map.

Skill 19.4   Identify the major groups of rocks, examples of each, and the processes of their formation

Rocks

Rocks are simply aggregates of minerals. Rocks are classified by their differences in chemical composition and mode of formation. Generally, three classes are recognized: igneous, sedimentary and metamorphic; however, it is common that one type of rock is transformed into another and this is known as the rock cycle.

Igneous rocks are formed from molten magma. There are two types of igeneous rock: volcanic and plutonic. As the name suggest, volcanic rock is formed when magma reaches the Earth's surface as lava. Plutonic rock is also derived from magma, but it is formed when magma cools and crystallizes beneath surface of the Earth. Thus, both types of igneous rock are magma that has cooled either above (volcanic) or below (plutonic) the Earth's crust. Examples of this type of rock include granite and obsidian glass.

Sedimentary rocks are formed by the layered deposition of inorganic and/or organic matter. Layers, or strata, of rock are laid down horizontally to form sedimentary rocks. Sedimentary rocks that form as mineral solutions (i.e.: sea water) evaporate are called precipitate. Those that contain the remains of living organisms are termed biogenic. Finally, those that form from the freed fragments of other rocks are called clastic. Because the layers of sedimentary rocks reveal chronology and often contain fossils, these types of rock have been key in helping scientists understand the history of the earth. Chalk, limestone, sandstone and shale are all examples of sedimentary rock.

Metamorphic rocks are created when rocks are subjected to high temperatures and pressures. The original rock, or protolith, may have been igneous, sedimentary or even an older metamorphic rock. The temperatures and pressures necessary to achieve transformation are higher than those observed on the Earth's surface and are high enough to alter the minerals in the protolith. Because these rocks are formed within the Earth's crust, studying metamorphic rocks gives us clues to conditions in the Earth's mantle. In some metamorphic rocks, different colored bands are apparent. These result from strong pressures being applied from specific directions and is termed foliation. Examples of metamorphic rock include slate and marble.

The three major subdivisions of rocks are sedimentary, metamorphic and igneous.

Lithification of sedimentary rocks

When fluid sediments are transformed into solid sedimentary rocks, the process is known as **lithification**. One very common process affecting sediments is compaction where the weights of overlying materials compress and compact the deeper sediments. The compaction process leads to cementation.
Cementation is when sediments are converted to sedimentary rock.

Factors in crystallization of igneous rocks

Igneous rocks can be classified according to their texture, their composition, and the way they formed.

Molten rock is called magma. When molten rock pours out onto the surface of Earth, it is called lava.

As magma cools, the elements and compounds begin to form crystals. The slower the magma cools, the larger the crystals grow. Rocks with large crystals are said to have a coarse-grained texture. Granite is an example of a coarse grained rock. Rocks that cool rapidly before any crystals can form have a glassy texture such as obsidian, also commonly known as volcanic glass.

Metamorphic rocks are formed by high temperatures and great pressures. The process by which the rocks undergo these changes is called metamorphism. The outcome of metamorphic changes include deformation by extreme heat and pressure, compaction, destruction of the original characteristics of the parent rock, bending and folding while in a plastic stage, and the emergence of completely new and different minerals due to chemical reactions with heated water and dissolved minerals.

Metamorphic rocks are classified into two groups, foliated (leaflike) rocks and unfoliated rocks. Foliated rocks consist of compressed, parallel bands of minerals, which give the rocks a striped appearance. Examples of such rocks include slate, schist and gneiss. Unfoliated rocks are not banded and examples of such include quartzite, marble and anthracite rocks.

Skill 19.5 Identify atmospheric conditions (e.g., air masses, wind patterns, cloud types and storms) and properties of air

El Niño refers to a sequence of changes in the ocean and atmospheric circulation across the Pacific Ocean. The water around the equator is unusually hot every two to seven years. Trade winds normally blow east to west across the equatorial latitudes, piling warm water into the western Pacific. A huge mass of heavy thunderstorms usually forms in the area and produces vast currents of rising air that displace heat poleward. This helps create the strong mid-latitude jet streams. The world's climate patterns are disrupted by this change in location of thunderstorm activity.

Air masses moving toward or away from the Earth's surface are called air currents. Air moving parallel to Earth's surface is called **wind**. Weather conditions are generated by winds and air currents carrying large amounts of heat and moisture from one part of the atmosphere to another. Wind speeds are measured by instruments called anemometers.

The wind belts in each hemisphere consist of convection cells that encircle Earth like belts. There are three major wind belts on Earth: 1) Trade Winds, 2) Prevailing Westerlies, and 3) Polar Easterlies. Wind belt formation depends on the differences in air pressures that develop in the doldrums, the Horse Latitudes, and the Polar Regions. The Doldrums surround the equator. Within this belt heated air usually rises straight up into Earth's atmosphere. The Horse Latitudes are regions of high barometric pressure with calm and light winds and the Polar Regions contain cold dense air that sinks to the Earth's surface.

Winds caused by local temperature changes include sea breezes, and land breezes.

Sea breezes are caused by the unequal heating of the land and an adjacent, large body of water. Land heats up faster than water. The movement of cool ocean air toward the land is called a sea breeze. Sea breezes usually begin blowing about mid-morning; ending about sunset.

A breeze that blows from the land to the ocean or a large lake is called a **land breeze.**

Monsoons are huge wind systems that cover large geographic areas and that reverse direction seasonally. The monsoons of India and Asia are examples of these seasonal winds. They alternate wet and dry seasons. As denser cooler air over the ocean moves inland, a steady seasonal wind called a summer or wet monsoon is produced.

The air temperature at which water vapor begins to condense is called the **dew point**.

Relative humidity is the actual amount of water vapor in a certain volume of air compared to the maximum amount of water vapor this air could hold at a given temperature.

Knowledge of types of storms

A **thunderstorm** is a brief, local storm produced by the rapid upward movement of warm, moist air within a cumulo-nimbus cloud. Thunderstorms always produce lightning and thunder and are accompanied by strong wind gusts and heavy rain or hail.

A severe storm with swirling winds that may reach speeds of hundreds of km per hour is called a **tornado**. Such a storm is also referred to as a "twister." The sky is covered by large cumulo-nimbus clouds and violent thunderstorms; a funnel-shaped swirling cloud may extend downward from a cumulo-nimbus cloud and reach the ground. Tornadoes are storms that leave a narrow path of destruction on the ground.
A swirling, funnel-shaped cloud that **extends** downward and touches a body of water is called a **waterspout**.

Hurricanes are storms that develop when warm, moist air carried by trade winds rotates around a low-pressure "eye." A large, rotating, low-pressure system accompanied by heavy precipitation and strong winds is called a tropical cyclone (better known as a hurricane). In the Pacific region, a hurricane is called a typhoon.

Storms that occur only in the winter are known as blizzards or ice storms. A **blizzard** is a storm with strong winds, blowing snow and frigid temperatures. An **ice storm** consists of falling rain that freezes when it strikes the ground, covering everything with a layer of ice.

Skill 19.6   Identify the movement of water in the water cycle, including types of precipitation and causes of condensation

Water that falls to Earth in the form of rain and snow is called **precipitation**. Precipitation is part of a continuous process in which water at the Earth's surface evaporates, condenses into clouds, and returns to Earth. This process is termed the **water cycle**. The water located below the surface is called groundwater.

The impacts of altitude upon climatic conditions are primarily related to temperature and precipitation. As altitude increases, climatic conditions become increasingly drier and colder. Solar radiation becomes more severe as altitude increases while the effects of convection forces are minimized. Climatic changes as a function of latitude follow a similar pattern (as a reference, latitude moves either north or south from the equator). The climate becomes colder and drier as the distance from the equator increases. Proximity to land or water masses produces climatic conditions based upon the available moisture. Dry and arid climates prevail where moisture is scarce; lush tropical climates can prevail where moisture is abundant. Climate, as described above, depends upon the specific combination of conditions making up an area's environment. Man impacts all environments by producing pollutants in earth, air and water. It follows then, that man is a major player in world climatic conditions.

Skill 19.7   Identify ways in which land and water interact (e.g., soil absorption, runoff, leaching, percolation, sinkholes, aquifers and reservoirs)

Soil types and properties

Soils are composed of particles of sand, clay, various minerals, tiny living organisms and humus, plus the decayed remains of plants and animals.

Soils are divided into three classes according to their texture. These classes are sandy soils, clay soils and loamy soils.

Sandy soils are gritty and their particles do not bind together firmly. Sandy soils are porous; water passes through them rapidly. Therefore, sandy soils do not hold much water and therefore have poor **absorption.**

Clay soils are smooth and greasy; their particles bind together firmly. Clay soils are moist and usually do not allow water to pass through easily. This type of soil has the lowest potential for run off.

Loamy soils feel somewhat like velvet and their particles clump together. Loamy soils are made up of sand, clay and silt. Loamy soils hold water but some water can pass through. **Percolation** is best in this type of soil.

Sinkholes

Large features formed by dissolved limestone (calcium carbonate), include sinkholes, caves and caverns. **Sinkholes** are funnel-shaped depressions created by dissolved limestone. Many sinkholes started life as a limestone cavern. Erosion weakens the cavern roof causing it to collapse, forming a sinkhole.

Groundwater usually contains large amounts of dissolved minerals, especially if the water flows through limestone. As groundwater drips through the roof of a cave, gases dissolved in the water can escape into the air. A deposit of calcium carbonate is left behind. Stalactites are icicle-like structures of calcium carbonate that hang from the roofs of caves. Water that falls on a constant spot on the cave floor and evaporates leaving a deposit of calcium carbonate, builds a stalagmite.

Groundwater provides drinking water for 53% of the population in the United States. Much groundwater is clean enough to drink without any type of treatment. Impurities in the water are filtered out by the rocks and soil through which it flows; however, many groundwater sources are becoming contaminated. Septic tanks, broken pipes, agriculture fertilizers, garbage dumps, rainwater runoff, leaking underground tanks, all pollute groundwater. Toxic chemicals from farmland mix with groundwater. Removal of large volumes of groundwater can cause collapse of soil and rock underground, causing the ground to sink.

Along shorelines, excessive depletion of underground water supplies allows the intrusion of salt water into the fresh water field. The groundwater supply becomes undrinkable.

Karst topography

Karst topography is a specific type of rock formation with distinctive surface shapes. These structures are formed when mildly acidic water dissolves bedrock (such as limestone or dolostone). The water is made acidic by carbonic acid that forms when water combines with carbon monoxide in the atmosphere. This water then dissolves surface rock and causes fractures. These fractures enlarge over time and as large gaps are formed, underground drainage systems develop that allow even more water to flow in and dissolve the rock. Complex underground drainage systems and caves are important features of karst topography.

Over thousand of years, karsification of a landscape will eventually form features of varied size. Giant spikes, "limestone pavements," and other striking features commonly form on the surface. Sinkholes, springs and shafts are common below the surface. In the United States, large visible surface structures and complex underground caves formed by karst topography can be found in Missouri and Arkansas.

Run-off

Surface run-off is water that flows over land before reaching a river, lake or ocean. Run-off occurs when precipitation falls faster than the soil can absorb it and/or when the soil becomes saturated with precipitation. Certain human activities have increased run-off by making surfaces increasingly impervious to precipitation. Water is prevented from flowing in the ground by pavement and buildings in urban areas and by heavily tilled farmland in rural areas. Instead of renewing the ground water supplies, this precipitation is channeled directly to streams and other bodies of water. Not only does this reduce ground water supplies, it can trigger increased erosion, siltation and flooding. The increased rate of erosion is particularly damaging to agricultural endeavors, since fertile topsoil is carried away at a higher rate.

Another important environmental aspect of the effect of human activity on run-off is the additional contribution to water pollution. As the run-off flows across land, it picks up and carries particulates and soil contaminants. The pollutants, including pesticides and fertilizers used agriculturally, then accumulate in the body of water to which the run-off flows. Increased run-off means even more pollutants in the water supply and that even more fertilizer and pesticides must be applied to grow crops efficiently.

Leaching

Leaching is the extraction of substances from a solid by a liquid. Leaching includes the natural processes by which water removes soluble nutrients from soil and minerals from rocks. Agriculturally, the process of leaching is often exploited to lower high salt concentrations in soil. The nutrient loss caused by leaching can be mitigated by crop planting and fertilizer application techniques.

Leaching may have negative environmental consequences because it can lead to contamination of soil when water liberates contaminates in buried waste (nuclear waste or that in landfills, etc.). Water can also dissolve agricultural chemicals and carry them to under- and above-ground water sources.

COMPETENCY 20.0 KNOWLEDGE OF EARTH AND SPACE

Skill 20.1 Identify the components of Earth's solar system and compare their individual characteristics

There are eight established planets in our solar system: Mercury, Venus, Earth, Mars, Jupiter, Saturn, Uranus and Neptune. Pluto was an established planet in our solar system, but as of summer 2006, its status is being reconsidered. The planets are divided into two groups based on distance from the sun. The inner planets include: Mercury, Venus, Earth and Mars. The outer planets include: Jupiter, Saturn, Uranus and Neptune.

Planets

Mercury -- the closest planet to the sun, Mercury's surface has craters and rocks. The atmosphere is composed of hydrogen, helium and sodium. Mercury was named after the Roman messenger god.

Venus -- has a slow rotation when compared to Earth. Venus and Uranus rotate in opposite directions from the other planets. This opposite rotation is called retrograde rotation. The surface of Venus is not visible due to the extensive cloud cover. The atmosphere is composed mostly of carbon dioxide. Sulfuric acid droplets in the dense cloud cover give Venus a yellow appearance. Venus has a greater greenhouse effect than observed on Earth. The dense clouds combined with carbon dioxide trap heat. Venus was named after the Roman goddess of love.

Earth -- considered a water planet with 70% of its surface covered by water. Gravity holds the masses of water in place. The different temperatures observed on earth allow for the different states (solid, liquid, gas) of water to exist. The atmosphere is composed mainly of oxygen and nitrogen. Earth is the only planet that is known to support life.

Mars -- the surface of Mars contains numerous craters, active and extinct volcanoes, ridges and valleys with extremely deep fractures. Iron oxide found in the dusty soil makes the surface seem rust colored and the skies seem pink in color. The atmosphere is composed of carbon dioxide, nitrogen, argon, oxygen and water vapor. Mars has Polar Regions with ice caps composed of water. Mars has two satellites. Mars was named after the Roman war god.

Jupiter -- largest planet in the solar system. Jupiter has 16 moons. The atmosphere is composed of hydrogen, helium, methane and ammonia. There are white colored bands of clouds indicating rising gas and dark colored bands of clouds indicating descending gases. The gas movement is caused by heat resulting from the energy of Jupiter's core. Jupiter has a Great Red Spot that is thought to be a hurricane type cloud. Jupiter has a strong magnetic field.

Saturn -- the second largest planet in the solar system. Saturn has rings of ice, rock and dust particles circling it. Saturn's atmosphere is composed of hydrogen, helium, methane and ammonia. Saturn has 20 plus satellites. Saturn was named after the Roman god of agriculture.

Uranus -- the second largest planet in the solar system with retrograde revolution. Uranus is a gaseous planet. It has 10 dark rings and 15 satellites. Its atmosphere is composed of hydrogen, helium and methane. Uranus was named after the Greek god of the heavens.

Neptune -- another gaseous planet with an atmosphere consisting of hydrogen, helium and methane. Neptune has 3 rings and 2 satellites. Neptune was named after the Roman sea god because its atmosphere is the same color as the seas.

Pluto – once considered the smallest planet in the solar system; its status as a planet is being reconsidered. Pluto's atmosphere probably contains methane, ammonia and frozen water. Pluto has 1 satellite. Pluto revolves around the sun every 250 years. Pluto was named after the Roman god of the underworld.

Comets, asteroids and meteors

Astronomers believe that rocky fragments may have been the remains of the birth of the solar system that never formed into a planet. **Asteroids** are found in the region between Mars and Jupiter.

Comets are masses of frozen gases, cosmic dust and small rocky particles. Astronomers think that most comets originate in a dense comet cloud beyond Pluto. Comet consists of a nucleus, a coma and a tail. A comet's tail always points away from the sun. The most famous comet, **Halley's Comet**, is named after the person whom first discovered it in 240 B.C. It returns to the skies near earth every 75 to 76 years.

Meteoroids are composed of particles of rock and metal of various sizes. When a meteoroid travels through the earth's atmosphere, friction causes its surface to heat up and it begins to burn. The burning meteoroid falling through the earth's atmosphere is called a **meteor** (also known as a "shooting star").

Meteorites are meteors that strike the earth's surface. A physical example of a meteorite's impact on the earth's surface can be seen in Arizona. The Barringer Crater is a huge meteor crater. There are many other meteor craters throughout the world.

Oort Cloud and Kuiper Belt

The **Oort Cloud** is a hypothetical spherical cloud surrounding our solar system. It extends approximately 3 light years or 30 trillion kilometers from the Sun. The cloud is believed to be made up of materials ejected out of the inner solar system because of interaction with Uranus and Neptune, but is gravitationally bound to the Sun. It is named the Oort Cloud after Jan Oort who suggested its existence in 1950. Comets from the Oort Cloud exhibit a wide range of sizes, inclinations and eccentricities and are often referred to as Long-Period Comets because they have a period of greater than 200 years.

It seems that the Oort Cloud objects were formed closer to the Sun than the Kuiper Belt objects. Small objects formed near the giant planets would have been ejected from the solar system by gravitational encounters. Those that didn't escape entirely formed the distant Oort Cloud. Small objects formed farther out had no such interactions and remained as the Kuiper Belt objects.

The **Kuiper Belt** is the name given to a vast population of small bodies orbiting the sun beyond Neptune. There are more than 70,000 of these small bodies with diameters larger than 100 km extending outwards from the orbit of Neptune to 50AU. They exist mostly within a ring or belt surrounding the sun. It is believed that the objects in the Kuiper Belt are primitive remnants of the earliest phases of the solar system. It is also believed that the Kuiper Belt is the source of many Short-Period Comets (periods of less then 200 years). It is a reservoir for the comets in the same way that the Oort Cloud is a reservoir for Long-Period Comets.

Occasionally, the orbit of a Kuiper Belt object will be disturbed by the interactions of the giant planets in such a way as to cause the object to cross the orbit of Neptune. It will then very likely have a close encounter with Neptune sending it out of the solar system or into an orbit crossing those of the other giant planets or even into the inner solar system. Prevailing theory states that scattered disk objects began as Kuiper belt objects, which were scattered through gravitational interactions with the giant planets.

Skill 20.2   Demonstrate knowledge of space exploration (e.g., history, purposes and benefits)

Though outer space has been a subject of fascination throughout human history, **space exploration refers particularly to the travel into outer space to discover new features and facts**. Though space exploration continues today, it was at its height in the late 20th century, when much progress was made over just a few years.

Telescopes are one of the oldest technologies used to gain information about space. **Most telescopes are optical, though spectrum telescopes for gathering all types of electromagnetic radiation also exist**. Optical telescopes have been used for hundreds of years to observe bodies and phenomena in outer space. As technology has allowed telescopes to be **launched into outer space**, even more detailed information has been obtained. Particularly, these telescopes have **allowed observation unhindered by the interference of the Earth's atmosphere**. The **Hubble telescope**, which is in orbit around Earth, is one famous optical telescope that has been utilized in this manner. The **Chandra X-ray observatory** is another famous telescope, though it collects X-rays. These and other telescopes have gleaned much information about distant bodies in outer space.

Some of earliest forays into true space exploration were unmanned missions involving space probes. The **probes are controlled remotely** from Earth and have been shot into outer space and immediately returned, placed into orbit around our planet, and sent to and past the other planets in our solar system. The first was the USSR's **Sputnik I in October of 1957**. It was the first man-made object ever launched into space. This was the beginning of the **"space race" between the USSR and USA**. The USA's first successful launch of a space probe occurred with **Vanguard I in December of 1957**. A few early unmanned missions were space **probes carrying animals**, such as the Soviet dog Laika that became the first animal in orbit in November of 1957. Animals are included only for research purposes in current missions. **Space probes are still used for certain applications where risk, cost or duration makes manned missions impractical**. The **Voyager probes** are among the most famous probes. They were launched to take advantage of the favorable planetary alignment in the late 1970s. They returned data and fascinating pictures from Jupiter and Saturn as well as information from beyond our solar system. It is hoped that, as technology continues to improve, space probes will be allow us to investigate space even farther away from Earth.

The first manned mission occurred in 1961, when the USSR launched Yuri Gagarin aboard Vostok I into space. A year later, the American John Glenn became the first man to orbit the Earth. The USA finally pulled well ahead in the space race in 1969, when Neil Armstrong and Buzz Aldrin became the first men to reach the moon aboard Apollo 11. Reusable space shuttles were a large step forward in allowing manned missions. The first space shuttle to enter outer space was the Columbia, though other famous US shuttles include the Challenger, Atlantis and Endeavour. Shuttles are now used to conduct experiments and to transport astronauts to and from space stations. Space stations now serve as key tool in space exploration. A space station is any artificial structure designed to house, but not transport humans living in space. The first space station was Salyut 1, launched by the USSR in 1971.

This, like all space stations up to the present, was a low earth orbital station. Other space stations include Skylab, Salyuts 2-7, Mir and the International Space Station. Only the International Space Station is currently in use. Space stations offer an excellent environment to run long-term experiments in outer space; however, they are not suitable for human life beyond a few months because of the low gravity, high radiation and other less understood factors. Much progress needs to be made before human beings will be able to live permanently in space. In fact, the future of manned missions is somewhat uncertain, as there is some debate about how necessary they are. Many speculate that significant cost and risk could be avoided with the use of robots. Currently, humans in space perform many experiments and conduct necessary repairs on equipment.

Benefits of Space Exploration

Space exploration, like all scientific endeavors, provides the expansion of our knowledge about how the universe works; however, given the relatively high cost of space exploration, further justification is needed. First, money spent on space research creates many jobs and so has economic benefits. Second, as space exploration has become an increasingly international affair, it has served to increase cooperation between nations and generate goodwill. Note that such cooperation also decreases the financial burden for individual countries; however, one of the greatest benefits of space exploration is the potential for transfer of technology. Vast arrays of technologies developed to further space exploration have found broader applications. These include communication devices, satellite operations, electronics, fabrics and other materials. For instance, the technology used in smoke detectors was developed for NASA's Skylab spacecraft in the 1970s and quartz timing crystals used in nearly all wristwatches were developed as timing devices for the Apollo lunar missions.

Skill 20.3   Identify the phases of the moon and the moon's effect on Earth

Lunar Phases

The Earth's orientation in respect to the solar system is also responsible for our perception of the phases of the moon. As the Earth orbits the Sun with a period of 365 days, the Moon orbits the Earth every 27 days. As the moon circles the Earth, its shape in the night sky appears to change. The changes in the appearance of the moon from Earth are known as "lunar phases." These phases vary cyclically according to the relative positions of the Moon, the Earth and the Sun. At all times, half of the Moon is facing the Sun and is thus illuminated by reflecting the Sun's light. As the Moon orbits the Earth and the Earth orbits the Sun, the half of the moon that faces the Sun changes; however, the Moon is in synchronous rotation around the Earth, meaning that nearly the same side of the moon faces the Earth at all times. This side is referred to as the near side of the moon. Lunar phases occur as the Earth and Moon orbit the Sun and the fractional illumination of the Moon's near side changes.

When the Sun and Moon are on opposite sides of the Earth, observers on Earth perceive a "full moon," meaning the moon appears circular because the entire illuminated half of the moon is visible. As the Moon orbits the Earth, the Moon "wanes" as the amount of the illuminated half of the Moon that is visible from Earth decreases. A gibbous moon is between a full moon and a half moon, or between a half moon and a full moon. When the Sun and the Moon are on the same side of Earth, the illuminated half of the moon is facing away from Earth, and the moon appears invisible. This lunar phase is known as the "new moon." The time between each full moon is approximately 29.53 days.

A list of all lunar phases includes:

- New Moon: the moon is invisible or the first signs of a crescent appear

- Waxing Crescent: the right crescent of the moon is visible

- First Quarter: the right quarter of the moon is visible

- Waxing Gibbous: only the left crescent is not illuminated

- Full Moon: the entire illuminated half of the moon is visible

- Waning Gibbous: only the right crescent of the moon is not illuminated

- Last Quarter: the left quarter of the moon is illuminated

- Waning Crescent: only the left crescent of the moon is illuminated

Viewing the moon from the Southern Hemisphere would cause these phases to occur in the opposite order.

Tides

The orientation of and gravitational interaction between the Earth and the Moon are responsible for the ocean tides that occur on Earth. The term "tide" refers to the cyclic rise and fall of large bodies of water. Gravitational attraction is defined as the force of attraction between all bodies in the universe. At the location on Earth closest to the Moon, the gravitational attraction of the Moon draws seawater toward the Moon in the form of a tidal bulge. On the opposite side of the Earth, another tidal bulge forms in the direction away from the Moon because at this point, the Moon's gravitational pull is the weakest. "Spring tides" are especially strong tides that occur when the Earth, Sun and Moon are in line, allowing both the Sun and the Moon to exert gravitational force on the Earth and increase tidal bulge height. These tides occur during the full moon and the new moon. "Neap tides" are especially weak tides occurring when the gravitational forces of the Moon and the Sun are perpendicular to one another. These tides occur during quarter moons

Skill 20.4   Identify Earth's orbital pattern and its effect on the seasons

Earth is the third planet away from the sun in our solar system. Earth's numerous types of motion and states of orientation greatly effect global conditions, such as seasons, tides and lunar phases. The Earth orbits the Sun with a period of 365 days. During this orbit, the average distance between the Earth and Sun is 93 million miles. The shape of the Earth's orbit around the Sun deviates from the shape of a circle only slightly. This deviation, known as the Earth's eccentricity, has a very small affect on the Earth's climate. The Earth is closest to the Sun at perihelion, occurring around January 2nd of each year, and farthest from the Sun at aphelion, occurring around July 2nd. Because the Earth is closest to the sun in January, the northern winter is slightly warmer than the southern winter.

Seasons

The rotation axis of the Earth is not perpendicular to the orbital (ecliptic) plane. The axis of the Earth is tilted 23.45° from the perpendicular. The tilt of the Earth's axis is known as the obliquity of the ecliptic and is mainly responsible for the four seasons of the year by influencing the intensity of solar rays received by the Northern and Southern Hemispheres. The four seasons, spring, summer, fall and winter are extended periods of characteristic average temperature, rainfall, storm frequency and vegetation growth or dormancy. The effect of the Earth's tilt on climate is best demonstrated at the solstices, the two days of the year when the Sun is farthest from the Earth's equatorial plane. At the Summer Solstice (June Solstice), the Earth's tilt on its axis causes the Northern Hemisphere to the lean toward the Sun, while the southern hemisphere leans away. Consequently, the Northern Hemisphere receives more intense rays from the Sun and experiences summer during this time, while the Southern Hemisphere experiences winter. At the Winter Solstice (December Solstice), it is the Southern Hemisphere that leans toward the sun and thus experiences summer. Spring and fall are produced by varying degrees of the same leaning toward or away from the Sun.

COMPETENCY 21.0   KNOWLEDGE OF THE PROCESSES OF LIFE

Skill 21.1   Compare and contrast living and nonliving things

The organization of living systems builds by levels from small to increasingly more large and complex. All aspects, whether it is a cell or an ecosystem, have the same requirements to sustain life. Life is organized from simple to complex in the following way:

- **Organelles** make up **cells** that make up **tissues** that make up **organs**. Groups of organs make up **organ systems**. Organ systems work together to provide life for the **organism.**

Several characteristics have been described to identify living versus non-living substances.

1. **Living things are made of cells**; they grow, are capable of reproduction and respond to stimuli.
2. **Living things must adapt to environmental changes or perish**.
3. **Living things carry on metabolic processes**. They use and make energy.

All organic life has a common element: Carbon. Carbon is recycled through the ecosystem through both biotic and abiotic means. It is the link between biological processes and the chemical make-up of life.

Skill 21.2   Distinguish among microorganisms (i.e.: viruses, bacteria and protozoans)

The cell is the basic unit of all living things. There are three types of cells. They are prokaryotes, eukaryotes and archaea. Archaea have some similarities with prokaryotes, but are as distantly related to prokaryotes as prokaryotes are to eukaryotes.

PROKARYOTES

Prokaryotes (Monera) consist only of bacteria and cyanobacteria (formerly known as blue-green algae). Bacteria are then further divided into 19 groups.

Prokaryote cells have no defined nucleus or nuclear membrane. The DNA, RNA and ribosomes float freely within the cell. The cytoplasm has a single chromosome condensed to form a nucleoid. Prokaryotes have a thick cell wall made up of amino sugars (glycoproteins). This is for protection, to give the cell shape, and to keep the cell from bursting. It is the cell wall of bacteria that is targeted by the antibiotic penicillin. Penicillin works by disrupting the cell wall, thus killing the cell.

The cell wall surrounds the cell membrane (plasma membrane). The cell membrane consists of a lipid bilayer that controls the passage of molecules in and out of the cell. Some prokaryotes have a capsule made of polysaccharides that surrounds the cell wall for extra protection from higher organisms.

Many bacterial cells have appendages used for movement called flagella. Some cells also have pili, which are a protein strand used for attachment of the bacteria. Pili may also be used for sexual conjugation (where the DNA from one bacterial cell is transferred to another bacterial cell).

Prokaryotes are the most numerous and widespread organisms on earth. Bacteria were most likely the first cells and date back in the fossil record to 3.5 billion years ago. Their ability to adapt to the environment allows them to thrive in a wide variety of habitats.

EUKARYOTES

Eukaryotic cells are found in protists, fungi, plants and animals. Most eukaryotic cells are larger than prokaryotic cells. They contain many organelles, which are membrane bound areas for specific functions. Their cytoplasm contains a cytoskeleton that provides a protein framework for the cell. The cytoplasm also supports the organelles and contains the ions and molecules necessary for cell function. The cytoplasm is contained by the plasma membrane. The plasma membrane allows molecules to pass in and out of the cell. The membrane can bud inward to engulf outside material in a process called endocytosis. Exocytosis is a secretory mechanism, the reverse of endocytosis.

The most significant differentiation between prokaryotes and eukaryotes is that eukaryotes have a nucleus.

ARCHAEA

There are three kinds of organisms with archaea cells: 1) methanogens are obligate anaerobes that produce methane, 2) halobacteria can live only in concentrated brine solutions, and 3) thermoacidophiles can only live in acidic hot springs.

VIRUSES

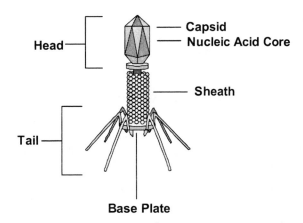

Bacteriophage

All viruses have a head or protein capsid that contains genetic material. This material is encoded in the nucleic acid and can be DNA, RNA or even a limited number of enzymes. Some viruses also have a protein tail region. The tail aids in binding to the surface of the host cell and penetrating the surface of the host in order to introduce the virus's genetic material.

Other examples of viruses and their structures:

Adenovirus (DNA virus)

Eastern equine encephalitis (RNA virus)

Herpes virus (DNA virus)

HIV retrovirus (RNA virus)

Influenza virus (RNA virus)

Rotavirus (RNA virus)

Skill 21.3   Differentiate structures and functions of plant and animal cells

The structure of the cell is often related to the cell's function. Root hair cells differ from flower stamens or leaf epidermal cells. They all have different functions.

Animal cells – begin a discussion of the nucleus as a round body inside the cell. It controls the cell's activities. The nuclear membrane contains threadlike structures called chromosomes. The genes are units that control cell activities found in the nucleus. The cytoplasm has many structures in it. Vacuoles contain the food for the cell. Other vacuoles contain waste materials. Animal cells differ from plant cells because they have cell membranes.

Plant cells – have cell walls. A cell wall differs from cell membranes. The cell membrane is very thin and is a part of the cell. The cell wall is thick and is a nonliving part of the cell. Chloroplasts are bundles of chlorophyll.

Skill 21.4   Identify the major steps of the plant physiological processes of photosynthesis, transpiration, reproduction and respiration

Photosynthesis is the process by which plants make carbohydrates from the energy of the sun, carbon dioxide, and water. Oxygen is a waste product. Photosynthesis occurs in the chloroplast where the pigment chlorophyll traps sun energy. It is divided into two major steps:

- **Light Reactions** - Sunlight is trapped, water is split, and oxygen is given off. ATP is made and hydrogens reduce NADP to $NADPH_2$. The light reactions occur in light. The products of the light reactions enter into the dark reactions (Calvin cycle).
- **Dark Reactions** - Carbon dioxide enters during the dark reactions can occur with or without the presence of light. The energy transferred from $NADPH_2$ and ATP allow for the fixation of carbon into glucose.

Respiration - during times of decreased light, plants break down the products of photosynthesis through cellular respiration. Glucose, with the help of oxygen, breaks down and produces carbon dioxide and water as waste. Approximately fifty percent of the products of photosynthesis are used by the plant for energy.

Transpiration - water travels up the xylem of the plant through the process of transpiration. Water sticks to itself (cohesion) and to the walls of the xylem (adhesion). As it evaporates through the stomata of the leaves, the water is pulled up the column from the roots. Environmental factors such as heat and wind increase the rate of transpiration. High humidity will decrease the rate of transpiration.

Reproduction - Angiosperms are the largest group in the plant kingdom. They are the flowering plants and produce true seeds for reproduction. They arose about seventy million years ago when the dinosaurs were disappearing. The land was drying up and their ability to produce seeds that could remain dormant until conditions became acceptable allowed for their success. When compared to other plants, they also had more advanced vascular tissue and larger leaves for increased photosynthesis. Angiosperms reproduce through a method of **double fertilization**. An ovum is fertilized by two sperm. One sperm produces the new plant, the other forms the food supply for the developing plant.

Seed dispersal - success of plant reproduction involves the seed moving away from the parent plant to decrease competition for space, water and minerals. Seeds may be carried by wind (maple trees), water (palm trees), carried by animals (burrs) or ingested by animals and released in their feces in another area.

Skill 21.5   Identify the structures and functions of organs and systems of animals, including humans

Skeletal System - The skeletal system functions in support. Vertebrates have an endoskeleton, with muscles attached to bones. Skeletal proportions are controlled by area to volume relationships. Body size and shape is limited due to the forces of gravity. Surface area is increased to improve efficiency in all organ systems.

Muscular System – Its function is for movement. There are three types of muscle tissue. Skeletal muscle is voluntary. These muscles are attached to bones. Smooth muscle is involuntary. It is found in organs and enable functions such as digestion and respiration. Cardiac muscle is a specialized type of smooth muscle.

Nervous System - The neuron is the basic unit of the nervous system. It consists of an axon, which carries impulses away from the cell body, the dendrite, which carries impulses toward the cell body and the cell body, which contains the nucleus. Synapses are spaces between neurons. Chemicals called neurotransmitters are found close to the synapse. The myelin sheath, composed of Schwann cells, covers the neurons and provides insulation.

Digestive System - The function of the digestive system is to break down food and absorb it into the blood stream where it can be delivered to all cells of the body for use in cellular respiration. As animals evolved, digestive systems changed from simple absorption to a system with a separate mouth and anus, capable of allowing the animal to become independent of a host.

Respiratory System - This system functions in the gas exchange of oxygen (needed) and carbon dioxide (waste). It delivers oxygen to the bloodstream and picks up carbon dioxide for release out of the body. Simple animals diffuse gases from and to their environment. Gills allow aquatic animals to exchange gases in a fluid medium by removing dissolved oxygen from the water. Lungs maintain a fluid environment for gas exchange in terrestrial animals.

Circulatory System - The function of the circulatory system is to carry oxygenated blood and nutrients to all cells of the body and return carbon dioxide waste to be expelled from the lungs. Animals evolved from an open system to a closed system with vessels leading to and from the heart.

HUMAN BODY

Skeletal System - The skeletal system functions in support. Vertebrates have an endoskeleton, with muscles attached to bones. Skeletal proportions are controlled by area to volume relationships. Body size and shape are limited due to the forces of gravity. Surface area is increased to improve efficiency in all organ systems.

The **axial skeleton** consists of the bones of the skull and vertebrae. The **appendicular skeleton** consists of the bones of the legs, arms, tail and shoulder girdle. Bone is a connective tissue. Parts of the bone include compact bone which gives strength, spongy bone which contains red marrow to make blood cells, yellow marrow in the center of long bones to store fat cells, and the periosteum, which is the protective covering on the outside of the bone.

A **joint** is defined as a place where two bones meet. Joints enable movement. **Ligaments** attach bone to bone. **Tendons** attach bones to muscles.

Muscular System - Functions in movement. There are three types of muscle tissue. Skeletal muscle is voluntary. These muscles are attached to bones. Smooth muscle is involuntary. It is found in organs and enables functions such as digestion and respiration. Cardiac muscle is a specialized type of smooth muscle and is found in the heart. Muscles can only contract; therefore they work in antagonistic pairs to allow back and forward movement. Muscle fibers are made of groups of myofibrils which are made of groups of sarcomeres. Actin and myosin are proteins which make up the sarcomere.

Physiology of muscle contraction - A nerve impulse strikes a muscle fiber. This causes calcium ions to flood the sarcomere. Calcium ions allow ATP to expend energy. The myosin fibers creep along the actin, causing the muscle to contract. Once the nerve impulse has passed, calcium is pumped out and the contraction ends.

Nervous System - The neuron is the basic unit of the nervous system. It consists of an axon, which carries impulses away from the cell body, the dendrite, which carries impulses toward the cell body, and the cell body, which contains the nucleus. Synapses are spaces between neurons. Chemicals called neurotransmitters are found close to the synapse. The myelin sheath, composed of Schwann cells, covers the neurons and provides insulation.

Physiology of the nerve impulse - Nerve action depends on depolarization and an imbalance of electrical charges across the neuron. A polarized nerve has a positive charge outside the neuron. A depolarized nerve has a negative charge outside the neuron. Neurotransmitters turn off the sodium pump which results in depolarization of the membrane. This wave of depolarization (as it moves from neuron to neuron) carries an electrical impulse. This is actually a wave of opening and closing gates that allows for the flow of ions across the synapse. Nerves have an action potential. There is a threshold of the level of chemicals that must be met or exceeded in order for muscles to respond. This is called the "all or none" response.

The **reflex arc** is the simplest nerve response. The brain is bypassed. When a stimulus (like touching a hot stove) occurs, sensors in the hand send the message directly to the spinal cord. This stimulates motor neurons that contract the muscles to move the hand.

Voluntary nerve responses involve the brain. Receptor cells send the message to sensory neurons that lead to association neurons. The message is taken to the brain. Motor neurons are stimulated and the message is transmitted to effector cells that cause the end effect.

Organization of the Nervous System - The somatic nervous system is controlled consciously. It consists of the central nervous system (brain and spinal cord) and the peripheral nervous system (nerves that extend from the spinal cord to the muscles). The autonomic nervous system is unconsciously controlled by the hypothalamus of the brain. Smooth muscles, the heart and digestion are some processes controlled by the autonomic nervous system. The sympathetic nervous system works opposite of the parasympathetic nervous system. For example, if the sympathetic nervous system stimulates an action, the parasympathetic nervous system would end that action.

Neurotransmitters - these are chemicals released by exocytosis. Some neurotransmitters stimulate, while others inhibit, action.

Acetylcholine - the most common neurotransmitter; it controls muscle contraction and heartbeat. The enzyme acetylcholinesterase breaks it down to end the transmission.

Epinephrine - responsible for the "fight or flight" reaction. It causes an increase in heart rate and blood flow to prepare the body for action. It is also called adrenaline.

Endorphins and enkephalins - these are natural pain killers and are released during serious injury and childbirth.

Digestive System - The function of the digestive system is to break food down and absorb it into the blood stream where it can be delivered to all cells of the body for use in cellular respiration. The teeth and saliva begin digestion by breaking food down into smaller pieces and lubricating it so it can be swallowed. The lips, cheeks and tongue form a bolus (ball) of food. It is carried down the pharynx by the process of peristalsis (wave like contractions) and enters the stomach through the cardiac sphincter which closes to keep food from going back up. In the stomach, pepsinogen and hydrochloric acid form pepsin, the enzyme that breaks down proteins. The food is broken down further by this chemical action and is turned into chyme. The pyloric sphincter muscle opens to allow the food to enter the small intestine. Most nutrient absorption occurs in the small intestine. Its large surface area, accomplished by its length and protrusions called villi and microvilli allow for a great absorptive surface. Upon arrival into the small intestine, chyme is neutralized to allow the enzymes found there to function. Any food left after the trip through the small intestine enters the large intestine. The large intestine functions to reabsorb water and produce vitamin K. The feces, or remaining waste, are passed out through the anus.

Accessory organs - although not part of the digestive tract, these organs function in the production of necessary enzymes and bile. The pancreas makes many enzymes to break down food in the small intestine. The liver makes bile which breaks down and emulsifies fatty acids.

Respiratory System - This system functions in the gas exchange of oxygen (needed) and carbon dioxide (waste). It delivers oxygen to the bloodstream and picks up carbon dioxide for release out of the body. Air enters the mouth and nose, where it is warmed, moistened, and filtered of dust and particles. Cilia in the trachea trap unwanted material in mucus, which can be expelled. The trachea splits into two bronchial tubes and the bronchial tubes divide into smaller and smaller bronchioles in the lungs. The internal surface of the lung is composed of alveoli, which are thin walled air sacs. These allow for a large surface area for gas exchange. The alveoli are lined with capillaries. Oxygen diffuses into the bloodstream and carbon dioxide diffuses out to be exhaled. The oxygenated blood is carried to the heart and delivered to all parts of the body. The thoracic cavity holds the lungs. A muscle, the diaphragm, below the lungs is an adaptation that makes inhalation possible. As the volume of the thoracic cavity increases, the diaphragm muscle flattens out and inhalation occurs. When the diaphragm relaxes, exhalation occurs.

Circulatory System - The function of the circulatory system is to carry oxygenated blood and nutrients to all cells of the body and return carbon dioxide waste to be expelled from the lungs. Be familiar with the parts of the heart and the path blood takes from the heart to the lungs, through the body and back to the heart. Unoxygenated blood enters the heart through the inferior and superior vena cava. The first chamber it encounters is the right atrium. It goes through the tricuspid valve to the right ventricle, on to the pulmonary arteries, and then to the lungs where it is oxygenated. It returns to the heart through the pulmonary vein into the left atrium. It travels through the bicuspid valve to the left ventricle where it is pumped to all parts of the body through the aorta.

Sinoatrial node (SA node) - the pacemaker of the heart. Located on the right atrium, it is responsible for contraction of the right and left atrium.

Atrioventricular node (AV node) - located on the left ventricle, it is responsible for contraction of the ventricles.

Blood vessels include:

- **Arteries** - lead away from the heart. All arteries carry oxygenated blood except the pulmonary artery going to the lungs. Arteries are under high pressure.

- **Arterioles** - arteries branch off to form these smaller passages.

- **Capillaries** - arterioles branch off to form tiny capillaries that reach every cell. Blood moves slowest here due to the small size; only one red blood cell may pass at a time to allow for diffusion of gases into and out of cells. Nutrients are also absorbed by the cells from the capillaries.

- **Venules** - capillaries combine to form larger venules. The vessels are now carrying waste products from the cells.

- **Veins** - venules combine to form larger veins, leading back to the heart. Veins and venules have thinner walls than arteries, because they are not under as much pressure. Veins contain valves to prevent the backward flow of blood due to gravity.

Components of the blood include:

- **Plasma** – 60% of the blood is plasma. It contains salts called electrolytes, nutrients and waste. It is the liquid part of blood.
- **Erythrocytes** - also called red blood cells; they contain hemoglobin which carries oxygen molecules.
- **Leukocytes** - also called white blood cells. White blood cells are larger than red cells. They are phagocytic and can engulf invaders. White blood cells are not confined to the blood vessels and can enter the interstitial fluid between cells.
- **Platelets** - assist in blood clotting. Platelets are made in the bone marrow.

Blood clotting - the neurotransmitter that initiates blood vessel constriction following an injury is called serotonin. A material called prothrombin is converted to thrombin with the help of thromboplastin. The thrombin is then used to convert fibrinogen to fibrin which traps red blood cells to form a scab and stop blood flow.

Lymphatic System (Immune System)

Nonspecific defense mechanisms – They do not target specific pathogens, but are a whole body response. Results of nonspecific mechanisms are seen as symptoms of an infection. These mechanisms include the skin, mucous membranes and cells of the blood and lymph (ie: white blood cells, macrophages). Fever is a result of an increase of white blood cells. Pyrogens are released by white blood cells which set the body's thermostat to a higher temperature. This inhibits the growth of microorganisms. It also increases metabolism to increase phagocytosis and body repair.

Specific defense mechanisms - They recognize foreign material and respond by destroying the invader. These mechanisms are specific in purpose and diverse in type. They are able to recognize individual pathogens. They are able to differentiate between foreign material and self. Memory of the invaders provides immunity upon further exposure.

- **Antigen** - any foreign particle that invades the body.
- **Antibody** - manufactured by the body, they recognize and latch onto antigens, hopefully destroying them.
- **Immunity** - this is the body's ability to recognize and destroy an antigen before it causes harm. Active immunity develops after recovery from an infectious disease (chicken pox) or after a vaccination (mumps, measles and rubella). Passive immunity may be passed from one individual to another. It is not permanent. A good example is the immunities passed from mother to nursing child.

Excretory System - The function of the excretory system is to rid the body of nitrogenous wastes in the form of urea. The functional units of excretion are the nephrons, which make up the kidneys. Antidiuretic hormone (ADH), which is made in the hypothalamus and stored in the pituitary, is released when differences in osmotic balance occur. This will cause more water to be reabsorbed. As the blood becomes more dilute, ADH release ceases.

The Bowman's capsule contains the glomerulus, a tightly packed group of capillaries. The glomerulus is under high pressure. Waste and fluids leak out due to pressure. Filtration is not selective in this area. Selective secretion by active and passive transport occur in the proximal convoluted tubule. Unwanted molecules are secreted into the filtrate. Selective secretion also occurs in the loop of Henle. Salt is actively pumped out of the tube and much water is lost due to the hyperosmosity of the inner part (medulla) of the kidney. As the fluid enters the distal convoluted tubule, more water is reabsorbed. Urine forms in the collecting duct which leads to the ureter then to the bladder where it is stored. Urine is passed from the bladder through the urethra. The amount of water reabsorbed back into the body is dependent upon how much water or fluids an individual has consumed. Urine can be very dilute or very concentrated if dehydration is present.

Endocrine System - The function of the endocrine system is to manufacture proteins called hormones. Hormones are released into the bloodstream and are carried to a target tissue where they stimulate an action. Hormones may build up over time to cause their effect, as in puberty or the menstrual cycle.

Hormone activation - Hormones are specific and fit receptors on the target tissue cell surface. The receptor activates an enzyme which converts ATP to cyclic AMP. Cyclic AMP (cAMP) is a second messenger from the cell membrane to the nucleus. The genes found in the nucleus turn on or off to cause a specific response.

There are two classes of hormones. **Steroid hormones** come from cholesterol. Steroid hormones cause sexual characteristics and mating behavior. Hormones include estrogen and progesterone in females and testosterone in males. **Peptide hormones** are made in the pituitary, adrenal glands (kidneys) and the pancreas. They include the following:

- **Follicle stimulating hormone (FSH)** - production of sperm or egg cells
- **Luteinizing hormone (LH)** - functions in ovulation
- **Luteotropic hormone (LTH)** - assists in production of progesterone
- **Growth hormone (GH)** - stimulates growth
- **Antidiuretic hormone (ADH)** - assists in retention of water
- **Oxytocin** - stimulates labor contractions at birth and let-down of milk
- **Melatonin** - regulates circadian rhythms and seasonal changes
- **Epinephrine (adrenaline)** - causes fight or flight reaction of the nervous system
- **Thyroxin** - increases metabolic rate
- **Calcitonin** - removes calcium from the blood
- **Insulin** - decreases glucose level in blood
- **Glucagon** - increases glucose level in blood

Hormones work on a feedback system. The increase or decrease in one hormone may cause the increase or decrease in another. Release of hormones cause a specific response.

Reproductive System - Sexual reproduction greatly increases diversity due to the many combinations possible through meiosis and fertilization. Gametogenesis is the production of the sperm and egg cells. Spermatogenesis begins at puberty in the male. One spermatozoa produces four sperm. The sperm mature in the seminiferous tubules located in the testes. Oogenesis, the production of egg cells is usually complete by the birth of a female. Egg cells are not released until menstruation begins at puberty. Meiosis forms one ovum with all the cytoplasm and three polar bodies, which are reabsorbed by the body. The ovum are stored in the ovaries and released each month from puberty to menopause.

Path of the sperm - sperm are stored in the seminiferous tubules in the testes where they mature. Mature sperm are found in the epididymis located on top of the testes. After ejaculation, the sperm travels up the vas deferens where they mix with semen made in the prostate and seminal vesicles and travel out the urethra.

Path of the egg - eggs are stored in the ovaries. Ovulation releases the egg into the fallopian tubes, which are ciliated to move the egg along. Fertilization normally occurs in the fallopian tube. If pregnancy does not occur, the egg passes through the uterus and is expelled through the vagina during menstruation. Levels of progesterone and estrogen stimulate menstruation. In the event of pregnancy, hormonal levels are affected by the implantation of a fertilized egg, so menstruation does not occur.

Pregnancy - if fertilization occurs, the zygote implants in about two to three days in the uterus. Implantation promotes secretion of human chorionic gonadotropin (HCG). This is what is detected in pregnancy tests. The HCG keeps the level of progesterone elevated to maintain the uterine lining in order to feed the developing embryo until the umbilical cord forms. Labor is initiated by oxytocin which causes labor contractions and dilation of the cervix. Prolactin and oxytocin cause the production of milk.

Skill 21.6   Identify the major steps of the animal physiological processes (e.g., respiration, reproduction, digestion and circulation)

Animal respiration takes in oxygen and gives off waste gases. For instance, a fish uses its gills to extract oxygen from the water. Bubbles are evidence that waste gasses are expelled. Respiration without oxygen is called anaerobic respiration. Anaerobic respiration in animal cells is also called lactic acid fermentation. The end product is lactic acid.

Animal reproduction can be asexual or sexual. Geese lay eggs. Animals such as bear cubs, deer and rabbits are born alive. Some animals reproduce frequently while others do not. Some animals only produce one baby yet others produce many (clutch size).

Animal digestion – some animals only eat meat (carnivores) while others only eat plants (herbivores). Many animals do both (omnivores). Nature has created animals with structural adaptations so they may obtain food through sharp teeth or long facial structures. Digestion's purpose is to break down carbohydrates, fats and proteins. Many organs are needed to digest food. The process begins with the mouth. Certain animals, such as birds, have beaks to puncture wood or allow for large fish to be consumed. The tooth structure of a beaver is designed to cut down trees. Tigers are known for their sharp teeth used to rip hides from their prey. Enzymes are catalysts that help speed up chemical reactions by lowering effective activation energy. Enzyme rate is affected by temperature, pH, and the amount of substrate. Saliva is an enzyme that changes starches into sugars.

Animal circulation – The blood temperature of all mammals stays constant regardless of outside temperature. This is called warm-blooded, while cold-blooded animals' (amphibians) circulation will vary with the temperature.

COMPETENCY 22.0   KNOWLEDGE OF HOW LIVING THINGS INTERACT WITH THE ENVIRONMENT

Skill 22.1   Identify parts and sequences of biogeochemical cycles of common elements in the environment (e.g., carbon, oxygen, hydrogen and nitrogen)

Essential elements are recycled through an ecosystem. At times, the element needs to be "fixed" in a useable form. Cycles are dependent on plants, algae and bacteria to fix nutrients for use by animals.

Water cycle - 2% of all the available water is fixed and held in ice or the bodies of organisms. Available water includes surface water (lakes, ocean, and rivers) and ground water (aquifers, wells). 96% of all available water is from ground water. Water is recycled through the processes of evaporation and precipitation. The water present now is the water that has been here since our atmosphere formed.

Carbon cycle - Ten percent of all available carbon in the air (from carbon dioxide gas) is fixed by photosynthesis. Plants fix carbon in the form of glucose; animals eat the plants and are able to obtain their source of carbon. When animals release carbon dioxide through respiration, the plants again have a source of carbon to fix.

Nitrogen cycle - Eighty percent of the atmosphere is in the form of nitrogen gas. Nitrogen must be fixed and taken out of the gaseous form to be incorporated into an organism. Only a few genera of bacteria have the correct enzymes to break the triple bond between nitrogen atoms. These bacteria live within the roots of legumes (peas, beans, alfalfa) and add bacteria to the soil so it may be taken up by the plant. Nitrogen is necessary to make amino acids and the nitrogenous bases of DNA.

Phosphorus cycle - Phosphorus exists as a mineral and is not found in the atmosphere. Fungi and plant roots have structures called mycorrhizae that are able to fix insoluble phosphates into useable phosphorus. Urine and decayed matter returns phosphorus to the earth where it can be fixed in the plant. Phosphorus is needed for the backbone of DNA and for the manufacture of ATP.

Skill 22.2   Identify causes and effects of pollution

Pollutants are impurities in air and water that may be harmful to life. Spills from barges carrying large quantities of oil pollute beaches and harm fish.

All acids contain hydrogen. Acidic substances from factories and car exhausts dissolve in rain water forming **acid rain**. Acid rain forms predominantly from pollutant oxides in the air (usually nitrogen-based NO_x or sulfur-based SO_x), which become hydrated into their acids (nitric or sulfuric acid). When the rain falls into stone, the acids can react with metallic compounds and gradually wear the stone away.

Radioactivity is the breaking down of atomic nuclei by releasing particles or electromagnetic radiation. Radioactive nuclei give off radiation in the form of streams of particles or energy. Alpha particles are positively charged particles consisting of two protons and two neutrons. It is the slowest form of radiation. It can be stopped by paper! Beta particles are electrons. It is produced when a neutron in the nucleus breaks up into a proton and an electron. The proton remains inside the nucleus, increasing its atomic number by one. But the electron is given off. They can be stopped by aluminum. Gamma rays are electromagnetic waves with extremely short wavelengths. They have no mass. They have no charge so they are not deflected by an electric field.

Gamma rays travel at the speed of light. It takes a thick block of lead to stop them. Uranium is the source of radiation and therefore is radioactive. Marie Curie discovered new elements called radium and polonium that actually give off more radiation than uranium.

The major concern with radioactivity is in the case of a nuclear disaster. Medical misuse is also a threat. Radioactivity ionizes the air it travels through. It is strong enough to kill cancer cells or dangerous enough to cause illness or even death. Gamma rays can penetrate the body and damage cells. Protective clothing is needed when working with gamma rays. Electricity from nuclear energy uses uranium 235. The devastation of the Russian nuclear power plant disaster has evacuated entire regions as the damage to the land and food source will last for hundreds of years.

Skill 22.3   Identify the living and nonliving factors that influence population density (e.g., food, space, predators and climate)

Charles Darwin proposed a mechanism for his theory of evolution, which he termed natural selection. Natural selection describes the process by which favorable traits accumulate in a population, changing the population's genetic make-up over time. Darwin theorized that all individual organisms, even those of the same species, are different and those individuals that happen to possess traits favorable for survival would produce more offspring. Thus, in the next generation, the number of individuals with the favorable trait increases and the process continues. Darwin, in contrast to other evolutionary scientists, did not believe that traits acquired during an organism's lifetime (e.g., increased musculature) or the desires and needs of the organism affected evolution of populations. For example, Darwin argued that the evolution of long trunks in elephants resulted from environmental conditions that favored those elephants that possessed longer trunks. The individual elephants did not stretch their trunks to reach food or water and pass on the new, longer trunks to their offspring.

Jean Baptiste Lamarck proposed an alternative mechanism of evolution. Lamarck believed individual organisms developed traits in response to changing environmental conditions and passed on these new, favorable traits to their offspring. For example, Lamarck argued that the trunks of individual elephants lengthen as a result of stretching for scarce food and water, and elephants pass on the longer trunks to their offspring. Thus, in contrast to Darwin's relatively random natural selection, Lamarck believed the mechanism of evolution followed a predetermined plan and depended on the desires and needs of individual organisms.

Different molecular and environmental processes and conditions drive the evolution of populations. The various mechanisms of evolution either introduce new genetic variation or alter the frequency of existing variation.

Mutations, random changes in nucleotide sequence, are a basic mechanism of evolution. Mutations in DNA result from copying errors during cell division, exposure to radiation and chemicals, and interaction with viruses. Simple point mutations, deletions or insertions can alter the function or expression of existing genes, but do not contribute greatly to evolution. On the other hand, gene duplication, the duplication of an entire gene, often leads to the creation of new genes that may contribute to the evolution of a species. Because gene duplication results in two copies of the same gene, the extra copy is free to mutate and develop without the selective pressure experienced by mutated single-copy genes. Gene duplication and subsequent mutation often leads to the creation of new genes. When new genes resulting from mutations lend the mutated organism a reproductive advantage relative to environmental conditions, natural selection and evolution can occur.

Recombination is the exchange of DNA between a pair of chromosomes during meiosis. Recombination does not introduce new genes into a population, but does affect the expression of genes and the combination of traits expressed by individuals. Thus, recombination increases the genetic diversity of populations and contributes to evolution by creating new combinations of genes that nature selects for or against.

Isolation is the separation of members of a species by environmental barriers that the organisms cannot cross. Environmental change, either gradual or sudden, often results in isolation. An example of gradual isolation is the formation of a mountain range or dessert between members of a species. An example of sudden isolation is the separation of species members by a flood or earthquake. Isolation leads to evolution because the separated groups cannot reproduce together and differences arise. In addition, because the environment of each group is different, the groups adapt and evolve differently. Extended isolation can lead to speciation, the development of new species.

Sexual reproduction and selection contributes to evolution by consolidating genetic mutations and creating new combinations of genes. Genetic recombination during sexual reproduction, as previously discussed, introduces new combinations of traits and patterns of gene expression. Consolidation of favorable mutations through sexual reproduction speeds the processes of evolution and natural selection. On the other hand, consolidation of deleterious mutations creates completely unfit individuals that are readily eliminated from the population.

Genetic drift is, along with natural selection, one of the two main mechanisms of evolution. Genetic drift refers to the chance deviation in the frequency of alleles (traits) resulting from the randomness of zygote formation and selection. Because only a small percentage of all possible zygotes become mature adults, parents do not necessarily pass all of their alleles on to their offspring. Genetic drift is particularly important in small populations because chance deviations in allelic frequency can quickly alter the genotypic make-up of the population. In extreme cases, certain alleles may completely disappear from the gene pool. Genetic drift is particularly influential when environmental events and conditions produce small, isolated populations.

Plate tectonics is the theory that the Earth's surface consists of large plates. Movement and shifting of the plates dictate the location of continents, formation of mountains and seas and volcanic and earthquake activity. Such contributions to environmental conditions influence the evolution of species. For example, tectonic activity resulting in mountain formation or continent separation can cause genetic isolation. In addition, the geographic distribution of species is indicative of evolutionary history and related tectonic activity.

Population Factors

A limiting factor is the component of a biological process that determines how quickly or slowly the process proceeds. Photosynthesis is the main biological process determining the rate of ecosystem productivity, the rate at which an ecosystem creates biomass. Thus, in evaluating the productivity of an ecosystem, potential limiting factors are light intensity, gas concentrations and mineral availability. The Law of the Minimum states that the required factor in a given process that is most scarce controls the rate of the process.

One potential limiting factor of ecosystem productivity is light intensity because photosynthesis requires light energy. Light intensity can limit productivity in two ways. First, too little light limits the rate of photosynthesis, because the required energy is not available. Second, too much light can damage the photosynthetic system of plants and microorganisms thus slowing the rate of photosynthesis. Decreased photosynthesis equals decreased productivity.

Another potential limiting factor of ecosystem productivity is gas concentrations. Photosynthesis requires carbon dioxide. Thus, increased concentration of carbon dioxide often results in increased productivity. While carbon dioxide is often not the ultimate limiting factor of productivity, increased concentration can indirectly increase rates of photosynthesis in several ways. First, increased carbon dioxide concentration often increases the rate of nitrogen fixation (available nitrogen is another limiting factor of productivity). Second, increased carbon dioxide concentration can decrease the pH of rain, improving the water source of photosynthetic organisms.

Finally, mineral availability also limits ecosystem productivity. Plants require adequate amounts of nitrogen and phosphorus to build many cellular structures. The availability of the inorganic minerals phosphorus and nitrogen often is the main limiting factor of plant biomass production. In other words, in a natural environment phosphorus and nitrogen availability most often limits ecosystem productivity, rather than carbon dioxide concentration or light intensity.

Interrelationships among organisms within a community

There are many interactions that may occur between different species living together. Predation, parasitism, competition, commensalisms and mutualism are the different types of relationships populations have amongst each other.

Predation and **parasitism** result in a benefit for one species and a detriment for the other. Predation is when a predator eats its prey. The common conception of predation is of a carnivore consuming other animals. This is one form of predation. Although not always resulting in the death of the plant, herbivory is a form of predation. Some animals eat enough of a plant to cause death. Parasitism involves a predator that lives on or in their hosts, causing detrimental effects to the host. Insects and viruses living off and reproducing in their hosts is an example of parasitism. Many plants and animals have defenses against predators. Some plants have poisonous chemicals that will harm the predator if ingested and some animals are camouflaged so they are harder to detect.

Competition is when two or more species in a community use the same resources. Competition is usually detrimental to both populations. Competition is often difficult to find in nature because competition between two populations is not continuous. Either the weaker population will no longer exist, or one population will evolve to utilize other available resources.

Symbiosis is when two species live close together. Parasitism is one example of symbiosis described above. Another example of symbiosis is commensalisms. **Commensalism** occurs when one species benefits from the other without harmful effects. **Mutualism** is when both species benefit from the other. Species involved in mutualistic relationships must coevolve to survive. As one species evolves, the other must as well if it is to be successful in life. The grouper and a species of shrimp live in a mutualistic relationship. The shrimp feed off parasites living on the grouper; thus the shrimp are fed and the grouper stays healthy. Many microorganisms are in mutualistic relationships.

Skill 22.4   Analyze various conservation methods and their effectiveness in relation to renewable and nonrenewable natural resources

A **renewable resource** is one that is replaced naturally. Living renewable resources would be plants and animals. Plants are renewable because they grow and reproduce. Sometimes renewal of the resource doesn't keep up with the demand. Such is the case with trees. Since the housing industry uses lumber for frames and homebuilding they are often cut down faster than new trees can grow. Now there are specific tree farms. Special methods allow trees to grow faster.

A second renewable resource is animals. They renew by the process of reproduction. Some wild animals need protection on refuges. As the population of humans increases resources are used faster. Cattle are used for their hides and for food. Some animals like deer are killed for sport. Each state has an environmental protection agency with divisions of forest management and wildlife management.

Non-living renewable resources would be water, air and soil. Water is renewed in a natural cycle called the water cycle. Air is a mixture of gases. Oxygen is given off by plants and taken in by animals that in turn expel the carbon dioxide that the plants need. Soil is another renewable resource. Fertile soil is rich in minerals. When plants grow they remove the minerals and make the soil less fertile. Chemical treatments are one way or renewing the composition. It is also accomplished naturally when the plants decay back into the soil. The plant material is used to make compost to mix with the soil.

Nonrenewable resources are not easily replaced in a timely fashion. Minerals are nonrenewable resources. Quartz, mica, salt and sulfur are some examples. Mining depletes these resources so society may benefit. Glass is made from quartz, electronic equipment from mica, and salt has many uses. Sulfur is used in medicine, fertilizers, paper and matches.

Metals are among the most widely used nonrenewable resource. Metals must be separated from the ore. Iron is our most important ore. Gold, silver and copper are often found in a more pure form called native metals.

COMPETENCY 23.0   KNOWLEDGE OF NATURE AND HISTORY OF SCIENCE

Skill 23.1   **Demonstrate knowledge of basic science processes (e.g., observing, classifying, communicating, qualifying, inferring and predicting)**

Science may be defined as a body of knowledge that is systematically derived from study, observations and experimentation. Its goal is to identify and establish principles and theories that may be applied to solve problems. Pseudoscience, on the other hand, is a belief that is not warranted. There is no scientific methodology or application. Some of the more classic examples of pseudoscience include witchcraft, alien encounters or any topics that are explained by hearsay.

Scientific inquiry starts with observation. Observation is a very important skill by itself, since it leads to experimentation and finally communicating the experimental findings to the society / public. After observing, a question is formed, which starts with "why" or "how." To answer these questions, experimentation is necessary. Between observation and experimentation, there are three more important steps. These are: gathering information (or researching about the problem), hypothesis, and designing the experiment.

Designing an experiment is very important since it involves identifying control, constants, independent variables and dependent variables. A control / standard is something we compare our results with at the end of the experiment. It is like a reference. Constants are the factors we have to keep constant in an experiment to get reliable results. Independent variables are factors we change in an experiment. It is very important to bear in mind that there should be more constants than variables to obtain reproducible results in an experiment.

Classifying is grouping items according to their similarities. It is important for students to realize relationships and similarity as well as differences to reach a reasonable conclusion in a lab experience.

After the experiment is done, it is repeated and results are graphically presented. The results are then analyzed and conclusions drawn.

It is the responsibility of the scientists to share the knowledge they obtain through their research.

After the conclusion is drawn, the final step is communication. In this age, lot of emphasis is put on the way and the method of communication. The conclusions must be communicated through clearly described information using accurate data, visual presentation like graphs (bar/line/pie), tables/charts, diagrams, artwork and other appropriate media like power point presentation. Modern technology must be used whenever it is necessary. The method of communication must be suitable to the audience.

Written communication is as important as oral communication. This is essential for submitting research papers to scientific journals, newspapers, other magazines and etc.

Skill 23.2   Apply knowledge of the integrated science processes of manipulating variables, defining operationally, forming hypotheses, measuring (metric) and graphing, and interpreting data

The scientific method is the basic process behind science. It involves several steps beginning with hypothesis formulation and working through to the conclusion.

Posing a question
Although many discoveries happen by chance, the standard thought process of a scientist begins with forming a question to research. The more limited the question, the easier it is to set up an experiment to answer it.

Form a hypothesis
Once the question is formulated take an educated guess about the answer to the problem or question. This 'best guess' is your hypothesis.

Doing the test
To make a test fair, data from an experiment must have a **variable** or any condition that can be changed such as temperature or mass. A good test will try to manipulate as few variables as possible so as to see which variable is responsible for the result. This requires a second example of a **control**. A control is an extra setup in which all the conditions are the same except for the variable being tested.

Observe and record the data
Reporting of the data should state specifics of how the measurements were calculated. A graduated cylinder needs to be read with proper procedures. As beginning students, technique must be part of the instructional process so as to give validity to the data.

Drawing a conclusion
After recording data, you compare your data with that of other groups. A conclusion is the judgment derived from the data results.

Graphing data

Graphing utilizes numbers to demonstrate patterns. The patterns offer a visual representation, making it easier to draw conclusions.

Apply knowledge of designing and performing investigations

Normally, knowledge is integrated in the form of a lab report. A report has many sections. It should include a specific **title** and tell exactly what is being studied. The **abstract** is a summary of the report written at the beginning of the paper. The **purpose** should always be defined and will state the problem. The purpose should include the **hypothesis** (educated guess) of what is expected from the outcome of the experiment. The entire experiment should relate to this problem.

It is important to describe exactly what was done to prove or disprove a hypothesis. A **control** is necessary to prove that the results occurred from the changed conditions and would not have happened normally. Only one variable should be manipulated at a time. **Observations** and **results** of the experiment should be recorded including all results from data. Drawings, graphs and illustrations should be included to support information. Observations are objective, whereas analysis and interpretation is subjective. A **conclusion** should explain why the results of the experiment either proved or disproved the hypothesis.

A scientific theory is an explanation of a set of related observations based on a proven hypothesis. A scientific law usually lasts longer than a scientific theory and has more experimental data to support it.

Science uses the metric system as it is accepted worldwide and allows easier comparison among experiments done by scientists around the world. Learn the following basic units and prefixes:

- **Meter** - measure of length
- **Liter** - measure of volume
- **Gram** - measure of mass
- **Deca**-(meter, liter, gram)= 10X the base unit   **deci** = 1/10 the base unit
- **Hecto**-(meter, liter, gram)= 100X the base unit **centi** = 1/100 the base unit
- **Kilo**-(meter, liter, gram) = 1000X the base unit **milli**   = 1/1000 the base unit

Graphing is an important skill to visually display collected data for analysis. The two types of graphs most commonly used are the **line graph** and the **bar graph** (histogram). Line graphs are set up to show two variables represented by one point on the graph. The X axis is the horizontal axis and represents the dependent variable. Dependent variables are those that would be present independently of the experiment. A common example of a dependent variable is time. Time proceeds regardless of anything else occurring. The Y axis is the vertical axis and represents the independent variable. Independent variables are manipulated by the experiment, such as the amount of light, or the height of a plant. Graphs should be calibrated at equal intervals. If one space represents one day, the next space may not represent ten days. A "best fit" line is drawn to join the points and may not include all the points in the data. Axes must always be labeled, for the graph to be meaningful. A good title will describe both the dependent and the independent variable. Bar graphs are set up similarly in regards to axes, but points are not plotted. Instead, the dependent variable is set up as a bar where the X axis intersects with the Y axis. Each bar is a separate item of data and is not joined by a continuous line.

Skill 23.3 Apply knowledge of inquiry approaches to learning science concepts

Learning can be broadly divided into two kinds - active and passive. Active learning involves, as the name indicates, a learning atmosphere full of action whereas in passive learning students are taught in a nonstimulating and inactive atmosphere. Active learning involves and draws students into it, thereby interesting them to the point of participating and purposely engaging in learning.

It is crucial that students are actively engaged, not entertained. They should be taught the answers for "How" and "Why" questions and encouraged to be inquisitive and interested.

Active learning is conceptualized as follows:

A Model of Active Learning

Experience of	Dialogue with
Doing	Self
Observing	Others

This model suggests that all learning activities involve some kind of experience or some kind of dialogue. The two main kinds of dialogue are "Dialogue with self" and "Dialogue with others." The two main kinds of experience are "Observing" and "Doing."

Dialogue with self: This is what happens when a learner thinks reflectively about a topic. They ask themselves a number of things about the topic.

Dialogue with others: When the students are listening to a book being read by another student or when the teacher is teaching, a partial dialogue takes place because the dialogue is only one sided. When they are listening to an adult, and when there is an exchange of ideas back and forth, it is said to be a dialogue with others.

Observing: This is a most important skill in science. This occurs when a learner is carefully watching or observing someone else doing an activity or experiment. This is a good experience, although it is not quite like doing it for themselves.

Doing: This refers to any activity where a learner actually does something, giving the learner a firsthand experience that is very valuable.

Inquiry is invaluable to teaching in general and especially to teaching science. The steps involved in scientific inquiry are discussed in the following section.

The scientific attitude is to be curious, open to new ideas, and skeptical. In science, there is always new research, new discoveries, and new theories proposed. Sometimes, old theories are disproved. To view these changes rationally, one must have such openness, curiosity and skepticism (skepticism is a Greek word that means a method of obtaining knowledge through systematic doubt and continual testing). A scientific skeptic is one who refuses to accept certain types of claims without subjecting them to a systematic investigation.

The students may not have these attitudes inherently, but it is the responsibility of the teacher to encourage, nurture and practice these attitudes so that students will have a good role model.

Skill 23.4   Identify the appropriate laboratory equipment for specific activities

Bunsen burners - Hot plates should be used whenever possible to avoid the risk of burns or fire. If Bunsen burners are used, the following precautions should be followed:

1. Know the location of fire extinguishers and safety blankets and train students in their use. Long hair and long sleeves should be secured and out of the way.
2. Turn the gas all the way on and make a spark with the striker. The preferred method to light burners is to use strikers rather than matches.
3. Adjust the air valve at the bottom of the Bunsen burner until the flame shows an inner cone.
4. Adjust the flow of gas to the desired flame height by using the adjustment valve.
5. Do not touch the barrel of the burner (it is hot).

Graduated Cylinder - These are used for precise measurements. They should always be placed on a flat surface. The surface of the liquid will form a meniscus (lens-shaped curve). The measurement is read at the <u>bottom</u> of this curve.

Balance - Electronic balances are easier to use, but more expensive. An electronic balance should always be tarred (returned to zero) before measuring and used on a flat surface. Substances should always be placed on a piece of paper to avoid spills and/or damage to the instrument. Triple beam balances must be used on a level surface. There are screws located at the bottom of the balance to make any adjustments. Start with the largest counterweight first and proceed toward the last notch that does not tip the balance. Do the same with the next largest, etc until the pointer remains at zero. The total mass is the total of all the readings on the beams. Again, use paper under the substance to protect the equipment.

Buret – A buret is used to dispense precisely measured volumes of liquid. A stopcock is used to control the volume of liquid being dispensed at a time.

Light microscopes are commonly used in laboratory experiments. Several procedures should be followed to properly care for this equipment:
- Clean all lenses with lens paper only.
- Carry microscopes with two hands; one on the arm, and one on the base.
- Always begin focusing on low power, then switch to high power.
- Store microscopes with the low power objective down.
- Always use a coverslip when viewing wet mount slides.
- Bring the objective down to its lowest position then focus by moving up to avoid breaking the slide or scratching the lens.

Wet mount slides should be made by placing a drop of water on the specimen and then putting a glass coverslip on top of the drop of water. Dropping the coverslip at a forty-five degree angle will help in avoiding air bubbles. Total magnification is determined by multiplying the ocular (usually 10X) and the objective (usually 10X on low, 40X on high).

Skill 23.5 **Identify state safety procedures for teaching science, including the care of living organisms and the accepted procedures for the safe preparation, use, storage and disposal of chemicals and other materials**

Dissections - Animals that are not obtained from recognized sources should not be used. Decaying animals or those of unknown origin may harbor pathogens and/or parasites. Specimens should be rinsed before handling. Latex gloves are desirable. If gloves are not available, students with sores or scratches should be excused from the activity. Formaldehyde is a carcinogen and should be avoided or disposed of according to district regulations. Students objecting to dissections for moral reasons should be given an alternative assignment.
Live specimens - No dissections may be performed on living mammalian vertebrates or birds. Lower order life and invertebrates may be used.

Biological experiments may be done with all animals except mammalian vertebrates or birds. No physiological harm may result to the animal. All animals housed and cared for in the school must be handled in a safe and humane manner. Animals are not to remain on school premises during extended vacations unless adequate care is provided. Many state laws stipulate that any instructor who intentionally refuses to comply with the laws may be suspended or dismissed.

Microbiology - Pathogenic organisms must never be used for experimentation. Students should adhere to the following rules at all times when working with microorganisms to avoid accidental contamination:

1. Treat all microorganisms as if they were pathogenic.
2. Maintain sterile conditions at all times.

If you are taking a national level exam you should check the Department of Education for your state for safety procedures. You will want to know what your state expects of you not only for the test but also for performance in the classroom and for the welfare of your students.

All science labs should contain the following items of safety equipment. The following are requirements by law.

- Fire blanket which is visible and accessible
- Ground Fault Circuit Interrupters (GFCI) within two feet of water supplies
- Emergency shower capable of providing a continuous flow of water
- Signs designating room exits
- Emergency eye wash station, which can be activated by the foot or forearm
- Eye protection for every student and a means of sanitizing equipment
- Emergency exhaust fans providing ventilation to the outside of the building
- Master cut-off switches for gas, electric and compressed air. Switches must have permanently attached handles. Cut-off switches must be clearly labeled.
- An ABC fire extinguisher
- Storage cabinets for flammable materials

Also recommended, but not required by law:
- Chemical spill control kit
- Fume hood with a motor which is spark proof
- Protective laboratory aprons made of flame retardant material
- Signs which will alert people to potential hazardous conditions
- Containers for broken glassware, flammables, corrosives and waste
- Containers should be labeled

It is the responsibility of teachers to provide a safe environment for their students. Proper supervision greatly reduces the risk of injury and a teacher should never leave a class for any reason without providing alternate supervision. After an accident, two factors are considered: foreseeability and negligence.

Foreseeability is the anticipation that an event may occur under certain circumstances. **Negligence** is the failure to exercise ordinary or reasonable care. Safety procedures should be a part of the science curriculum and a well managed classroom is important to avoid potential lawsuits.

The **"Right to Know Law" statutes** cover science teachers who work with potentially hazardous chemicals. Briefly, the law states that employees must be informed of potentially toxic chemicals. An inventory must be made available if requested. The inventory must contain information about the hazards and properties of the chemicals. Training must be provided in the safe handling and interpretation of the Material Safety Data Sheet.

The following chemicals are potential carcinogens and are not allowed in school facilities: Acrylonitriel, Arsenic compounds, Asbestos, Bensidine, Benzene, Cadmium compounds, Chloroform, Chromium compounds, Ethylene oxide, Ortho-toluidine, Nickel powder, Mercury.

All laboratory solutions should be prepared as directed in the lab manual. Care should be taken to avoid contamination. All glassware should be rinsed thoroughly with distilled water before using and cleaned well after use. Safety goggles should be worn while working with glassware in case of an accident. All solutions should be made with distilled water as tap water contains dissolved particles which may affect the results of an experiment. Chemical storage should be located in a secured dry area. Chemicals should be stored in accordance with reactability. Acids are to be locked in a separate area. Used solutions should be disposed of according to local disposal procedures. Any questions regarding safe disposal or chemical safety may be directed to the local fire department.

COMPETENCY 24.0   KNOWLEDGE OF THE RELATIONSHIP OF SCIENCE AND TECHNOLOGY

Skill 24.1   Identify the interrelationship of science and technology

Biological science is closely connected to technology and the other sciences and greatly impacts society and everyday life. Scientific discoveries often lead to technological advances and, conversely, technology is often necessary for scientific investigation and advances in technology often expand the reach of scientific discoveries. In addition, biology and the other scientific disciplines share several unifying concepts and processes that help unify the study of science. Finally, because biology is the science of living systems, biology directly impacts society and everyday life.

Science and technology and their distinct concepts are closely related. Science attempts to investigate and explain the natural world, while technology attempts to solve human adaptation problems. Technology often results from the application of scientific discoveries and advances in technology can increase the impact of scientific discoveries. For example, Watson and Crick used science to discover the structure of DNA and their discovery led to many biotechnological advances in the manipulation of DNA. These technological advances greatly influenced the medical and pharmaceutical fields; however, the success of Watson and Crick's experiments was dependent on the technology available. Without the necessary technology, the experiments would have failed.

The combination of biology and technology has improved the human standard of living in many ways; however, the negative impact of increasing human life expectancy and population on the environment is problematic. In addition, advances in biotechnology (e.g., genetic engineering, cloning) produce ethical dilemmas that society must consider. Biologists use a variety of tools and technologies to perform tests, collect and display data and analyze relationships. Examples of commonly used tools include computer-linked probes, spreadsheets and graphing calculators.

Biologists use computer-linked probes to measure various environmental factors including temperature, dissolved oxygen, pH, ionic concentration and pressure. The advantage of computer-linked probes, as compared to more traditional observational tools, is that the probes automatically gather data and present it in an accessible format. This property of computer-linked probes eliminates the need for constant human observation and manipulation.

Biologists use spreadsheets to organize, analyze and display data. For example, conservation ecologists use spreadsheets to model population growth and development, apply sampling techniques, and create statistical distributions to analyze relationships. Spreadsheet use simplifies data collection and manipulation and allows the presentation of data in a logical and understandable format.

Graphing calculators are another technology with many applications to biology. For example, biologists use algebraic functions to analyze growth, development and other natural processes. Graphing calculators can manipulate algebraic data and create graphs for analysis and observation. In addition, biologists use the matrix function of graphing calculators to model problems in genetics. The use of graphing calculators simplifies the creation of graphical displays including histograms, scatter plots and line graphs. Biologists can also transfer data and displays to computers for further analysis. Finally, biologists connect computer-linked probes, used to collect data, to graphing calculators to ease the collection, transmission and analysis of data.

Skill 24.2   Identify the tools and techniques of science and technology used for data collection and problem solving

Processes by which hypotheses are generated and tested

Science may be defined as a body of knowledge that is systematically derived from study, observations and experimentation. Its goal is to identify and establish principles and theories that may be applied to solve problems. Pseudoscience, on the other hand, is a belief that is not warranted. There is no scientific methodology or application. Some of the more classic examples of pseudoscience include witchcraft, alien encounters or any topic that is explained by hearsay.

Scientific theory and experimentation must be repeatable. It is possible to be disproved and is capable of change. Science depends on communication, agreement and disagreement among scientists. It is composed of theories, laws and hypotheses:

- **Theory -** the formation of principles or relationships which have been verified and accepted.
- **Law -** an explanation of events that occur with uniformity under the same conditions (laws of nature, law of gravitation).
- **Hypothesis -** an unproved theory or educated guess followed by research to best explain a phenomena. A theory is a proven hypothesis.

Science is limited by the available technology. An example of this would be the relationship of the discovery of the cell and the invention of the microscope. As our technology improves, more hypotheses will become theories, and possibly laws. Science is also limited by the data that is able to be collected. Data may be interpreted differently on different occasions. Science limitations cause explanations to be changeable as new technologies emerge.

The first step in scientific inquiry is posing a question to be answered. Next, a hypothesis is formed to provide a plausible explanation. An experiment is then proposed and performed to test this hypothesis. A comparison between the predicted and observed results is the next step. Conclusions are then formed and it is determined whether the hypothesis is correct or incorrect. If incorrect, the next step is to form a new hypothesis and the process is repeated.

Methods or procedures for collecting data

The procedure used to obtain data is important to the outcome. Experiments consist of **controls** and **variables**. A control is the experiment run under normal conditions. The variable includes a factor that is changed. In biology, the variable may be light, temperature, pH, time and etc. The differences in tested variables may be used to make a prediction or form a hypothesis. Only one variable should be tested at a time. One would not alter both the temperature and pH of the experimental subject.

An **independent variable** is one that is changed or manipulated by the researcher. This could be the amount of light given to a plant or the temperature at which bacteria is grown. The **dependent variable** is influenced by the independent variable.

Procedures and Tools

See also Skill 23.4.

Chemicals should not be stored on bench tops or heat sources. They should be stored in groups based on their reactivity with one another and in protective storage cabinets. All containers within the lab must be labeled. Suspect and known carcinogens must be labeled as such and segregated within trays to contain leaks and spills. Chemical waste should be disposed of in properly labeled containers. Waste should be separated based on their reactivity with other chemicals.

Biological material should never be stored near food or water used for human consumption. All biological material should be appropriately labeled. All blood and body fluids should be put in a well-contained container with a secure lid to prevent leaking. All biological waste should be disposed of in biological hazardous waste bags.

Material safety data sheets are available for every chemical and biological substance. These are available directly from the company of acquisition or the internet. The manuals for equipment used in the lab should be read and understood before using them.

Use of live specimens

No dissections may be performed on living mammalian vertebrates or birds. Lower order life and invertebrates may be used. Biological experiments may be done with all animals except mammalian vertebrates or birds. No physiological harm may result to the animal. All animals housed and cared for in the school must be handled in a safe and humane manner. Animals are not to remain on school premises during extended vacations unless adequate care is provided. Any instructor who intentionally refuses to comply with the laws may be suspended or dismissed.

Pathogenic organisms must never be used for experimentation. Students should adhere to the following rules at all times when working with microorganisms to avoid accidental contamination:

1. Treat all microorganisms as if they were pathogenic.
2. Maintain sterile conditions at all times.

Dissection and alternatives to dissection

Animals that are not obtained from recognized sources should not be used. Decaying animals, or those of unknown origin, may harbor pathogens and/or parasites. Specimens should be rinsed before handling. Latex gloves are desirable. If not available, students with sores or scratches should be excused from the activity. Formaldehyde is likely carcinogenic and should be avoided or disposed of according to district regulations. Students objecting to dissections for moral reasons should be given an alternative assignment. Interactive dissections are available online or from software companies for those students who object to performing dissections. There should be no penalty for those students who refuse to physically perform a dissection.

Laboratory safety procedures

Students should wear safety goggles when performing dissections, heating, or while using acids and bases. Hair should always be tied back and objects should never be placed in the mouth. Food should not be consumed while in the laboratory. Hands should always be washed before and after laboratory experiments. In case of an accident, eye washes and showers should be used for eye contamination or a chemical spill that covers the student's body. Small chemical spills should only be contained and cleaned by the teacher. Kitty litter or a chemical spill kit should be used to clean spill. For large spills, the school administration and the local fire department should be notified. Biological spills should also be handled only by the teacher. Contamination with biological waste can be cleaned by using bleach when appropriate.

Accidents and injuries should always be reported to the school administration and local health facilities. The severity of the accident or injury will determine the course of action to pursue.

It is the responsibility of the teacher to provide a safe environment for their students. Proper supervision greatly reduces the risk of injury and a teacher should never leave a class for any reason without providing alternate supervision. After an accident, two factors are considered; **foreseeability** and **negligence**. Foreseeability is the anticipation that an event may occur under certain circumstances. Negligence is the failure to exercise ordinary or reasonable care. Safety procedures should be a part of the science curriculum and a well managed classroom is important to avoid potential lawsuits.

COMPETENCY 25.0   KNOWLEDGE OF TECHNOLOGY PROCESSES AND APPLICATIONS

Skill 25.1   Identify the purposes and functions of common computer software (e.g., word processor, spreadsheet, database, multimedia, communication and publishing)

o   *See Skill 25.1*

Skill 25.2   Identify ways technology can be used by students to represent understanding of science concepts (should be out there by a writer)

While a certain amount of information will always be presented in lecture form or using traditional written materials (i.e.: textbooks) technology, both new and old, can help students understand concepts and become more engaged in discovering new facts and the scientific method. Below are some examples:

Hands-on experiments and demonstrations

Some of the most simple and oldest technologies can be used to demonstrate concepts for students. These include simple chemical equipment such as Bunsen burners and devices that display physical phenomenon such as gyroscopes. Some simple experiments may be appropriate for elementary aged students and newer safety technology makes this true even more so. Ideas for experiments can be found in many places including:

> <u>http://sciencepage.org/teachers.htm</u>
> <u>http://www.anachem.umu.se/eks/pointers.htm</u>
> <u>http://www.csun.edu/science/</u>

Software and simulations

When hands-on experiments are costly, complicated, dangerous or otherwise not possible, students may benefit from software programs that simulate them. While these experiences are less "hands-on" than actual experiments, much current software is highly interactive and so does allow the students to become more involved in what they are learning. Multimedia software packages can be used to expose students to video and sounds of subjects they are they are studying. The following website lists many publishers of such software:

> <u>http://www.educational-software-directory.net/science/</u>

Online Resources

Similar to the software discussed above, there are many science-focused websites directed to grade school aged children. Web resources can be of particular use when following a current event in science. For instance, the NASA website frequently allows tracking of space missions in progress, which can be an exciting experience for students.

Skill 25.3   Identify telecommunications terminology, processes and procedures

Telecommunications is defined as the use of wire, radio, optical or other electromagnetic channels to transmit or receive signals for voice, data and video communications.

There are three basic parts of a telecommunications system:

- The **transmitter** is an electronic device that transmits an electromagnetic signal with the aid of an antenna. This may be radio, television or other telecommunications signals.

- The **transmission medium** is the medium over which the signal is transmitted. It may be optical fiber, twisted pair wires, coaxial cable, water, air, glass or concrete.

- The **receiver** is the system that receives the signal and converts it into usable information. Examples include a radio, television, modem, hearing aids and etc.

An example would be a radio broadcast. The broadcast tower is the transmitter, the radio is the receiver and the transmission medium is free space (air). Often, the telecommunications device serves as both the transmitter and the receiver. A mobile phone is an example of such a two-way device, also called a transceiver.

Telecommunications signals can be digital or analogue. In a digital signal, the information is encoded as a set of discrete values. In an analogue signal, the signal is varied continuously with respect to the information; the transmitter coverts different types of information, sound or video, into electrical or optical signals. Electrical signals travel along a medium such as copper wire or are carried over the air as radio waves. Optical signals travel along a medium such as strands of glass fibers. When the signal reaches its destination, the receiver converts the signal back into an understandable message, such as a sound, an image or words and pictures.

Skill 25.4   Demonstrate knowledge of legal and ethical practices as they relate to information and technological systems (e.g., copyright, privacy and plagiarism)

In both research science and technology innovation, it is extremely important that credit for work is properly assigned. Whether in the development of technology or in pure research, there are both financial and scientific issues at stake. In fact, an entire branch of law, intellectual property law, deals with the legal issues surrounding ownership of ideas and information.

In both commercial and academic research environments, scientists keep careful records in laboratory notebooks. These serve as primary documents bearing witness to new discoveries and developments. In academic and pure research settings these findings are typically published in peer reviewed journals and student theses. Occasionally, cases of falsification of data and/or plagiarism occur. Plagiarism means that the work has been presented as original when, in fact, it incorporates the work of others. Both these occurrences are highly undesirable and may results in disciplinary action and/or loss of reputation within the scientific community. It should be noted that when preparing documents, it is acceptable to include information and even direction quotations from other sources, so long as they are always *properly cited*.

In contrast, new inventions and technology developed by commercial enterprises are typically patented or copyrighted. A patent gives an individual or organization exclusive rights to a device, method or process. A copyright serves an analogous purpose for an idea or image (a trademark is similar but specifically distinguishes a specific business or type of product). Copyrights and patents allow an inventor/designer (or the company for which they are employed) to exclusively use, sell or license their design. Both typically grant exclusive use for only a limited period of time. If others attempt to produce or sell the patented or copyrighted design, they can be challenged under the law. Because patents are published (everyone can view them, but not use them), some companies prefer not to patent their designs, but keep them as trade secrets. Such trade secrets, of course, cannot be legally protected; however, patents expire at which point the technology is available to all; the exclusivity of trade secrets does not expire. There is much debate over the utility of patents and copyrights. Some believe they offer economic incentive and so encourage innovation while others say they lead to monopolies and provide no protection for inventions developed simultaneously.

DOMAIN V. MUSIC, VISUAL ARTS, PHYSICAL EDUCATION AND HEALTH

COMPETENCY 26.0 KNOWLEDGE OF SKILLS AND TECHNIQUES IN MUSIC AND VISUAL ART

Skill 26.1 Identify appropriate vocal literature (e.g., age-appropriate range and vocal ability; diverse cultures, genres and styles)

"Genre," originating from the French for "kind," refers to a style or category of work, characterized by content or artistic style. For example, in the visual arts, various genres include, among others, the content areas of seascape, still lives, portraiture and religious works. Specific examples for each of these include the following:

- **Seascape**- Turner's *The Slave Ship*
- **Still life**- Cezanne's *Still Life*
- **Portraiture**- Reynold's *Lord Heathfield*
- **Religious**- Rembrandt van Riji's *The Three Crosses*

Genres of artistic style include, among others, realism, abstract expressionism and non-objective compositions. Specific examples for each of these include the following:

- **Realism**- Wyeth's *Christina's World*
- **Abstract expressionism**- de Kooning's *Woman I*
- **Non-objective painting**- Kelly's *Red, Blue, Green*

In the visual arts, "genre" also refers to a specific style of realistic painting, which illustrates scenes of everyday life, an example of which is Kalf's *Still Life*. (See 1.3 and 2.10 for more information.)

In the field of music, various genres include, among others, the forms of cantata, concerto, mass, motet, opera, oratorio, overture, sonata, suite and symphony. Examples for each of these include the following:
- **Cantata**- Orff's *Carmina Burana*
- **Concerto**- Vivaldi's *Concerto for Two Trumpets*
- **Mass**- Palestrina's *Veni sponsa Christi*
- **Motet**- Gabrieli's *In Ecclesiis*
- **Opera**- Mozart's *Marriage of Figaro*
- **Oratorio**- Handel's *Messiah*
- **Overture**- Mozart's *Cosi Fan Tutte Overture*
- **Sonata**- Hayden's *String Quartet in F Major, movements 1,2*
- **Suite**- Stravinsky's *The Rite of Spring*
- **Symphony**- Beethoven's *Ninth Symphony*

In the visual arts, one type of genre is based on subject matter, therefore leading to genre headings such as seascape, landscape, still life, portraiture, religious and interiors and etc. Most of these headings are merely descriptive and self-explanatory. A work of visual art falls into one of these categories merely based on subject content.

Another definition of genre in the field of the visual arts is more specific. A "genre" scene is a realistically portrayed scene that depicts everyday life in a casual, informal, non-monumental way. This type of genre appears throughout the history of art.

Yet another genre in the visual arts is based on the artist's style of work, such as realism, abstraction, impressionism, expressionism and etc. For an example, a painting done by Picasso utilizing the concepts of cubism is said to belong to the cubist genre, while another painting, also by Picasso, but reflecting the concepts of neoclassicism, will fall into that genre. (See 1.5 and 2.10 for more information.)

In the fields of music and literature, genre refers to established forms of compositions. Many of these forms have precise definitions and parameters, as given here.

Vocal music is probably the oldest form of music, since it does not require any instrument besides the human voice. Unaccompanied music is referred to as acappella. The human voice consists of sound made by using the vocal folds (vocal chords) used for talking. The vocal folds, in combination with the lips, the tongue, the lower jaw and the palate are capable of producing highly intricate sound. The tone (i.e.: pitch, intensity and modulation) of voice may be modified to suggest various emotions, such as happiness and sadness. Tone quality is the quality of a note or sound that distinguishes different types of musical instruments.

Vocal music is the study and performance of repertoires of vocal music. It includes instruction in proper technique and skills, and the cultural and historical context of vocal literature. Vocal music encourages self-expression through performance and creation of music. The broadest definition of vocal range is the span of the highest to the lowest note a particular voice can produce. Choral music is less stringent than opera in that the large number of voices that can be deployed in each group make it somewhat less important that each individual voice be flawlessly produced and completely audible.

Skill 26.2 Identify developmentally appropriate singing techniques (e.g., posture, breath support, tone quality and vocal range)

Vocal music is probably the oldest form of music, since it does not require any instrument besides the human voice. Unaccompanied music is referred to as acappella. The human voice consists of sound made by using the vocal folds (vocal chords) used for talking. The vocal folds, in combination with the lips, the tongue, the lower jaw and the palate are capable of producing highly intricate sound. The tone (i.e.: pitch, intensity and modulation) of voice may be modified to suggest various emotions, such as happiness and sadness. Tone quality is the quality of a note or sound that distinguishes different types of musical instruments. Tone quality is what people use to distinguish the saxaphone from a trumpet, even when both instruments are playing notes at the same pitch.

Vocalists use the human voice as an instrument to create music and is complex. The vocal folds can loosen, tighten or change their thickness, transferring breath at various pressures. The position of the tongue and tightening of the muscles in the neck can result in changes of pitch and volume. Breath control, tone and posture all require different techniques.

Breathing technique is very important for proper voice projection. To talk we use air from the top of the lungs and the muscles from the back of the throat. To properly project our voices, we pull air from the bottom of the lungs, and the diaphragm (or stomach area) is used to push it out. Finding ways to exercise and lift the diaphragm such as singing musical scales can help singers reacher higher or lower notes. Stance is also important. It is recommended to stand up straight with your feet shoulder width apart, and your foot slightly forward. This improves your balance. This also improves your breathing.

Skill 26.3 Identify correct performance techniques for rhythmic and melodic classroom instruments (e.g., nonpitched percussion, recorder, autoharp and/or keyboard)

In music, a "devisive" rhythm is when a larger period of time is divided into smaller units. "Additive" rhythms are when larger periods of time are made from smaller units of time added to a previous unit.

Any single strike or series of beats on a percussion instrument creates a rhythmic pattern, sometimes called a "drum beat." Percussion instruments are sometimes referred to as nonpitched, or untuned. This occurs when the sound of the percussion instrument has no pitch that can be heard by the ear. Examples of percussion instruments that are nonpitched are the snare drum, cymbals and whistles.

The autoharp, or lyre, is a stringed instrument which has 30 to 40 strings stretched across a flat soundboard and is usually plucked rather than strummed. In the acoustic version, the autoharp has no neck. Chord bars are attached to dampers which mute all the other strings except the desired chord. An autoharp is sometimes called a zither. The zither is mainly used in folk music, most common in German-speaking Alpine Europe.

A keyboard instrument is any musical instrument played using a musical keyboard. The harpsichord and pipe organ was used in early European countries. The organ is the oldest, appearing in the 3rd century BC and until the 14th century was the only keyboard instrument. The harpsichord appeared at this time and was very common until the arrival of the piano in the 18th century.

The piano is popular because the player can vary the volume of the sound by varying the amount of intensity in which the keys were struck. Volume can also be adjusted with pedals which act as dampers. Other widely used keyboard instruments include electrictronicinstruments, which are largely referred to as keyboard-style synthesizers. Significant development of the synthesizer occurred in the 1960's when digital synthesizers became more common.

Skill 26.4 Read and interpret simple, traditional and nontraditional music notation (e.g., melodic, rhythmic and harmonic)

When music is written down, it is generally notated so that there are instructions regarding how the composer wants listeners to hear, and what the musician should do to perform the music. This is referred to as musical notation. Music notation is used by composers for writing music. Present standard music notation is based on a five-line staff called the clefs. The upper clef is called treble and the lower clef is called bass. Pitch is shown by placing notes on the staff. These notes are modified by additional symbols called sharps, flats and naturals. The duration is shown with different note shapes and additional symbols such as ties, dotted notes and rests. Besides notations developed for human performers, there are also computer generated representations of music designed to either be turned into conventional notation or designed to be read directly by the computer.

Melodic music covers music that is characterized by a single strong melody line. The melody line or tune, is easily memorable and followed without much difficulty. Melodic music may be performed by a singer and orchestra, a single instrument or any combination of the three. Opera is considered to be a classical form, the lighter operetta is considered borderline, while the musical is placed in the popular category.

Harmonic notation is commonly referred to as the "key" in which music is written. Keys can be major or minor, depending on the combination of whole and half steps used in the scale, and are indicated by sharp signs and flat signs after the clef signs in the signature. There are twelve pitches in the musical scale, with each pitch a degree of the scale. An interval is the relationship between two separate musical pitches. "Harmony" is the result of more than one note being played simultaneously (e.g., chord) and is created by the combination of notes making intervals.

Rhythmic notation refers to the exact rhythm the indicated notes or chords are played or sung. The rhythm key is written above the staff and is indicated in the traditional manner. Rhythms are usually arranged by using a time signature - signifying a meter. The top number of the time signature reflects the number of beats in each measure, whereas the bottom number reflects which type of note uses a single beat (e.g., 1 on the bottom reflects a whole note, 2 on the bottom reflects a half note, 4 reflects a quarter note and etc.). The speed of the underlying beat is the tempo (e.g., Allegro, Allegretto, Presto, Moderato, Lento and Largo) used singly or with any combination within a selection. Some music makes different use of rhythm than others. Most Western music is based on **divisive** rhythm, while non-Western music uses more **additive** rhythm.

Skill 26.5 Select safe and developmentally appropriate media, techniques, and tools to create both two-dimensional and three-dimensional works of art

Students should create and experience works of art that will explore different types of subject matter, themes and topics. Students need to understand the sensory elements and organizational principles of art and expression of images.

Students should be able to select and using mediums and processes that actively communicate and express the intended meaning or their art works, exhibits and prove competence in at least two mediums. For example, students are able to select a process or medium for their intended work of art and describe their reasons for that selection.

Students must also use the computer and electronic media to express their visual ideas and demonstrate a variety of different approaches to their selected medium. An excellent example for students to produce works using mixed media or a work of art that uses the computer, the camera and the copy machine or other types of electronic equipment.

At any age, students should be asked to compile a variety of their best works of art using different types of media. This is typically referred to as a portfolio. Early Childhood students all the way through High School students benefit from uses of a portfolio. Teachers are then able to explain choices of media and how it was chosen and used in a variety of ways using many different topics. The portfolio should begin with an early sample of the student's work, what is called a rough draft or a sketch. It can then be tracked to see the progress of each individual throughout the course of building the portfolio. By the end of the portfolio experience the growth in uses of medium and techniques should be clear and progress can be tracked through a use of a rubric or by observation.

Some of the areas that should be mastered by students and can be modeled by the teacher include the following:
- Experimentation through works of art using a variety of mediums, drawing, painting, sculpture, ceramics, printmaking and video
- Producing a collection of art works (portfolio) and using a variety of mediums, topics, themes and subject matter
- Convey meaning through which art works were chosen
- Create and evaluate different art works and which types of mediums chosen
- Reflection on work and others works

Some examples should include:
- Mixing paint in ranges of shades and tints
- Use the computer to design an idea for sculpting
- Include in the portfolio works that display at least two mediums
- Try to include at least ten works of art in each portfolio
- Include early sketches, research and development of each project with each entry
- Research a design such as a building or a landmark and design it based on the research
- Paint a picture using tempra or watercolor recalling a specific experience or memory

Skill 26.6   Identify appropriate uses of art materials and tools for developing basic processes and motor skills

It is vital that students learn to identify characteristics of visual arts that include materials, techniques and processes necessary to establish a connection between art and daily life. Early ages should begin to experience art in a variety of forms. It is important to reach many areas at an early age to establish a strong artistic foundation for young students. Students should be introduced to the simple recognition of simple patterns found in the art environment. They must also identify art materials such as clay, paint and crayons. Each of these types of material should be introduced and explained for use in daily lessons with young children.

Young students may need to be introduced to items that are developmentally appropriate for their age and for their fine motor skills. Many Pre-Kindergarten and Kindergarten students use oversized pencils and crayons for the first semester. Typically, after this first semester, development occurs to enable children to gradually develop into using smaller sized materials.

Students should begin to explore artistic expression at this age using colors and mixing. The color wheel is a vital lesson for young children and students begin to learn the uses of primary colors and secondary colors. By the middle of the school year students should be able to explain this process. For example, a student needs orange paint, but only has a few colors. Students should be able to determine that by mixing red and yellow that orange is created.

Teachers should begin to plan and use variation using line, shape, texture and many different principles of design. By using common environmental figures such as people, animals and buildings teachers can base many art lessons on characteristics of readily available examples. Students should be introduced to as many techniques as possible to ensure that all strands of the visual arts and materials are experienced at a variety of levels.

By using original works of arts students should be able to identify visual and actual textures of art and based their judgments of objects found in everyday scenes. Other examples that can be described as subjects could include landscapes, portraits and still life.

The major areas that young students should experience should include the following:

1. Painting-using tempra or watercolors.
2. Sculpture-typically using clay or play-dough.
3. Architecture-building or structuring design using 3D materials such as cardboard and poster board to create a desired effect.
4. Ceramics- another term for pottery using a hollow clay sculpture and pots made from clay and fired in a kiln using high temperature to strengthen them.
5. Metalworking-another term for engraving or cutting design or letters into metal with a sharp tool printmaking.
6. Lithography is an example of planographics, where a design is drawn on a surface and then the print is lifted from the surface.

COMPETENCY 27.0   KNOWLEDGE OF CREATION AND COMMUNICATION IN MUSIC AND VISUAL ARTS

Skill 27.1   Identify the elements of music (e.g., rhythm, melody, form, texture, timbre and dynamics) and ways they are used in expressing text; ideas; emotions; and settings, time and place

Music

Cantata - Developed in the baroque era, these compositions were written for solo and chorus voices, with orchestral accompaniment. With either secular or sacred lyrics, cantatas contain several movements.

Concerto - A musical work written for one or more solo instruments with orchestral accompaniment, the concerto usually is comprised of three movements in a fast-slow-fast order.

Mass - This choral type is usually associated with the Roman Catholic Church service, thus following the form of that service and including six musical parts: the Kyrie Eleison, Gloria in Excelsis Deo, Credo in Unum Deum, Sanctus, Benedictus and Agnus Dei. Specific masses for the dead are known as "requiem" masses; however, not all masses are written for church services. Since the Medieval period, "concert masses" have been an accepted form of composition.

Motet - From the French for "word," a motet is a choral work, utilizing a polyphonic approach. Motets from the thirteenth century were often written for three voices (triplum, motetus and tenor), and combined texts from both sacred and secular sources. During the fifteenth and sixteenth centuries (Renaissance), the motet expanded to a contrapuntal work for four or five voices a cappella, utilizing a sacred text. The motet also appears in the Baroque and Romantic periods with both orchestral and a cappella variations.

Opera- Originating from the Italian word for "work," opera is appropriately named. It is a musical work that incorporates many of the other arts as well. Technically, it is a play in which all the dialogue (libretto) is sung, with orchestral accompaniment. The origins of opera were founded in Renaissance Florence by intellectuals reviving Greek and Roman drama. Since then, operatic forms have evolved through many stages. Major ones include "grand opera" or "opera seria," which consists of five acts and is serious in nature, "opera comique," which, regardless of emotional content, has spoken dialogue, "opera buffa," which is the comic opera usually based on farce, and "operetta," also with spoken dialogue and characterized by a light, romantic mood and popular theme.

Oratorio - Developed during the Baroque era, an oratorio is a choral work of large scale, including parts for soloists, chorus and orchestra alike. Themes are usually epic or religious in nature. Although the soloists may take the role of various characters and there may be a plot, an oratorio is usually presented in concert form, without action, costumes or set design.

Overture - Usually an overture is the introductory composition to an opera, written to capture the mood of the opera, and even to showcase a musical motif from the opera; however, since in concerts overtures are often performed out-of-context, composers have now begun to write "concert overtures," meant to stand alone, without a larger body of music to follow.

Sonata - A sonata is a succession of movements which have loosely related tonalities. The first of these movements usually is composed in a specific pattern, which is known as "sonata form." Sonata form, or sonata-allegro form, follows the pattern of development ABA or AABA, where A is the exposition, B is the development, and the final section of A is the recapitulation.

Suite - A musical suite is a group of dances, usually written for keyboards or an ensemble of stringed or wind instruments. The dances are usually unrelated except for a common key.

Symphony - Fully refined by the eighteenth century, a symphony is a large scale work composed for a full orchestra; however, the various historic and stylistic periods, in addition to the development of instruments, have produced an evolution of this form. Because of this, "symphony" also refers to compositions for chamber orchestras and string quartets. Although some symphonies vary in the number of movements, in general, the four symphonic movements follow the tempo pattern of fast, slow, moderate and fast with a minuet included in the third movement.

Skill 27.2   Demonstrate knowledge of strategies to develop creative responses through music to ideas drawn from text, speech, movement and visual images

Students can explore creating moods with music, analyzing stories and creating musical compositions that reflect or enhance it. Their daily routines can include exploration, interpretation, and understanding of musical sound. Immersing them in musical conversations as we sing, speak rhythmically, and walk in-step stimulates their awareness of the beauty and structure of musical sound.

As students acquire the skills and knowledge that music brings to their lives, they go through the similar stages of developing language skills. Singing, chanting and moving, exposing them to many different sound sources, including a variety of styles of music in play, reinforcing rhythm through patting, tapping and moving will enhance their awareness of musical sound. Involvement in music is thought to teach basic skills such as concentration, counting, listening and promoting understanding of language.

Skill 27.3   Demonstrate knowledge of strategies to develop creative responses through art to ideas drawn from text, music, speech, movement and visual images

In early years, students engage in many activities that help them develop their oral language skills and help them begin to read and write. Early Childhood students take part in language activities that extend their vocabulary and conceptual knowledge. Students learn to follow directions and develop the language of schooling. Students discuss the meanings of words from familiar and conceptually challenging selections read aloud. Students express themselves in complete thoughts.

In Kindergarten, students listen to a wide variety of children's literature, including selections from classic and contemporary works. Students listen to nonfiction and informational material. Students learn to listen attentively and ask and respond to questions and retell stories. Students know simple story structure and distinguish fiction from nonfiction. Kindergarten students identify and write the letters of the alphabet. Students learn that individual letters are different from printed words that words have spaces between them, and that print is read from left-to-right and from top-to-bottom. Through meaningful and organized activities, Kindergarten students learn that spoken language is composed of sequences of sounds.

Students learn to segment and identify the sounds in spoken words. Students name each letter of the alphabet, begin to associate spoken sounds with the letter or letters that represent them, and begin to use this knowledge to read words and simple stories. In Kindergarten, students write the letters of the alphabet, their names, and other words. Initially, students dictate messages and stories for others to write. Students begin to use their knowledge of sounds and letters to write by themselves.

Some of the knowledge and skills for developing creative responses could include:

- Listening/speaking/purposes. The student listens attentively and engages actively in a variety of oral language experiences. The student is expected to:

  a) determine the purpose(s) for listening such as to get information, to solve problems, and to enjoy and appreciate

  b) respond appropriately and courteously to directions and questions

  c) participate in rhymes, songs, conversations, and discussions

  d) listen critically to interpret and evaluate

  e) listen responsively to stories and other texts read aloud, including selections from classic and contemporary works

  f) identify the musical elements of literary language such as its rhymes or repeated sounds

- Listening/speaking/culture. The student listens and speaks to gain knowledge of his/her own culture, the culture of others, and the common elements of cultures. The student is expected to:

  a) connect experiences and ideas with those of others through speaking and listening and

  b) compare language and oral traditions (family stories) that reflect customs, regions and cultures

- Listening/speaking/audiences/oral grammar. The student speaks appropriately to different audiences for different purposes and occasions. The student is expected to:

  a) choose and adapt spoken language appropriate to the audience, purpose and occasion, including use of appropriate volume and rate

  b) use verbal and nonverbal communication in effective ways when making announcements, giving directions or making introductions

  c) ask and answer relevant questions and make contributions in small or large group discussions

  d) present dramatic interpretations of experiences, stories, poems or plays and

  e) gain increasing control of grammar when speaking such as using subject-verb agreement, complete sentences and correct tense

- Learn the vocabulary of school such as numbers, shapes, colors, directions and categories

  a) use vocabulary to describe clearly ideas, feelings and experiences

  b) clarify and support spoken messages using appropriate props such as objects, pictures or charts and

  c) retell a spoken message by summarizing or clarifying

Skill 27.4 **Identify the elements of art and principles of design (e.g., line, color, shape, form, texture, balance and movement) and ways they are used in expressing text, ideas, meanings and emotions**

Western Principles of design in western art include the following:

1) Unity
2) Balance
3) Center of Interest
4) Movement
5) Repetition
6) Variation
7) Rhythm
8) Contrast
9) Space
10) Tension

These principles are apparent in artistic works throughout all historical time periods, although emphasis may shift from period to period, or from location to location, or from artist to artist.

There are different types of visual balance and artists use these types to create art work that convey a particular message or idea to a view. Balance is a fundamental of design seen as a visual weight and counterweight. That is apparent in a single image or in the organization of images and objects in a composition. Examples of balance are:

- **Symmetrical Balance** - The same objects or arrangement are on both sides.

- **Asymmetrical Balance** - Objects or arrangements on are on different sides.

- **Radial Balance** - The axis design or pattern appear to radiate from the center axis.

- **Horizontal Balance** - Works which utilise the picture plane from left to right.

Lines are the marks left by the painting tools that define the edges of objects in artwork. Their shape and thickness may express movement or tone. Texture in a painting is the "feel" of the canvas based on the paint used and its method of application. There are two forms of texture in painting, visual and tactile. Because texture uses two different senses it is a unique element of art.

Color refers to the hue (e.g., red vs. orange) and intensity or brightness (e.g., neon-green vs. yellow-green) of the colors used. Shapes are formed from the meeting of lines and the enclosing of areas in a two-dimensional space.

COMPETENCY 28.0   KNOWLEDGE OF CULTURAL AND HISTORICAL CONNECTIONS IN MUSIC AND VISUAL ARTS

SKILL 28.1   Identify characteristics of style in musical selections

Music is a form of art that involves organized and audible sounds (notes) and silence (rests). It is normally expressed in terms of pitch, rhythm and tone. Musical style is the basic musical language. A musical genre is a collection of music that shares a style.

Classical music is a class of music covering compositions and performances by professionally trained artists. Classical music is written traditionally. It is composed and written using music notation (see Skill VOID #12) and as a rule is performed exactly as written. Classical music often refers to instrumental music in general, although opera is also considered classical.

Jazz is a form of music that grew out of a combination of folk music, ragtime and band music. It has been called the first native art form to develop in the United States. The music has gone through a series of developments since its inception. In rough chronological order they are: Dixieland, swing, big band, bebop, cool jazz and smooth jazz.

Blues is a vocal and instrumental music form which came from West African spirituals, work songs and chants. This musical form has been a major influence on later American popular music, finding expression in jazz, rock and roll and country music. Due to its powerful influence that originated from America, blues can be regarded as the root of pop as well as American music. Elvis Presley and Eric Clapton feel they found their niche in the music industry from their predecessors in the blues industry.

Rock and roll, in its broadest sense, can refer to almost all pop music recorded since the early 1950's. Its main features include an emphasis on rhythm, and the use of percussion and amplified instruments like the bass and guitar. Elvis Presley in the 1950's shocked the nation with his rhythm and gyrating hips in what was the early stages of rock and roll. Starting the mid-1960s, a group of British bands, sometime referred to as the British Invasion, formed folk rock, as well as a variety of less-popular genres. The British Invasion evolved into psychedelic rock, which in turn gave birth to jam bands and progressive rock.

Skill 28.2   Demonstrate knowledge of how music reflects particular cultures, historical periods, and places

The resources available to man to make music have varied throughout different ages and eras and have given the chance for a musical style or type to be created or invented due to diverse factors. Social changes, cultural features and historical purpose have all shared a part in giving birth to a multitude of different musical forms in every part of the earth.

Music can be traced to the people who created it by the instruments, melodies, rhythms and records of performance (songs) that are composed in human communities. Starting from early musical developments, as far back as nomadic cave dwellers playing the flute and beating on hand drums, to the different electric instruments and recording technology of the modern music industry, the style and type of music produced have been closely related to the human beings who choose it for their particular lifestyle and way of existence.

Western music, arising chiefly from the fusion of classical and folkloric forms, has always included a large variety of instruments and generated new techniques to fit the change in expression provided by the expansion of its possibilities. Instruments such as the piano and the organ; stringed instruments like the violin, viola, cello, guitar and bass; wind instruments like the flute, saxophone, trumpet, trombone, tuba and saxophone; and electronic instruments like the synthesizer and electric guitar have all provided for the invention of new styles and types of music created and used by different people in different times and places.

The rites of Christinianity during the early middle ages were the focus of social and cultural aspiration and became a natural meeting place for communities to come together consistently for the purpose of experiencing God through preaching and music. Composers and performers fulfilled their roles with sacred music, including Gregorian chants and Oratorios. The art patron's court in the 15th and 14th centuries provided a venue for talented composers; the opera house of the 19th century satisfied the need of nascent, progressive society looking to experience grander and more satisfying music. New forms were generated such as the *concerto*, *symphony*, *sonata* and *string quartet* that employed a zeal and zest for creation typical of the burgeoning intellect at the end of the middle ages and the beginning of modern society.

Traditional types and styles of music in America, India, China, throughout the Middle East and Africa—using a contrasting variety of stringed instruments and percussion from typical Western instruments—began a long and exciting merger with the Western musical world. With the beginning of widespread colonialism came the eventual integration of different musical styles between disparate cultures. Western musical instruments were adopted to play the traditional musical styles of different cultures.

Blues music, arising from the southern black community in the United States would morph into *Rock n' Roll* and *Hip Hop,* alongside the progression of the traditional folk music of European settlers.

Hispanic music would come about by Western musical instruments being imbued with African rhythms throughout the Caribbean in different forms like *Salsa*, *Merengue*, *Cumbia* and *Son Cubano*.

Call-and-response songs are a form of verbal and non-verbal interaction between a speaker and a listener, in which statements by a speaker are responded to by a listener. In West African cultures, call-and-response songs were used in religious rituals and gatherings, and are now used in other forms such as gospel, blues, and jazz, as a form of musical expression. In certain Native American tribes, call-and-response songs are used to preserve and protect the tribe's cultural heritage and can be seen and heard at modern-day "pow-wows". The men would begin the song as the speaker with singing and drumming and the women would respond with singing and dancing.

A **ballad** is a song that contains a story. Instrumental music forms a part of folk music, especially dance traditions. Much folk music is vocal, since the instrument (the voice) that makes such music is usually handy. As such, most folk music has lyrics and is descriptive about something. Any story form can be a ballad, such as fairy tales or historical accounts. Ballads usually have simple repeating rhymes and often contain a refrain (or repeating sections) that are played or sung at regular intervals throughout. Ballads could be called hymns when they are based on religious themes. In the 20th century, "ballad" took on the meaning of a popular song "especially of a romantic or sentimental nature".

Folk music is music that has endured and been passed down by oral tradition and emerges spontaneously from ordinary people. In early societies, it arose in areas that were not yet affected by mass communication. It was normally shared by the entire community and was transmitted by word of mouth. A folk song is usually seen as an expression of a way of life now, past, or about to disappear. In the 1960's, folk songs were sung as a way of protesting political themes.

The **work song** is typically a song sung acappella by people working on a physical and often repetitive task. It was probably intended to reduce feelings of boredom. Rhythms of work songs also serve to synchronize physical movement in a gang or the movement in marching. Frequently, the verses of work songs are improvised and sung differently each time. Examples of work songs could be heard from slaves working in the field, prisoners on chain gangs, and soldiers in the military.

Skill 28.3   Identify characteristics of style in works of art

Teachers should be able to utilize and teach various techniques when analyzing works of art. Students will learn and then begin to apply what they have learned in the arts to all subjects across the curriculum. Using problem solving techniques and creative skills, students will begin to master the techniques necessary to derive meaning from both visual and sensory aspects of art. Students will be asked to review, respond to, and analyze various types of art. Students should be critical and it is necessary that students relate to art in terms of life and human aspects of life.

Students should be introduced to the wide range of opportunities to explore such art. Examples may include exhibits, galleries, museums, libraries, and personal art collections. It is imperative that students learn to research and locate such artistic opportunities that are common in today's society. Some opportunities for research include the following: reproductions, art slides, films, print materials, and electronic media. Once students are taught how to effectively research and use sources, students should be expected to graduate to higher level thinking skills. Students should be able to begin to reflect on, interpret, evaluate, and explain how works of art and various styles of art work explain social, psychological, cultural, and environmental aspects of life.

Several areas that must be mastered for students to explore and identify styles in the arts include:
- understanding various types of media (two-dimensional, three-dimensional & electronic images) that are appropriate for learning
- developing skills using electronic media to express visual ideas
- awareness of cultural, environmental, community opportunities that will provide options for exploring art images and consulting artists
- awareness of potential careers and professions in the field of arts
- develop a variety of ways to use art material/medium

Some examples of mastery include:
- drawing or painting a computer graphics program
- visiting a museum or art festival and writing a report telling about the experience
- engage in an interview or conversation with an artist regarding what s/he does and why s/he has chosen art as a profession.\
- mixing and painting with a range of colors

Skill 28.4   Knowledge of how visual arts reflect particular cultures, historical periods, and places

Art history is relatively new to academics. True art history relies on faithful reproductions of artworks as a springboard of discussion and study. Photography techniques after World War II made this possible; however, the appreciation and study of the visual arts has intrigued man for hundreds of years. Art history features the study of biographies of individual artists. The most renowned of these was **Michelangelo**. In the 18th century, scholars began arguments that the real emphasis in the study of art belonged on the views of the learned beholder and not the unique viewpoint of the charismatic artist. By comparing visual arts to each other, one is able to make distinctions of style.

Art history has added to political history by using approaches to show how art interacts with power structures in society. The first critical approach was Marxism. Marxist art history attempted to show how art was tied to specific classes, how images contain information about the economy, and how images can make the status quo seem natural. In the book titled *The Social History of Art,* an attempt was made to show how class consciousness was reflected in major art periods. This book was very controversial when it was published during the 1950s because it makes gross generalizations about entire eras. However, it remains in print as a classic art historical text.

Cultural art predates history as sculptures, cave paintings, and rock paintings have been found that are roughly 40,000 years old, but the precise meaning of such art is often disputed because we know so little about the cultures that produced them. Most art traditions have a foundation in the great ancient civilizations of Egypt, Persia, India, China or Rome. Each of these early civilizations developed a unique and characteristic style of art. Because of their size and the duration of these civilizations, more art works from these eras have survived and more influence has been transmitted to other cultures and later times. The 18th century is referred to as the Age of Enlightenment with artistic renderings of the physical universe as well as politically revolutionary visions. The late 19th century saw numerous artistic movements such as Symbolism and Impressionism which were torn down by the search for new standards and did not last much past the time of their invention. In the latter 20th century came Modernism, or the search for truth, which later led to the period of Contemporary Art.

COMPETENCY 29.0 KNOWLEDGE OF AESTHETIC AND CRITICAL ANALYSIS OF MUSIC AND VISUAL ARTS

Skill 29.1 Identify strategies for developing students' analytical skills to evaluate musical performance

Students can take music courses, which typically takes the form of an overview course on the history of music, or a music appreciation course that focuses on listening to music and learning about different musical styles.

A musical performance (a concert or a recital) may take place indoors in a hall or theatre or outdoors in a field, and may require the audience to remain very quiet, or encourage them to sing or dance along with the music. Although music cannot contain emotions, it is sometimes designed to encourage the emotion of the listener/listeners. Music created for movies is a good example of its use to manipulate emotions.

Performance analysis works through and for the ear. The greatest analysts are those with the keenest ears; their insights reveal how a piece of music should be heard, which in turn implies how it should be played. Analysis consists of 'putting oneself in the composer's shoes,' and explaining what he was experiencing as he was writing.

Skill 29.2 Identify strategies for developing students' analytical skills to evaluate works of art

Art criticism is one of the four foundational disciplines of Discipline-Based Art Education (DBAE), along with art production, art history, and aesthetics. Art criticism is responding to, interpreting meaning, and making critical judgments about specific works of art. Usually art criticism focuses on individual, contemporary works of art.

When initially introduced to art criticism, many people associate negative connotations with the word "criticism." This is understandable; the first definition given for criticism in *Webster's Ninth New Collegiate Dictionary* is "the act of criticizing, usually unfavorably." Yet Webster's second definition is more appropriate for art criticism: "the art of evaluating or analyzing works of art." Art criticism, in practice, generally is positive.

Any agreement on a simple definition of art criticism is difficult to obtain. In *Practical Art Criticism*, Edmund Feldman writes that art criticism is "spoken or written 'talk' about art" and that "the central task of criticism" is interpretation. Feldman developed a widely used sequential approach to art criticism based on description, analysis, interpretation, and judgment.

Stephen Dobbs, writing in *The DBAE Handbook: An Overview of Discipline-Based Art Education*, states that, through art criticism, people "look at art, analyze the forms, offer multiple interpretations of meaning, make critical judgments, and talk or write about what they see, think, and feel."

Terry Barrett, author of *Criticizing Art: Understanding the Contemporary*, bases his approach to art criticism on the four activities of describing, interpreting, judging, and theorizing about art. Barrett suggests that, although all four overlap, "Interpretation is the most important activity of criticism, and probably the most complex." Though interwoven with description, analysis, and judgment, interpretation of the meaning of individual works of art is of foremost concern in contemporary art criticism.

The Role of the Art Critic

In all four disciplines of DBAE, the practice of each is based upon the roles of each discipline's practitioner or expert. For art criticism, the role model is the art critic. A professional art critic may be a newspaper reporter assigned to the art beat, a scholar writing for professional journals or texts, or an artist writing about other artists.

Journalistic criticism, written for the general public, includes reviews of art exhibitions in galleries and museums. Most people are familiar with journalistic art criticism because it appears in newspapers, popular magazines, and on radio and television. Feldman suggests that journalistic criticism deals with art mainly to the extent that it is newsworthy.

Scholarly art criticism is written for a more specialized art audience and appears in art journals, such as *Art in America*, *Art Papers*, and *Art News*, as well as presentations at professional conferences or seminars. Scholar-critics may be college and university professors or museum curators, often with particular knowledge about a style, period, medium, or artist.

In both journalistic and scholarly art criticism, the viewer, according to Feldman, "confronts works of art and determines what they mean, whether they are any good, and, if so, why."

Art Criticism in the Classroom

Through art criticism activities in the classroom, students interpret and judge individual works of art. Interpretation is the most critical task of art criticism, but we recommend no prescribed order to follow. The work of art itself should guide the approach to inquiry. For example, a non-objective painting initially may be approached through description, while a highly-detailed, symbol-filled realistic painting probably would be best approached first through possible interpretations of meaning.

Critic's descriptions are lively. Critics write to be read, and they must capture their readers' attention and engage their readers' imaginations. Critics want to persuade their readers to see a work of art as they do. If they are enthused, they try to communicate their enthusiasm through their choice of descriptors and how they put them together in a sentence, a paragraph, and an article."

Written art criticism can be thought of as persuasive writing, with interpretations of meaning supported by reasoned judgments. Critic Terry Barrett calls for "good, lively, interpretive writing about art" that may take many forms in the classroom. Similarly, Feldman states that words are virtually indispensable for communicating a critic's understanding and that "words enable us to build bridges between sensory impressions, prior experience, logical inferences, and the tasks of interpretation and explanation."

Guidelines and Strategies for the Classroom

Use learning activities and vocabulary appropriate for students' grade levels. Whole class or small group discussions are beneficial as brainstorming and prewriting activities. Allowing students to work in pairs or small groups fosters collaborative learning.

Art criticism strategies for the classroom include comparing/contrasting works of art, writings based on questions on activity cards, and narratives, poetry, cinquains, and other forms of writing.

Interpretation of works of art may extend to dramatic presentations through reader's theater (students write dialogue for the people in an artwork, then perform the parts with different voices), "living paintings" or tableaux, and sound symphonies (students act out the sounds that are suggested by the artwork). A variety of approaches will lead students to enter and interpret many works of art from multiple perspectives.

COMPETENCY 30.0 KNOWLEDGE OF APPROPRIATE ASSESSMENT STRATEGIES IN MUSIC AND VISUAL ARTS

Skill 30.1 Identify a variety of developmentally appropriate strategies and materials to assess skills, techniques, creativity, and communication in music

As students acquire the skills and knowledge that music brings to their lives, they go through the similar stages of developing language skills. Singing, chanting, and moving; exposing them to many different sound sources, including a variety of styles of music in play; andreinforcing rhythm through patting, tapping, and moving will enhance their awareness of musical sound. Involvement in music is thought to teach basic skills such as concentration, counting, listening, and promoting understanding of language.

Analysis of music works through and for the ear. The greatest analysts are those with the keenest ears; their insights reveal how a piece of music should be heard, which in turn implies how it should be played. Analysis consists of 'putting oneself in the composer's shoes, and explaining what he was experiencing as he was writing.

An assessment based on performance of music would require students to create, produce, or do something in the music field. Proficiency would be demonstrated by a performance such as a musical recital.

Skill 30.2 Identify a variety of developmentally appropriate strategies and materials to assess skills, techniques, creativity, and communication in art

Art is creativity that has some form of appreciative value, usually on the basis of aesthetic value or emotional impact. The purpose of works of art may be to communicate ideas, (e.g., as in politically-, spiritually-, or philosophically-motivated art), to create a sense of beauty, to explore the nature of perception, for pleasure, or to generate strong emotions. Art is something that visually stimulates an individual's thoughts, emotions, beliefs or ideas and is a realized expression of an idea.

An assessment based on artistic ability would require students to create, produce, or do something in the visual arts field. Proficiency would be demonstrated by an exhibit such as art projects or drawings, paintings, or sculptures.

COMPETENCY 31.0   KNOWLEDGE OF PERSONAL HEALTH AND WELLNESS

Skill 31.1   Demonstrate knowledge of the interrelatedness of physical activity, fitness, and health

ROLE OF EXERCISE IN HEALTH MAINTENANCE

The health risk factors improved by physical activity include cholesterol levels, blood pressure, stress related disorders, heart diseases, weight and obesity disorders, early death, certain types of cancer, musculoskeletal problems, mental health, and susceptibility to infectious diseases.

PHYSIOLOGICAL BENEFITS OF EXERCISE

Physiological benefits of physical activity include:
- improved cardio-respiratory fitness
- improved muscle strength
- improved muscle endurance
- improved flexibility
- more lean muscle mass and less body fat
- quicker rate of recovery
- improved ability of the body to utilize oxygen
- lower resting heart rate
- increased cardiac output
- improved venous return and peripheral circulation
- reduced risk of musculoskeletal injuries
- lower cholesterol levels
- increased bone mass
- cardiac hypertrophy and size and strength of blood vessels
- increased number of red cells
- improved blood-sugar regulation
- improved efficiency of thyroid gland
- improved energy regulation
- increased life expectancy

Skill 31.2 Demonstrate basic knowledge of nutrition and its role in promoting health

EXERCISE AND DIET

Exercise and diet maintain proper body weight by equalizing caloric intake to caloric output.

Nutrition and exercise are closely related concepts important to student health. An important responsibility of physical education instructors is to teach students about proper nutrition and exercise and how they relate to each other. The two key components of a healthy lifestyle are consumption of a balanced diet and regular physical activity. Nutrition can affect physical performance. Proper nutrition produces high energy levels and allows for peak performance. Inadequate or improper nutrition can impair physical performance and lead to short-term and long-term health problems (e.g. depressed immune system and heart disease, respectively). Regular exercise improves overall health. Benefits of regular exercise include a stronger immune system, stronger muscles, bones, and joints, reduced risk of premature death, reduced risk of heart disease, improved psychological well-being, and weight management.

NUTRITION AND WEIGHT CONTROL

Identify the components of nutrition

The components of nutrition are **carbohydrates, proteins, fats, vitamins, minerals, and water.**

Carbohydrates – the main source of energy (glucose) in the human diet. The two types of carbohydrates are simple and complex. Complex carbohydrates have greater nutritional value because they take longer to digest, contain dietary fiber, and do not excessively elevate blood sugar levels. Common sources of carbohydrates are fruits, vegetables, grains, dairy products, and legumes.

Proteins – are necessary for growth, development, and cellular function. The body breaks down consumed protein into component amino acids for future use. Major sources of protein are meat, poultry, fish, legumes, eggs, dairy products, grains, and legumes.

Fats – a concentrated energy source and important component of the human body. The different types of fats are saturated, monounsaturated, and polyunsaturated. Polyunsaturated fats are the healthiest because they may lower cholesterol levels, while saturated fats increase cholesterol levels. Common sources of saturated fats include dairy products, meat, coconut oil, and palm oil. Common sources of unsaturated fats include nuts, most vegetable oils, and fish.

Vitamins and minerals – organic substances that the body requires in small quantities for proper functioning. People acquire vitamins and minerals in their diets and in supplements. Important vitamins include A, B, C, D, E, and K. Important minerals include calcium, phosphorus, magnesium, potassium, sodium, chlorine, and sulfur.

Water – makes up 55 – 75% of the human body. Essential for most bodily functions. Attained through foods and liquids.

Determine the adequacy of diets in meeting the nutritional needs of students

Nutritional requirements vary from person-to-person. General guidelines for meeting adequate nutritional needs are: no more than 30% total caloric intake from fats (preferably 10% from saturated fats, 10% from monounsaturated fats, 10% from polyunsaturated fats), no more than 15% total caloric intake from protein (complete), and at least 55% of caloric intake from carbohydrates (mainly complex carbohydrates).

Exercise and diet help maintain proper body weight by equalizing caloric intake and caloric output.

Skill 31.3   Identify the process of decision making and goal setting in promoting individual health and wellness

GOAL SETTING

Goal setting is an effective way of achieving progress. In order to preserve and/or increase self-confidence, you and your students must set goals that are frequently reachable. One such way of achieving this is to set several small, short-term goals to attain one long-term goal. Be realistic in goal setting to increase fitness levels gradually. As students reach their goals, set more in order to continue performance improvement. Keep in mind that maintaining a current fitness level is an adequate goal provided the individual is in a healthy state. Reward your students when they reach goals. Rewards serve as motivation to reach the next goal. Also, be sure to prepare for lapses. Try to get back on track as soon as possible.

WELLNESS

Wellness has two major components: understanding the basic human body functions and how to care for and maintain personal fitness, and developing an awareness and knowledge of how certain everyday factors, stresses, and personal decisions can affect one's health. Teaching fitness needs to go along with skill and activity instruction. Life-long fitness and the benefits of a healthy lifestyle need to be part of every P.E. teacher's curriculum. Cross-discipline teaching and teaching thematically with other subject matter in classrooms would be the ideal method to teach health to adolescents.

Incorporating wellness into the P.E. teacher's lesson plan doesn't need to take that much time or effort. For example, have students understand the idea that if you put more calories into your body than what you burn, you will gain weight. Teaching nutrition and the caloric content of foods in P.E. can be as simple as learning the amount of calories burned when participating in different sports for a set amount of time. To teach a more sophisticated lesson on nutrition that can have students understand the relationship between caloric intake and caloric expenditure, students could keep a food diary, tabulating the caloric content of their own diets while comparing it to an exercise diary that keeps track of the calories they've burned.

Another example of incorporating wellness into the P.E. curriculum would be when participating in endurance running activities. Having students run a set distance and then giving them a finish time rewards the faster students and defeats the slower students. In addition to a final time, teach students a more beneficial way of measuring one's cardiovascular fitness by understanding pulse rate.

Teach students how to take their own pulse, how pulse rates vary at different stages of exercise (i.e. resting pulse, target pulse, recovery pulse, etc.), how pulse rates can differ between boys and girls, and encourage them to keep track of their own figures. As students gather their data, teacher-led discussions amongst classmates about similarities, differences and patterns that are developing would teach students how to monitor their own vital signs effectively and easily.

Skill 31.4 Demonstrate knowledge of common health problems and risk behaviors associated with them

MALFUNCTIONS OF THE BODY SYSTEMS AND COMMON HEALTH PROBLEMS

Malfunctions of the respiratory and excretory systems

Emphysema is a chronic obstructive pulmonary disease (COPD, making it difficult for a person to breathe. Partial obstruction of the bronchial tubes limits airflow, making breathing difficult. The primary cause of emphysema is smoking. People with a deficiency in alpha$_1$-antitrypsin protein production have a greater risk of developing emphysema and at an earlier age. This protein helps protect the lungs from damage done by inflammation. This genetic deficiency is rare and doctors can test for it in individuals with a family history of the deficiency. There is no cure for emphysema, but there are treatments available. The best prevention against emphysema is to refrain from smoking. (Wouldn't asthma be more appropriate here, for elem. ed?)

Nephritis usually occurs in children. Symptoms include hypertension, decreased renal function, hematuria, and edema. Glomerulonephritis (GN) is a more precise term to describe this disease. An antigen-antibody complex that causes inflammation and cell proliferation produces nephritis. Nephritis damages normal kidney tissue and, if left untreated, can lead to kidney failure and death.

Malfunctions of the circulatory system

Cardiovascular diseases are the leading cause of death in the United States. Cardiac disease usually results in either a heart attack or a stroke. A heart attack occurs when cardiac muscle tissue dies, usually from coronary artery blockage. A stroke occurs when nervous tissue in the brain dies due to the blockage of arteries in the head.

Atherosclerosis causes many heart attacks and strokes. Plaques form on the inner walls of arteries, narrowing the area in which blood can flow. Arteriosclerosis occurs when the arteries harden from the plaque accumulation. A healthy diet low in saturated fats and cholesterol and regular exercise can prevent atherosclerosis. High blood pressure (hypertension) also promotes atherosclerosis. Diet, medication, and exercise can reduce high blood pressure and prevent atherosclerosis.

Malfunctions of the immune system

The immune system attacks both microbes and cells that are foreign to the host. This is the problem with skin grafts, organ transplantations, and blood transfusions. Antibodies to foreign blood and tissue types already exist in the body. Antibodies will destroy the new blood cells in transfused blood that is not compatible with the host. There is a similar reaction with tissue and organ transplants.

The major histocompatibility complex (MHC) is responsible for the rejection of tissue and organ transplants. This complex is unique to each person. Cytotoxic T-cells recognize the MHC on the transplanted tissue or organ as foreign and destroy these tissues. Suppression of the immune system with various drugs can prevent this reaction. The complication with immune suppression is that the patient is more susceptible to infection.

Autoimmune disease occurs when the body's own immune system destroys its own cells. Lupus, Grave's disease, and rheumatoid arthritis are examples of autoimmune diseases. There is no way to prevent autoimmune diseases. Immunodeficiency is a deficiency in either the humoral or cell mediated immune defenses. HIV is an example of an immunodeficiency disease.

Malfunctions of the digestive system

Gastric ulcers are lesions in the stomach lining. Bacteria are the main cause of ulcers, but pepsin and acid can exacerbate the problem if the ulcers do not heal quickly enough.

Appendicitis is the inflammation of the appendix. The appendix has no known function, but is open to the intestine and hardened stool or swollen tissue can block it. The blocked appendix can cause bacterial infections and inflammation leading to appendicitis. The swelling cuts the blood supply, killing the organ tissue. If left untreated, this leads to rupture of the appendix allowing the stool and the infection to spill out into the abdomen. This condition is life threatening and requires immediate surgery. Symptoms of appendicitis include lower abdominal pain, nausea, loss of appetite, and fever.

Malfunctions of the nervous and endocrine systems

Diabetes is the best-known endocrine disorder. A deficiency of insulin resulting in high blood glucose is the primary cause of diabetes. Type I diabetes is an autoimmune disorder. The immune system attacks the cells of the pancreas, ending the ability to produce insulin. Treatment for Type I diabetes consists of daily insulin injections. Type II diabetes usually occurs with age and/or obesity. There is usually a reduced response in target cells due to changes in insulin receptors or a deficiency of insulin. Type II diabetics need to monitor their blood glucose levels. Treatment usually consists of dietary restrictions and exercise.

Hyperthyroidism is another disorder of the endocrine system. Excessive secretion of thyroid hormones is the cause. Symptoms are weight loss, high blood pressure, and high body temperature. The opposite condition, hypothyroidism, causes weight gain, lethargy, and intolerance to cold.

There are many nervous system disorders. The degeneration of the basal ganglia in the brain causes Parkinson's disease. This degeneration causes a decrease in the motor impulses sent to the muscles. Symptoms include tremors, slow movement, and muscle rigidity. Progression of Parkinson's disease occurs in five stages: early, mild, moderate, advanced, and severe. In the severe stage, the person is confined to a bed or chair. There is no cure for Parkinson's disease. Private research with stem cells is currently underway to find a cure for Parkinson's disease.

COMPETENCY 32.0 KNOWLEDGE OF PHYSICAL, SOCIAL, AND EMOTIONAL GROWTH AND DEVELOPMENT

Skill 32.1 Identify the structure, function, and interrelatedness of the systems of the human body

HUMAN NERVOUS AND ENDOCRINE SYSTEMS

The **central nervous system (CNS)** consists of the brain and spinal cord. The CNS is responsible for the body's response to environmental stimuli. The spinal cord is located inside the spine. It sends out motor commands for movement in response to stimuli. The brain is where responses to more complex stimuli occur. The meninges are the connective tissues that protect the CNS. The CNS contains fluid filled spaces called ventricles. These ventricles are filled when cerebrospinal fluid which is formed in the brain. This fluid cushions the brain and circulates nutrients, white blood cells, and hormones. The CNS's response to stimuli is a reflex. A reflex is an unconscious, automatic response.

The **peripheral nervous system (PNS)** consists of the nerves that connect the CNS to the rest of the body. The sensory division brings information to the CNS from sensory receptors and the motor division sends signals from the CNS to effector cells. The motor division consists of the somatic nervous system and the autonomic nervous system. The body consciously controls the somatic nervous system in response to external stimuli. The hypothalamus in the brain unconsciously controls the autonomic nervous system to regulate the internal environment. This system is responsible for the movement of smooth muscles, cardiac muscles, and the muscles of other organ systems.

Understand the major endocrine glands and the function of their hormones

The function of the **endocrine system** is to manufacture proteins called hormones. **Hormones** circulate in the bloodstream and stimulate actions when they interact with target tissue. There are two classes of hormones: steroid and peptide. Steroid hormones come from cholesterol and include the sex hormones. Amino acids are the source of peptide hormones. Hormones are specific and fit receptors on the target tissue cell surface. The receptor activates an enzyme that converts ATP to cyclic AMP. Cyclic AMP (cAMP) is a second messenger from the cell membrane to the nucleus. The genes found in the nucleus turn on or off to cause a specific response.

Endocrine cells, which make up endocrine glands, secrete hormones. The major endocrine glands and their hormones include:

Hypothalamus – located in the lower brain; signals the pituitary gland.

Pituitary gland – located at the base of the hypothalamus; releases growth hormones and antidiuretic hormone (retention of water in kidneys).

Thyroid gland – located on the trachea; lowers blood calcium levels (calcitonin) and maintains metabolic processes (thyroxine).

Gonads – located in the testes of the male and the ovaries of the female; testes release androgens to support sperm formation and ovaries release estrogens to stimulate uterine lining growth and progesterone to promote uterine lining growth.

Pancreas – secretes insulin to lower blood glucose levels and glucagon to raise blood glucose levels.

ROLE OF NERVE IMPULSES AND NEURONS

The **neuron** is the basic unit of the nervous system. It consists of an axon, which carries impulses away from the cell body to the tip of the neuron; the dendrite, which carries impulses toward the cell body; and the cell body, which contains the nucleus. Synapses are spaces between neurons. Chemicals called neurotransmitters are found close to the synapse. The myelin sheath, composed of Schwann cells, covers the neurons and provides insulation.

Nerve action depends on depolarization and an imbalance of electrical charges across the neuron. A polarized nerve has a positive charge outside the neuron. A depolarized nerve has a negative charge outside the neuron. Neurotransmitters turn off the sodium pump which results in depolarization of the membrane. This wave of depolarization (as it moves from neuron to neuron) carries an electrical impulse. This is actually a wave of opening and closing gates that allows for the flow of ions across the synapse. Nerves have an action potential. There is a threshold of the level of chemicals that must be met or exceeded in order for muscles to respond. This is the "all or nothing" response.

STRUCTURE AND FUNCTION OF THE SKIN

The skin consists of two distinct layers, the epidermis and the dermis. The epidermis is the thinner outer layer and the dermis is the thicker inner layer. Layers of tightly packed epithelial cells make up the epidermis. The tight packaging of the epithelial cells supports the skin's function as a protective barrier against infection.

The top layer of the epidermis consists of dead skin cells and contains keratin, a waterproofing protein. The dermis layer consists of connective tissue. It contains blood vessels, hair follicles, sweat glands, and sebaceous glands. The body releases an oily secretion called sebum, produced by the sebaceous gland, to the outer epidermis through the hair follicles. Sebum maintains the pH of the skin between 3 and 5, which inhibits most microorganism growth.

The skin also plays a role in thermoregulation. Increased body temperature causes skin blood vessels to dilate, causing heat to radiate from the skin's surface. Increased temperature also activates sweat glands, increasing evaporative cooling. Decreased body temperature causes skin blood vessels to constrict. This results in blood from the skin diverting to deeper tissues and reduces heat loss from the surface of the skin.

HUMAN RESPIRATORY AND EXCRETORY SYSTEMS

Surface area, volume, and function of the respiratory and excretory systems

The lungs are the respiratory surface of the human respiratory system. A dense net of capillaries contained just beneath the epithelium form the respiratory surface. The surface area of the epithelium is about $100m^2$ in humans. Based on the surface area, the volume of air inhaled and exhaled is the tidal volume. This is normally about 500mL in adults. Vital capacity is the maximum volume the lungs can inhale and exhale. This is usually around 3400mL.

The kidneys are the primary organ in the excretory system. Each of the two kidneys in humans is about 10cm long. Despite their small size, they receive about 20% of the blood pumped with each heartbeat. The function of the excretory system is to rid the body of nitrogenous wastes in the form of urea.

Knowledge of process of breathing and gas exchange

The respiratory system functions in the gas exchange of oxygen and carbon dioxide waste. It delivers oxygen to the bloodstream and picks up carbon dioxide for release from the body. Air enters the mouth and nose, where it is warmed, moistened and filtered of dust and particles. Cilia in the trachea trap and expel unwanted material in mucus. The trachea splits into two bronchial tubes and the bronchial tubes divide into smaller and smaller bronchioles in the lungs. The internal surface of the lung is composed of alveoli, which are thin-walled air sacs. These allow for a large surface area for gas exchange. Capillaries line the alveoli. Oxygen diffuses into the bloodstream and carbon dioxide diffuses out of the capillaries and is exhaled from the lungs due to partial pressure. Hemoglobin, a protein-containing iron, carries the oxygenated blood to the heart and all parts of the body.

The thoracic cavity holds the lungs. The diaphragm muscle below the lungs is an adaptation that makes inhalation possible. As the volume of the thoracic cavity increases, the diaphragm muscle flattens out and inhalation occurs. When the diaphragm relaxes, exhalation occurs.

HUMAN CIRCULATORY AND IMMUNE SYSTEMS

Structure, function, and regulation of the heart

The function of the closed circulatory system (**cardiovascular system**) is to carry oxygenated blood and nutrients to all cells of the body and return carbon dioxide waste to the lungs for expulsion. The heart, blood vessels, and blood make up the cardiovascular system. The following diagram shows the structure of the heart:

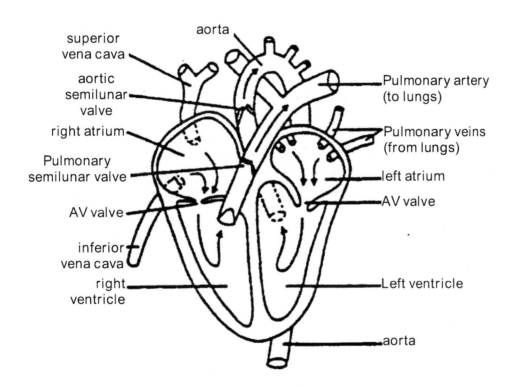

The atria are the chambers that receive blood returning to the heart and the ventricles are the chambers that pump blood out of the heart. There are four valves, two atrioventricular (AV) valves and two semilunar valves. The AV valves are located between each atrium and ventricle. The contraction of the ventricles closes the AV valve to keep blood from flowing back into the atria. The semilunar valves are located where the aorta leaves the left ventricle and the pulmonary artery leaves the right ventricle. Ventricular contraction opens the semilunar valves, pumping blood out into the arteries, and ventricular relaxation closes the valves.

The cardiac output is the volume of blood per minute that the left ventricle pumps. This output depends on the heart rate and stroke volume. The **heart rate** is the number of times the heart beats per minute and the **stroke volume** is the amount of blood pumped by the left ventricle each time it contracts. Humans have an average cardiac output of about 5.25 L/min. Heavy exercise can increase cardiac output up to five times. Epinephrine and increased body temperature also increase heart rate and, thus, the cardiac output. Cardiac muscle can contract without any signal from the nervous system. The sinoatrial node is the pacemaker of the heart. It is located on the wall of the right atrium and generates electrical impulses that make the cardiac muscle cells contract in unison. The atrioventricular node briefly delays the electrical impulse to ensure the atria empty before the ventricles contract.

Structure, function, and regulation of the immune system

The immune system is responsible for defending the body against foreign invaders. There are two defense mechanisms: non-specific and specific.

The **non-specific** immune mechanism has two lines of defense. The first line of defense is the physical barriers of the body. These include the skin and mucous membranes. The skin prevents the penetration of bacteria and viruses as long as there are no abrasions on the skin. Mucous membranes form a protective barrier around the digestive, respiratory, and genitourinary tracts. In addition, the pH of the skin and mucous membranes inhibit the growth of many microbes. Mucous secretions (tears and saliva) wash away many microbes and contain lysozyme that kills microbes.

The second line of defense includes white blood cells and the inflammatory response. **Phagocytosis** is the ingestion of foreign particles. Neutrophils make up about seventy percent of all white blood cells. Monocytes mature to become macrophages, which are the largest phagocytic cells. Eosinophils are also phagocytic. Natural killer cells destroy the body's own infected cells instead of the invading the microbe directly.

The other second line of defense is the inflammatory response. The blood supply to the injured area increases, causing redness and heat. Swelling also typically occurs with inflammation. Basophils and mast cells release histamine in response to cell injury. This triggers the inflammatory response.

The **specific** immune mechanism recognizes specific foreign material and responds by destroying the invader. These mechanisms are specific and diverse. They are able to recognize individual pathogens. An **antigen** is any foreign particle that elicits an immune response. The body manufactures **antibodies** that recognize and latch onto antigens, hopefully destroying them. They also discriminate between foreign material versus self material. Memory of the invaders provides immunity upon further exposure.

Immunity is the body's ability to recognize and destroy an antigen before it causes harm. Active immunity develops after recovery from an infectious disease (e.g. chicken pox) or after a vaccination (e.g. mumps, measles, rubella). Passive immunity may be passed from one individual to another and is not permanent. A good example is the immunity passed from mother to nursing child. A baby's immune system is not well developed and the passive immunity received through nursing protects health.

There are two main responses made by the body after exposure to an antigen:

1. **Humoral response** - Free antigens activate this response and B cells (lymphocytes from bone marrow) give rise to plasma cells that secrete antibodies and memory cells that will recognize future exposures to the same antigen. The antibodies defend against extracellular pathogens by binding to the antigen and making them an easy target for phagocytes to engulf and destroy. Antibodies are in a class of proteins called immunoglobulins. There are five major classes of immunoglobulins (Ig) involved in the humoral response: IgM, IgG, IgA, IgD, and IgE.

2. **Cell mediated response** – Infected cells activate T cells (lymphocytes from the thymus). These activated T cells defend against pathogens in the cells or cancer cells by binding to the infected cell and destroying them along with the antigen. T cell receptors on the T helper cells recognize antigens bound to the body's own cells. T helper cells release IL-2, which stimulates other lymphocytes (cytotoxic T cells and B cells). Cytotoxic T cells kill infected host cells by recognizing specific antigens.

Vaccines are antigens given in very small amounts. They stimulate both humoral and cell mediated responses. After vaccination, memory cells recognize future exposure to the antigen so the body can produce antibodies much faster.

HUMAN DIGESTIVE SYSTEM

Mechanical and chemical digestion

The teeth and saliva begin digestion by breaking food down into smaller pieces and lubricating it to allow swallowing. The lips, cheeks, and tongue form a bolus or ball of food. The process of peristalsis (wave-like contractions) carries the food down the pharynx where it enters the stomach through the sphincter, which closes to keep food from going back up. In the stomach, pepsinogen and hydrochloric acid form pepsin, the enzyme that hydrolyzes proteins. This chemical action breaks the food down further and churns it into a semifluid mass called acid chyme. The pyloric sphincter muscle opens to allow the food to enter the small intestine. Most nutrient absorption occurs in the small intestine. Its large surface area, resulting from its length and protrusions called villi and microvilli, allows for a great absorptive surface into the bloodstream. Neutralization of the chyme after arrival from the acidic stomach allows the local enzymes to function. Accessory organs function in the production of necessary enzymes and bile. The pancreas makes many enzymes to break down food in the small intestine. The liver makes bile, which breaks down and emulsifies fatty acids. Any food left after the trip through the small intestine enters the large intestine. The large intestine functions to reabsorb water and produce vitamin K. The feces, or remaining waste, pass out through the anus.

HUMAN REPRODUCTIVE SYSTEM

Hormone control and development and function of male and female reproductive systems

Hormones regulate sexual maturation in humans. Humans cannot reproduce until puberty, about the age of 8-14, depending on the individual. The hypothalamus begins secreting hormones that help mature the reproductive system and develop the secondary sex characteristics. Reproductive maturity in girls occurs with their first menstruation and occurs in boys with the first ejaculation of viable sperm.

Hormones also regulate reproduction. In males, the primary sex hormones are the androgens, testosterone being the most important. The testes produce androgens that dictate the primary and secondary sex characteristics of the male. Female hormone patterns are cyclic and complex. Most women have a reproductive cycle length of about 28 days. The menstrual cycle is specific to the changes in the uterus. The ovarian cycle results in ovulation and occurs in parallel with the menstrual cycle. Hormones regulate this parallelism. Five hormones participate in this regulation, most notably estrogen and progesterone. Estrogen and progesterone play an important role in signaling to the uterus and the development and maintenance of the endometrium. Estrogens also dictate the secondary sex characteristics of females.

Gametogenesis, fertilization, and birth control

Gametogenesis is the production of the sperm and egg cells.

Spermatogenesis begins at puberty in the male. One spermatogonia, the diploid precursor of sperm, produces four sperm. The sperm mature in the seminiferous tubules located in the testes. **Oogenesis**, the production of egg cells (ova), is usually complete by the birth of a female. Females do not release egg cells until menstruation begins at puberty. Meiosis forms one ovum with all the cytoplasm and three polar bodies that the body reabsorbs. The ovaries store the ovum and release them each month from puberty to menopause.

Seminiferous tubules in the testes house sperm, where they mature. The epididymis, located on top of the testes, contains mature sperm. After ejaculation, the sperm travel up the **vas deferens** where they mix with semen made in the prostate and seminal vesicles and travel out the urethra. Ovulation releases the egg into the fallopian tubes where cilia move the egg along the length of the tubes. Fertilization of the egg by the sperm normally occurs in the fallopian tube. If pregnancy does not occur, the egg passes through the uterus and is expelled through the vagina during menstruation. Levels of progesterone and estrogen stimulate menstruation. Implantation of a fertilized egg downregulates the levels, stopping menstruation.

There are many methods of contraception (birth control) that affect different stages of fertilization. Chemical contraception (birth control pills) prevents ovulation by synthetic estrogen and progesterone. Several barrier methods of contraception are available. Male and female condoms block semen from contacting the egg. Sterilization is another method of birth control. Tubal ligation in women prevents eggs from entering the uterus. A vasectomy in men involves the cutting of the vas deferens. This prevents the sperm from entering the urethra. The most effective method of birth control is abstinence. Programs exist worldwide that promote abstinence, especially amongst teenagers.

Skill 32.2   Identify the principles of sequential progression of motor skill development

The development of motor skills in children is a sequential process. We can classify motor skill competency into stages of development by observing children practicing physical skills. The sequence of development begins with simple reflexes and progresses to the learning of postural elements, locomotor skills, and, finally, fine motor skills. The stages of development consider both innate and learned behaviors.

STAGES OF MOTOR LEARNING

Stage 1 – Children progress from simple reflexes to basic movements such as sitting, crawling, creeping, standing, and walking.

Stage 2 – Children learn more complex motor patterns including running, climbing, jumping, balancing, catching, and throwing.

Stage 3 – During late childhood, children learn more specific movement skills. In addition, the basic motor patterns learned in stage 2 become more fluid and automatic.

Stage 4 – During adolescence, children continue to develop general and specific motor skills and master specialized movements. At this point, factors including practice, motivation, and talent begin to affect the level of further development.

SEQUENTIAL DEVELOPMENT FOR LOCOMOTOR SKILLS ACQUISITION

Sequential Development = crawl, creep, walk, run, jump, hop, gallop, slide, leap, skip, step-hop.

SEQUENTIAL DEVELOPMENT FOR NONLOCOMOTOR SKILL ACQUISITION

Sequential Development = stretch, bend, sit, shake, turn, rock and sway, swing, twist, dodge, and fall.

SEQUENTIAL DEVELOPMENT FOR MANIPULATIVE SKILL ACQUISITION

Sequential Development = striking, throwing, kicking, ball rolling, volleying, bouncing, catching, and trapping.

Skill 32.3.   Demonstrate knowledge of human growth and development and its relationship to physical, social, and emotional well-being

Physical development – Small children (ages 3-5) have a propensity for engaging in periods of a great deal of physical activity, punctuated by a need for a lot of rest. Children at this stage lack fine motor skills and cannot focus on small objects for very long. Their bones are still developing. At this age, girls tend to be better coordinated, and boys tend to be stronger.

The lag in fine motor skills continues during the early elementary school years (ages 6-8).

Pre-adolescent children (ages 9-11) become stronger, leaner, and taller. Their motor skills improve, and they are able to sit still and focus for longer periods of time. Growth during this period is constant. This is also the time when gender-specific physical predispositions will begin to manifest. Pre-adolescents are at risk of obesity without proper nutrition and adequate activity.

Young adolescents (ages 12-14) experience drastic physical growth (girls earlier than boys), and are highly preoccupied with their physical appearance.

As children proceed to the later stages of adolescence (ages 15-17), girls will reach their full height, while boys will still have some growth remaining. The increase in hormone levels will cause acne, which coincides with a slight decrease of preoccupation with physical appearance. At this age, children may begin to initiate sexual activity (boys generally more motivated by hormones, and girls more by peer pressure). There is a risk of teen pregnancy and sexually transmitted diseases.

Cognitive development – Language development is the most important aspect of cognitive development in small children (ages 3-5). Allowing successes, rewarding mature behavior, and allowing the child to explore can improve confidence and self-esteem at this age.

Early elementary school children (ages 6-8) are eager to learn and love to talk. Children at this age have a very literal understanding of rules and verbal instructions and must develop strong listening skills.

Pre-adolescent children (ages 9-11) display increased logical thought, but their knowledge or beliefs may be unusual or surprising. Differences in cognitive styles develop at this age (e.g. field dependant or independent preferences).

In early adolescence (ages 12-14), boys tend to score higher on mechanical/spatial reasoning, and girls on spelling, language, and clerical tasks. Boys are better with mental imagery, and girls have better access to and retrieval of information from memory. Self-efficacy (the ability to self-evaluate) becomes very important at this stage.

In later adolescence (ages 15-17), children are capable of formal thought, but don't always apply it. Conflicts between teens' and parents' opinions and worldviews will arise. Children at this age may become interested in advanced political thinking.

Social development – Small children (ages 3-5) are socially flexible. Different children will prefer solitary play, parallel play, or cooperative play. Frequent minor quarrels will occur between children, and boys will tend to be more aggressive (children at these ages are already aware of gender roles).

Early elementary school children (ages 6-8) are increasingly selective of friends (usually of the same sex). Children at this age enjoy playing games, but are excessively preoccupied by the rules. Verbal aggression becomes more common than physical aggression, and adults should encourage children of this age to solve their own conflicts.

Pre-adolescent children (ages 9-11) place great importance on the (perceived) opinions of their peers and of their social stature, and will go to great lengths to "fit in." Friendships at this age are very selective, and usually of the same sex.

Young adolescents (ages 12-14) develop greater understanding of the emotions of others, which results in increased emotional sensitivity and impacts peer relationships. Children at this age develop an increased need to perform.

In the later stages of adolescence (ages 15-17), peers are still the primary influence on day-to-day decisions, but parents will have increasing influence on long-term goals. Girls' friendships tend to be close and intimate, whereas boys' friendships are based on competition and similar interests. Many children this age will work part-time, and educators should be alert to signs of potential school dropouts.

Emotional development – Small children (ages 3-5) express emotions freely and have a limited ability to understand how emotions influence behavior. Jealousy at this age is common.

Early elementary school children (ages 6-8) have easily bruised feelings and are just beginning to recognize the feelings of others. Children this age will want to please teachers and other adults.

Pre-adolescent children (ages 9-11) develop a global and stable self-image (self-concept and self-esteem). Comparisons to their peers and the opinions of their peers are important. An unstable home environment at this age contributes to an increased risk of delinquency.

Young adolescence (ages 12-14) can be a stormy and stressful time for children, but, in reality, this is only the case for roughly 20% of teens. Boys will have trouble controlling their anger and will display impulsive behavior. Girls may suffer depression. Young adolescents are very egocentric and concerned with appearance, and will feel very strongly that "adults don't understand."

In later stages of adolescence (ages 15-17), educators should be alert to signs of surfacing mental health problems (e.g. eating disorders, substance abuse, schizophrenia, depression, and suicide).

Skill 32.4 Identify major factors associated with social and emotional health (e.g., communication skills, self-concept, fair play, conflict resolution, character development, and stress management)

There is an important relationship to consider between physical activity and the development of personal identity and emotional and mental well-being—most notably the impact of positive body image and self-concept. Instructors can help children develop a positive body image and self-concept by creating opportunities for the children to experience successes in physical activities and to develop a comfort level with their bodies. This is an important contributor to their personal and physical confidence. The following are lists of the emotional, behavioral, and physical signs of stress:

Emotional signs of stress include: depression, lethargy, aggressiveness, irritability, anxiety, edginess, fearfulness, impulsiveness, chronic fatigue, hyper excitability, inability to concentrate, frequent feelings of boredom, feeling overwhelmed, apathy, impatience, pessimism, sarcasm, humorlessness, confusion, helplessness, melancholy, alienation, isolation, numbness, purposelessness, isolation, self-consciousness, inability to maintain an intimate relationship.

Behavioral signs of stress include: elevated use of substances (alcohol, drugs, tobacco), crying, yelling, insomnia or excessive sleep, excessive TV watching, school/job burnout, panic attacks, poor problem-solving capability, avoidance of people, aberrant behavior, procrastination, accident proneness, restlessness, loss of memory, indecisiveness, aggressiveness, inflexibility, phobic responses, tardiness, disorganization, sexual problems.

Physical signs of stress: pounding heart, stuttering, trembling/nervous tics, excessive perspiration, teeth grinding, gastrointestinal problems (constipation, indigestion, diarrhea, queasy stomach), dry mouth, aching lower back, migraine/tension headaches, stiff neck, asthma attacks, allergy attacks, skin problems, frequent colds or low grade fevers, muscle tension, hyperventilation, high blood pressure, amenorrhea, nightmares, cold intolerance.

IDENTIFY BOTH POSITIVE AND NEGATIVE COPING STRATEGIES FOR INDIVIDUALS UNDER STRESS

Positive coping strategies to cope with stress include: using one's social support system, spiritual support, managing time, initiating direct action, re-examining priorities, active thinking, acceptance, meditation, imagery, biofeedback, progressive relaxation, deep breathing, massage, sauna, Jacuzzi, humor, recreation and diversions, and exercise.

Negative coping strategies to cope with stress include: using alcohol or other mind-altering substances, smoking, excessive caffeine intake, poor eating habits, negative "self-talk," expressing feelings of distress, anger, and other feelings in a destructive manner.

SOCIAL HEALTH

For most people, the development of social roles and appropriate social behaviors occurs during childhood. Physical play between parents and children, as well as between siblings and peers, serves as a strong regulator in the developmental process. Chasing games, roughhousing, wrestling, or practicing sport skills such as jumping, throwing, catching, and striking, are some examples of childhood play. These activities may be competitive or non-competitive and are important for promoting social and moral development of both boys and girls. Unfortunately, fathers will often engage in this sort of activity more with their sons than their daughters. Regardless of the sex of the child, both boys and girls enjoy these types of activities.

Physical play during infancy and early childhood is central to the development of social and emotional competence. Research shows that children who engage in play that is more physical with their parents, particularly with parents who are sensitive and responsive to the child, exhibited greater enjoyment during the play sessions and were more popular with their peers. Likewise, these early interactions with parents, siblings, and peers are important in helping children become more aware of their emotions and to learn to monitor and regulate their own emotional responses. Children learn quickly through watching the responses of their parents which behaviors make their parents smile and laugh and which behaviors cause their parents to frown and disengage from the activity.

If children want the fun to continue, they engage in the behaviors that please others. As children near adolescence, they learn through rough-and-tumble play that there are limits to how far they can go before hurting someone (physically or emotionally), which results in termination of the activity or later rejection of the child by peers. These early interactions with parents and siblings are important in helping children learn appropriate behavior in the social situations of sport and physical activity.

Children learn to assess their social competence (i.e., ability to get along with and receive acceptance from peers, family members, teachers and coaches) in sport through the feedback received from parents and coaches. Initially, authority figures teach children, "You can't do that because I said so." As children approach school age, parents begin the process of explaining why a behavior is right or wrong because children continuously ask, "why?"

Similarly, when children engage in sports, they learn about taking turns with their teammates, sharing playing time, and valuing rules. They understand that rules are important for everyone and without these regulations, the game would become unfair. The learning of social competence is continuous as we expand our social arena and learn about different cultures. A constant in the learning process is the role of feedback as we assess the responses of others to our behaviors and comments.

In addition to the development of social competence, sport participation can help youth develop other forms of self-competence. Most important among these self-competencies is self-esteem. Self-esteem is how we judge our worth and indicates the extent to which an individual believes he is capable, significant, successful and worthy. Educators have suggested that one of the biggest barriers to success in the classroom today is low self-esteem.

Children develop self-esteem by evaluating their own abilities and by evaluating the responses of others. Children actively observe parents' and coaches' responses to their performances, looking for signs of approval or disapproval of their behavior. Children often interpret feedback and criticism as either a negative or a positive response to the behavior. In sports, research shows that the coach is a critical source of information that influences the self-esteem of children.

Little League baseball players whose coaches use a "positive approach" to coaching (e.g. more frequent encouragement; positive reinforcement for effort; and corrective, instructional feedback), had significantly higher self-esteem ratings over the course of a season than children whose coaches used these techniques less frequently. The most compelling evidence supporting the importance of coaches' feedback was found for those children who started the season with the lowest self-esteem ratings and increased considerably their self-assessment and self-worth. In addition to evaluating themselves more positively, low self-esteem children evaluated their coaches more positively than did children with higher self-esteem who played for coaches who used the "positive approach." Moreover, studies show that 95 percent of children who played for coaches trained to use the positive approach signed up to play baseball the next year, compared with 75 percent of the youth who played for untrained adult coaches.

We cannot overlook the importance of enhanced self-esteem on future participation. A major part of the development of high self-esteem is the pride and joy that children experience as their physical skills improve. Children will feel good about themselves as long as their skills are improving. If children feel that their performance during a game or practice is not as good as that of others, or as good as they think Mom and Dad would want, they often experience shame and disappointment.

Some children will view mistakes made during a game as a failure and will look for ways to avoid participating in the task if they receive no encouragement to continue. At this point, it is critical that adults (e.g., parents and coaches) intervene to help children to interpret the mistake positively. We must teach children that a mistake is not synonymous with failure. Rather, a mistake shows us that we need a new strategy, more practice, and/or greater effort to succeed at the task.

Physical education activities can promote positive social behaviors and traits in a number of different ways. Instructors can foster improved relations with adults and peers by making students active partners in the learning process and delegating responsibilities within the class environment to students. Giving students leadership positions (e.g. team captain) can give them a heightened understanding of the responsibilities and challenges facing educators.

Team-based physical activities like team sports promote collaboration and cooperation. In such activities, students learn to work together, both pooling their talents and minimizing the weaknesses of different team members, in order to achieve a common goal. The experience of functioning as a team can be very productive for the development of loyalty between children, and seeing their peers in stressful situations that they can relate to can promote a more compassionate and considerate attitude among students. Similarly, the need to maximize the strengths of each student on a team (who can complement each other and compensate for weaknesses) is a powerful lesson about valuing and respecting diversity and individual differences. Varying students between leading and following positions in a team hierarchy is a good way to help students gain a comfort level being both followers and leaders.

Fairness is another trait that physical activities, especially rules-based sports, can foster and strengthen. Children are by nature very rules-oriented, and have a keen sense of what they believe is and isn't fair. Fair play, teamwork, and sportsmanship are all values that stem from proper practice of the spirit of physical education classes. Of course, a pleasurable physical education experience goes a long way towards promoting an understanding of the innate value of physical activity throughout the life cycle.

Finally, communication is another skill that improves enormously through participation in sports and games. Students will come to understand that skillful communication can contribute to a better all-around outcome, whether it be winning the game or successfully completing a team project. They will see that effective communication helps to develop and maintain healthy personal relationships; organize and convey information; and reduce or avoid conflict.

Skill 32.5 Identify problems associated with physical, social, and emotional health.

PHYSICAL

o   *See Section 32, Skill 4*

SOCIAL AND EMOTIONAL

Children are susceptible to a wide array of social and emotional health problems. Common emotional health problems include depression, Attention Deficit Hyperactivity Disorder (ADHD), anxiety, and stress. Common social health problems for children include social anxiety, shyness, and aggression.

Depression – The most common mental health problem among adults also affects up to 5% of American children. Symptoms of depression in children include withdrawal from friends or activities, loss of interest in activities, frequent sadness and crying, low energy, increased irritability, poor concentration, and frequent complaints of physical illnesses such as stomachaches and headaches. Possible treatments include counseling and antidepressant medication.

ADHD – Affecting between 4% and 12% of school-age children, ADHD is the name for a group of behaviors found in many children and adults. ADHD behaviors prevent proper concentration and make paying attention and following instructions difficult. Common symptoms of ADHD include short attention span, fidgetiness, inability to stay still or stay in seat, difficulty following directions, and inability to plan ahead. The most common treatment for ADHD is medication.

Social Health Problems – Many children suffer from social anxiety and shyness. Social anxiety is an extreme phobia of one or more social situations. Symptoms of social anxiety include avoidance of social situations, extreme shyness, inability to make new friends, and complaints of physical ailments during social interaction.

SKILL 32.6   Identify factors related to responsible sexual behavior

There are many possible consequences for students who become sexually active. Possible consequences include HIV infection, infection with other sexually transmitted diseases, unintended pregnancies, and emotional difficulties.

The human immunodeficiency virus (HIV) is the virus that causes AIDS. Currently, there is no cure for AIDS. Many young adults infected with HIV acquired the infection during sexual activity in their adolescent years. In addition to HIV, there are also numerous other sexually transmitted diseases. Sexually transmitted diseases frequently reported in adolescents include gonorrhea, syphilis, pelvic inflammatory disease, bacterial vaginosis, genital herpes, chlamydia, genital warts, and human papillomavirus (HPV). Some of these diseases can result in infertility, and HPV can result in a deadly form of cervical cancer. Some of these diseases, such as genital herpes, are chronic. Additionally, condom use cannot prevent HPV and genital herpes.

Sexually transmitted disease infection can occur without having sexual intercourse. Oral or anal sex can cause infection with a sexually transmitted disease as easily as sexual intercourse. The only guaranteed method to prevent these diseases is abstinence.

In addition to possible infection with a sexually transmitted disease, adolescents who choose to become sexually active may also face the consequences of an unplanned pregnancy. Rates of child abuse and neglect are much higher among adolescent parents. Babies born to teenage parents are also more likely to have a lower birth weight, which can affect the babies' overall well-being. The suicide rate among teen mothers is significantly higher than among other teens, as well.

There is no doubt that teachers must encourage students to choose abstinence and responsible sexual behavior. Abstinence is choosing not to engage in sexual activity. Choosing abstinence is often a difficult decision for a teenager. In order to stand firm against the pressures to become sexually active, adolescents can become involved in activities in their school and community; work to develop strong family relationships; socialize with other teens who have chosen abstinence; avoid situations that increase sexual feelings and temptation; avoid using alcohol and other drugs; and select wholesome entertainment.

COMPETENCY 33.0 KNOWLEDGE OF COMMUNITY HEALTH AND SAFETY ISSUES

Skill 33.1   Identify factors contributing to substance use and abuse and identify signs, symptoms, effects, and prevention strategies

SUBSTANCE ABUSE

Substance abuse can lead to adverse behaviors and increased risk of injury and disease. Any substance affecting the normal functions of the body, illegal or not, is potentially dangerous and students and athletes should avoid them completely. Factors contributing to substance abuse include peer pressure, parental substance abuse, physical or psychological abuse, mental illness, and physical disability. Education, vigilance, and parental oversight are the best strategies for the prevention of substance abuse. Some of more commonly abused substances include:

Anabolic steroids – The alleged benefit is an increase in muscle mass and strength. However, this substance is illegal and produces harmful side effects. Premature closure of growth plates in bones can occur if abused by a teenager, limiting adult height. Other effects include bloody cysts in the liver, increased risk of cardiovascular disease, increased blood pressure, and dysfunction of the reproductive system.

Alcohol – This is a legal substance for adults but is very commonly abused. Moderate to excessive consumption can lead to an increased risk of cardiovascular disease, nutritional deficiencies, and dehydration. Alcohol also causes ill effects on various aspects of performance such as reaction time, coordination, accuracy, balance, and strength.

Nicotine – Another legal but often abused substance that can increase the risk of cardiovascular disease, pulmonary disease, and cancers of the mouth. Nicotine consumption through smoking severely hinders athletic performance by compromising lung function. Smoking especially affects performance in endurance activities.

Marijuana – This is the most commonly abused illegal substance. Adverse effects include a loss of focus and motivation, decreased coordination, and lack of concentration.

Cocaine – Another illegal and somewhat commonly abused substance. Effects include increased alertness and excitability. This drug can give the user a sense of overconfidence and invincibility, leading to a false sense of one's ability to perform certain activities. A high heart rate is associated with the use of cocaine, leading to an increased risk of heart attack, stroke, potentially deadly arrhythmias, and seizures.

Skill 33.2 **Demonstrate knowledge of resources from home, school, and community that provide valid health information, products, and services**

We can find information relating to physical activity at local public and university libraries and online. Educators should regularly inform themselves about updates in the field, and should periodically search for new resources that they can use with their students. Instructors should encourage students to make use of free resources like libraries, and especially the Internet, to expand their own knowledge and understanding of the subject matter.

We can find products relating to physical activity at sporting goods stores, gym boutiques, nutritional supplement stores, and wholesalers. Local community centers may also sell or rent equipment, and prices may be more favorable.

We can find services for promoting consumer awareness skills in relation to physical activity, recreation, fitness, and wellness online and at local community centers. Many community centers have outreach programs to increase public participation in physical activities. Health food stores may also offer seminars on fitness and wellness. Physical education professionals can work to build ties between these publicly offered services and their own curricula.

There is generally a wide array of information available related to health, fitness and recreational activities, products, facilities, and services. It can be difficult for the untrained consumer to sort through it all to find information that is pertinent and accurate.

When evaluating information relating to fitness and sports equipment, consumers (for example, parents of students who are seeking to equip their home with training facilities for themselves and their children) should ask the sales staff about the differences between their choices. It is important to make comparisons not just in terms of prices, but also in terms of potential fitness benefits and especially safety (Is the equipment in question safe to use? Is it safe for all ages? Is a spotter required for its use?).

When evaluating weight control products and programs, consumers should ask sales staff to explain the mechanism by which the program functions (e.g. does it limit caloric intake, maximize caloric expenditure, or function by means of some other process?). The word of the sales staff is not sufficient, however, and consumers should investigate further using the tools at their disposal, which include public and university libraries, the internet, and physical education professionals at their children's schools.

When evaluating fitness-training facilities, consumers should consider several factors. These factors are quality and availability of training equipment, hygiene of the facility, and overall atmosphere. You can determine the general quality of the equipment by its age and you can glean further information from a discussion with the training staff on-site. You can investigate the availability of the equipment by visiting the facility at peak training times (which vary depending on the demographics of the facility – again, you should ask the training staff for the appropriate times). If it takes too long for equipment to become available and lines seem to form, this may not be the best facility for your needs (unless you're not interested in visiting the facility during those hours). Most important, though, is the atmosphere at the facility. The best way to get a feel for this is to have short conversations with some customers about their experiences there.

Skill 33.3 Identify appropriate violence prevention strategies in the home, school, and community

Violence is a primary concern of educators. Assault, rape, suicide, gang violence, and weapons in school are major issues confronting educators in today's schools. Violence is no longer an issue confined to secondary schools in large urban areas. Violence involving younger students at the elementary level and in rural areas is also on the rise. Additionally, more adolescents are regularly witnessing violence in their schools and communities. Clearly, violence poses a serious threat to students' personal safety; however, violence also creates another challenge for schools. The fear of possible violence negatively affects students' growth, development, and ability to learn. In order to promote learning and healthy growth and development, schools must be violence-free. In order to accomplish this, schools must enact policies and procedures that promote an environment free from crime, drugs, and weapons. For some schools, this may include locker searches, full-time school security officers, and metal detectors. Some school systems may choose to utilize separate alternative schools for students proven to be violent or abusive.

In addition to experiencing violence at school, students may also be involved in various forms of harmful relationships in their homes or communities. Harmful relationships may include abuse, violence, and co-dependence. Students can use self-protection strategies to decrease the risk of becoming a victim of violence in their school, home, and community. Students should learn to have faith in their feelings about people and situations. If their instincts indicate that a person or situation is potentially dangerous, they should trust their feeling and remove themselves from the situation. They should always be attentive and aware of the actions of the people near them. They should avoid situations that increase the chance that something harmful will happen. Lastly, adult mentors can play a vital role in helping young people to stay safe. Educators are in a unique position to mentor young people and to act as a resource to help students avoid violence.

Skill 33.4   Identify appropriate safety and injury prevention strategies in the home, school, and community

STRATEGIES FOR INJURY PREVENTION

Participant screenings – evaluate injury history, anticipate and prevent potential injuries, watch for hidden injuries and reoccurrence of an injury, and maintain communication.

Standards and discipline – ensure that athletes obey rules of sportsmanship, supervision, and biomechanics.

Education and knowledge – stay current in knowledge of first aid, sports medicine, sport technique, and injury prevention through clinics, workshops, and communication with staff and trainers.

Conditioning – programs should be yearlong and participants should have access to conditioning facilities in and out of season to produce more fit and knowledgeable athletes who are less prone to injury.

Equipment – perform regular inspections; ensure proper fit and proper use.

Facilities – maintain standards and use safe equipment.

Field care – establish emergency procedures for serious injury.

Rehabilitation – use objective measures such as power output on an isokinetic dynamometer.

PREVENTION OF COMMON ATHLETIC INJURIES

Foot – start with good footwear, foot exercises.

Ankle – use high top shoes and tape support; strengthen plantar (calf), dorsiflexor (shin), and ankle eversion (ankle outward).

Shin splints – strengthen ankle dorsiflexors.

Achilles tendon – stretch dorsiflexion and strengthen plantar flexion (heel raises).

Knee – increase strength and flexibility of calf and thigh muscles.

Back – use proper body mechanics.

Tennis elbow – lateral epicondylitis caused by bent elbow, hitting late, not stepping into the ball, heavy rackets, and rackets with strings that are too tight.

Head and neck injuries – avoid dangerous techniques (i.e. grabbing facemask) and carefully supervise dangerous activities like using a trampoline.

School officials and instructors should base **equipment selection** on quality and safety; goals of physical education and athletics; participants' interests, age, sex, skills, and limitations; and trends in athletic equipment and uniforms. Knowledgeable personnel should select equipment, keeping in mind continuous service and replacement considerations (i.e. what's best in year of selection may not be best the following year). One final consideration is the possibility of reconditioning versus the purchase of new equipment.

ACTIONS THAT PROMOTE SAFETY AND INJURY PREVENTION

The following is a list of practices that promote safety in all types of physical education and athletic activities.

1.   Having an instructor who is properly trained and qualified.

2.   Organizing the class by size, activity, and conditions of the class.

3.   Inspecting buildings and other facilities regularly and immediately giving notice of any hazards.

4.   Avoiding overcrowding.

5.   Using adequate lighting.

6.   Ensuring that students dress in appropriate clothing and shoes.

7.   Presenting organized activities.

8.   Inspecting all equipment regularly.

9.   Adhering to building codes and fire regulations.

10.   Using protective equipment.

11.   Using spotters.

12.   Eliminating hazards.

13.   Teaching students correct ways of performing skills and activities.

14.   Teaching students how to use the equipment properly and safely.

COMPETENCY 34.0 KNOWLEDGE OF SUBJECT CONTENT AND APPROPRIATE CURRICULUM DESIGN

Skill 34.1 Distinguish between developmentally appropriate and inappropriate instructional practices that consider the interaction of cognitive, affective, and psychomotor domains

INSTRUCTIONAL METHODS FOR VARIOUS OBJECTIVES, SITUATIONS, AND DEVELOPMENTAL LEVELS

When selecting instructional methods, it is essential that the physical educator understands that the use of well-planned, sequential unit and lesson plans will maximize the value of the instruction. Additionally, the unit and lesson plans should not only build upon the students' prior physical education experience, but should also accommodate the various ability levels of the students and maximize the practice time for all students. When selecting an instructional format, the physical educator may choose to utilize more than one configuration in any given lesson. The physical educator can select from five basic instructional formats: cognitive structuring, large-group skill instruction, small-group skill instruction, individual skill instruction, and testing.

When utilizing cognitive structuring, the teacher addresses the whole class through lecture, demonstration, or questioning. This method is particularly effective for imparting basic knowledge in a short amount of time. Large-group skill instruction involves all of the students in the class in the related activities. In small-group skill instruction (also called stations), the instructor divides students into groups, each of which works on a different skill or activity. A significant advantage of this instructional format is the ability to maximize instruction in situations where equipment is limited. In addition, small-group activities increase the amount of practice time for each student. In the individual skill instruction format, the instructor asks each student to select a skill on which to work. The students independently decide when they are ready to progress to the next skill. When ready to progress, the students simply put away their equipment, gather equipment for the next selected skill, and work at their own pace on the next skill. This self-paced arrangement allows for the greatest chance of skill mastery. The final instructional format is testing. During testing, the instructor assesses the students utilizing a written or skills test.

Finally, the physical educator may choose to supplement his or her teaching with the use of instructional devices. Examples of instructional devices include basic physical education equipment such as cones or targets, but may also include other types of technology such as pedometers, DVDs, computer programs, or interactive white boards.

Teaching methods to facilitate psychomotor learning include:

1. **Task/Reciprocal** - The instructor integrates task learning into the learning setting by utilizing stations.

2. **Command/Direct** - Task instruction is teacher-centered. The teacher clearly explains the goals, explains and demonstrates the skills, allocates time for practice, and frequently monitors student progress.

3. **Contingency/Contract** - A task style of instruction that rewards completion of tasks.

Techniques that facilitate psychomotor learning include:

1. **Reflex movements** - Activities that create an automatic response to some stimuli. Responses include flexing, extending, stretching, and postural adjustment.

2. **Basic fundamental locomotor movements** - Activities that utilize instinctive patterns of movement established by combining reflex movements.

3. **Perceptual abilities** - Activities that involve interpreting auditory, visual, and tactile stimuli in order to coordinate adjustments.

4. **Physical abilities** - Activities to develop physical characteristics of fitness providing students with the stamina necessary for highly advanced, skilled movement.

5. **Skilled movements** - Activities that involve instinctive, effective performance of complex movement including vertical and horizontal components.

6. **Nondiscursive communication** - Activities necessitating expression as part of the movement.

Teaching methods that facilitate cognitive learning include:

1. **Problem Solving** - The instructor presents the initial task and students come to an acceptable solution in unique and divergent ways.

2. **Conceptual Theory** - The instructor's focus is on acquisition of knowledge.

3. **Guided Inquiry** – Stages of instructions strategically guide students through a sequence of experiences.

Initially, performing skills will be variable, inconsistent, error-prone, "off-time," and awkward. Students' focus will be on remembering what to do. Instructors should emphasize clear information of the skill's biomechanics and correct errors in gross movement that affect significant parts of the skill. So students will not be overburdened with too much information, they should perform one or two elements at a time. Motivation results from supportive and encouraging comments.

Techniques to facilitate cognitive learning include:

1. **Transfer of learning** – Identifying similar movements of a previous learned skill present in a new skill.

2. **Planning for slightly longer instructions and demonstrations** as students memorize cues and skills.

3. **Using appropriate language** for the level of the students.

4. **Conceptual Thinking** - giving more capable students more responsibility for their learning.

Aids to facilitate cognitive learning include:

1. Frequent assessments of student performance

2. Movement activities incorporating principles of biomechanics

3. Laser discs, computers and software

4. Video recordings of student performance

Teaching methods and techniques that facilitate affective development include:

1. **Fostering a positive learning environment** – Instructors should create a comfortable, positive learning environment by encouraging and praising effort and emphasizing respect for others.

2. **Grouping students appropriately** – Instructors should carefully group students to best achieve equality in ability, age, and personalities.

3. **Ensure all students achieve some level of success** – Instructors should design activities that allow students of all ability levels to achieve success and gain confidence.

Skill 34.2   Identify various factors (e.g., environment, equipment, facilities, space, safety, and group diversity) to consider when planning physical activities

IDENTIFY CLASS MANAGEMENT TECHNIQUES TO ENHANCE THE LEARNING EXPERIENCE.

The first few weeks of the school year are the most effective time for teaching class management structure (behavioral rules, terms for compliance and violation of rules, and classroom routines).

Instructors must manage all essential procedures and routines (roll call, excuses, tardiness, changing, and showering) to use available class time productively. Good class management also ensures the safety of the group through procedures and routines, provides a controlled classroom atmosphere to make instruction easier, promotes individual self-discipline and self-motivation, develops a sense of responsibility towards others, develops rapport between teacher and students that promotes learning, creates a group camaraderie where each student feels good about him/herself and feels at ease within the group, uses the instructor's time and energy productively, and organizes and coordinates classes for the most effective instruction and learning.

Long-term planning for the semester and year, as well as daily, weekly, and seasonal planning, is necessary. Instructors must effectively plan activities so that they proceed with precision, minimize "standing-around time", and allow for maximum activity time for each student. Instructors should arrange activities in advance and prepare any necessary line markings.

To determine student progress and effectiveness of teaching, instructors must plan appropriate measurement and evaluation opportunities. Instructors also must wear suitable clothing, have good knowledge of the subject, and promote desirable attitudes toward and understanding of fitness, skill learning, sportsmanship, and other physical education objectives.

PROPER USE OF EQUIPMENT, FACILITIES, SPACE, AND COMMUNITY RESOURCES

In addition to providing a safe, education-friendly environment that maximizes the use of class time, physical education instructors must use equipment, facilities, space, and community resources effectively.

Instructors must have a thorough understanding of athletic equipment to demonstrate proper usage to students and ensure student safety during activities. Instructors should expose students to a variety of activities and related equipment. Instructors must also consider the feasibility of certain activities as determined by the availability and costliness of equipment.

Instructors must consider available facilities and space when planning physical education curricula. Facilities and space may limit the types of activities in which students can engage. For example, sports like golf require large open spaces and specific equipment to which schools may not have access.

Finally, physical education instructors should investigate and research community resources. Community organizations and athletic clubs often will provide equipment, facilities, and volunteer instructors to schools for reduced or no cost.

Skill 34.3 Analyze the influence of culture, media, technology, and other factors when planning health and wellness instruction

A variety of influences affects a student's motor development and fitness level:

Societal – We cannot separate students from the societies in which they live. The general perceptions around them about the importance of fitness activities will necessarily have an effect on their own choice regarding physical activity. We should consider the "playground to PlayStation" phenomenon and the rising levels of obesity among Americans as negative societal influences on motor development and fitness.

Psychological – Psychological influences on motor development and fitness include a student's mental well-being, perceptions of fitness activities, and level of comfort in a fitness-training environment (both alone and within a group). Students experiencing psychological difficulties, such as depression, will tend to be apathetic and lack both the energy and inclination to participate in fitness activities. As a result, their motor development and fitness levels will suffer. Factors like the student's confidence level and comfort within a group environment, related to both the student's level of popularity within the group and the student's own personal insecurities, are also significant. It is noteworthy, though, that in the case of psychological influences on motor development and fitness levels, there is a more reciprocal relationship than with other influences. While a student's psychology may negatively affect his fitness levels, proper fitness training has the potential to positively affect the student psychologically, thereby reversing a negative cycle.

Cultural – Culture is a significant and sometimes overlooked influence on a student's motor development and fitness, especially in the case of students belonging to minority groups. Students may not feel motivated to participate in certain physical activities, either because they are not associated with the student's sense of identity or because the student's culture discourages these activities. For example, students from cultures with strict dress codes may not be comfortable with swimming activities. On the same note, students (especially older children) may be uncomfortable with physical activities in inter-gender situations. Educators must keep such cultural considerations in mind when planning physical education curricula.

Economic – The economic situation of students can affect their motor development and fitness because lack of resources can detract from the ability of parents to provide access to extra-curricular activities that promote development, proper fitness training equipment (ranging from complex exercise machines to team sport uniforms to something as simple as a basketball hoop), and even adequate nutrition.

Familial – Familial factors that can influence motor development and fitness relate to the student's home climate concerning physical activity. A student's own feelings toward physical activity often reflect the degree to which caregivers and role models (like older siblings) are athletically inclined and have a positive attitude towards physical activity. It isn't necessary for the parents to be athletically inclined, so much as it is important for them to encourage their child to explore fitness activities that could suit them.

Environmental and Health – Genetic make-up (i.e. age, gender, ethnicity) has a big influence on growth and development. Various physical and environmental factors directly affect one's personal health and fitness. Poor habits, living conditions, and afflictions such as disease or disability can impact a person in a negative manner. A healthy lifestyle with adequate conditions and minimal physical or mental stresses will enable a person to develop towards a positive, healthy existence. A highly agreed upon motor development theory is the relationship between one's own heredity and environmental factors.

Instructors should place students in rich learning situations, regardless of previous experience or personal factors, which provide plenty of positive opportunities to participate in physical activity. For example, prior to playing a game of softball, have students practice throwing by tossing the ball to themselves, progressing to the underhand toss, and later to the overhand toss.

Sample Test

Reading, Language & Literature

1. Which of the following is not a characteristic of a fable?

A. Animals that feel and talk like humans.

B. Happy solutions to human dilemmas.

C. Teaches a moral or standard for behavior.

D. Illustrates specific people or groups without directly naming them.

2. All of the following are true about phonological awareness EXCEPT:

A. It may involve print.

B. It is a prerequisite for spelling and phonics.

C. Activities can be done by the children with their eyes closed.

D. Starts before letter recognition is taught.

3. If a student has a poor vocabulary the teacher should recommend that:

A. The student read newspapers, magazines and books on a regular basis.

B. The student enroll in a Latin class.

C. The student writes the words repetitively after looking them up in the dictionary.

D. The student use a thesaurus to locate synonyms and incorporate them into his/her vocabulary.

4. Which definition below is the best for defining diction?

A. The specific word choices of an author to create a particular mood or feeling in the reader.

B. Writing which explains something thoroughly.

C. The background, or exposition, for a short story or drama.

D. Word choices which help teach a truth or moral.

5. Which is an untrue statement about a theme in literature?

A. The theme is always stated directly somewhere in the text.

B. The theme is the central idea in a literary work.

C. All parts of the work (plot, setting, mood) should contribute to the theme in some way.

D. By analyzing the various elements of the work, the reader should be able to arrive at an indirectly stated theme.

6. Which is not a true statement concerning an author's literary tone?

A. Tone is partly revealed through the selection of details.

B. Tone is the expression of the author's attitude toward his/her subject.

C. Tone in literature is usually satiric or angry.

D. Tone in literature corresponds to the tone of voice a speaker uses.

7. The arrangement and relationship of words in sentences or sentence structure best describes:

A. Style.

B. Discourse.

C. Thesis.

D. Syntax.

8. Which of the following is a complex sentence?

A. Anna and Margaret read a total of fifty-four books during summer vacation.

B. The youngest boy on the team had the best earned run average, which mystifies the coaching staff.

C. Earl decided to attend Princeton; his twin brother Roy, who aced the ASVAB test, will be going to Annapolis.

D. "Easy come, easy go," Marcia moaned.

9. **Followers of Piaget's learning theory believe that adolescents in the formal operations period:**

A. Behave properly from fear of punishment rather than from a conscious decision to take a certain action.

B. See the past more realistically and can relate to people from the past more than preadolescents.

C. Are less self-conscious and thus more willing to project their own identities into those of fictional characters.

D. Have not yet developed a symbolic imagination.

10. **Which of the following is a formal reading level assessment?**

A. A standardized reading test.

B. A teacher-made reading test.

C.   An interview.

D. A reading diary.

11. **Middle and high school students are more receptive to studying grammar and syntax:**

A. Through worksheets and end - of-lesson practices in textbooks.

B. Through independent homework assignments.

C. Through analytical examination of the writings of famous authors.

D. Though application to their own writing.

12. **Which of the following is not a technique of prewriting?**

A. Clustering.

B. Listing.

C. Brainstorming.

D. Proofreading.

13. **Which of the following is not an approach to keep students ever conscious of the need to write for audience appeal?**

 A. Pairing students during the writing process.

 B. Reading all rough drafts before the students write the final copies.

 C. Having students compose stories or articles for publication in school literary magazines or newspapers.

 D. Writing letters to friends or relatives.

14. **The children's literature genre came into its own in the:**

 A. Seventeenth century.

 B. Eighteenth century.

 C. Nineteenth century.

 D. Twentieth century.

15. **Which of the following should not be included in the opening paragraph of an informative essay?**

 A. Thesis sentence.

 B. Details and examples supporting the main idea.

 C. A broad general introduction to the topic.

 D. A style and tone that grabs the reader's attention.

16. **Which aspect of language is innate?**

 A. Biological capability to articulate sounds understood by other humans.

 B. Cognitive ability to create syntactical structures.

 C. Capacity for using semantics to convey meaning in a social environment.

 D. Ability to vary inflections and accents.

17. **Which of the following contains an error in possessive inflection?**

 A. Doris's shawl

 B. Mother's-in-law frown

 C. Children's lunches

 D. Ambassador's briefcase

18. To decode is to:

A. Construct meaning.

B. Sound out a printed sequence of letters.

C. Use a special code to decipher a message.

D. None of the above.

19. To encode means that you:

A. Decode a second time.

B. Construct meaning from a code.

C. Tell someone a message.

D. None of the above.

20. A teacher has taught his students several strategies to monitor their reading comprehension. These strategies include identifying where in the passage they are having difficulty, identifying what the difficulty is, and restating the difficult sentence or passage in their own words. These strategies are examples of:

A. Graphic and semantic organizers.

B. Metacognition.

C. Recognizing story structure.

D. Summarizing.

21. All of the following are examples of ongoing informal assessment techniques used to observe student progress EXCEPT:

A. Analyses of student work product.

B. Collection of data from assessment tests.

C. Effective questioning.

D. Observation of students.

22. A student has written a paper with the following characteristics: written in first person; characters, setting, and plot; some dialogue; events organized in chronological sequence with some flashbacks. In what genre has the student written?

A. Expository writing.

B. Narrative writing.

C. Persuasive writing.

D. Technical writing.

23. Which of the following indicates that a student is a fluent reader?

A. Reads texts with expression or prosody.

B. Reads word-to-word and haltingly.

C. Must intentionally decode a majority of the words.

D. In a writing assignment, sentences are poorly-organized, structurally.

24. Which of the following is an essential characteristic of effective assessment?

A. Students are the ones being tested; they are not involved in the assessment process.

B. Testing activities are kept separate from the teaching activities.

C. Assessment should reflect the actual reading for which the classroom instruction has prepared the student.

D. Tests should use entirely different materials than those used in teaching so the result will be reliable.

25. To understand the origins of a word, one must study the:

A. Synonyms.

B. Inflections.

C. Phonetics.

D. Etymology.

History & Social Science

26. Which two Native American nations or tribes inhabited the Mid-Atlantic and Northeastern regions at the time of the first European contact?

A. Pueblo and Inuit.

B. Algonquian and Cherokee.

C. Seminoles and Sioux.

D. Algonquian and Iroquois.

27. Which of the following were results of the Age of Exploration?

A. More complete and accurate maps and charts.

B. New and more accurate navigational instruments.

C. Proof that the earth is round.

D. All of the above.

28. What was "triangular trade"?

A. It was regulated trade between the colonies, England and France.

B. It was an approach to trade that transported finished goods from the mother country to the African colonies, slaves and goods from Africa to the North American Colonies, and raw materials and tobacco or rum back to the mother country.

C. It was an approach to trade that resulted in colonists obtaining crops and goods from the Native tribes in exchange for finished goods from England.

D. It was trade between the colonists of the three regions (Southern, mid Atlantic, and New England).

29. What intellectual movement during the period of North American colonization contributed to the development of public education and the founding of the first colleges and universities?

A. Enlightenment.

B. Great Awakening.

C. Libertarianism.

D. The Scientific Revolution.

30. Which of the following contributed to the severity of the Great Depression in California?

A. An influx of Chinese immigrants.

B. The dust bowl drove people out of the cities.

C. An influx of Mexican immigrants.

D. An influx of Oakies.

31. During the period of Spanish colonialism, which of the following was not a key to the goal of exploiting, transforming and including the native people?

A. Missions.

B. Ranchos.

C. Presidios.

D. Pueblos.

32. The first European to see Florida and sail along its coast was:

A. Cabot

B. Columbus.

C. Ponce de Leon.

D. Narvaez.

33. How did the United States gain Florida from Spain?

A. It was captured from Spain after the Spanish-American War.

B. It was given to the British and became part of the original thirteen colonies.

C. America bought it from Spain.

D. America acquired it after the First World War.

34. What is the form of local government that acts as an intermediary between the state and the city?

A. Metropolitan government.

B. Limited government.

C. The Mayor-Council system.

D. County Commission system.

35. New York was initially inhabited by what two native peoples?

A. Sioux and Pawnee.

B. Micmac and Wampanoag.

C. Iroquois and Algonquin.

D. Nez Perce and Cherokee.

36. What was the name of the cultural revival that took place in New York after the Civil War?

A. The Revolutionary War.

B. The Second Great Awakening.

C. The Harlem Renaissance.

D. The Gilded Age.

37. Which one of the following is not a reason why Europeans came to the New World?

A. To find resources in order to increase wealth.

B. To establish trade.

C. To increase a ruler's power and importance.

D. To spread Christianity.

38. **The year 1619 was a memorable one for the colony of Virginia. Three important events occurred, resulting in lasting effects on U.S. history. Which one of the following is not one of the events?**

A. Twenty African slaves arrived.

B. The London Company granted the colony a charter making it independent.

C. The colonists were given the right by the London Company to govern themselves through representative government in the Virginia House of Burgesses.

D. The London Company sent to the colony 60 women who were quickly married, establishing families and stability in the colony.

39. **The "divine right" of kings was the key political characteristic of:**

A. The Age of Absolutism.

B. The Age of Reason.

C. The Age of Feudalism.

D. The Age of Despotism.

40. **During the 1920s, the United States almost completely stopped all immigration. One of the reasons was:**

A. Plentiful, cheap, unskilled labor was no longer needed by industrialists.

B. War debts from World War I made it difficult to render financial assistance.

C. European nations were reluctant to allow people to leave since there was a need to rebuild populations and economic stability.

D. The United States did not become a member of the League of Nations.

41. **Which one of the following would not be considered a result of World War II?**

A. Economic depressions and slow resumption of trade and financial aid.

B. Western Europe was no longer the center of world power.

C. The beginnings of new power struggles not only in Europe but in Asia as well.

D. Territorial and boundary changes for many nations, especially in Europe.

42. **The belief that the United States should control all of North America was called:**

A. Westward Expansion.

B. Pan Americanism.

C. Manifest Destiny.

D. Nationalism.

43. **Capitalism and communism are alike in that they are both:**

A. Organic systems.

B. Political systems.

C. Centrally planned systems.

D. Economic systems.

44. **An economist might engage in which of the following activities?**

A. An observation of the historical effects of a nation's banking practices.

B. The application of a statistical test to a series of data.

C. Introduction of an experimental factor into a specified population to measure the effect of the factor.

D. An economist might engage in all of these.

45. **The advancement of understanding in dealing with human beings has led to a number of interdisciplinary areas. Which of the following interdisciplinary studies would NOT be considered under the social sciences?**

A. Molecular biophysics.

B. Peace studies.

C. African-American studies.

D. Cartographic information systems.

46. **For the historian studying ancient Egypt, which of the following would be least useful?**

A. The record of an ancient Greek historian on Greek-Egyptian interaction.

B. Letters from an Egyptian ruler to his/her regional governors.

C. Inscriptions on stele of the Fourteenth Egyptian Dynasty.

D. Letters from a nineteenth century Egyptologist to his wife.

MATH

47. $\left(\dfrac{^-4}{9}\right) + \left(\dfrac{^-7}{10}\right) =$

A. $\dfrac{23}{90}$

B. $\dfrac{^-23}{90}$

C. $\dfrac{103}{90}$

D. $\dfrac{^-103}{90}$

48. $(5.6) \times (^-0.11) =$

A. $^-0.616$

B. 0.616

C. $^-6.110$

D. 6.110

49. An item that sells for $375 is put on sale at $120. What is the percent of decrease?

A. 25%

B. 28%

C. 68%

D. 34%

50. Two mathematics classes have a total of 410 students. The 8:00 am class has 40 more than the 10:00 am class. How many students are in the 10:00 am class?

A. 123.3

B. 370

C. 185

D. 330

51. What measure could be used to report the distance traveled in walking around a track?

A. degrees

B. square meters

C. kilometers

D. cubic feet

52. What is the area of a square whose side is 13 feet?

A. 169 feet

B. 169 square feet

C. 52 feet

D. 52 square feet

53. What is the greatest common factor of 16, 28, and 36?

A. 2

B. 4

C. 8

D. 16

54. If $4x - (3 - x) = 7(x - 3) + 10$, then

A. $x = 8$

B. $x = -8$

C. $x = 4$

D. $x = -4$

55. Given the formula $d = rt$, (where d = distance, r =rate, and t =time), calculate the time required for a vehicle to travel 585 miles at a rate of 65 miles per hour.

A. 8.5 hours

B. 6.5 hours

C. 9.5 hours

D. 9 hours

56. The following chart shows the yearly average number of international tourists visiting Palm Beach for 1990-1994. How may more international tourists visited Palm Beach in 1994 than in 1991?

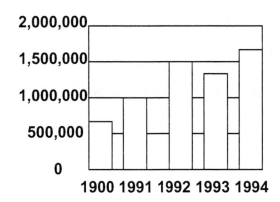

A. 100,000

B. 600,000

C. 1,600,000

D. 8,000,000

57. What is the probability of drawing 2 consecutive aces from a standard deck of cards?

A. $\dfrac{3}{51}$

B. $\dfrac{1}{221}$

C. $\dfrac{2}{104}$

D. $\dfrac{2}{52}$

58. A sofa sells for $520. If the retailer makes a 30% profit, what was the wholesale price?

A. $400

B. $676

C. $490

D. $364

59. Which of the following is an irrational number?

A.   .362626262...

B. $4\frac{1}{3}$

C. $\sqrt{5}$

D. $-\sqrt{16}$

60. Corporate salaries are listed for several employees. Which would be the best measure of central tendency?

$24,000 $24,000 $26,000
$28,000 $30,000 $120,000

A.   Mean

B.   Median

C.   Mode

D.   No difference

61. Which statement is true about George's budget?

A.   George spends the greatest portion of his income on food.

B.   George spends twice as much on utilities as he does on his mortgage.

C.   George spends twice as much on utilities as he does on food.

D.   George spends the same amount on food and utilities as he does on mortgage.

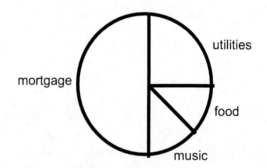

62. Given a drawer with 5 black socks, 3 blue socks, and 2 red socks, what is the probability that you will draw two black socks in two draws in a dark room?

A.   2/9

B.   1/4

C.   17/18

D.   1/18

63. Solve for x: $|2x+3| > 4$

A. $-\frac{7}{2} > x > \frac{1}{2}$

B. $-\frac{1}{2} > x > \frac{7}{2}$

C. $x < \frac{7}{2}$ or $x < -\frac{1}{2}$

D. $x < -\frac{7}{2}$ or $x > \frac{1}{2}$

64. Graph the solution:
   $|x| + 7 < 13$

A.

B.

C.

D.

65. A boat travels 30 miles upstream in three hours. It makes the return trip in one and a half hours. What is the speed of the boat in still water?

A. 10 mph

B. 15 mph

C. 20 mph

D. 30 mph

66. Given segment AC with B as its midpoint find the coordinates of C if A = (5,7) and B = (3, 6.5).

A. (4, 6.5)

B. (1, 6)

C. (2, 0.5)

D. (16, 1)

67. 3 km is equivalent to

A. 300 cm

B. 300 m

C. 3000 cm

D. 3000 m

68. The mass of a cookie is closest to:

A. 0.5 kg .

B. 0.5 grams

C. 15 grams

D. 1.5 grams

69. If the radius of a right circular cylinder is doubled, how does its volume change?

A. No change.

B. Also is doubled.

C. Four times the original.

D. Pi times the original.

70. In similar polygons, if the perimeters are in a ratio of x:y, the sides are in a ratio of

A. x : y

B. $x^2 : y^2$

C. 2x : y

D. 1/2 x : y

71. Find the midpoint of (2,5) and (7,-4).

A. (9,-1)

B. (5,9)

C. (9/2 , -1/2)

D. (9/2, 1/2)

72. 3x + 2y = 12
    12x + 8y = 15

A. all real numbers

B. x = 4, y = 4

C. x = 2, y = -1

D. ∅

Science
73. Carbon bonds with hydrogen by _____

A. ionic bonding

B. non-polar covalent bonding

C. polar covalent bonding

D. strong nuclear force.

74. Which skill refers to quantifying data, performing graphic analysis, making charts, and writing summaries?

A. Recording.

B. Data gathering.
C. Data processing.

D. Evaluating.

75. When several computers are connected together by a modem or telephone it is a:

A. Processor.

B. Network.

C. Online.

D. Hard drive.

76. Computer simulations are most appropriate for:

A. Replicatingdangerous experiments.

B. Mastering basic facts.

C. Emphasizing competition and entertainment.

D. Providing motivational feedback.

77. Accepted procedures for preparing solutions should be made with _____ .

A.   Alcohol.

B.   Hydrochloric acid.

C.   Distilled water.

D.   Tap water.

78. Enzymes speed up reactions by _____ .

A.   Utilizing ATP.

B.   Lowering pH, allowing reaction speed to increase.

C.   Increasing volume of substrate.

D.   Lowering energy of activation.

79. The transfer of heat by electromagnetic waves is called _____ .

A. Conduction.

B. Convection.

C. Phase change.

D. Radiation.

80. Which of the following is *not* considered ethical behavior for a scientist?

A.   Using unpublished data and citing the source.

B.   Publishing data before other scientists have had a chance to replicate results.

C.   Collaborating with other scientists from differentlaboratories.

D.   Publishing work with an incomplete list of citations.

81. Sound waves are produced by _____ .

A. Pitch.

B. Noise.

C. Vibrations.

D. Sonar..

82. Chemicals should be stored:

A.   In the principal's office.

B.   In a dark room.

C.   According to their reactivity with other substances.

D.   In a double locked room.

83. In an experiment measuring the growth of bacteria at different temperatures, what is the independent variable?

A. Number of bacteria.

B. Growth rate of bacteria.

C. Temperature.

D. Size of bacteria.

84. Which is the correct order of methodology?

1. collecting data
2. planning a controlled experiment
3. drawing a conclusion
4. hypothesizing a result
5. re-visiting a hypothesis to answer a question

A. 1,2,3,4,5

B. 4,2,1,3,5

C. 4,5,1,3,2

D. 1,3,4,5,2

85. What cell organelle contains the cell's stored food?

A. Vacuoles.

B. Golgi Apparatus.

C. Ribosomes.

D. Lysosomes.

86. Identify the correct sequence of organization of living things from lower to higher order:

A. Cell, Organelle, Organ, Tissue, System, Organism.

B. Cell, Tissue, Organ, Organelle, System, Organism.

C. Organelle, Cell, Tissue, Organ, System, Organism.

D. Organelle, Tissue, Cell, Organ, System, Organism.

87. Which of the following is a correct explanation for scientific "evolution"?

A. Giraffes need to reach higher for leaves to eat, so their necks stretch. The giraffe babies are then born with longer necks. Eventually, there are more long-necked giraffes in the population.

B. Giraffes with longer necks are able to reach more leaves, so they eat more and have more babies than other giraffes. Eventually, there are more long-necked giraffes in the population.

C. Giraffes want to reach higher for leaves to eat, so they release enzymes into their bloodstream, which in turn causes fetal development of longer-necked giraffes. Eventually, there are more long-necked giraffes in the population.

D. Giraffes with long necks are more attractive to other giraffes, so they get the best mating partners and have more babies. Eventually, there are more long-necked giraffes in the population.

88. Which of the following is the most accurate definition of a non-renewable resource?

A. A nonrenewable resource is never replaced once used.

B. A nonrenewable resource is replaced on a timescale that is very long relative to human life spans.

B. A nonrenewable resource is a resource that can only be manufactured by humans.

D. A nonrenewable resource is a species that has already become extinct.

89. Which kingdom is comprised of organisms made of one cell with no nuclear membrane?

A. Monera.

B. Protista.

C. Fungi.

D. Algae.

90. **What are the most significant and prevalent elements in the biosphere?**

A.   Carbon, Hydrogen, Oxygen, Nitrogen, Phosphorus.

B.   Carbon, Hydrogen, Sodium, Iron, Calcium.

C.   Carbon, Oxygen, Sulfur, Manganese, Iron.

D.   Carbon, Hydrogen, Oxygen, Nickel, Sodium, Nitrogen.

91. **Which of the following types of rock are made from magma?**

A. Fossils.

B. Sedimentary.

C. Metamorphic.

D. Igneous.

92. **What is the most accurate description of the Water Cycle?**

A.   Rain comes from clouds, filling the ocean. The water then evaporates and becomes clouds again.

B.   Water circulates from rivers into groundwater and back, while water vapor circulates in the atmosphere.

C.   Water is conserved except for chemical or nuclear reactions, and any drop of water could circulate through clouds, rain, ground water, and surface-water.

D.   Weather systems cause chemical reactions to break water into its atoms.

93. **Which of the following is the best definition for 'meteorite'?**

A.   A meteorite is a mineral composed of mica and feldspar.

B.   A meteorite is material from outer space that has struck the earth's surface.

C.   A meteorite is an element that has properties of both metals and nonmetals.

D.   A meteorite is a very small unit of length measurement.

94. The measure of the pull of the earth's gravity on an object is called _____

A. Mass number.

B. Atomic number.

C. Mass.

D. Weight.

95. Which parts of an atom are located inside the nucleus?

A. Electrons and neutrons.

B. Protons and neutrons.

C. Protons only.

D. Neutrons only.

Physical Education & Health

96. A physical education teacher emphasizes healthy attitudes and habits. She conducts her classes so that students acquire and interpret knowledge and learn to think/analyze, which is necessary for physical activities. The goals and values utilized and the philosophy applied by this instructor is:

A. Physical Development Goals and Realism Philosophy.

B. Affective Development Goals and Existentialism.

C. Motor Development Goals and Realism Philosophy.

D. Cognitive Development Goals and Idealism Philosophy.

97. Social skills and values developed by activity include all of the following except:

A. Winning at all costs.

B. Making judgments in groups.

C. Communicating and cooperating.

D. Respecting rules and property.

98. **Activities that enhance team socialization include all of the following except:**

A. Basketball.

B. Soccer.

C. Golf.

D. Volleyball.

99. **Through physical activities, John has developed self-discipline, fairness, respect for others, and new friends. John has experienced which of the following?**

A. Positive cooperation psycho-social influences.

B. Positive group psycho-social influences.

C. Positive individual psycho-social influences.

D. Positive accomplishment psycho-social influences.

100. **Which of the following psycho-social influences is not negative?**

A. Avoidance of problems.

B. Adherence to exercise.

C. Ego-centeredness.

D. Role conflict.

101. **The most effective way to promote the physical education curriculum is to:**

A. Relate physical education to higher thought processes.

B. Relate physical education to humanitarianism.

C. Relate physical education to the total educational process.

D. Relate physical education to skills necessary to preserve the natural environment.

102. **The affective domain of physical education contributes to all of the following except:**

A. Knowledge of exercise, health, and disease.

B. Self-actualization.

C. An appreciation of beauty.

D. Good sportsmanship.

103. A physical education instructor anticipates and prevents potential injuries, watches for hidden injuries, and takes an injury evaluation of the entire class. Which of the following strategies to prevent injuries is the teacher demonstrating?

A. Maintaining hiring standards.

B. Proper use of equipment.

C. Proper procedures for emergencies.

D. Participant screening.

Visual Art

104. A combination of three or more tones sounded at the same time is called a

A. Harmony.

B. Consonance.

C. A chord.

D. Dissonance.

105. A series of single tones which add up to a recognizable sound is called a:

A. Cadence.

B. Rhythm.

C. Melody.

D. Sequence.

106. Which is a true statement about crafts?

A. Students experiment with their own creativity.

B. Products are unique and different.

C. Self-expression is encouraged.

D. Outcome is predetermined.

107. The following is not a good activity to encourage fifth graders' artistic creativity:

A. Ask them to make a decorative card for a family member.

B. Have them work as a team to decorate a large wall display.

C. Ask them to copy a drawing from a book, with the higher grades being awarded to those students who come closest to the model.

D. Have each student try to create an outdoor scene with crayons, giving them a choice of scenery.

108. During the early childhood years (ages 3-5), drama and theatre experiences are especially beneficial to children because they provide the opportunity for students to:

A. Apply the concept of turn-taking.

B. Learn the importance of listening skills.

C. Acquire the skills needed to become a proficient reader.

D. Learn early drama skills using their five senses.

109. In the area of Performing Arts, specifically dance, primary grades are expected to have a gross understanding of their motor movements. Which of the following movements would not be age-appropriate?

A. Basic rhythm.

B. Early body awareness.

C. Imagery.

D. Listening skills.

110. Creating movements in response to music helps students to connect music and dance in which of the following ways?

A. Rhythm.

B. Costuming.

C. Speed.

D. Vocabulary skills.

111. Often local elected officials and guest or resident artists are brought into the classroom to:

A. Explain their jobs or trades.

B. Observe teaching skills.

C. Enrich and extend arts curriculum.

D. Entertain students and Teachers.

112. Early childhood students are expected to be able to complete tasks using basic loco-motor skills. Which of the following would not be included?

A. Walking.

B. Galloping.

C. Balancing.

D. Jogging.

113. **Which of the following skills is not applicable to the importance of developing dance skills?**

A.   Body awareness.

B.   Time and space.

C.   Balance.

D.   None of the above.

114. **The American Indian cultures developed a highly technical and aesthetic art form known as_____?**

A.   Beading.

B.   Coil pottery.

C.   Basketry.

D.   Weaving.

115. **In visual arts such as music and dance, the intentional, regular reputation of a given element most commonly serves as a feeling of:**

A.   Rhythm.

B.   Dissonance.

C.   Contrast.

D.   Dominance.

116. **Sculpting without using realistic detail is best defined as which of the twentieth century styles of art?**

A.   Futurism.

B.   Cubism.

C.   Abstraction.

D.   None of the above.

117. **The following are all historically recognized styles of dance except which one?**

A.   Ballet.

B.   Folk.

C.   Hip hop.

D.   Modern.

118. **Which of the following type and style of music is described as a large musical work consisting of four movements, or sections?**

A.   Cantata.

B.   Symphony.

C.   Sonata.

D.   Chorale.

119. In visual art studies students are expected to be able to interact in all of the following exercises except which one:

A. Clap out rhythmic patterns found in music lyrics.

B. Compare and contrast various art pieces.

C. Recognize related dance vocabulary.

D. Identify and sort pictures organized by shape, size, and color.

120. A six year old student in Mrs. Brack's first grade class has exhibited a noticeable change in behavior over the last month. The child was usually outgoing, alert, but she has become quiet and withdrawn, and appears to be unable to concentrate on her work. Yesterday, bruises were evident on the child's arm and right eye. Mrs. Brack should:

A. Ignore the situation.

B. Provide remedial work.

C. Immediately report the suspected abuse to the authorities.

D. Call the girl's parents.

Answer Key

1.	D	25.	D	49.	C	73.	C	97.	A
2.	A	26.	A	50.	C	74.	C	98.	C
3.	A	27.	D	51.	C	75.	B	99.	B
4.	A	28.	B	52.	B	76.	A	100.	B
5.	A	29.	A	53.	B	77.	C	101.	C
6.	C	30.	D	54.	C	78.	D	102.	A
7.	D	31.	B	55.	D	79.	D	103.	D
8.	B	32.	A	56.	B	80.	D	104.	C
9.	B	33.	C	57.	B	81.	C	105.	C
10.	A	34.	A	58.	A	82.	C	106.	D
11.	D	35.	C	59.	C	83.	C	107.	C
12.	D	36.	C	60.	B	84.	B	108.	D
13.	D	37.	B	61.	C	85.	A	109.	C
14.	A	38.	B	62.	A	86.	C	110.	A
15.	B	39.	A	63.	D	87.	B	111.	C
16.	A	40.	A	64.	A	88.	B	112.	D
17.	B	41.	A	65.	B	89.	A	113.	D
18.	B	42.	C	66.	B	90.	A	114.	D
19.	B	43.	D	67.	D	91.	D	115.	A
20.	B	44.	B	68.	C	92.	C	116.	B
21.	B	45.	A	69.	C	93.	B	117.	C
22.	B	46.	D	70.	A	94.	D	118.	B
23.	A	47.	D	71.	D	95.	B	119.	C
24.	C	48.	A	72.	D	96.	D	120.	C

Rationales for Sample Questions

1. D. Illustrates specific people or groups without directly naming them.

A fable is a short tale with animals, humans, gods, or even inanimate objects as characters. Fables often conclude with a moral, delivered in the form of an epigram (a short, witty, and ingenious statement in verse). Fables are among the oldest forms of writing in human history: it appears in Egyptian papyri of c1,500 BC. The most famous fables are those of Aesop, a Greek slave living in about 600 BC. In India, the Pantchatantra appeared in the third century. The most famous modern fables are those of seventeenth century French poet Jean de La Fontaine.

2. The key word here is EXCEPT which will be highlighted in upper case on the test as well. All of the options are correct aspects of phonological awareness except the first one, **A,** because phonological awareness DOES NOT involve print.

3. A. The student read newspapers, magazines and books on a regular basis.

It is up to the teacher to help the student choose reading material, but the student must be able to choose where s/he will search for the reading pleasure indispensable for enriching vocabulary.

4. A. The specific word choices of an author to create a particular mood or feeling in the reader.

Diction refers to an author's choice of words, expressions and style to convey his/her meaning.

5. A. The theme is always stated directly somewhere in the text.

The theme may be stated directly, but it can also be implicit in various aspects of the work, such as the interaction between characters, symbolism, or description.

6. C. Tone in literature is usually satiric or angry.

Tone in literature conveys a mood and can be as varied as the tone of voice of a speaker (see D., e.g. sad, nostalgic, whimsical, angry, formal, intimate, satirical, sentimental, etc.)

7. D. Syntax.

Syntax is the grammatical structure of sentences.

8. B. The youngest boy on the team had the best earned run average which mystifies the coaching staff.

Here, the use of the relative pronoun "which", whose antecedent is "the best run average," introduces a clause that is dependent on the independent clause "The youngest boy on the team had the best run average". The idea expressed in the subordinate clause is subordinate to the one expressed in the independent clause.

9. B. See the past more realistically and can relate to people from the past more than preadolescents.

Since, according to Piaget, adolescents 12-15 years old begin thinking beyond the immediate and obvious, and theorizing, their assessment of events shifts from considering an action as "right" or "wrong" to considering the intent and behavior in which the action was performed. Fairy tale or other kinds of unreal characters have ceased to satisfy them and they are able to recognize the difference between pure history and historical fiction.

10. A. A standardized reading test

If assessment is standardized, it has to be objective, whereas B, C and D are all subjective assessments.

11. D. Through application to their own writing.

The answer is D. At this age, students learn grammatical concepts best through practical application in their own writing.

12. D. Proofreading.

Proofreading cannot be a method of prewriting, since it is done on already written texts only.

13. D. Writing letters to friends or relatives.

The answer is D. Reading all rough drafts will not encourage the students to take control of their text and might even inhibit their creativity. On the contrary, pairing students will foster their sense of responsibility, and having them compose stories for literary magazines will boost their self esteem as well as their organizational skills. As far as writing letters is concerned, the work of authors such as Madame de Sevigne in the seventeenth century is a good example of the epistolary literary style.

14. A. Seventeenth century.

In the seventeenth Century, authors such as Jean de La Fontaine and his *Fables*, Pierre Perreault's *Tales*, Mme d'Aulnoye's Novels based on old folktales and Mme de Beaumont's *Beauty and the Beast* all created a children's literature genre. In England, Perreault was translated and a work allegedly written by Oliver Smith, *The Renowned History of Little Goody Two Shoes*, also helped to establish children's literature in England.

15. B. Details and examples supporting the main idea.

The introductory paragraph should introduce the topic, capture the reader's interest, state the thesis and prepare the reader for the main points in the essay. Details and examples, however, should be given in the second part of the essay, so as to help develop the thesis presented at the end of the introductory paragraph, following the inverted triangle method consisting of a broad general statement followed by some information, and then the thesis at the end of the paragraph.

16. A. Biological capability to articulate sounds understood by other humans.

Language ability is innate and the biological capability to produce sounds lets children learn semantics and syntactical structures through trial and error. Linguists agree that language is first a vocal system of word symbols that enables a human to communicate his/her feelings, thoughts, and desires to other human beings.

17. B. Mother's-in-law frown.

Mother-in-Law is a compound common noun and the inflection should be at the end of the word, according to the rule.

18. The answer is "**B**" and, again, the definition of this word in reading is what you have to know from your coursework.

19. The answer is "**B**." You need to memorize these special definitions.

20. B. Metacognition.

Metacognition may be defined as "thinking about thinking." Good readers use metacognitive strategies to think about and have control over their reading. Before reading, they might clarify their purpose for reading and preview the text. During reading, they might monitor their understanding, adjusting their reading speed to fit the difficulty of the text and fixing any comprehension problems they have. After reading, they check their understanding of what they have read.

21. B. Collection of data from assessment tests.

Assessment tests are formal progress-monitoring measures.

22. B. Narrative writing.

These are all characteristics of narrative writing. Expository writing is intended to give information, such as an explanation or directions, and the information is logically organized. Persuasive writing gives an opinion in an attempt to convince the reader that this point of view is valid or tries to persuade the reader to take a specific action. The goal of technical writing is to clearly communicate a select piece of information to a targeted reader or group of readers for a particular purpose in such a way that the subject can readily be understood. It is persuasive writing that anticipates a response from the reader.

23. A. Reads texts with expression or prosody.

The teacher should listen to the children read aloud, but there are also clues to reading levels in their writing.

24. C. Assessment should reflect the actual reading for which the classroom instruction has prepared the student.

The only reliable measure of the success of a unit will be based on the reading the instruction has focused on.

25. D. Etymology.

A synonym is an equivalent of another word and can substitute for it in certain contexts. Inflection is a modification of words according to their grammatical functions, usually by employing variant word-endings to indicate such qualities as tense, gender, case, and number. Phonetics is the science devoted to the physical analysis of the sounds of human speech, including their production, transmission, and perception.

26. D. Algonquian and Iroquois.

The Algonquian and Iroquois nations inhabited the Mid-Atlantic and Northeastern regions of the U.S. These Native Americans are classified among the Woods Peoples. Some of the most famous of these nations are Squanto, Pocahontas, Chief Powhatan, Tecumseh, and Black Hawk. These two nations were frequently at odds over territory. The people of these nations taught early settlers about the land and survival in the new world. They introduced the settlers to maize and tobacco. The settlers and the Native Americans gradually developed respect and opened trade and cultural sharing.

27. D. All of the above.

The importance of the Age of Exploration was not only the discovery and colonization of the New World, but also better maps and charts, new accurate navigational instruments, increased knowledge, great wealth, new and different foods and items not known in Europe, a new hemisphere as a refuge from poverty and persecution and a place to start a new and better life. The Age of Exploration also provided proof that Asia could be reached by sea and that the earth was round; ships and sailors would not sail off the edge of a flat earth and disappear forever into nothingness.

28. B. It was an approach to trade that transported finished goods from the mother country to the African colonies, slaves and goods from Africa to the North American colonies, and raw materials and tobacco or rum back to the mother country.

The New England and Middle Atlantic colonies at first felt threatened by these laws as they had started producing many of the same products being produced in Britain. But they soon found new markets for their goods and began what was known as a **"triangular trade."** Colonial vessels started the first part of the triangle by sailing for Africa loaded with kegs of rum from colonial distilleries. On Africa's West Coast, the rum was traded for either gold or slaves. The second part of the triangle was from Africa to the West Indies where slaves were traded for molasses, sugar, or money. The third part of the triangle was home, bringing sugar or molasses (to make more rum), gold, and silver.

29. A. Enlightenment.

Enlightenment thinking quickly made the voyage across the Atlantic Ocean. Enlightenment thinking valued human reason and the importance of education, knowledge, and scholarly research. Education in the middle colonies was influenced largely by the Enlightenment movement, which emphasized scholarly research and public service. Benjamin Franklin embodied these principles in Philadelphia, which became a center of learning and culture, owing largely to its economic success and ease of access to European books and tracts.

30. D. An influx of Oakies.

The Dust Bowl of the Great Plains destroyed agriculture in the area. People living in the Plains areas lost their livelihood and many lost their homes and possessions in the great dust storms that resulted from a period of extended drought. People from all of the states affected by the Dust Bowl made their way to California in search of a better life. Because the majority of the people were from Oklahoma, they were all referred to as "Oakies." These migrants brought with them their distinctive Plains culture. The great influx of people seeking jobs exacerbated the effects of the Great Depression in California.

31. B. Ranchos.

The goal of Spanish colonialism was to exploit, transform and include the native people of California. The Spanish empire sought to do this first by gathering the native people into communities where they could both be taught Spanish culture and be converted to Roman Catholicism and its value system. The social institutions by which this was accomplished was the encouragement of the Mission System, which established a number of Catholic missions a day's journey apart. Once the native people were brought to the missions, they were incorporated into a mission society and indoctrinated in the teachings of Catholicism. The Presidios were fortresses that were constructed to protect Spanish interests and the communities from invaders. The Pueblos were small civilian communities that attracted settlers with the gift of land, seed, and farming equipment. The function of the Pueblos was to produce food for the missions and for the presidios.

32. A. Cabot.

John Cabot (1450-1498) was the English explorer who gave England claim to North American and the first European to see Florida and sail along its coast. (B) Columbus (1451-1506) was sent by the Spanish to the New World and has received false credit for "discovering America" in 1492, although he did open up the New World to European expansion, exploitation, and Christianity. (C) Ponce de Leon (1460-1521), the Spanish explorer, was the first European to actually land on Florida. (D) Panfilo de Narvaez (1470-1528) was also a Spanish conquistador, but he was sent to Mexico to force Cortes into submission. He failed and was captured.

33. C. America bought it from Spain.

Spain received $5 million dollars for Florida, mostly to pay for damagesincurred during the war. Following the War of 1812, Spain actually ceded Florida to the United States as part of the treaty. Florida, while under Spanish control, had been a difficult issue for the United States. Runaway slaves would often seek refuge there and the Seminole Indians of Florida would attack Georgia from the South. Therefore, in 1819, the Spanish agreed to put Florida into U.S. hands as part of a treaty to stop the fighting between the two nations. Andrew Jackson, the hero of the War of 1812 became the first governor of Florida.

34. A. Metropolitan Government.

Metropolitan Government was the form of local government that acts as an intermediary between the state and the city and comes from the idea of municipal home rule first enacted by Missouri in 1875. As suburbs grew and cities declined a bit, it became more important to have an intermediary between the city and state governments.

35. C. Iroquois and Algonquin.

The area now known as the State of New York was initially inhabited by several tribes that were part of one of two major Native American Nations. These were the Iroquois Nation and the Algonquian Nation. (A) Sioux and Pawnee tribal lands were found primarily in Minnesota and Nebraska, respectively. (B) Micmac and Wampanoag are tribes primarily found in New England and Canada. (D) Nez Perce and Cherokee were found in the Pacific Northwest and the Eastern parts of the United States, respectively.

36. C. The Harlem Renaissance.

As African Americans left the rural South and migrated to the North in search of opportunity, many settled in Harlem in New York City. By the 1920s, Harlem had become a center of life and activity for persons of color. The music, art, and literature of this community gave birth to a cultural movement known as the Harlem Renaissance. (A) The Revolution War (1776) occurred prior to the Civil War. (B) The Second Great Awakening occurred in the 1920s but like the (D) Gilded Age (1878 – 1889), affected the entire United States.

37. B. To establish trade.

The Europeans came to the New World for a number of reasons; often, they came to find new natural resources to extract for manufacturing. The Portuguese, Spanish and English were sent over to increase the monarch's power and spread influences such as religion (Christianity) and culture. Therefore, the only reason given that Europeans didn't come to the New World for was to establish trade.

38. B. The London Company granted the colony a charter making it independent.

In the year 1619, the Southern colony of Virginia had an eventful year including the first arrival of twenty African slaves, the right to self-governance through representative government in the Virginia House of Burgesses (their own legislative body), and the arrival of sixty women sent to marry and establish families in the colony. The London Company did not, however, grant the colony a charter in 1619.

39. A. The Age of Absolutism.

The "divine right" of kings was the key political characteristic of The Age of Absolutism and was most visible in the reign of King Louis XIV of France, as well as during the times of King James I and his son, Charles I. The divine right doctrine claims that kings and absolute leaders derive their right to rule by virtue of their birth alone. They see this both as a law of God and of nature.

40. A. Plentiful cheap, unskilled labor was no longer needed by industrialists.

The primary reason that the United States almost completely stopped all immigration during the 1920s was because immigrants' once, much-needed, cheap, unskilled labor, made necessary by the formerly booming, industrial economy, were no longer needed. This has much to do with the increased use of machines to do the work once done by cheap, unskilled laborers.

41. A. Economic depressions and slow resumption of trade and financial aid.

Following World War II, the economy was vibrant and flourished from the stimulant of war and an increased dependence of the world on United States' industries. Therefore, World War II didn't result in economic depressions and slow resumption of trade and financial aid. Western Europe was no longer the center of world power. New power struggles arose in Europe and Asia and many European nations underwent changing territories and boundaries.

42. C. Manifest Destiny.

The belief that the United States should control all of North America was called (B) Manifest Destiny. This idea fueled much of the violence and aggression towards those already occupying the lands, such as the Native Americans. Manifest Destiny was certainly driven by sentiments of (D) nationalism and gave rise to (A) westward expansion.

43. C. Utility.

As used in the social science of economics, (C) utility is the measurement of happiness or satisfaction a person receives from consuming a good or service. The decision of the student to increase his satisfaction by buying a second candy bar relates to this concept because he is spending money to increase his happiness.

44. B. Historiography.

Historiography is a term used to refer to the actual writing of history as well as to the study of this type of writing. (A) Public policy analysis is part of political science. (B) Historical perspective refers to the prevailing viewpoint of a historical time, and (D) historical analysis concerns the interpretation of historical events.

45. A. Molecular biophysics.

Molecular biophysics is an interdisciplinary field combining the fields of biology, chemistry and physics. These are all natural sciences, and not social sciences.

46. D. Letters from a nineteenth century Egyptologist to his wife.

Historians use primary sources from the actual time they are studying whenever possible. (A) Ancient Greek records of interaction with Egypt, (B) letters from an Egyptian ruler to regional governors, and (C) inscriptions from the Fourteenth Egyptian Dynasty are all primary sources created at or near the actual time being studied. (D) Letters from a nineteenth century Egyptologist would not be considered primary sources, as they were created thousands of years after the fact and may not actually be about the subject being studied.

47. Find the LCD of $\dfrac{^-4}{9}$ and $\dfrac{^-7}{10}$. The LCD is 90, so you get

$\dfrac{^-40}{90} + \dfrac{^-63}{90} = \dfrac{^-103}{90}$, which is answer **D.**

48. Simple multiplication. The answer will be negative because a positive times a negative is a negative number. $5.6 \times {}^-0.11 = {}^-0.616$, which is answer **A.**

49. Use $(1 - x)$ as the discount. $375x = 120$.
$375(1-x) = 120 \rightarrow 375 - 375x = 120 \rightarrow 375x = 255 \rightarrow x = 0.68 = 68\%$ which is answer **C.**

50. Let x = # of students in the 8 am class and $x - 40$ = # of student in the 10 am class. $x + (x - 40) = 410 \rightarrow 2x - 40 = 410 \rightarrow 2x = 450 \rightarrow x = 225$. So there are 225 students in the 8 am class, and $225 - 40 = 185$ in the 10 am class, which is answer **C**.

51. Degrees measure angles, square meters measure area, cubic feet measure volume, and kilometers measure length. Kilometers is the only reasonable answer, which is **C**.

52. Area = length times width (lw).
Length = 13 feet
Width = 13 feet (square, so length and width are the same).
Area = $13 \times 13 = 169$ square feet.
Area is measured in square feet. So the answer is **B**.

53. The smallest number in this set is 16; its factors are 1, 2, 4, 8 and 16. 16 in the largest factor, but it does not divide into 28 or 36. Neither does 8. 4 does factor into both 28 and 36. The answer is **B**.

54. Solve for x.
$$4x - (3 - x) = 7(x - 3) + 10$$
$$4x - 3 + x = 7x - 21 + 10$$
$$5x - 3 = 7x - 11$$
$$5x = 7x - 11 + 3 \qquad \text{The answer is } \textbf{C.}$$
$$5x - 7x = {}^{-}8$$
$${}^{-}2x = {}^{-}8$$
$$x = 4$$

55. We are given d = 585 miles and r = 65 miles per hour and $d = rt$. Solve for t. $\quad 585 = 65t \rightarrow t = 9$ hours, which is answer **D**.

56. The number of tourists in 1991 was 1,000,000 and the number in 1994 was 1,600,000. Subtract to get a difference of 600,000, which is answer **B**.

57. **There are 4 aces in the 52 card deck.**

P(first ace) = $\dfrac{4}{52}$. P(second ace) = $\dfrac{3}{51}$.

P(first ace and second ace) = P(one ace)xP(second ace|first ace)
$= \dfrac{4}{52} \times \dfrac{3}{51} = \dfrac{1}{221}$. This is answer **B**.

58. A. $400

Let x be the wholesale price, then x + .30x = 520, 1.30x = 520. divide both sides by 1.30.

59. A. $500

12(40) = 480 which is closest to $500.

60. B. Median.

The median provides the best measure of central tendency in this case where the mode is the lowest number and the mean would be disproportionately skewed by the outlier $120,000.

61. C. George spends twice as much on utilities as he does on food.

George spends twice as much on utilities as on food.

62. A. 2/9

In this example of conditional probability, the probability of drawing a black sock on the first draw is 5/10. It is implied in the problem that there is no replacement, therefore the probability of obtaining a black sock in the second draw is 4/9. Multiply the two probabilities and reduce to lowest terms.

63. D. $x < -\frac{7}{2}$ or $x > \frac{1}{2}$

The quantity within the absolute value symbols must be either > 4 or < -4. Solve the two inequalities 2x + 3 > 4 or 2x + 3 < -4.

64. A.

Solve by adding -7 to each side of the inequality. Since the absolute value of x is less than 6, x must be between -6 and 6. The end points are not included so the circles on the graph are hollow.

65. B. 15 mph

Let x = the speed of the boat in still water and c = the speed of the current.

	rate	time	distance
upstream	x - c	3	30
downstream	x + c	1.5	30

Solve the system:
$$3x - 3c = 30$$
$$1.5x + 1.5c = 30$$

66. B. (1, 6)

67. D. 3000 m

To change kilometers to meters, move the decimal 3 places to the right.

68. C. 15 grams. A cookie is measured in grams.

69. C. Four times the original.

If the radius of a right circular cylinder is doubled, the volume is multiplied by four because in the formula, the radius is squared. Therefore, the new volume is 2 x 2 or four times the original.

70. A. x : y   The sides are in the same ratio.

71. D. (9/2, 1/2)   Using the midpoint formula:

$$x = (2 + 7)/2 \quad y = (5 + -4)/2$$

72. D. $\varnothing$

Multiplying the top equation by -4 and adding results in the equation 0 = -33. Since this is a false statement, the correct choice is the null set.

73. C. Polar covalent bonding.

Each carbon atom contains four valence electrons, while each hydrogen atom contains one valence electron. A carbon atom can bond with one or more hydrogen atoms, such that two electrons are shared in each bond. This is covalent bonding, because the electrons are shared. (In ionic bonding, atoms must gain or lose electrons to form ions. The ions are then electrically attracted in oppositely charged pairs.) Covalent bonds are always polar when between two non-identical atoms, so this bond must be polar. ("Polar" means that the electrons are shared unequally, forming a pair of partial charges, i.e. poles.) In any case, the strong nuclear force is not relevant to this problem. The answer to this question is therefore (C).

74. C. Data Processing.

Data processing is any process that converts data into information.

75. B. Network.

A collection of computers and related devices, connected in a way that allows them to share data, hardware, and software is a network. Thus, the **answer is (B)**.

76. A. Replicating a dangerous experiment.

A computer simulation is a computer program that attempts to simulate an abstract model of a particular system.

77. C. Distilled water.

Alcohol and hydrochloric acid should never be used to make solutions unless instructed to do so. All solutions should be made with distilled water, since tap water contains dissolved particles which may affect the results of an experiment. The correct **answer is (C)**.

78. D. Lowering energy of activation.

Because enzymes are catalysts, they work the same way—they cause the formation of activated chemical complexes, which require a lower activation energy. Therefore, the **answer is (D)**. ATP is an energy source for cells, and pH or volume changes may or may not affect reaction rate, so these answers can be eliminated.

79. D. Radiation.

Heat transfer via electromagnetic waves (which can occur even in a vacuum) is called radiation. (Heat can also be transferred by direct contact [conduction], by fluid current [convection], and by matter changing phase, but these are not relevant here.) The answer to this question is therefore (D).

80. D. Publishing work with an incomplete list of citations.

One of the most important ethical principles for scientists is to cite all sources of data and analysis when publishing work. It is reasonable to use unpublished data (A), as long as the source is cited. Most science is published before other scientists replicate it (B), and frequently scientists collaborate with each other, in the same or different laboratories (C). These are all ethical choices. However, publishing work without the appropriate citations is unethical. Therefore, the **answer is (D).**

81. C. Vibrations.

Sound waves are produced by a vibrating body. The vibrating object moves forward and compresses the air in front of it, then reverses direction so that pressure on the air is lessened and expansion of the air molecules occurs. The vibrating air molecules move back and forth parallel to the direction of motion of the wave as they pass the energy from adjacent air molecules closer to the source to air molecules farther away from the source. Therefore, the answer is (C).

82. D. According to their reactivity with other substances.

Chemicals should be stored with other chemicals of similar properties (e.g. acids with other acids), to reduce the potential for either hazardous reactions in the storeroom, or mistakes in reagent use. Certainly, chemicals should not be stored in anyone's office, and the light intensity of the room is not very important because light-sensitive chemicals are usually stored in dark containers. In fact, good lighting is desirable in a storeroom, so that labels can be read easily. Chemicals may be stored off-site, but that makes their use inconvenient. Therefore, the best answer is (D).

83. C. Temperature.

To answer this question, recall that the independent variable in an experiment is the entity that is changed by the scientist, in order to observe the effects (the dependent variable(s). In this experiment, temperature is changed in order to measure growth of bacteria, so (C) is the answer. Note that answer (A) is the dependent variable, and neither (B) nor (D) is directly relevant to the question.

84. B. 4.2.1.3.5.

The correct methodology for the scientific method is first to make a meaningful hypothesis (educated guess), then to plan and execute a controlled experiment to test that hypothesis. Using the data collected in that experiment, the scientist then draws conclusions and attempts to answer the original question related to the hypothesis. This is consistent only with answer (B).

85. A. Vacuoles.

 In a cell, the sub-parts are called organelles. Of these, the vacuoles hold stored food (and water and pigments). The Golgi Apparatus sorts molecules from other parts of the cell; the ribosomes are sites of protein synthesis; the lysosomes contain digestive enzymes. This is consistent only with answer (A).

86. C. Organelle, Cell, Tissue, Organ, System, Organism.

Organelles are parts of the cell; cells make up tissue, which makes up organs. Organs work together in systems (e.g. the respiratory system), and the organism is the living thing as a whole. Therefore, the answer must be (C).

87. B. Giraffes with longer necks are able to reach more leaves, so they eat more and have more babies than other giraffes. Eventually, there are more long-necked giraffes in the population.

Although evolution is often misunderstood, it occurs via natural selection. Organisms with a life/reproductive advantage will produce more offspring. Over many generations, this changes the proportions of the population. In any case, it is impossible for a stretched neck (A) or a fervent desire (C) to result in a biologically mutated baby. Although there are traits that are naturally selected because of mate attractiveness and fitness (D), this is not the primary situation here, so answer (B) is the best choice.

88. B. A nonrenewable resource is replaced on a timescale that is very long relative to human life- spans.

Renewable resources are those that are renewed, or replaced, in time for humans to use more of them. Examples include fast-growing plants, animals, or oxygen gas. (Note that while sunlight is often considered a renewable resource, it is actually a nonrenewable but extremely abundant resource.) Nonrenewable resources are those that renew themselves only on very long—usually geologic—timescales. Examples include minerals, metals, or fossil fuels. Therefore, the correct answer is (B).

89. A. Monera

To answer this question, first note that algae are not a kingdom of their own. Some algae are in monera, the kingdom that consists of unicellular prokaryotes with no true nucleus. Protista and fungi are both eukaryotic, with true nuclei, and are sometimes multi-cellular. Therefore, the answer is (A).

90. A. Carbon, Hydrogen, Oxygen, Nitrogen, Phosphorus

Organic matter (and life as we know it) is based on Carbon atoms, bonded to Hydrogen and Oxygen. Nitrogen and Phosphorus are the next most significant elements, followed by Sulfur and then trace nutrients such as Iron, Sodium, Calcium, and others. Therefore, the answer is (A). If you know that the formula for any carbohydrate contains Carbon, Hydrogen, and Oxygen, that will help you narrow the choices to (A) and (D) in any case.

91. D. Igneous

Few fossils are found in metamorphic rock and virtually none found in igneous rocks. Igneous rocks are formed from magma and magma is so hot that any organisms trapped by it are destroyed. Metamorphic rocks are formed by high temperatures and great pressures. When fluid sediments are transformed into solid sedimentary rocks, the process is known as lithification. The answer is (D).

92. C. Water is conserved except for chemical or nuclear reactions, and any drop of water could circulate through clouds, rain, ground water, and surface- water.

All natural chemical cycles, including the Water Cycle, depend on the principle of Conservation of Mass. (For water, unlike for elements such as Nitrogen, chemical reactions may cause sources or sinks of water molecules.) Any drop of water may circulate through the hydrologic system, ending up in a cloud, as rain, or as surface- or ground-water. Although answers (A) and (B) describe parts of the water cycle, the most comprehensive answer is (C).

93. B. A meteorite is material from outer space that has struck the earth's surface.

Meteoroids are pieces of matter in space, composed of particles of rock and metal. If a meteoroid travels through the earth's atmosphere, friction causes burning and a "shooting star"—i.e. a meteor. If the meteor strikes the earth's surface, it is known as a meteorite. Note that although the suffix –ite often means a mineral, answer (A) is incorrect. Answer (C) refers to a 'metalloid' rather than a 'meteorite', and answer (D) is simply a misleading pun on 'meter'. Therefore, the answer is (B).

94. D. Weight

To answer this question, recall that mass number is the total number of protons and neutrons in an atom, atomic number is the number of protons in an atom, and mass is the amount of matter in an object. The only remaining choice is (D), weight, which is correct because weight is the force of gravity on an object.

95. B. Protons and Neutrons

Protons and neutrons are located in the nucleus, while electrons move around outside the nucleus. This is consistent only with answer (B).

Physical Education

96. D.

Educators use cognitive development goals to describe the act of teaching children in a manner that will help them develop as personal and social beings. Concepts that fall under this term include social and emotional learning, moral reasoning/cognitive development, life-skills education, health education, violence prevention, critical thinking, ethical reasoning, and conflict resolution and mediation. This form of education involves teaching children and teenagers such values as honesty, stewardship, kindness, generosity, courage, freedom, justice, equality, and respect. Idealism is an approach to philosophical inquiry that asserts direct and immediate knowledge can only be had as ideas or mental pictures. We can only know the objects that are the basis of these ideas indirectly.

97. A.

Winning at all costs is not a desirable social skill. Instructors and coaches should emphasize fair play and effort over winning. Answers B, C, and D are all positive skills and values developed in physical activity settings.

98. C.

Golf is mainly an individual sport. Though golf involves social interaction, it generally lacks the team element inherent in basketball, soccer, and volleyball.

99. B. Through physical activities, John developed his social interaction skills.

Social interaction is the sequence of social actions between individuals (or groups) that modify their actions and reactions due to the actions of their interaction partner(s). In other words, they are events in which people attach meaning to a situation, interpret what others mean, and respond accordingly. Through socialization with other people, John feels the influence of the people around him.

100. B.

The ability of an individual to adhere to an exercise routine due to her/his excitement, accolades, etc. is not a negative psycho-social influence. Adherence to an exercise routine is healthy and positive.

101. C. The government treats the physical education curriculum as one of the major subjects.

Because of all of the games that we now participate in, many countries have focused their hearts and set their minds on competing with rival countries. Physical education is now one of the major, important subjects and instructors should integrate physical education into the total educational process.

102. A.

The affective domain encompasses emotions, thoughts, and feelings related to physical education. Knowledge of exercise, health, and disease is part of the cognitive domain.

103. D. In order for the instructor to know each student's physical status, she takes an injury evaluation.

Such surveys are one way to know the physical status of an individual. It chronicles past injuries, tattoos, activities, and diseases the individual may have or had. It helps the instructor to know the limitations of each individual. Participant screening covers all forms of surveying and anticipation of injuries.

Art

104. C. Identifying tones, music, beats etc. can be related to the Artistic Perception module 1.2

105. C. Using crafting and artistic lessons can be related to Artistic Perception 1.2

106. D. Creativity and teaching upper level thinking, reasoning, and creativity lessons can be related to Creative Expression threads 2.1-2.7

107. C. Encouraging artistic creativity can be located in the framework threads 2.2

108. D.

Students in Early Childhood ages are introduced to drama and theatre using their 5 senses. Smell, feel, sound, touch, and taste are all senses that even at the earliest ages children know and are able to relate to.

109. C.

Early Childhood students are expected to have limited understanding of their bodies and general movement of them. However, early imagery is a tool that is only developed once a student begins to mature and doesn't typically happen until late elementary or early middle school age.

110. A.

Students should be able to understand the connections made between movement and music is related by rhythm.

111. C.

Teachers often look for outside sources to help aid in their students' understanding of lessons and concepts. There are many programs utilized and the artist in residence program is an example of how artists enrich the art program of study.

112. D.

Early childhood students are only expected to complete basic motor skills at ages 3-5.

113. D

All skills are applicable when developing dance skills. Students must be aware of their bodies and their surroundings, and they must learn elements such as time and space in order to dance alone and with other dancers. And finally students must have listening skills in order to be taught important dance skills.

114. D

Weaving is a highly concentrated art form that was developed by Native American cultures and used as a livelihood toward their survival and barter with other cultures.

115. A

Rhythm is the basis of dance and is developed through repetition and practice.

116. B

Cubism is a school of painting and sculpture in which the subject matter is portrayed by geometric forms without realistic detail.

117. C

Hip Hop dance is a slang term that is often heard in today's society but is not a style that has long been recognized and taught by instructors.

118. B

A symphony is defined as a large musical work consisting of four movements, or sections.

119. C.

Dance is not a related area in visual arts.

120. C

Teachers are required by law to report suspected cases of child abuse.

XAMonline, INC. 21 Orient Ave. Melrose, MA 02176

Toll Free number 800-301-4647

TO ORDER Fax 781-662-9268 OR www.XAMonline.com

FLORIDA TEACHER CERTICATION EXAMINATIONS
- FTCE - 2007

PO#   Store/School:

Attention

Bill to Address 1   Ship to address

City, State Zip

Credit card number_____-_____-_____-_____   expiration_____

EMAIL _____

PHONE   **FAX**

13# ISBN 2007	TITLE	Qty	Retail	Total
978-1-58197-900-8	Art Sample Test K-12		$15.00	
978-1-58197-801-8	Biology 6-12		$59.95	
978-1-58197-099-9	Chemistry 6-12		$73.50	
978-1-58197-923-7	Earth/Space Science 6-12		$34.95	
978-1-58197-921-3	Educational Media Specialist PK-12		$34.95	
978-1-58197-908-4	Elementary Ed. Sample Questions		$34.95	
978-1-58197-907-7	Elementary Education K-6		$59.95	
978-1-58197-915-2	English 6-12		$59.95	
978-1-58197-904-6	Exceptional Student Ed. K-12		$59.95	
978-1-51897-905-3	Family and Consumer Science		$34.95	
978-1-58197-906-0	FELE Florida Ed. Leadership		$59.95	
978-1-58197-919-0	French Sample Test K-12		$15.00	
978-1-58197-902-2	General Knowledge		$34.95	
978-1-58197-916-9	Guidance and Counseling PK-12		$34.95	
978-1-58197-089-0	Humanities K-12		$34.95	
978-1-58197-914-5	Mathematics 6-12		$59.95	
978-1-58197-911-4	Middle Grades English 5-9		$34.95	
978-1-58197-912-1	Middle Grades General Science 5-9		$59.95	
978-1-58197-924-4	Middle Grades Integrated Curriculum		$59.95	
978-1-58197-910-7	Middle Grades Math 5-9		$34.95	
978-1-58197-913-8	Middle Grades Social Science 5-9		$34.95	
978-1-58197-920-6	Physical Education K-12		$34.95	
978-1-58197-922-0	Physics 6-12		$15.00	
978-1-58197-903-9	Professional Educator		$34.95	
978-1-58197-909-1	Reading K-12		$34.95	
978-1-58197-917-6	Social Science 6-12		$59.95	
978-1-58197-918-3	Spanish K-12		$34.95	
			SUBTOTAL	
	Add ship/handling $8.25 one title, $11.00 two titles, $15.00 three or more titles			
			TOTAL	